LEISURE IN CONTEMPORARY SOCIETY

Second Edition

LEISURE IN CONTEMPORARY SOCIETY
Second Edition

Ken Roberts

www.cabi.org

CABI is a trading name of CAB International

CABI Head Office
Nosworthy Way
Wallingford
Oxfordshire OX10 8DE
UK

Tel: +44 (0)1491 832111
Fax: +44 (0)1491 833508
E-mail: cabi@cabi.org
Website: www.cabi.org

CABI North American Office
875 Massachusetts Avenue
7th Floor
Cambridge, MA 02139
USA

Tel: +1 617 395 4056
Fax: +1 617 354 6875
E-mail: cabi-nao@cabi.org

A catalogue record for this book is available from the British Library, London, UK.

A catalogue record for this book is available from the Library of Congress, Washington, DC.

Library of Congress Cataloging-in-Publication Data
Roberts, Kenneth, 1940-
Leisure in contemporary society / Ken Roberts.-- 2nd ed.
    p. cm.
Includes bibliographical references and index.
  ISBN-13: 978-1-84593-069-1 (alk. paper)
  ISBN-10: 1-84593-069-X (alk. paper)
  1. Leisure—Sociological aspects. 2. Recreation—Sociological aspects. I. Title.

GV14.45.R63 2006
306.4'812--dc22

                                                    2005023099

Typeset by AMA DataSet Ltd, UK
Printed and bound in the USA by Integrated Books International, Dulles, Virginia

Contents

Tables

Boxes

Preface

I wrote my first text on leisure in 1970, a second in 1978 (Roberts, 1970, 1978), and the first edition of this book was published in 1999. Several topics – the hardy perennials on 'leisure and society' syllabuses – have been prominent in all these books. These are work and leisure, the family and leisure, and the relationships between uses of leisure and age and gender divisions. The growth of leisure has been another constant theme. The quantitative growth of leisure in terms of time, the money that is spent and participation rates in leisure activities is ongoing and beyond argument. However, there have always been suggestions that leisure is also becoming more important in qualitative senses, and here the claims have changed in subtle ways over time. It used to be argued (not by myself) that life would become more leisurely as the demands of work were progressively rolled back, as 3-day working weeks became standard and people were blessed or cursed by oceans of free time. Nowadays work–life balance and mounting time pressure are leading issues. It used to be argued (again, not by myself) that an old work ethic would be replaced by a new leisure ethic, that leisure time would become pivotal in people's lives, meaning that, instead of leisure being time left over, other things would be slotted in around leisure commitments and that leisure values (doing things for their own sake, for the intrinsic satisfactions) would spread from leisure into other areas of life, including work. None of these forecasts look as plausible today as they did 30–40 years ago. Nowadays the favoured sense in which leisure is said to be gaining importance in a qualitative sense is as a source of our identities – our own and other people's conceptions of who we are. These claims can be relied on to inject excitement into leisure studies but I have always been, and remain, thoroughly sceptical of claims that leisure is growing and becoming more important in anything other than the strictly quantitative senses.

Some issues that were hotly debated in the 1960s and 1970s appear to have sunk without trace but have actually metamorphosed. We no longer debate whether the mass media are creating a mass society and spreading a mass culture in which atomized individuals can be manipulated by whoever controls the media. These fears and forecasts have been undermined by the growth of the media, the splintering of both ownership and control, and the now well-known fact that different sections of the population are able to use the same media in different ways, for their own purposes. However, there are contemporary versions of the mass society theory – for example, the McDonaldization thesis and its variants – which claim that our leisure choices are increasingly limited to 'brands' that are all based on the same tedious rational principles. In a similar way, older arguments about class domination, in which the interests of a ruling class were said to shape everyone's leisure time and preferences and the values of the same ruling class were said to pervade all leisure activities, have metamorphosed into present-day claims about the suffocating embrace of consumer culture. I have never been persuaded by any of these rather pessimistic views about the role of leisure. The alternative 'pluralist scenario' (as I described it in 1978) no longer appears to need explicit defence because in leisure studies its propositions are now generally accepted. My constant position, affirmed in this book, is that the best explanations of how people use their leisure are not in terms of how they are manipulated 'from above' but in terms of the different combinations of constraints and opportunities associated with different types of employment or lack of employment, gender and family roles and life stages, all operating in the contexts of ethnic, national and religious cultures.

A big change, probably the biggest change over the last 30–40 years, is that we now have many more data on leisure behaviour. This is due to improvements in information processing technology. There are more large-scale surveys based on representative samples, and the findings are more accessible than in the pre-silicon chip, pre-Internet era. We now have a wealth of information on time use, how money is spent and participation rates in different leisure activities, which can all be analysed with the population subdivided by age, gender, ethnic group and socio-economic class. This means, I hope, that, while most of the positions adopted in this book are basically similar to those that I occupied many years ago, they are now much more securely grounded, the data required to address matters that are still subject to debate (of which there are many) can be defined more precisely than formerly and there are far better prospects of the relevant information being assembled.

Topics in leisure research have waxed and waned in popularity over the last 40 years and then in some cases waxed again:

- Work and leisure were the source of the field's big questions in the 1960s. Interest then declined, partly because some questions were answered (about the effects of shift work, for example) and in other cases because the theories (about spillover and compensation, for instance) turned out to explain less than was hoped. In the 1980s a flurry of enquiries addressed the leisure implications of unemployment (which had then returned as a public and political issue in most Western countries). These questions were answered and the projects (though not necessarily unemployment itself) dried up. The issues that keep 'work and leisure' a prominent issue today have to do with work–life balance, the general destandardization of working time and the implications of the new contours of inequality in post-industrial, globalized market economies.

- Community studies, which were a rich source of information about the ways of life of specific groups in the 1950s and 1960s, have become virtually extinct, probably due to the changing significance of 'place' in societies where people have become more mobile (geographically) than in the past and where, in some respects, lifestyles have become home- rather than neighbourhood-centred.

- Marxism provoked heated debates among leisure scholars (and elsewhere in the social sciences) in the 1970s and 1980s and then suffered long-range and rapid downward intellectual mobility, largely as a result of the world-wide collapse of communism between 1989 and 1991.

- Second-wave feminism elevated gender, women and leisure into leading research issues in the 1980s, which is what they have remained.

- Snapshots of leisure at different stages in the life course have been comple-mented by the investigation of developmental patterns and the impact of life events (made possible by the availability of longitudinal data sets), and the earlier preoccupation with young people's leisure is now balanced by grow-ing attention to leisure in later life (an example of research interest following the demographic trend towards ageing populations in all the world's older modern societies).

- During the 1990s, postmodern thought and the related 'cultural turn' gave a now fading boost to fact-free theory and a welcome and hopefully more enduring boost to in-depth qualitative studies.

- There has been a steady growth of interest in the leisure of ethnic minority groups, which is due to the growth in size of these groups, another outcome of population mobility, in Western Europe and North America.

Throughout all the above developments, leisure research and teaching have grown considerably. In the 1960s there were critical masses of leisure researchers only in North America, in France (and French Canada), and in communist east-ern and central Europe. Subsequently critical masses were formed in Britain, the Netherlands, Scandinavia, Australasia, Latin America, India, Japan, South Korea and China, while the east-central European group disintegrated when communism collapsed. The expansion of leisure as an academic enterprise in most parts of the world has been partly in response to leisure's growth, but also to the worldwide expansion of higher education and the 'graduatization' of emergent professions and semi-professions, which include many occupations in leisure. We have discovered that leisure is among the most naturally interna-tional social science topics, similar to social theory in this respect. This is because so many leisure activities are international – sports, television, films, music and, of course, tourism. Moreover, it just so happens that all the main relationships between leisure and other social roles are found to exist everywhere. Most of the hard evidence presented in this book is from Britain, my own country, and the one that I know best, but there are equally powerful relationships (and very simi-lar relationships) between types of employment, gender and life stages, on the one hand, and uses of leisure, on the other, in every country about which we possess the relevant information. Leisure evidence and the related theories travel remarkably well. This will be a reason why international networks in the study of leisure tend to be as sturdy as, if not stronger than, their national counterparts. Perhaps surprisingly, this has not yet led to a large volume of international comparative leisure research. Maybe this is an enterprise for the future. We still lack typologies that depict cross-national differences in uses of leisure, but, as noted above, the similarities in leisure practices and patterns in all modern societies appear to outweigh the differences. Maybe there are no counterparts in leisure to the continental European and Anglo-American versions of a market economy or the various types of state welfare regimes.

Leisure researchers today face some problems that have not changed over the last 30–40 years. There are still arguments about whether the subject is a discipline or a multidisciplinary field (which is my own view). The field tends to lack status when accommodated within other academic disciplines and has low status if treated as a subject in its own right. The field constantly threatens to fragment into specialist studies of sport, the arts, the media, tourism, etc. There are constant tensions between those who want the study of leisure to be based on the qualitative methods of cultural studies, those who favour the techniques of quantitative social science and those (like myself) who hope to draw from both. The upside is that all research fields and disciplines profit from controversy, and leisure studies have always benefited from open borders – by importing issues and linking up with researchers with what turn out to be cognate interests in economic change, health, the gender wars, delinquency, social inclusion and so on.

A stance adopted in the first edition of this book can be repeated here: the study of leisure now has strong roots, which are major assets, and fresh ventures will be strongest if based squarely on these foundations.

Ken Roberts
Liverpool University
2005

1   Leisure: Past and Present

Introduction

This book is about leisure in present-day Britain and similar societies: Western societies with market economies, democratic political systems and written or unwritten constitutions that protect citizens' rights from encroachment by the state. The leisure in our lives is a product of the modern organization of work, our market economies, the civil liberties that we enjoy and the weakening of the family, community and religious controls that prescribed and enforced common ways of life in earlier times. There are plenty of comparisons with other types of societies in the following chapters, and the above comments are not meant to imply that other people had and still have no leisure, only that a rather different concept is needed to convey the main features. It was only towards the end of the 19th century that the term leisure began to be applied to the lives of Britain's industrial workers (Cunningham, 1980). It is no accident that this was when Britain had become the first modern industrial society.

    This chapter opens by considering what we mean by leisure. As signalled above, it will be argued that the best course for analysts is to allow leisure to be defined by its economic, political and social contexts. The following section explains why leisure matters and why it deserves serious thought and investigation. We shall see that there are overwhelming economic, psychological and social grounds for taking leisure seriously. We shall also see that nowadays our uses of leisure make a big difference to the overall quality of our lives. These are among the reasons why, all over the world, present-day governments have become heavily involved in leisure. The chapter then introduces our main sources of information about leisure and, on the basis of this evidence, distinguishes major and minor uses of our leisure time and money. The chapter ends by posing this book's big question. If leisure can improve the quality of people's lives, how can it be that, despite the growth of leisure since the Second World War, people today appear no happier, no more satisfied with their lives, than when the relevant assessments were first made in the 1950s and 1960s?

Modern Leisure

Leisure is highly context-dependent. This will become clearer throughout the following chapters. Even within Western societies it can be argued that men and women and the employed, unemployed and retired, for example, do not share one common type of leisure. What leisure is can vary from group to group within a country depending on each group's circumstances, but the variations between societies, certainly between types of civilizations, are even more profound. Within Western countries, despite the internal variations, it is possible to identify a dominant form of leisure, which is produced by four contextual features.

The organization of work

Our leisure is a product, first and foremost, of the modern organization of work. Some work has not been modernized; housework is an example. But in all modern societies work is ordinarily taken to mean paid work, and most paid work is modernized, meaning here that it is compartmentalized and rationalized.

Paid work is usually done at specific times, at workplaces and under work-specific authority. This is what is meant by compartmentalization. Work thereby becomes a part of life rather than being embedded in multifunctional groups such as families. With the development of modern industries, work was taken from its former family and community contexts and located in offices and factories. Business is organized by the clock in these modern work organizations. People do not work when nature decrees that things can or have to be done. There are specified hours of work. The clock dictates when each working day begins and ends. While at work most people are subject to the orders of bosses, whose authority stops at the factory or office doors and at the end of each working day. This is different from the relationships that prevailed between lords and serfs in feudal times. Garhammer (1999) has argued that this 'modern' division of life into work and leisure is currently breaking down. This is just one of the trends (others are discussed in later chapters) that are said to be creating a new 'postmodern' condition. Garhammer argues that information technology (specifically the personal computer (PC), the mobile phone and the Internet) is leading to more people doing more of their work at home, where the hours when they perform tasks are variable. There is evidence to support this claim. Throughout the European Union in 2003 (just 15 countries at that time), approximately a quarter of all employees claimed to work regularly outside their core hours (European Commission, 2003). In Britain in 2000, around a fifth of all employees worked at home at least occasionally (Hogarth *et al.*, 2001). However, we should note that these figures show that most employees never or very rarely work outside their core hours or when they are at home, and that most of the exceptions still have core hours and other places – workplaces – where they go to do their paid work. This seems unlikely to change. Employers insist that it is necessary to have their staff working together face to face, not so much in order to supervise them as to facilitate the development of cohesion and trust (see Britton *et al.*, 2004).

Modern work is compartmentalized and also rationalized. Business is organized so that things are done efficiently. Work is not governed by tradition. If a new machine will perform more effectively, then custom and practice are discarded. This does not mean that work has to be disagreeable, but when people like their jobs this is more likely to be a fortuitous by-product rather than the prime objective. Good human relations and job satisfaction are deliberately promoted only insofar as they contribute to efficiency. This means that opportunities to play, to do things purely for fun, for the intrinsic satisfaction, tend to be squeezed out of working life. They must be sought outside the workplace, in the after hours: hence the modern division of life into work and leisure.

In any society where work has been modernized there will be a recognizable domain of leisure. This domain does not extend across all the time that is not accounted for by paid work. There are other things which, like paid jobs, just have to be done. Sleeping, feeding, bathing, household chores and other self-maintenance activities usually fall into this category. Leisure is the time left over. At any rate, it is located in this time. There are 'grey areas' (shopping, gardening and DIY, for example) which may be regarded by the actors as part work, part leisure, or as pure work by one person and pure leisure by another. Despite this, all those concerned are most likely to resort to the concepts of work and leisure in making sense of these uses of time. The money that is available to help them use their own time is the other key resource with which individuals develop leisure interests, engage in leisure activities and seek fun, diversion, relaxation or whatever experiences they prefer.

The market economy

Everyone who visited the former communist countries became aware that their leisure was different. In the holiday resorts that catered for Western tourists, careful efforts were made to provide these visitors with what they were believed to want. There was plenty of pop music, sunbathing or skiing, alcohol and souvenir shops. But when a single state authority operated all the hotels, restaurants and souvenir stores the effect was never quite the same as when a variety of suppliers compete for business. Market economies allow consumers to make more significant choices than were possible under state socialism. In market economies suppliers offer a variety of goods, services and environments. Each business tries to persuade customers that it is offering what they really want. It can be argued that powerful suppliers can sometimes manipulate people's desires and that markets systematically fail to satisfy the wants of many customers. These arguments are considered fully in later chapters, especially in Chapter 7. The current points are that markets create leisure environments in which individuals feel that they can choose how to use the time and money at their disposal, and this kind of experience is not guaranteed simply by having work-free time and money; it also depends on a surrounding market economy.

Liberal democracy

Multiparty democracies allow voters to choose their governments but an even more significant feature of these political systems for the character of leisure is that they permit freedom of association. The governments do not try to run everything. Citizens have civil rights. They are able to operate businesses and to form churches, political parties and pressure groups, trade unions and professional associations that run their own affairs. These same civil liberties allow people to organize their own leisure activities in voluntary associations: sports teams and clubs, art societies, gardening clubs, dramatic societies and so on. In any medium-sized town there are hundreds of such associations (see Bishop and Hoggett, 1986). In Toxteth alone, just one district in Liverpool, Ruby Dixon (1991) was able to identify 54 voluntary arts organizations. The district appeared to be a hotbed of arts activity, but a systematic investigation would almost certainly have identified just as many sports organizations, and there is no reason to believe that Toxteth was a particular hotbed.

Voluntary organizations are not profit-seeking businesses that are subject to the rules of the marketplace. Nor are they branches of the state, though they may sometimes receive state subsidies. Voluntary associations are formed and die according to their members' wishes and enthusiasm or apathy. The voluntary sector offers a distinctive kind of leisure experience and adds to the variety of leisure opportunities that are available. Once again, leisure is inevitably different in societies where all organizations are subject to state, party or church regulation.

The decline of community

The modern organization of work, economic markets and civil rights all conspire to weaken extended families, neighbourhood communities, churches and other belief-propagating movements, which, in other societies, have prescribed ways of life for everyone. When individuals can obtain their own jobs, locally or elsewhere, and earn their own money, they are able to spend their incomes without necessarily respecting the opinions of other family members, neighbours or church leaders. Voluntary associations and commercial enterprises offer leisure options that may not be part of family, neighbourhood or church traditions. Prior to these modern developments most people had little choice but to share the ways of life of the groups in which they lived, whereas with modern leisure individuals have greater scope to make their own lifestyle choices. Young people can live quite differently from their parents. Members of different households who live side by side can nurture entirely different leisure interests. DeLisle (2004) has argued that the tolerance that followed the Reformation in Roman Catholic Europe was important historically in allowing modern leisure to develop. Post-Reformation we have been tolerant towards different opinions and beliefs and towards other people's uses of their 'own time'. It can be argued that, in countries where there have been no equivalents of the Reformation, civil societies and multiparty political systems are less easily developed. That said, once up and running anywhere, these formations and practices, like modern leisure, can by adopted by other societies.

The kind of leisure that Western societies make available, and which most of their citizens can take for granted, does not occur naturally, as a straightforward expression of human nature, but has arisen in specific economic, political and social contexts. This kind of leisure has not existed in all societies. What used to be specifically Western leisure is currently becoming more widespread as more countries modernize and as the populations in their modern centres expand. The collapse of communism has also contributed to the globalization of Western leisure. But this kind of leisure is still far from universal. And just as the leisure that we know has not been around from the beginning of history, it is unlikely to last until the end of history, whenever that might be.

Why Study Leisure?

The very idea of taking leisure seriously and studying it systematically still produces sniggers in some quarters. Sceptics wonder why leisure scholars do not switch to something more important and worthwhile. 'Farce of Useless Degrees' was the *Daily Express* front-page headline on 21 August 1996. It was followed up by an editorial deploring 'supposed higher education that offers degrees and diplomas in leisure and recreation studies . . . Can you imagine for one minute that if university education were paid for directly and in full by parents or students there would be this laughable inflation of subjects?' Well, the students and parents who, since 1998 (when student fees were reintroduced in the UK), have been paying for degrees in these subjects have answered this question.

Twenty years ago this kind of tabloid outcry was quite common. Nowadays it is widely recognized that the jibes are wrongly targeted. It is true that no one needs even to be able to spell leisure in order to enjoy it, but the crucial fact is that leisure is important and needs to be investigated and studied thoroughly for economic, psychological, social and political reasons.

Economic

Leisure today is big business. Tourism alone can claim to be the world's biggest industry. In Britain leisure accounts for between 25% and 38% of all consumer spending, depending on exactly how many objects of spending are treated as leisure (Martin and Mason, 1998). Leisure may be just fun for some but it is a field in which others invest and where millions earn their living. Leisure is more likely to be a vocational subject for its students than most other social science specialisms. When all the vested interests are taken into account, it becomes easier to understand some of the imagery that surrounds leisure activities – why we are told that we will enjoy the experience of a lifetime if we visit a certain place and how our social acceptability will soar if only we drink or wear a certain thing, for example.

Leisure is an important source of employment, and it is now one of the few business sectors where some countries can be confident that employment will continue to grow. These countries include Britain. The economically advanced societies all experienced agricultural revolutions many years ago, in which jobs on the land were decimated while, in many cases, agricultural output actually increased. These societies are already well into their second industrial revolutions, in which manufacturing is following the path of agriculture – stable or even rising output alongside a steep decline in employment. Up to now, in most of these countries, the expansion of service sector employment has fully compensated for job reductions elsewhere, but some service sectors now appear set to follow agriculture and manufacturing. Public sector employment is no longer growing inexorably; voters have become resistant to forever rising taxes. The financial services are introducing computer technology and rationalizing their operations to reduce labour costs. Leisure remains one of the few economic sectors in which more employment is envisaged almost everywhere: hence the interest of villages, towns, cities, regions and countries throughout the world in gaining the largest possible shares of the leisure market.

The growth of tourism has made it an increasingly important factor in countries' trade balances. No country today can afford to ignore the economic impact of inward and outward tourism. Much the same applies to most towns and cities. It is no longer only traditional resorts that want to attract tourists, day trippers and people who are intent on enjoying an evening out. Former industrial, mining and commercial centres are now keen to present their heritages as tourist attractions. They take leisure seriously and are thirsty for information about trends in tourism and leisure more generally and the features that attract people with time and money to spend. Public leisure services used to be targeted primarily at local populations, whereas nowadays local and central governments seem more likely to invest in mega-projects that will attract visitors (see Bianchini and Parkinson, 1993; Street, 1993). In some cases the developers feel it necessary to shield the visitors from the local populations, or to train the latter to behave in the manner that the tourists expect, lest the locals blight the attractions. Developing World peoples in tourist resorts have become accustomed to this treatment; sections of the First World population are now tasting the medicine.

Psychological

Leisure has an important economic dimension and it is also important for the well-being of individuals. First, leisure enables people to relax and to refresh and literally recreate themselves so that they can then return, suitably restored, to other roles in their workplaces and families.

Secondly, leisure permits people to express desires and drives that would otherwise remain hidden and even suppressed. In everyday language, leisure allows people to 'let off steam' and give vent to their emotions. This is often achieved by playing games. Every game has its own particular rules and there are many different kinds of games, but the rules always serve to separate the activities from the rest of life. This separation is crucial. It means that people can become absorbed in the games that they play. Sports and quizzes can be taken very seriously. The same applies to artistic forms of play. But because it is 'only a game' the outcome does not really matter. People can emerge defeated or having crushed an opponent without there being any drastic implications for anyone's family or working life. This is why, in leisure, people are able to 'let themselves go', act adventurously, take risks and place themselves in the hands of fate (Vester, 1987).

Thirdly, leisure can be educative. People can develop skills and discover abilities that would otherwise have been untapped. Once again, this is possible because in leisure people can experiment and take risks without failure having devastating consequences. Through leisure activities, children and adults can develop motor, language and social skills, which may then be transported into other areas of their lives. Play methods work in classrooms and in many other places as well.

It will be clear from the above that there is immense variety in the experiences, including the satisfactions (psychic benefits) that people can derive from their leisure activities. Uses of leisure can be valued for diversion, entertainment, fun and relaxation. However, two particular kinds of satisfaction that may be obtained through leisure activities deserve special mention.

Mihaly Csikszentmihalyi (1990, 1993), an American social psychologist, has conducted a series of investigations to explore what people mean when they claim that something is enjoyable. Csikszentmihalyi's proposition is that enjoyment depends on the balance between the challenge that a situation or task poses and an individual's skill in the relevant area (see Box 1.1). When an individual's skill is overwhelmed by the immensity of a challenge, Csikszentmihalyi argues that anxiety will be experienced. If their skills are such that a challenge can be met almost effortlessly, he argues that people will soon become bored. When both an individual's skills and the challenge are modest, people are said to become apathetic. Peak enjoyment is said to arise from challenges in areas where individuals are highly skilled and when their capabilities are stretched to the utmost. In such situations Csikszentmihalyi argues that people will become wholly absorbed and 'lost' in the activities and that they will become unaware of other issues and incidents in their environments and of the passage of time. Csikszentmihalyi has adopted the term 'flow' to describe this state. No one argues that flow is the normal, let alone the definitive, leisure experience. Nor is it

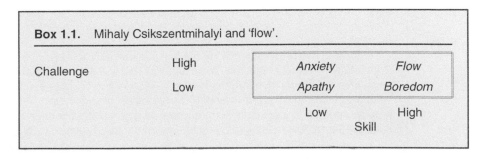

Box 1.1.   Mihaly Csikszentmihalyi and 'flow'.

Challenge	High	Anxiety	Flow
	Low	Apathy	Boredom
		Low	High
			Skill

argued that leisure alone can produce flow experiences: these are just as likely to arise when people are at work. However, it can be claimed that everyone is capable, in principle, of seeking and achieving flow experiences through leisure activities. People may experience flow in sporting contests, where optimal experience depends on meeting an opponent of equal ability, or they can become thoroughly absorbed in dancing, playing music, listening to music, reading or whatever. An implication is that making things easy, or doing things because they are easy, will not be the best way of gaining optimal leisure experience. Some writers argue that we have gone too far in trying to exclude risk (danger) from our leisure activities (see Dickson, 2004). Are ocean sailing and mountaineering as exciting and as satisfying as formerly when a combination of technology and regulations has virtually eliminated the risks? Is commerce guilty of making leisure activities so easy that the experiences are typically bland and hollow? As we shall see repeatedly in what follows, deeply satisfying leisure is most likely to be a product of people working hard at it (see Harper, 1997).

Serious leisure (see Box 1.2) also demands hard and sustained work and delivers special satisfactions of a kind that are different from 'flow'. Robert Stebbins (2001) does not denigrate casual leisure (the opposite of the serious type). He notes that casual leisure can refresh, amuse and so on – all valuable experiences in their own ways (Stebbins, 2001). He has also identified, and praised the virtues of, 'project-based leisure', which is midway between the really serious and the casual (Stebbins, 2005). Serious leisure, however, is said to deliver especially deep and sustained psychic and social (see below) benefits, which become more and more fulfilling the longer a serious leisure career is developed. In recent years, inspired by Stebbins's own case studies, there has been a stream of research into various types of serious leisure. For example, Gillespie and his colleagues (2002) have examined the extent to which show dog

---

Box 1.2.   Serious leisure.

This is a term coined by Robert Stebbins (1992), a Canadian sociologist. Stebbins defines serious leisure as 'the systematic pursuit of an amateur, hobbyist or volunteer activity that is sufficiently substantial and interesting for the participant to find a career there in the acquisition of its special skills and knowledge' (Stebbins, 1992, p. 3).

Instead of dividing uses of leisure into tourism, sport, television viewing and so on, it becomes possible to distinguish the serious from the casual and to recognize that serious leisure may link experiences in ostensibly different domains, such as listening to radio programmes about and taking holidays that are devoted to an interest.

Stebbins has drawn attention to the fact that some people grow so involved in their leisure interests that they become as skilled and knowledgeable as professionals in astronomy, sport, drama and so on. He argues that serious leisure enables people to derive a long-term sense of accomplishment, which may, provided people have such leisure, operate as a functional alternative to work during retirement or in the event of unemployment (see Stebbins, 1998).

enthusiasts often allow this interest to dominate their entire lives. Stanley Parker and a team of colleagues studied the serious leisure of a group of Australians. There were only 30 subjects in this study, but they were able to supply information about 222 of their leisure activities. Of these, only 17% were judged to be serious and another 18% were judged partly serious. Arts, handicrafts and volunteering were the leisure activities which were most likely to be serious. Sport was rarely more than partly serious, while watching television, reading and socializing were nearly always casual. Middle-class males aged over 50 were more likely to report serious leisure interests than other respondents (Parker *et al.*, 1993). We shall return below to the infrequency of people using their leisure in ways that are likely to be or to become serious or to generate flow.

Social

Most leisure has a social dimension and is therefore socially important. A common feature of leisure activities is their ability to bind people together. Leisure can contribute to personal health, well-being and fulfilment, and it can also promote trust, cooperation and bonding (see Arai and Pedlar, 2003). Common leisure interests and the related interaction in hobbies, sports and the arts can make groups gel. Shared leisure normally helps groups to cohere. This can work in families, neighbourhoods, schools and firms and for cities and countries. The solidarity engendered by shared leisure is likely to be most intense when, as in sport, one group competes against others. Employers, head teachers, urban planners and many other 'social engineers' have tried to benefit from leisure's bonding capacities.

It is important to bear in mind that what can unite can also divide. Thus home-centred leisure can privatize and isolate nuclear families. Leisure-based loyalties can set interest groups, schools, cities and countries at 'war' with one another. Provided this is treated as 'just a game', the outcomes need not be distressing for anyone except that the isolation of games from the rest of life is never total. Leisure relationships may arise from and within, and may sharpen, other social divisions. Leisure occasions can be times of harmony and fun, but they can also be stressful. Some people fear going out after dark. Northern Ireland's communal (separate Catholic and Protestant) celebrations can be occasions of jubilation, but for some they mean trauma and the threat of physical violence and injury (see Bairner and Shirlow, 2003; Murphy, 2003). Hence the need always to enquire which groups are strengthened and which divisions are highlighted and reinforced by a society's leisure activities.

Leisure and the quality of life

Leisure's psychological and social functions make it an important contributor to the quality of people's lives, meaning how good, satisfied, happy and content they feel. Here we face a paradox. Most people do not rate their leisure activities as highly important. All the relevant surveys show that most people prioritize their health, jobs and families (see Hall and Perry, 1974; Pronovost, 1988). Popular attitudes to leisure mirror the status of its study in some traditional academic circles. Yet objective measurements invariably find positive relationships between leisure activity and life satisfaction. There is some dispute about the confidence that can be placed in replies to questions such as 'How satisfied are you with your life?' (see Abrams, 1977). Expressed satisfaction may be a product of low expectations and aspirations. However, for what the measurements are worth (and we have no superior methods of diagnosis), life satisfaction appears to be additive – the product of how satisfied people are with their jobs, places of residence, family lives, health and so on (Andrews and Withey, 1976). Leisure activities are found to be related to general life satisfaction when other contributors are controlled. Indeed, leisure is usually found to be a better predictor of overall life satisfaction than income levels and health. Leisure's contribution to life satisfaction varies between socio-demographic groups. The relationship is particularly strong among people in later life (see Chapter 5, p. 155) but it contributes to life satisfaction in all sections of the population (see Kelly *et al.*, 1987; Melendez, 1992). All uses of leisure seem capable of making people feel better provided the leisure is structured and involves activity and social contact (see Hendry *et al.*, 1993; Isao-Ahola and Mannell, 2004). In other words, going regularly to the cinema with friends does people more good than staying alone at home and switching on a television film for want of anything better to do. Leisure contributes to life satisfaction by providing 'basic' experiences that are beneficial wherever they are obtained – activity, social contact, achieving goals and being appreciated by others.

That said, it appears to be the case that people need interests and goals and, in particular, group memberships to celebrate in their leisure, which in itself appears unable to generate sufficiently powerful and stable bonds to give people a sense of purpose and security. There are occupational communities, neighbourhood communities and religious communities. Are there comparable leisure communities? Groups with other bases can be strengthened through shared leisure, whereas groups that are formed specifically for leisure purposes appear far less likely to become multifunctional. It seems that people's social and psychological needs must be structured elsewhere otherwise their leisure becomes meaningless.

People today have more leisure time, and more money to spend in this time, than in the past. Chapter 2 warns against exaggerating the pace and extent to which leisure has grown, but we have in fact experienced a 'historical inversion' (Dumazedier, 1989). We are now in an era when most people's leisure time exceeds their hours at paid work. On average, UK adults (aged 16 and over) spend just 13% of their lifetime in paid work and study combined, whereas 22% of their lifetime is spent at leisure (see Table 1.1). Rojek (2000a) concludes from evidence such as this that we now live in a post-work society in which the work ethic has become dysfunctional and needs to be replaced by ethical principles that make us value free time and direct our uses of it. Subsequent chapters explain how recent economic and social changes have destabilized many people's occupational careers and neighbourhood and family lives. These have become

Table 1.1. UK 2000 Time Use Survey (all adults, all days, in percentages).

Sleep	35
Eating	6
Personal care (wash, dress)	3
Paid work and study	13
Housework and childcare (including shopping)	13
Leisure	22
Social life and entertainment	6
Sport	1
Hobbies and games	1
Watching TV	10
Other leisure	4
Travel	6
Not specified	1
Total	100

less reliable for many people. Such trends underline the importance of recognizing and using leisure's ability to contribute to personal and social well-being.

Political

All governments become interested in leisure, if only on account of the functions described above. Nowadays no government can afford to be indifferent to the economic significance of leisure. Most national governments have tourism policies and programmes designed to promote the import of tourists. Nowadays regional and local government bodies are most likely to have similar concerns and policies. Governments have become equally alert to the value of leisure in social bonding. Specifically, governments have sought to foster national solidarity and with this, they have usually hoped, support for their regimes. Pride in national heritage and culture can help to strengthen, if not create, a sense of national identity. International sporting success has been pursued by governments as a means of raising their countries' profiles and boosting national esteem. However, such measures may be insufficient to save otherwise unpopular regimes. Some communist states were spectacularly successful in international (especially Olympic) sports, but most of the governments and their political systems have now been replaced (see Riordan, 1995). Some governments have also been alert to the functions of leisure for individuals and have sought to provide all sections of their populations with opportunities to participate in 'desirable' leisure activities. In the 1960s and 1970s there were some signs of leisure gaining recognition as a branch of the welfare state and of all citizens becoming entitled, as of right, to take part in sport, appreciate the arts, visit the countryside and even go on holidays away from home (Bramham and Henry, 1985; Henry, 1993). Today it seems doubtful whether any governments, in the foreseeable future, will be able to raise the funds to bear the costs of such aspirations.

Governments inevitably become involved in leisure, irrespective of whether they wish to encourage particular uses of free time, if only because they are the ultimate custodians of social order and 'Leisure is part of the struggle for the control of space and time in which social groups are continuously engaged' (Wilson, 1988, p. 12). Leisure time and money have not been delivered automatically to the people by economic growth. They have usually needed to be won in labour markets, by bargaining with employers or by persuading governments to regulate hours of work and rates of pay (see Cunningham, 1980; Rosenweig, 1983). Governments must decide which demands to endorse, and they must define the limits of what is tolerable and may need, if only as a last resort, to arbitrate between competing claims on resources – for the use of water space by anglers and skiers, for example, to protect coastal or rural areas from industrial encroachment or to protect sensitive citizens from spectacles they find offensive. One group's innocent pleasure may offend others. When prohibiting or discouraging particular uses of leisure, governments appear prone to argue that they are acting in the real interests of those whose behaviour is being curbed. Whether declaring a war on drugs, curbing binge drinking, restricting gambling or discouraging public smoking, governments are likely to claim that the relevant actors are addicted, compulsive or irrational rather than making perfectly rational pleasure-seeking choices (see O'Malley and Valverde, 2004). Leisure is unavoidably political. Various groups constantly stake claims on physical and sociocultural space, sometimes within the existing politico-legal framework and at other times by resisting its demands and seeking changes. Bennett (2001) claims that since the 1950s all popular music genres have been part of, if not the basis of, broader cultures, usually with a political message, broadly defined.

Governments do not always win the leisure wars on which they embark. By the 1990s, despite the efforts of successive UK governments, drug use among Britain's young people had been 'normalized' (see Chapter 5, p. 143). Roughly a third of young people were then regular users of illegal drugs at some stage in their lives and most others were occasional or one-off users (Parker *et al.*, 2002). Pornography is another huge and highly controversial leisure industry (see Box 1.3), which has grown despite all the restrictions that governments have introduced.

Up to now most public leisure spending in Britain has been by local, not central, government. Leisure has, in fact, become the largest element in many a local authority's budget. Few members of the public may be aware of this because of their limited interest and involvement in local politics. In UK local elections people tend to vote, if they bother to do so, according to their national party sympathies. However, since 1992, most central government leisure spending has been channelled through a single department, originally the Department of National Heritage and, since 1997, the Department for Culture, Media and Sport, which is also responsible for the National Lottery. This is big money and how it is spent easily becomes politically controversial. Flops such as the Millennium Dome are politically embarrassing. Politicians also become embroiled in controversies about how Lottery funds are distributed between regions, between projects that are majority and minority and mainly middle-class as opposed to working-class interests, for example. Electoral pressures and government's own financial problems

---

Box 1.3.   Pornography.

This is a very large leisure industry.

Nowadays the main product is the sex video. In the USA 200 new titles are produced every week.

The Internet has become a major outlet. In 1997 there were around 22,000 porn websites; by 2003 there were an estimated 300,000.

US pornography has a larger turnover than:

- mainstream cinema;
- theatre;
- rock and country music.

US strip clubs have a larger cash turnover than Broadway, regional theatres and orchestral performances combined.

Sex tourism has become a distinct branch of the global holiday industry.

Sources: Sharkey (1997); Jeffreys (1999); Campbell (2003).

---

have already persuaded politicians that some Lottery funds should go to environmental, health and education projects rather than leisure facilities, which, as noted above, are not generally regarded as crucial, whatever the objective evidence says, to people's quality of life.

Mulgan and Wilkinson (1995) have forecast that time will become a major political issue during the 21st century. They have in mind people demanding parental leave, sabbaticals for re-education and training and ceilings on the hours that they can be expected to work in order to be considered serious candidates for promotion. During the 20th century governments came to be regarded as responsible for production issues – the extent to which economic output and standards of living grew. Governments are now held equally responsible for the overall distribution of society's resources and these include time and space (geographical and cultural) as well as money.

Information about Leisure

Nowadays leisure researchers face not a shortage but a wealth of basic information about the population's leisure activities, time and spending. These data mountains grow so fast that the material is never analysed exhaustively. There may be a shortage of small and medium-scale studies that explore the fine detail of the leisure of specific social groups and of carefully designed enquiries into specific leisure issues, but there is a wealth of information about the distribution of leisure time, leisure activities and spending throughout the entire population in the UK and most other modern societies. Most of this information has not been gathered to satisfy someone's disinterested thirst for knowledge. It has been collected routinely, usually at the behest of public and commercial leisure providers, who have wanted to establish the actual and potential sizes of their markets and audiences.

Participation surveys

These provide one kind of information about the population's leisure. Participation surveys usually present their samples with checklists of leisure activities and ask which have been done within a given time period and how often. The main British survey that has collected this type of information is the General Household Survey. This is conducted annually and covers a nationally representative sample of households. It is a general, multipurpose survey and carries any questions that government departments (and sometimes outside bodies) wish to have included and are willing to pay for. In 1973, and subsequently at various intervals, the General Household Survey has included a battery of questions about leisure activities. It has recorded, for example, the proportions of the population that do gardening, sport and dressmaking. Participation rates for different sections of the population can be calculated and compared, and since some of the same leisure questions have been asked periodically since 1973 trends over time can be established. This evidence shows, for example, that levels of sport participation rose during the 1970s and 1980s, remained steady during the early 1990s and have subsequently declined slightly (see Table 1.2). The steepest decline in all kinds of physically active recreation has been in walking (for at least 2 miles, for recreation). The decline in other forms of physically active recreation has been steepest in the young adult age groups (Table 1.3). Governments have neither envisaged nor encouraged these trends. The trends are not part of an all-round decline in leisure activity. In most leisure activities participation rates have been either constant or have risen (Table 1.4). Why are fewer of us going for long walks, and why are fewer young adults playing sports than in the early 1990s? Participation surveys have revealed these trends. Further enquiries (of a different type) are required to discover the reasons why.

Presentations of the type of information in the following tables are normally, and justifiably, accompanied by hazard warnings. The evidence is never quite as

Table 1.2. Trends in sport participation taken part in 4 weeks before interview (in percentages).

	1987	1990	1993	1996	2002
Walking	38	41	41	45	35
Swimming	13	15	15	15	14
Keep fit/yoga	9	12	12	12	12
Snooker/pool/billiards	15	14	12	11	9
Cycling	8	9	10	11	9
Weight training	5	5	5	6	5
Running	5	5	5	5	5
Soccer	5	5	4	5	5
At least one activity	61	65	64	64	58
At least one activity excluding walking	45	48	47	46	43

Source: Fox and Rickards (2004).

Table 1.3. Participation in at least one physical activity (excluding walking) in 4 weeks prior to interview by age (in percentages).

Age (years)	1987	1990	1993	1996	2002
16–19	80	82	81	78	72
20–24	69	72	71	70	61
25–29	63	67	65	63	60
30–44	56	59	58	57	54
45–59	35	42	43	40	40
60–69	23	28	28	30	27
70 and over	10	12	16	13	14

Source: Fox and Rickards (2004).

Table 1.4. Trends in participation in selected leisure activities: percentages taking part in 4 weeks prior to interview.

	1977	1980	1983	1986	1987	1990	1993	1996	2002
Watching TV	97	98	98	98	99	99	99	99	99
Visiting or entertaining friends or relatives	91	91	91	94	95	96	96	96	*
Listening to radio	87	88	87	86	88	89	89	88	88
Listening to records/tapes	62	64	63	67	73	76	77	78	83
Reading books	54	57	56	59	60	62	65	65	66
Gardening	42	43	44	43	46	48	48	48	*
DIY	35	37	36	39	43	43	42	42	*
Dressmaking, needlework or knitting	29	28	27	27	27	23	22	22	*

*Questions not asked.
Source: Fox and Rickards (2004).

hard as it can appear in tables of figures. The percentages shown to be taking part depend on the thresholds for being considered a participant: should this be at least once a month, less or more frequently? The specific activities that are included under certain broad headings also repay scrutiny. For example, the General Household Survey's list of sports contains non-strenuous activities, such as snooker, and all types of physical recreation are included – recreational swimming and walking, for example – not just those cases where there are sporting contests.

Participation surveys are more discriminating for some activities than for others. The measurements work quite well with structured activities such as sports, which may be played daily, weekly or more occasionally, but the findings are less useful in respect of activities such as watching television, which most people do daily, and with unstructured pastimes such as listening to radio music, with which people can have difficulty in recalling exactly how often they have participated.

Time budget studies

These have been conducted rather less frequently and less regularly than national participation surveys. Time budgets are expensive to administer and analyse, especially with large samples. They require subjects to keep diaries for specimen days (a week day and a weekend day in the UK 2000 Time Use Survey), but sometimes for as long as a week or a fortnight, recording their main activities in each 15- or 30-min period, and then usually seek additional information such as where the subjects were and who they were with.

Time budget evidence permits calculations of the total amount of leisure time that is available to the population as a whole (see Table 1.1, p. 11) and to various subgroups. The proportions and amounts of leisure time devoted to specific leisure activities can also be calculated. This kind of evidence discriminates levels of television viewing, which many people do daily, more effectively than participation surveys, but time budgets have their own limitations. Because it is unrealistic to expect people to maintain diaries for longer than a few days the method is likely to miss more occasional activities such as holidays. The method is also liable to miss activities that are not precisely time-bounded and which are often done alongside something else. Talking with other family members, which may happen while preparing or eating meals or watching television, is one example. Also, there will be activities that people prefer not to report, such as having sex, taking drugs and committing robberies.

Economic statistics

There is a wealth of information about the public's spending patterns, the most detailed in the UK being from the Family Expenditure Survey. Like the General Household Survey, this is conducted annually with a large, nationally representative sample. Like time budgets, it requires the subjects to keep records, of all their spending in this case, and to give details about their incomes. From this information it is possible to calculate the total amount of leisure spending and the amounts devoted to specific types of leisure. As with participation surveys and time budgets, these calculations can be made for the population as a whole and then subdivided in numerous ways.

These data also have inherent limitations. All survey evidence is subject to errors arising from respondents' imperfect memories or preferring not to disclose some of the things that they have done. We know that people tend to underestimate their spending on items often considered wasteful, such as alcohol and tobacco, and grossly exaggerate their participation in 'worthwhile' activities, such as sport (see Chase and Godbey, 1983; Cale and Almond, 1992). Economic statistics have additional blind spots. They do not pick up free uses of leisure, such as relaxing. Also, there are many types of spending within which it is

Table 1.5. Average household spending, Great Britain, 1974–2000/1.

	1974 (£s (at 2000/1 prices))	2000/1 (£s)	2000/1 as % of 1974 (in real terms)
Housing	38.8	63.9	164
Fuel and power	14.8	11.9	80
Food and non-alcoholic drink	68.8	61.9	90
Alcoholic drink	13.5	15.0	111
Tobacco	10.1	6.1	60
Clothing and footwear	25.5	22.0	86
Household goods	23.0	32.6	141
Household services	8.7	22.0	252
Personal goods and services	9.4	14.7	156
Motoring	30.2	55.1	182
Fares and other travel	7.6	9.5	125
Leisure goods	13.2	19.7	149
Leisure services	16.5	50.6	307
Miscellaneous	1.3	0.7	54
Total	281.3	385.7	137

Source: Family Expenditure Survey.

difficult, in practice impossible, to separate the leisure element. Spending on clothing, transport and telephones are examples.

We can see in Table 1.5 that between 1974 and 2001 the fastest-growing area of consumer spending in Britain was on leisure services. There were absolute declines (in real terms) in the amounts being spent on fuel and power, clothing and footwear and tobacco products. After leisure services, the steepest increases were in household services, motoring and housing.

A point to bear in mind when reading data such as in Table 1.5 is that the comparisons are not between strictly like and like. The composition of the UK population changed – more older people and relatively fewer in the younger age groups, and more single-person households as a result of young people tending to live singly on first leaving their parents' homes prior to marrying or cohabiting and of rising rates of divorce and separation. A net result is that the growth in average household spending lagged behind the rate of growth in spending by the entire population and in the typical employee's gross earnings. However, none of this modifies the picture of leisure as the fastest-growing area of consumer spending. By 2002/3 UK households, on average, were spending as much on restaurants and hotels as on fuel and power, and more on recreation and culture than on food and non-alcoholic drinks (Table 1.6).

Major uses of leisure

All the above types of information have characteristic limitations, but by combining the different kinds of evidence it is possible to identify the public's main

Table 1.6.   Average household spending: distribution between
various items, Great Britain 2002/3.

	%
Housing, fuel and power	9
Food and non-alcoholic drink	11
Alcohol and tobacco	3
Clothing and footwear	5
Household goods and services	7
Health	1
Travel	15
Communications	3
Recreation and culture	14
Education	1
Restaurants and hotels	9
Miscellaneous (specified)	8
Other	14
Total	100

Source: Family Expenditure Survey.

leisure activities – things that most people do and which account for considerable
proportions of their leisure time and/or spending. The big three that are identifiable in this way are the media, out-of-home eating and drinking and holidaymaking. Out-of-home eating and drinking (when combined) head the spending
league, tourism is in second place and home entertainment (mostly TV-related)
is third.

When people go out, the things that they are most likely to do and spend
money on are the consumption of food and drink (especially the alcoholic varieties). Participation in these activities and the sums spent vastly exceed the figures
for cinema admissions and sport spectating and playing. When people go out in
the evenings or at weekends, their most likely activities are eating and drinking.
Sometimes these are the central events in the outings but people are also likely to
purchase and consume food and alcohol when they go out for other leisure purposes – for day trips to the countryside or to concerts, for example. The result is
that out-of-home food and drink are leading leisure items.

In terms of time use, home entertainment is placed first. Since the 1970s
adults in Britain have been watching television for well over 20 h per week on
average. Time spent attending to all the mass media, when aggregated, amounts
to approximately a half of all leisure time. Television alone accounts for 40%
(see Table 1.1, p. 11). The media play a major role in most people's leisure and
since the 1950s, among all the media, television has been by far the most important, certainly in terms of time accounted for. The media are also major objects
of leisure spending. People may regard switching on the television or the radio as
free entertainment but in fact we spend substantial sums, relative to other leisure
items, on renting or purchasing the sets, on cable and satellite reception and

on video and DVD recordings. The home is most people's main leisure centre. The family is their main leisure group. And, when at home with their families, people are more likely to watch television or attend to other media than to engage in any other leisure activities.

Tourism is the third member of leisure's leading trio. Approximately three-fifths of the UK population take at least one holiday away from home each year. Participation is not as high as for television viewing and alcohol consumption, and tourism is not outstanding in terms of time accounted for since most people 'go away' only once or twice a year. In terms of expenditure, however, tourism is definitely among the population's leading uses of leisure. Over a 12-month period the typical household spends more on its holidays than on audio-visual media. Over time, spending on holidays has been rising more steeply than most other kinds of leisure spending. The proportion of UK households that do not take any holidays away from home – around 40% – has not declined since data collection began in 1970. Meanwhile, more of the 60% who do go away have been taking multiple holidays rather than just a single break. This is just one example of leisure polarization. We shall encounter further examples, mainly in Chapter 3. The explanation of the leisure polarization lies in the wider economic polarization that has occurred in the UK (and in many other countries) since the 1970s. The better-off have become even better-off both absolutely and relative to the less well-off, and the well-off have been using their additional resources, among other things, to take more holidays and to travel further. The extent to which so many of the people who are able to do so are willing to save for the greater part of the year in order to enjoy a week or two 'away' suggests that these occasions must be highlights to which individuals attach considerable importance.

Uses of Leisure and the Quality of Life

None of our main uses of leisure are likely to be sources of flow or bases for the development of serious leisure careers. It is true that holidays and TV programmes may be selected so as to extend a long-term interest in ecclesiastical buildings, Renaissance art or whatever, but this is not what usually happens. Despite the prominence of television in our time schedules, we rarely name it as a particularly enjoyable use of leisure (Robinson and Godbey, 1999). From what we know about how we have been using our increased free time and the money to spend in it, we can hardly claim surprise that the results have not included enhanced life satisfaction. This could be because, above the subsistence/poverty level, access to free time and levels of consumer spending can make no further impact on human well-being. However, it could also be on account of the particular ways in which we have been using our new leisure resources.

As acknowledged earlier, it is not easy to measure things like well-being and the quality of life. One day we may be able to measure relevant kinds of brain activity but these measurements will still need validation by correlating them with what people say. Here the evidence is unequivocal. In Western countries people feel no happier today than 50 years ago (Layard, 2003). Within countries, the higher income groups are consistently happier than poorer people, but between countries mean happiness scores cease to rise alongside rising incomes once the mean income exceeds US$15,000 per year (Layard, 2003). This has led even (some) economists to criticize the extent to which governments remain dedicated to achieving growth in GDP (gross domestic product). Two hundred years ago, in the age of Adam Smith, economists advocated markets and allowing individuals to pursue their self-interests because they believed (and they were probably right at the time) that this would lead to greater happiness for everyone. The 19th-century utilitarians advocated 'the greatest happiness for the greatest number' as the benchmark for assessing government policies. Since the Second World War, governments have prioritized GDP despite the mounting evidence that further gains on this index cannot be equated with gains in overall well-being. Radical social economists are now proposing alternative indices. The London-based New Economics Foundation (www.neweconomics.org) has developed a measure of domestic progress (MDP), which takes GDP and then subtracts sums for environmental costs, resource depletion and social factors, such as crime, inequality and family breakdown. Over the last 50 years, GDP in the UK has roughly tripled while MDP has hardly changed. Yet leisure has grown. Must we conclude that the growth of leisure has lost the ability that it might once have possessed to improve the quality of people's lives? Such pessimism must be judged premature, given all that we know about socially and physically active leisure improving mental and physical health among rich and poor, men and women and in all age groups, likewise feelings of leisure being self-determined and giving individuals a sense of autonomy (Isao-Ahola and Mannell, 2004). The problem seems to be that, if the goal is to improve the well-being of individuals and to create a better quality of life for all, we are using our increased leisure in perverse ways.

Far from promoting physical health, our major uses of leisure are more likely to inflict damage. Given that we spend so much of our leisure time watching television and that when we go out this is most likely to be to eat and/or drink, it should come as no surprise that we have become heavier. The proportions of adults who are obese or overweight have risen. In fact, the majority of adults in England are now in one of these categories (see Tables 1.7a and 1.7b). So are an increasing proportion of our children. Nearly a fifth of England's 4-year-olds are overweight and 8% have already grown clinically obese. This is not a

Table 1.7a. Body mass, males only, England 1993 and 1999 (percentages).

	1993	1999
Underweight	5	5
Desirable	38	33
Overweight	44	44
Obese	13	19

Table 1.7b. Body mass, males and females, England 2001 (percentages).

	Males	Females
Underweight	4	6
Desirable	28	38
Overweight	47	33
Obese	21	23

Source: Health Survey for England, Department for Health.

peculiarly British phenomena. Americans are the heaviest people on the planet. Obesity rates among France's 5–12-year-olds have risen from 6% in the 1980s to 12% today. In Finland the proportions of 14-year-olds who are overweight rose from 6% of boys and 4% of girls in 1977 to 17% and 10%, respectively, in 1999 (British Medical Association, 2003). The British Medical Association (2003) has warned that children's and young people's unhealthy lifestyles will inevitably result in higher rates of involuntary infertility and, further into the future, a decline in life expectancy (see also Chapter 5, p. 142).

Why do so many of us use our leisure in ways that are more likely to impair than to improve the quality of our lives? One possibility is that people are ignorant and need better information and leisure education. However, most people value their health, and they also know that physically active leisure will improve their health, and yet they fail to act on this knowledge (Isao-Ahola and Mannell, 2004). A second possibility is that the leisure industries, especially those that are driven by the profit motive, make things so easy and tempting that we succumb. Then there is a third possibility: that apparently perverse uses of leisure are enforced by the ways in which increased leisure time and spending power have been distributed between different sections of our population.

Chapter 2 considers how and why, exactly when and for whom leisure has grown over time. The distribution of leisure time and differences in participation rates in the various leisure activities among different sections of the population are considered in detail in Chapters 3–5. Chapter 3 deals with leisure differences related to people's types of jobs or lack of any employment, Chapter 4 deals with gender differences and Chapter 5 examines how uses of leisure change over the life course. The remaining chapters consider alleged consequences of the long-term growth of leisure, which, instead of or as well as the distribution of leisure throughout the population, may help to explain the failure of leisure's growth to convert into a better overall quality of life. Chapter 6 considers whether leisure has now become central to the lifestyles from which we derive our self-identities and from which we can be mobilized for 'political' action. Chapter 7 debates whether commerce, the profit-seeking economy and its consumer culture have become dominant influences on how we spend our leisure. Chapter 8 considers whether, in the light of these changes, we need to rethink our opening question, 'What is leisure?'

Summary

This chapter has argued that leisure is best defined in terms of how it has been created by modern market economies, democratic political systems and the surrounding social contexts.

We then examined the various reasons why leisure matters: because it is a major part of modern economies, on account of its psychological and social effects and because governments, partly in response to these considerations, inevitably become involved in leisure. We noted that leisure can offer benefits to individuals in terms of their physical and mental well-being, and to the entire population in terms of the quality of life to which people have access. We also noted that, if leisure can do good, it can also do harm – this depends on how leisure is used.

The chapter then reviewed our main sources of information about uses of leisure – participation surveys, time budgets and economic data. We saw that the main uses of leisure in modern Western countries are out-of-home eating and drinking, tourism and the media, none of which are likely to offer the fullest benefits of which leisure is capable.

The chapter concluded with a paradox: despite the benefits that leisure can offer, its growth since the Second World War has failed to translate into gains in life satisfaction in the world's richest countries. Possible answers to this paradox were noted. Its solution is probably the greatest challenge currently facing leisure theory and research.

Further Reading

On the historical development and necessary conditions for modern leisure

Cunningham, H. (1980) *Leisure in the Industrial Revolution*. Croom Helm, London.
DeLisle, L.J. (2004) Leisure and tolerance – an historical perspective. *World Leisure Journal* 46 (2), 55–63.

On leisure and the quality of life

Harper, W. (1997) The future of leisure: making leisure work. *Leisure Studies* 16, 189–198.
Isao-Ahola, S.E. and Mannell, R.C. (2004) Leisure and health. In: Haworth, J.T. and Veal, A.J. (eds) *Work and Leisure*. Routledge, London, pp. 184–199.

2 The Growth of Leisure

Introduction

This chapter begins with an overview of the long-term growth of leisure: how this has been an outcome of rolling back hours of paid work, rising incomes and changes in patterns of home and family life. We then see how modern leisure was shaped in what have usually proved enduring ways very early in industrial history. It was then that evenings, weekends and annual holidays became our major leisure occasions, when the commercial businesses, voluntary associations and public-sector bodies that still cater for our leisure were created and when most of our present-day leisure activities were either invented or adapted to conditions in industrial societies.

Next, the chapter identifies four long-term trends that have unfolded gradually during leisure's growth: commercialization, blurring social divisions, individualization and pacification.

The chapter then focuses on recent trends and how recent experiences have led some writers to reinterpret earlier history. They have noted that not all sections of the population have benefited equally, and that some have not benefited at all, from the long-term growth of leisure and that shorter hours of paid work (for some) have been at least partly offset by new obligations. We note that, compared with pre-industrial times, present-day societies are not blessed with an abundance of free time and that in some countries the rollback in hours of paid work appears to have ended (at least for the time being). Questions are then raised about the quality of the forms in which leisure has recently grown.

The final section of the chapter discusses possible future scenarios. It notes that recent gains in work-free time, on the one hand, and spending power, on the other, have gone to entirely different sections of the population. It also notes signs of frustration among both the time-rich, money-poor and the time-poor, money-rich, and that minorities, admittedly very tiny minorities as yet, are pioneering alternative lifestyles.

The Expansion of Modern Leisure

It has been customary, rightly so, for books on leisure to open by stressing the subject's importance: such regard for leisure still cannot be taken for granted. Subsequently the books normally and correctly explain how over time leisure has grown ever more important; that it has become a larger, more significant, more central element in people's day-to-day lives and in their overall quality of life. This book is true to type in all these respects. The growth of leisure is endemic in modern societies. Having created leisure by making work into a part of life, the economies generate more and more. This long-term trend is ongoing and no end is in sight.

All the quantitative indicators reveal long-term growth in leisure time, leisure spending and rates of participation in leisure activities. It is relatively easy to demonstrate leisure's quantitative growth. It is not quite as straightforward, but no less plausible, to postulate related qualitative trends: towards people's well-being – physical, mental and social – becoming increasingly dependent on their uses of leisure; towards leisure interests and activities becoming more central and pivotal in people's overall ways of life; towards people becoming more concerned about, and able to protect, their leisure by tailoring work and family commitments accordingly; and towards leisure becoming a base for people's self-concepts and social identities – how they regard themselves and how they are regarded by others. All this easily becomes an agreed credo among people with vested interests in leisure because they either cater for other people's or study and write about it. In fact, all these claims about qualitative shifts are extremely controversial, less firmly established than they can be made to sound. This book is sceptical towards these claims (which are discussed in detail in Chapters 6 and 7) and discriminating about the senses in which leisure is becoming more important.

The conventional (and correct) story of leisure's long-term growth invariably starts with the development of modern industries. In Britain this occurred between 1750 and 1850, when the country was transformed from a mainly rural into a predominantly urban society, when manufacturing replaced agriculture as the main economic activity and when Britain became the world's first industrial nation – the pioneer in the development of modern leisure. The far-reaching changes that took place in this period are usually summarized as 'the industrial revolution'.

Rolling back hours of work

All students of modern history learn about the long hours and hard labour that were imposed upon their workforces by the early industrialists (Malcolmson, 1973; Cunningham, 1980). During the first half of the 19th century a normal working day in the factories could last for 12 hours or more. In wintertime people commenced work before dawn and continued after sunset. This was before the age of electric lighting. At that time manual labour was often extremely heavy. Many tasks had still to be mechanized, let alone automated. Railway cuttings were excavated using human energy. During the industrial revolution the normal working week was extended to 6 days and Sunday remained the only generally recognized day of rest. Employers waged a long and ultimately unsuccessful struggle to discipline labour to accept such regimes.

The problem was that employers were seeking to impose not just long hours of work but also a new rhythm of working life. Previously most people's work had been governed by 'natural rhythms' (see Thompson, 1967). Work was done when it could be done or had to be done. In agriculture, there were periods such as harvests when there was much for everyone to do, but for most of the year the pace of life was more relaxed. The traditional English weekend had lasted 2 days, usually Sunday and Monday, and the calendar was liberally sprinkled with saints' days and feast days. People had participated in rural pastimes and sports and found amusement at fairs, and alcohol had flowed freely on all occasions of celebration. This was the background to the 19th-century campaigns for temperance, to encourage the working class to abandon traditional amusements and adopt sober ways of life (see Malcolmson, 1973). Employers struggled to discipline workforces that continued to recognize 'St Monday' and annual 'wakes', and who spent their free time in debauchery rather than physical and mental recovery. One advantage in employing child labour, according to some employers, was that the very young were easily moulded to industry's requirements. Adults who migrated from the countryside, bringing their blood sports and drinking with them, were less pliable. If children were too young to be employed, it was considered desirable that they should be schooled in the habits of discipline, punctuality and industriousness. These habits were in fact taught in the elementary schools, most of which were run by the churches, otherwise by private individuals and then, after 1870, by Britain's new local school boards. The churches and schools partnered employers and the temperance movements in propagating a work ethic consistent with industrial employment.

Prior to 1850 paid holidays were simply not part of industrial life. If workers continued to recognize traditional holiday weeks, their time off was unpaid. Most traditional saints' and feast days had no place in the new industrial calendar. Between 1761 and 1834 bank holidays were reduced from 47 to just four (Myerscough, 1974). Men, women and children were subjected to industrial hours and discipline in the mines and factories. There was no compulsory education or old-age pensions. People would work for as long as they were able. Thereafter they became dependent on their families, charity or, as a last resort, the workhouse. Poor relief operated on the principle of 'less eligibility'. In order to motivate and discipline labour it was considered essential that the conditions of those who resorted to charity or public assistance should be distinctly less attractive than those of the lowest-paid worker.

It would be misleading to create an impression that everyone worked 12 hours per day, 6 days a week, 52 weeks a year, from childhood to infirmity. For a start, employers could not guarantee regular work. Secondly, the workforces often preserved their traditional leisure occasions. This was in addition to individual absences. Thirdly, many young children were kept out of the factories and mines and were sent to school or remained at home assisting with the care of younger siblings. For many women, childbearing and child-rearing were necessarily full-time occupations. Subsequently employment has become more regular and workforces have become better disciplined, and these trends will have offset the impact of reductions in the standard working day, week and year, which have been one of three major trends responsible for the long-term growth of leisure.

After the mid-19th century, standard hours of work began to be rolled back and the long upward march of modern leisure commenced. There were several forces instigating this trend. First, legislators began to restrict hours of work, initially for vulnerable groups such as women and children and in industries which were considered especially hazardous, such as coal mining. Legal ceilings were introduced on the length of a working day and employers were required to give their staff breaks during otherwise long, unbroken, working stretches. National opinion was shocked by the reports of the factory inspectors on conditions of work in the mines and mills of industrial England. Child labour became an issue, a crusade, that lasted into the 20th century. Women and children had worked in rural Britain but this had usually been in the family or in family-like environments in the cases of domestic servants and apprentices. What outraged 19th-century opinion was not so much that women and children were working as that the new conditions included the long hours of work that were being imposed by employers, most of whom could not be described as paternal.

Trade unions were the second force behind the reduction in basic hours of work. Craft workers began to organize effectively in 'new model unions' from the 1850s onwards, and trade unionism spread to non-skilled labour in the 1880s. As soon as labour began to organize and confront employers with collective demands, these invariably included higher pay and shorter hours. It has remained so to the present day. Reductions in working time have not normally been bestowed on grateful workforces by benevolent employers. Such improvements in terms and conditions of work have usually been outcomes of workforce organization and struggle. Working hours have not been reduced gradually and smoothly from year to year. There have been major lurches, usually when employers have been able to afford the concession, namely, during upturns in business cycles and when trade unions have been especially keen to obtain shorter hours, typically in order to reduce the threat of unemployment, which remained at the forefront of negotiators' minds following their members' experiences during previous recessions (see Bienefeld, 1972).

It should be noted that, in bargaining for reduced hours of work, labour was implicitly accepting the 'payment for time' package. The industrial workforce came to accept industrial work discipline – the need to work reliably – in exchange for fair rewards. Labour learnt that time was money and tried to use the formula for its own advantage. Everything could be given a price. Shift systems and overtime proved acceptable if and when the price was right. By the time that trade unions were successfully negotiating for shorter hours, their employers' battles to industrialize their workforces had been won.

The third force behind the reduction of standard working hours was that from the mid-19th century onwards some employers began to adopt 'enlightened', 'progressive' approaches. Many realized that tired workers were neither efficient nor reliable and that the loss of working time could be at least partly compensated by increased productivity and fewer mistakes during the remaining hours of work. This became a more weighty consideration as industry became more capital-intensive and mistakes became more expensive and dangerous. When 'Taylorism' spread during the 20th century – so-called scientific management with its stop-watches and work study methods – employers became aware, because their own methods were producing the evidence, that long hours could be counterproductive. They discovered that work regimes could be intensified and quality standards maintained only by giving their workforces regular breaks and limiting their total hours of employment.

Moreover, employers began to realize that using leisure to motivate their workforces could be more effective than trying to suppress their pastimes. Employees, it was realized, could be persuaded to attend regularly and punctually and to work hard, in exchange for the promise of leisure. Needless to say, the employers wanted to ensure that their workers' free time was used 'sensibly'. Instead of just opposing the undesirable, 19th-century employers joined the churches and other social campaigners in urging 'rational recreation' (see Bailey, 1978). Workers were encouraged to adopt improving, edifying pastimes in preference to their blood sports and drink. Edifying pastimes included using the libraries that were being opened, attending the evening classes that were becoming available, going to the churches that were being built and playing the modern sports that were initially invented in the public schools and universities and then taken to the masses. Some employers developed work-based recreation. A few built their own model industrial villages. These campaigns were not 100% successful but they were a factor in the development of 'respectable' lifestyles among sections of the working classes, generally the more skilled and better paid and those whose jobs were the most secure (see Bailey, 1978). The middle classes more generally sought to use local government to civilize the industrial cities by laying out parks and playing fields, opening art galleries and museums and building concert halls. There were hopes that these facilities would civilize the labouring classes but by the time of the First World War the middle classes were in full flight to the suburbs, having largely abandoned their earlier aspirations (see Meller, 1976). Suburban living became an option as suburban railways were opened and when tram and bus services were introduced.

All the edges of working time have been trimmed. The standard working day was cut back to no more than 10 h in nearly all industries during the second half of the 19th century. Subsequently it has been reduced to its current norm of 7 or 8 h in a full working day. The contraction of the normal working day may now have ended. At some point, the time and money costs of travelling to work must cease to be recompensed from the worker's viewpoint. Employers too are bound to find at some point that their workforces can remain fully alert for a full working day and that there are no benefits to offset further reductions in working time.

The standard working week also began to shrink in the second half of the 19th century. An extra half-day of leisure was won. Saturday afternoons became leisure occasions. A reason why some employers preferred to release part of Saturday rather than restore 'St Monday' was that if workers became intoxicated on the Saturday they could recover on the Sunday. The 5½-day week remained the norm throughout industry until after the Second World War, when the 2-day weekend break became standard. There have been subsequent forecasts of a 4-day working week and a 3-day weekend (Poor, 1972). Early finishes on Fridays are now common, but as yet the 5-day working week has remained the most common pattern.

In the late 19th century employers began to recognize annual holidays. At first these were usually holidays without pay for manual workers. Until the First World War, paid holidays were non-manual perks in most businesses. Workers in Britain gained a statutory right to at least 2 weeks' paid annual holiday only at the outbreak of the Second World War. Public holidays have also increased – Spring, August, May and New Year Bank Holidays have been added to the leisure calendar. Until the 1950s most manual workers had no more than 2 weeks plus public holidays. Subsequently the working year has been the unit of working time that has been trimmed most heavily. In most occupations, holiday entitlement has risen to 4, 5 or even 6 weeks. The generous holidays that were once considered a privilege of prestigious professions have spread to virtually everyone.

The length of the typical working life has also shrunk. Childhood has been released for schooling. This began when elementary education was made compulsory, up to age 10 initially, between 1870 and 1880. Subsequently the statutory school-leaving age has been raised gradually, to 16 on the most recent occasion in 1972. Since then there has been a trend towards staying on for post-compulsory education. And there has been a parallel trend towards earlier retirement by men (which may be reversed in future decades – see Chapter 5). Up to now the trend towards earlier retirement has been despite people remaining healthier and living longer. State retirement pensions first became available in Britain in 1910 and this led to the institutionalization of retirement. Nearly all firms introduced retirement ages. It became accepted that on reaching a given age, usually 65 for men and 60 for women up to recently (it is now becoming the same – 65 – for both sexes), individuals should be entitled to give up work and yet retain an income. During their working lives they are deemed to earn the right to pensioned retirement. Compulsory retirement ages (when employers can force workers to retire) are currently being phased out in Europe (as required by European Union law) but workers retain their right to retire on pensions at a given age. State pensions alone have never ensured prosperity in retirement, but many UK employees now retire with private (usually occupational) pensions in addition to their state incomes. There has been no reduction in the age at which state pensions become available since 1910 but more men have been retiring earlier, many under severance schemes that provide full occupational pensions despite normal service being incomplete.

Since the mid-19th century working time has been assaulted from all sides and the net result is that today people have much more lifetime free from paid employment. The pace of change has not been so rapid that most people will ever have wondered whatever to do with their extra free time. The impact of the long-term historical trend will have been overridden in most people's experience by age effects – moving from being a student to being a worker, and later on into retirement, for example – and by the impact of short-term fluctuations, which have been liable to create overtime opportunities in one year and short-time working in the next. However, some people have experienced sudden gains in free time at specific points in their lives as standard working hours have taken one of their lurches downwards. This happened when I worked in a bank before entering university in the early 1960s, when Saturday morning opening was abolished (though it has subsequently been reintroduced at some bank branches) and bank employees won a 2-day weekend. Friday nights suddenly became different. So did Saturday afternoons, when one felt able to compete at sport on level terms with others who did not have to rush from work. Many employees will have had comparable one-off experiences, maybe following sudden increases in holiday entitlement, but no one can have experienced the combined impact of all the reductions in normal working time during the last 150 years because no one's life has spanned the entire period. However, the fact is that working time accounts for a much smaller proportion of lifetime today than when our great-grandparents were in the workforce.

Higher incomes

People are working less than formerly but earning more. This has been possible through improvements in labour productivity, sometimes linked to new technology and otherwise simply through more efficient working practices. Some of the benefits of economic growth have been taken in higher incomes; only a proportion has been taken in the form of increased free time. In fact, the growth in employees' personal incomes has been steeper than the growth of free time, from which one might infer that the population has wanted more free time and more money, but rather more of the latter than the former. People today have much more cash available for leisure spending than their parents and grandparents. Since the 1950s, standards of living in Britain have roughly tripled. Previously the rate of growth was more modest. Nevertheless, all generations since the 1850s have experienced improvements in their standards of living. Some have experienced temporary cutbacks, during the world wars, for example, but no generation has experienced an overall decline in its prosperity across its entire lifespan. Standards of living have risen so steeply that virtually everyone must have noticed the difference, certainly everyone who has lived this side of the 1930s.

Living standards have risen in all sections of the population. The workforce has benefited from higher wages and salaries. Other groups have benefited from the higher earnings of those on whom they have depended, the state welfare services that were created during the 20th century or their own ability to save or borrow so as to spread their personal spending throughout the life course. Many people are still extremely poor relative to average standards of living. This type of poverty, relative poverty, is as widespread and intense today as a century ago. And the poorest sections of the population in Britain, the bottom tenth, experienced no gains in their absolute standards of living during the 1980s and 1990s. But compared with their direct counterparts in earlier times – when workers are compared with workers and the retired of today with the retired in earlier generations – all groups have become considerably better off.

The feeling of being well off may not have become more widespread. During the 20th century we learnt how quickly hopes can become expectations and then necessities. Nowadays people feel that they need their motor cars, washing machines, telephones and holidays abroad. Life would become intolerable for many without them. History has confounded some earlier expectations. We now know that once our basic needs have been satisfied we are capable of acquiring an apparently infinite array of wants. It was once believed that, once their basic needs were met, people would become content and suffering, striving and conflict would be eradicated. Until the Second World War most occupational groups expressed their aspirations in terms of a 'fair day's pay' and protecting a traditional standard of living. This was in fact people's overriding concern in pre-modern times. Neither governments nor the people expected living standards to rise progressively from year to year. They hoped to protect their traditional ways of life from the ravages of drought, famine, plague and war. Improvements and declines in a country's fortunes were more likely to be regarded as acts of God than events over which the people themselves or their rulers had any control. It is different today; governments are judged by their ability to maintain rising living standards. Since the Second World War living standards have risen so rapidly that few people will have retained any conception of a normal way of life. The basic standards that earlier generations were anxious to protect are no longer threatened, but, rather than everyone feeling comfortable, anxiety over living standards has probably become more widespread and intense. People evaluate their own conditions not against a historical yardstick but by comparing their own circumstances with those of reference groups – people considered comparable to themselves. So, as everyone becomes better off, no one feels more prosperous. There are repeated forecasts that at some point people will see through the illusion of betterment and cease striving for more and that the engine that has driven industrial societies forward will splutter to a halt, but this does not appear to be an immediate prospect. Everyone settling for 3 acres and a cow is not a viable option. A steady state is no longer available. Modern economies either grow or shrink, and likewise people's standards of living. When the communist systems collapsed at the end of the 1980s, people who were already poor by Western standards became considerably poorer, and one indicator of this was a rise in mortality rates (see Jung, 1990, 1994; Gvozdeva, 1994). Seeking and obtaining improvements in living standards may not be a recipe for contentment but it is surely more satisfying than coping with objective impoverishment.

In Western countries rising standards of living have been reflected in rising levels of leisure activity and spending. Nearly all the participation and ownership graphs slope upwards. The exceptions are invariably cases where older favourites have been replaced by something similar but more attractive, as when radio was superseded by television. We spend considerably more than in the past on items that were once considered luxuries – overseas holidays, meals out and domestic entertainment equipment. Leisure has become a major industry, arguably the biggest industry, and it is one of the few economic sectors that is growing virtually everywhere, and growing in terms of not only investment, turnover and profits but also employment.

Home life

The third force that has fuelled the growth of leisure has been changes in home life. Birth rates and death rates have fallen since the 19th century. The fall in the birth rate had made the small planned family the norm by the 1930s. By then women were giving birth to far fewer children than their grandparents, only half as many on average, and child-rearing had been compressed. This has remained so to the present day. The typical ages of women having their first children fell in the 1950s and 1960s and have subsequently risen, but the norm of the small planned family, in which all the children are usually born within 10 years and often much more quickly, has continued. This amounts to a vast change from the time when childbearing and child-rearing were effectively full-time occupations for most adult women. When their own reproductive activities were over, the women who survived were once expected to continue using their skills and experience as grandmothers. Child-rearing has been made easier and is now a major occupation for a smaller proportion of most parents' lives than in the past.

The decline in the death rate means that more children survive into adulthood and more adults into old age. The death of a young child or sibling is no longer a common experience. Similarly, it is now rare for young children to lose their mothers or fathers through death. Divorce and separation are more common than in the 19th century, but in those earlier times families were more likely to be broken by mortality. People who are born fit and healthy can now expect to survive into old age and older people themselves are living longer. A consequence is that for some people retirement now lasts longer than working life. Most people can now expect a life phase beyond their careers in the labour market, during the greater part of which they will be fit, active and mentally alert. The advent of the small planned family means that many adults' principal responsibilities as parents are now completed well before they retire from employment: hence the creation of the so-called empty-nest life stage. This is a phase in their lives when many workers reach their peak earnings while their domestic responsibilities become less onerous, and a result is that many have time and money for leisure on an unprecedented scale.

A further set of changes in home life has followed the spread of domestic technology. Mains electricity and central heating have made homes more comfortable and have allowed rooms to be put to more uses. Bedrooms today are often used as studies and entertainment centres as well as for sleeping. The numerous gadgets that run on electricity have lightened housework. Deep freezers, refrigerators, cookers, microwave ovens, irons, washing machines, tumble dryers, vacuum cleaners and the availability of pre-prepared foods have made it easier to launder clothes, keep dwellings clean and feed a family. Gadgets that were once science fiction first became luxuries and are now standard domestic equipment. Simultaneously, homes have become more comfortable with the acquisition of soft furnishings, wall-to-wall carpets, instant heat and illumination and so on. In addition, dwellings have been equipped with an ever-expanding range of leisure equipment; several television sets, radios, video, DVD, audio cassette and compact disc players, and home computers and the Internet have joined or replaced the older card and board games.

All the trends that have generated more leisure are still operating. None has ground to a halt. The containment of working time that began in the 19th century is ongoing. So are economic growth and the rise in standards of living and likewise the additions to home equipment. The trends are endemic in modern societies. It is difficult to think of reasons why the trends should not continue indefinitely. 'All other relevant things remaining equal' does not appear to be an unwarranted assumption in this case. The growth of leisure is not a recent trend. It is well established, long-running and continuing. It is not just a desire to inflate the status of their subject that leads people who work in leisure – providing for other people's or researching and writing about it – to claim that this sphere of life really is becoming more and more important.

Shaping Modern Leisure

The 19th century

This was the creative period in shaping modern leisure: 'there is nothing in the leisure of today that was not visible in 1880' (Cunningham, 1980). All the basic forms were created by then, initially in Britain, the first industrial nation, and these basic forms have remained in place ever since. Work was modernized, life became divided into work and leisure and the spread of this modern form of time organization was accompanied by the diffusion of clocks and watches. These were not new inventions. The change was that with the modernization of the economy and life in general it became virtually impossible to live without them. Our main leisure occasions were also created during the second half of the 19th century – at the end of each working day, at the weekend and on annual holidays. All the subsequent growth has been on these foundations. People now have shorter working days, longer weekends and more holidays, but within recognizable forms. The major leisure provision systems were also created in the 19th century – commercial, voluntary and the public sector. What happened in the 19th century was revolutionary. Everything since, even the developments that some describe as postmodernization, has been evolutionary in comparison. Claims that we are now witnessing changes unprecedented in scale and pace are plain wrong.

During the second half of the 19th century, the working class became more prosperous. Many families were able to move into the new terraced housing that was built to conform with local authority by-laws. Some were able to buy their homes with the help of the recently created building societies. By the end of the 19th century, homes were being connected to mains gas supplies and had fresh water 'on tap'. The availability of fresh drinking water and, after the 1850s, the growing popularity of tea probably did as much as campaigns for temperance to spread sobriety. The promotion of non-alcoholic beverages – 'soft drinks', including dandelion and burdock – also had some success in replacing beer, especially as thirst quenchers for children and young people. Commerce began to cater for the leisure time and spending power of the industrial population. During the late 19th century, the urban pub was given a style and structure that present-day customers would recognize. The theatre and the music hall developed as alternative places of entertainment (see Bailey, 1986). The kinds of entertainment that they offered have subsequently been transferred to radio and screen, but the basic formats were 19th-century inventions. The holiday resorts also developed rapidly, with their boarding houses, piers and amusement parks. Their expansion was a product of prosperity, railway transport and employers recognizing holiday weeks (see Walton, 1977; Walvin, 1978). People today take more holidays and travel to more distant destinations, but the basic ingredients of the annual holiday have remained unchanged.

Modern leisure's voluntary sector also has 19th-century origins, and sport was the base for some of the most influential voluntary bodies. Modern sports were first developed in public schools and universities, where they became associated with physical, social and moral well-being. From their very beginning, the development of modern sports – fixing the rules and organizing competitions – was in the hands of voluntary associations. These bodies were remarkably effective in promoting their sports throughout the country. Association football caught on very quickly and spread as a participant and spectator sport. The sides that competed in the early years of the FA Cup and the Football League were run by committees of amateurs, as indeed were the national bodies. Football clubs that now compete in the Premier League and European competitions were often originally based in schools, colleges, churches and firms. Local teams fostered local pride and gave national reputations to many industrial towns. The 5½-day week, the railways and the development of a national popular press were all vital to the success of spectator sports, and by the end of the 19th century all the elements of the modern game of football were in place. The leading clubs had professional players, a transfer system was operating, international fixtures were being organized and crowd misbehaviour had already become an issue (see Dunning *et al.*, 1986; Mason, 1994). Sport was then run mainly on a voluntary basis, and so, by the end of the 19th century, were many other leisure activities. Working men's clubs were opening throughout the country. Youth organizations were beginning to develop. And a host of hobbies had their associations of enthusiasts.

The foundations of modern public-sector leisure provision were also laid during the second half of the 19th century. A mixture of civic pride and a desire to promote public health and 'worthwhile' uses of free time led towns and cities to build swimming baths, libraries, art galleries, concert halls and museums and to lay out urban parks. Present-day local government departments of leisure and recreation services have evolved directly from these beginnings.

Throughout this period, leisure was deeply class-divided. The middle and working classes lived in different districts and sent their children to different schools. The classes could usually be recognized instantly by their dress, and they spent their leisure in entirely different places, if not in different ways. When Seebohm Rowntree conducted his first study of poverty in York in 1899, he defined the working class (the subjects of his research) as households without servants. Middle-class households nearly always had domestic help. This was a common occupation for working-class females. Middle-class women expected such assistance. Within all social classes there were clear age and sex divisions in ways of life. For example, the new sports were designed by and for men and were played by very few women. The pubs and music halls were adult-dominated. Children and young people had to find their own spaces in the streets.

All the things that people do with their leisure nowadays had close 19th-century counterparts. Modern leisure occasions were created in the 19th century and were filled with what are still the modern range of leisure activities. The 19th century was a truly creative period. The subsequent growth of leisure may have been spectacular but it has been less creative. The developments that are currently claimed to be creating a postmodern condition, such as global mass communications, look modest in comparison.

From 1900 to 1945

The first half of the 20th century saw two world wars, and the interwar period is best remembered for its recession and mass unemployment, but overall there was economic growth and a rise in living standards. Even during the recession most people who remained in employment achieved increases in their real incomes. The growth of leisure that began in the 19th century continued during this period. Local government leisure provision was consolidated. Public baths were developed as recreational facilities rather than as places for washing bodies and clothes. Local authorities were made responsible for the development of the Youth Service, which addressed the social and recreational needs of 14–21-year-olds. The introduction of town and country planning made recreation space an issue within urban areas and on the fringes and in the countryside. The voluntary sector developed and was strengthened during the wars, which created unmet needs among civilians, and during the resettlement of ex-servicemen, while boosting social solidarity. Hobby and interest groups flourished. Working men's clubs became more widespread. Sport continued to develop as a mass participation activity and as mass entertainment. The voluntary youth movements grew to what was to be their peak strength.

Homes became leisure-friendly, especially when dwellings were connected to mains electricity and when a new range of 'white' consumer goods was marketed, most visibly in the department stores that opened in the major cities (see Bowden, 1994). Electric irons were bought by most households between the wars. Refrigerators and washing machines also became available, but these were luxury items at the time. The gramophone was another mass-marketed commodity, and as ownership spread the popularity of tunes and songs could be measured by sales of records as well as sheet music. However, the domestic gadget that made the greatest difference to home-based leisure was undoubtedly the wireless (as the radio was then called). Ownership spread rapidly following the creation of the British Broadcasting Company in 1922, which became the nationalized British Broadcasting Corporation (BBC) in 1927, and the radio became the population's principal source of news and entertainment (see Davies, 1994). Variety acts and drama were transferred from theatres and music halls to the radio, which rapidly became a new art form. The radio was a new medium through which performers could become national stars, and musical compositions could become instant 'hits', literally overnight. Television broadcasting began in Britain in 1936 but did not develop a mass audience until after the Second World War.

The other new medium that made stars was the cinema (see Davies, 1994). Between the wars picture palaces were constructed throughout the country. Most adults became cinema-goers, initially to silent and then to talking movies, and in the 1930s the typical cinema-goer went more than once a week (see Davies, 1994). The rapid progress of the radio and cinema was linked to a decline in the music hall and the live theatre. Alcohol consumption was another casualty. The cinema and radio proved more effective than preaching in reducing time spent in pubs. The decline in alcohol consumption, a long-established pre-modern pastime, was accelerated by the limited licensing hours that were introduced during the First World War, taxation and restrictions on the number and types of premises able to sell alcohol for in-house or outside consumption.

There were other growth areas in commercial leisure. 'Modern' types of dancing became popular among young people. The dance palais was a place for the young, whereas, up to the Second World War, cinemas, pubs and spectator sports attracted mainly adults. Spectator sports widened their appeal and the leading football clubs built new and larger stadiums, many of which remained little changed until the 1990s (see Mason, 1994). Between the wars, motoring and flying were pioneered as new leisure activities but these were restricted to the well-to-do (see Howkins and Lowerson, 1979). Cycling was the mass recreation. Rambling was another, made possible by a combination of the spread of prosperity, greater leisure time, rail and bus transport into and protection of public rights of access in the countryside. The major holiday resorts expanded as the annual holiday away from home became a normal expectation of working-class families.

Throughout this period leisure was becoming more commercial. Much leisure provision was straightforward private enterprise, and some nominally voluntary associations were increasingly operating on more commercial lines. The major spectator sports were leading examples of this. Much the same applied to some public-sector provisions. Access to the broadcasts of a public corporation, the BBC, depended on the purchase of radio sets, which were produced and marketed by private enterprise, and the 'light' entertainers who gained airtime did so on the basis of their mass appeal, and their fees were tailored accordingly.

Post-1945

After the Second World War the growth of leisure resumed. As in earlier decades, economic growth was the principal motor. The three decades following 1945 have been dubbed the '30 glorious years', during which the Western world enjoyed unprecedented sustained economic growth and full employment.

Since then, economic expansion has continued, but at a slower pace, and some sections of the population, mainly outside the paid workforce, have not shared in the growth in incomes. Even so, the overall growth of leisure has continued.

In the immediate post-war years the most visible beneficiaries of the new economic conditions were young people. The strong demand for labour eliminated youth unemployment in most regions and drew teenagers' earnings towards adult levels: hence the creation of affluent young workers, who became prime targets for a number of consumer industries, and a series of flamboyant youth styles and fashions was a high-profile outcome (Abrams, 1961). Subsequently other sections of the population have joined the consumer society.

The commercialization of leisure, involving the shaping of more leisure goods and services into commodities that can be bought and sold, has continued, accompanied by intellectuals' critiques of consumer culture and 'commodity fetishism', which, some argue, create wants that differ from people's real needs. These arguments are considered fully in Chapter 7. It is certainly true that leisure has become big business, and the major voluntary organizations increasingly operate on commercial lines, in running participant as well as spectator sports facilities (like Wembley Stadium), for example. It is also true that some older voluntary organizations have seen their roles diminish as their former members have turned to commercial alternatives. The traditional youth organizations have been prime examples of this. Some nominally voluntary bodies now depend heavily on state support: youth organizations and amateur sports associations, for instance. However, it is still the case that most participant sport is run on a genuinely voluntary basis, and virtually every leisure interest has enthusiasts who organize themselves in clubs and societies (see Bishop and Hoggett, 1986).

There is also a substantial public sector, which has grown rather than contracted alongside the development of commercial leisure since 1945. Since the 1970s most local authorities have rationalized the management of their leisure services into single departments and have sought overarching leisure policies. Central government has become more prominent in leisure provision. National councils and commissions with responsibilities for sport, the arts, the countryside and tourism have been created. Since 1992 the UK central government's leisure responsibilities have been drawn together in a Department of Culture, Media and Sport (its current title), and since 1994 the National Lottery has become a major source of public funding. The 'good causes' that benefit from the National Lottery include sport, the arts and heritage.

In some respects public provisions have become more commercial. Public providers have been encouraged to operate on business lines. Since 1992 local authorities have been obliged to submit the management of most of their leisure services to competitive tendering or equivalent 'best value' tests. But it remains the case that many public leisure provisions are subsidized from the National Lottery or from general central or local government budgets, thereby sustaining facilities that could not survive on a purely commercial basis or on voluntary effort. Participant sport and high culture would both be substantially reduced if all public subsidies were withdrawn.

Rising standards of living have enabled households to acquire more leisure equipment, and since 1945 one of the most significant of these acquisitions has been the television. The television set became a standard lounge fixture in the 1950s and ever since it has accounted for a substantial slice of leisure time. Radio and cinema audiences were decimated as television soared in popularity. These former leading media have subsequently adjusted by moving into market niches that television is less able to fill. Radio has targeted the audiences for various types of music and talk, and car drivers more generally. The cinema has adjusted by producing specialist products to be watched at multi-screen complexes by specific taste publics, mostly composed of young people rather than adults, who are more difficult to tempt from their homes and televisions. The press has also been affected by the rise of television. Newspapers have adjusted by offering either more detailed news coverage and analysis than other media (the quality papers) or entertainment – in particular, guides to other media, especially television programmes, and stories about media personalities (the popular tabloids). Most households now contain more than one television receiver and additional items that widen the choice of screen entertainment – videos, DVD players, camcorders, digital cameras, cable and satellite links. Most homes also have a range of audio equipment to play records, tapes and compact discs. The improved quality of furnishings has further enhanced the home as a leisure environment, as have central heating and telephones. The manner in which the telephone enables conversation to be purchased and the cost compared with a video rental or a glass of beer is an excellent example of commodification.

Despite the appeal of television, since 1945 leisure has not become more home-based. During the 1960s car ownership spread to the majority of households and made it easier for people (except those without cars) to go out. Cinema audiences have shrunk to a small fraction of their sizes in the 1930s and 1940s, and the film-making industry has adjusted by designing more of its products for video, DVD and television distribution. The crowds at some sports events have also shrunk and top sport is increasingly marketed to the television-viewing public (see Whannel, 1986). But there has been no decline since the 1950s in the audiences for live theatre and music or visits to art galleries, stately homes, coastal resorts, countryside beauty spots and other venues for trips out. The frequency with which people go out has made catering a leading leisure market. People have been going out more frequently for meals, sometimes as the main activity and sometimes while travelling to or from other leisure destinations. Alcohol consumption has also reversed its former long-term decline. Between the 1950s and 1980s per capita consumption doubled (see Goddard, 1991) and since then consumption has continued to rise (see Table 4.2, p. 102). Like food, drink can either be the focus of a leisure occasion or an incidental alongside other activities. The places where alcohol is available for consumption on the premises and for sale for consumption outside have multiplied. Alongside these trends, drinking has become socially acceptable, and often expected, within sections of the population (women and young people, for example) where it was once uncommon. By age 16 most young people are now drinking regularly, and the vast majority of their parents know about and condone their children's conduct (Sharp *et al.*, 1988).

The holiday industry has been another beneficiary of mass prosperity. Since the Second World War the holiday away from home has been an event in most

people's annual leisure calendars, and since the 1950s the numbers and proportion of holidays taken abroad have risen. Meanwhile the UK has been attracting
more tourists from overseas. The domestic population has been travelling further, to more exotic destinations, on main holidays, but it has also been taking
more second holidays and weekend breaks, most of which do not involve overseas travel. Camping holidays with tents and caravans have risen in popularity. It
is this all-round growth that has made tourism into a major industry, arguably the
biggest single industry in the world.

The growth in holidays away and going out more generally has expanded
the markets for leisure goods and clothing. Sports goods have become big business and sportswear even more so as the boundary between sports clothing and
general leisure attire has dissolved. The tendency nowadays is not for people to
'dress up' but to dress casually when they go out, which is just one of many
indications of how life in general has become more leisure-like.

Information technology

Contrasting views have been expressed on the most likely eventual impact
on our daily lives of the latest wave of new technology. There are two extreme
viewpoints and a variety of midway positions. At one extreme are writers who
predict a total change of epoch (Hassan, 2004), the demise of traditional civil
society and the creation of completely new kinds of political movements. Some
predict that information technology will turn us into stay-at-home 'anoraks' with
shrunken social networks and even more sedentary lifestyles than currently
(Kraut *et al.*, 1998; Albrechtsen, 2000). Others say that we shall be driven crazy
by the sheer volume of information and virtual interaction with which we allow
ourselves to be bombarded (Selwyn, 2003). These extreme schools of thought
draw their inferences from the potential of the new information technologies.
On the other hand, and at the other extreme, there are researchers who have
studied how new technology is actually being used at present. They have tended
to predict minimal change: that new technologies will simply facilitate and
supplement long-established social relationships and activities (Wellman and
Haythornwaite, 2002; Woolgar, 2002) and that web surfers will soon discover
that the constraints and frustrations in cyberspace are, if anything, more con-
straining than those in what was hitherto considered real life, with the end result
that real social networks and leisure practices hardly change in scale or composition (Franzen, 2000; Miah, 2000). We have also been reminded that escapes
into fantasy pre-date all the new technologies.

Diametrically opposed assessments are possible because it is really still too
early to draw any confident conclusions. In the 1970s the silicon chip gave us
personal computers and enabled us to play computer games either at home or in
amusement arcades. The mobile phone, the Internet and email have been available only since the early 1990s. It was only in the late 1990s in the UK that lift-off
commenced and the number of online households began to rise steeply so that
by 2004 over half were already connected to the web. By then well over
two-thirds of young people were experienced Internet users (Russell and Drew,

2001; Russell and Stafford, 2002). Maybe before long, assisted by the opening of public online centres (Hall Aitken Associates, 2002), Internet use will be as common as the TV and the landline telephone. Or maybe not. In the first years of the new millennium there were signs of a slowdown in the spread of the new technologies. People who wished to become so were already equipped with mobile phones and Internet access. Many of the remainder said that they were simply not interested (e-living, 2002): hence the warnings of a digital divide. A significant minority of young people have remained marginal to all the new technologies and may well remain so throughout their lives (Facer and Furlong, 2001).

This does not mean that current uses and impacts exhaust the social effects of the new technologies. Investigators who have made detailed studies of specific groups of new technology users have noted the emergence of some novel social forms and practices: the simultaneously public and anonymous character of Internet chat rooms encouraging reckless conversation (Lee, 2002); the spread of global music cultures with no local roots (Mattar, 2003); texting giving rise to new signs and rules of expression (Batan, 2002); the mobile phone giving women a new sense of security through being visibly in touch when out alone (Wearing and Foley, 2002); and live clubs (of Star Trek fans, for example) being deserted in favour of virtual communities (Lawrence, 2003).

Trivial changes or potentially momentous? It may still be too early to be certain, but will the likely changes in our daily and weekly lives be as momentous as those that accompanied the advent of mechanical transport, the creation of modern spectator and participant sports, holidaymaking and the music hall? Are our lives today changing as dramatically as they did for the interwar generations, who lived through the birth of radio and the cinema and the initial development of the recorded music industry? And what about the post-war generations, who experienced the advent of television, mass motoring and holidays abroad? Is new technology likely to divert or arrest any of the long-term trends that are discussed below, or to overturn hitherto persistent divisions and differences in uses of leisure by types of employment, age and gender?

Long-term Trends

Commercialization

Within the overall growth and the overall shape created in the 19th century, it is possible to identify several long-term trends in how people spend their leisure. One of these, commercialization, has already been highlighted. It is important to remember that this has been a trend, but remains a far from absolute condition. Leisure has not been totally commercialized. It is simply more commercial than 100 years ago and the basic reason for this is that people have more money. The commercialization of leisure and daily life has implications of which people may ordinarily remain unaware, if only because some of the associated changes have occurred so gradually and surreptitiously. Chaney (2002) argues that the rise of the commercial mass entertainment industries has led to 'radical democratization' and 'cultural fragmentation': democratization because there are no longer any clear cultural authorities – nowadays the market rules – and fragmentation on account of the large number of distinct cultures and audiences that have been created.

Blurred divisions

A second long-term trend has been a blurring of formerly clear divisions in leisure tastes and activities by age, sex, social class and region (see Howkins and Lowerson, 1979; Davies, 1992; Mason, 1994). Gershuny (2000), using evidence from 35 time budget surveys conducted in 20 different countries between the 1960s and the 1990s, argues that three great convergences are in process – between countries, social classes and the sexes. To these we might add age groups. Popular music was once (in the 1950s and 1960s) aimed primarily at and bought by young people. Today the over-40s buy more albums than the 12–19s (de Lisle, 2004). There are numerous reasons for all the blurring, many rooted outside leisure itself, but the development of national, often international, leisure markets has played a part, as has commodification. Private enterprise in general, though not every single merchandiser, has a vested interest in gaining access to the widest possible markets. Particular products, musical genres, for instance, may be targeted at specific groups. Some products, holiday resorts, for example, may cultivate exclusive reputations. But the tourist industry in general, and many resorts, can be relied on to seek customers from all age groups and social classes. As the population has grown more prosperous, more and more activities that were once confined to the well-to-do have become mass pastimes. Motoring and eating out are examples. Simultaneously, goods and services that were once considered coarse by groups who prided themselves on their more refined tastes have spread upmarket. People from all social classes now listen to popular music (see Longhurst, 1996). Classical fare is enjoyed as well as, not instead of, pop.

The blurring of divisions will have diffused leisure's bonding function. The blurring does not mean that everyone now does everything. Leisure has not been standardized and massified. Most leisure activities are minority interests that draw together their particular followers and separate them from other members of the public. Social divisions become blurred when interests attract participants from many age groups, regions and social classes and from both sexes. So the various taste publics in which people are involved all tend to have socially diverse memberships, and each of the many activities in which any person is involved creates a different set of peers. When this happens, the leisure networks in which people operate cease to be socially superimposed, with working-class people going to particular holiday resorts, wearing distinctive clothing, listening to 'their' types of music and so on. It thereby becomes more difficult to judge any individual's occupational class, age, sex or home region from a knowledge of what he or she does when at leisure.

Researchers into young people's leisure lives have remarked on the disappearance of older kinds of youth subcultures that developed among young

people, maybe among just one of the sexes and typically among those from specific social class backgrounds, maybe particular schools and neighbourhoods.
Present-day youth scenes do not contain such clearly defined groups as the
Teddy boys of the 1950s and the mods and rockers of the 1960s (see Chapter 5,
pp. 138–142). Nowadays there are more hybridity, individuality and mixed class
membership (see Muggleton, 2000). Steve Miles (2000) rejects 'subculture' in
favour of 'lifestyle' in examining present-day youth scenes. Lifestyles, according
to Miles, can be individual and do not necessarily have 'parents' (they are not
'subs' of anything else). New lifestyles, 'crowds' and 'tribes' (as they have also
been described) can appear and disappear rapidly, though some, skinheads and
goths, for example, have sustained themselves, developed histories, held on to
core members and recruited new ones for several decades (see Hodkinson,
2002).

Individualization

This trend is related to the blurring described above. It occurs as leisure ceases to
separate the population clearly into distinct groups. Again, it is important to
stress that individualization is a trend rather than an absolute state. In this case
the trend is towards every individual having a particular combination of leisure
interests and activities and a unique leisure career. Individuals develop personal
stocks of leisure skills and interests, some of which may be drawn from and others may subsequently be used in other spheres of life. No skill or interest will be
unique to any person, just the total package. Exactly how far these trends have
gone and their sources are explored in detail in Chapters 3, 4 and 5, which deal
with the relationships between leisure activities and individuals' occupations,
gender and age groups.

Pacification

A fourth long-term trend has been pacification. Eric Dunning has argued that
many developments in leisure are best understood as part of a broader civilizing
process (see Dunning and Rojek, 1992; Dunning *et al.*, 1992). It is said that the
development of modern societies has seen life become increasingly civil, peace-
ful and orderly. Sport is said to illustrate the civilizing process in two ways. First,
much aggression has been taken out of society and contained within sports. Secondly, sports themselves have become less violent. Hacking is no longer an
acceptable tactic in football and nowadays amateur boxers are fitted with head
guards. It can be argued that the concern about soccer hooliganism, which
mounted from the 1960s to the 1980s, was not so much a response to the
behaviour of spectators deteriorating as the wider society and the majority of those
who wanted to watch sport becoming less tolerant of such conduct. Pacification is
evident in many areas of leisure. Playground fighting is no longer an acceptable
schoolboy recreation. Street fights after closing time are no longer simply
accepted as part of weekend life. It is not only leisure that has been pacified.

Schoolteachers are no longer permitted to administer corporal punishment and its use within families has become controversial.

Reservations and Qualifications

All the above trends, like the growth of leisure, have been very long-term. No one seriously questions that the trends have occurred but in recent years a number of reservations have been expressed. These concern the extent to which leisure has grown, whether all sections of the population have been affected in the same way, whether people today really have historically unprecedented amounts of leisure, the type of leisure that is now playing a larger part in people's lives and whether the upward trend really is still in process and can be expected to continue indefintely.

More leisure for everyone or just for some?

One of the underlying forces behind the growth of leisure has been the containment of work, and this historical story is often told as if it applied to all sections of the population. In fact, it is male history. The history of women's lives during the last 150 years reads very differently. Presenting a male history of work and leisure time as if it were gender-neutral is one example of a gender blindness that has often left women hidden from view (see Chapter 4). During the latter part of the 19th century, the main trend among working-class married women in Britain was not a steady reduction in their hours of paid employment but their wholesale removal from the workforce (see Hakim, 1993). At that time, upper- and middle-class wives did not work outside their homes (or in their homes in some cases) and the bourgeois ideal was spread downwards. The woman as homemaker was promoted as an ideal. She was to provide a comfortable and nurturant base for children and male employees to return to at the end of each working day. Even with the benefit of hindsight, there are very different interpretations of this trend. Some see it as a reassertion of patriarchy, disempowering women and forcing them into economic servitude and therefore social and emotional dependence on men. Others argue that women benefited when employers accepted that men should be paid a 'family wage', thereby making it unnecessary for wives and mothers to seek employment in the mines and factories. By the beginning of the 20th century, unmarried females, mostly young women, were the only female group most of whom were in employment. During both world wars, single and married women were drawn into the workforce to do jobs vacated by male servicemen and to staff the munitions factories and other war industries. On both occasions, following the cessation of hostilities, most of these women returned to domesticity and their jobs were reoccupied by men. However, since the 1940s, there has been a steady rise in the proportion of married women in employment. Up to now most of these women have taken part-time jobs and have returned to the labour market only when their youngest children have become school-aged, but since the 1970s women have been shortening their career breaks. More have been taking maternity leave instead of terminating their employment and by the end of the 1980s the number of women in full-time employment was rising steadily (*see* Hakim, 1993). Rather than their hours of paid work steadily declining, for women there has been an overall increase during the last 50 years. There are many women today whose total working weeks, when their paid employment and unpaid domestic work are totalled, exceed 70 h. Such long work schedules have not been buried in 19th-century history. Of course, women have been affected, more than men, by the decline in fertility and the spread of domestic labour-saving technology. But the fact remains that one of the major strands in the story about the historical growth of leisure bears no resemblance to the experiences of women.

In general, men's hours of work have declined, but this has not applied among males in all occupations. In the professions and among the self-employed, there is no evidence of any overall decline in hours of work since the 19th century. Indeed, it is only during the 20th century that some professions have been transformed from bases for gentlemanly ways of life into modern occupations. Solicitors, barristers, accountants, bank managers, teachers, civil servants and local government officers have not experienced any reductions in their daily or weekly hours of work, increases in their holiday entitlement or reductions in the ages at which they have guaranteed retirement rights on full pensions. As the next chapter explains, in recent years typical working time in many jobs such as these has actually risen.

The story about the working day, week, year and life being gradually scaled down is in fact the history of male industrial manual workers. At the beginning of the 20th century the manual grades accounted for around three-quarters of the entire workforce. At that time the occupational class structure was bottom-heavy and it may have been reasonable to present the stories of manual workers as the history of 'the people', but today well under half of both male and female employees are in manual jobs. Employment has shifted towards occupations in which working time has not been in long-term decline and where it is currently tending to increase rather than decrease.

Since it bears little resemblance to women's history and does not apply in a substantial number of (typically) male occupations, is it legitimate to refer to the containment of work as a general historical trend? Statistically speaking, 'yes', but the fact of the matter is that the overall containment has been concentrated, if not confined, within particular occupations and the male half of the population.

Does less work mean more leisure?

During the 100 years following 1870, some of the time released from paid work was used to give employees shorter working days and weeks and longer holidays, but a greater quantity of the 'new' work-free lifetime increased the size of groups outside the paid workforce, mainly schoolchildren and the retired (*see* Wilenski, 1963). Since the children who were released from employment in the mines, factories and shops were expected to attend school, this product of the containment of working time can hardly be construed as a growth of leisure.

Although the case is less clear-cut, question marks can be placed against the leisure implications of the expansion of time spent in retirement (see Parker, 1979). Many of the retired have lived, and continue to subsist, on very low incomes, much lower than when they were in employment. Their reduced incomes inevitably reduce their leisure opportunities and will have done so more sharply as leisure has become more commercial. Is retirement really leisure time or is much of it literally spare time? This issue is taken up in Chapter 5. Such questions have become increasingly pertinent since the 1960s because virtually all the recent additions to work-free time have involved young people delaying their entry into employment and people retiring younger and living longer, plus the increase in the numbers unemployed. Whether there are any senses in which people who move from jobs into unemployment can be said to experience an increase in their leisure is discussed in Chapter 3. For present purposes it is sufficient to introduce serious reservations against any presumption that lifetime released from paid work must have led to an equivalent growth in leisure.

The time that people spend travelling to work is relevant here. Employees who have experienced reductions in the hours when they are at work may spend many hours per week travelling to and from their jobs. Long-distance commuting by road and rail has become widespread in south-east England. Working days of over 12 h have remained common when travelling time is included.

There have been comparable trends limiting the growth of leisure that would have followed the compression of child-rearing and the acquisition of domestic technology if all other things had remained equal. In the event, standards of home and childcare have risen. Many parents no longer consider it safe to allow their children to play outside without supervision or to travel to school or leisure unaccompanied. Between 1971 and 1991 the proportion of Britain's 7-year-olds who normally went to school on their own declined from 70% to just 7% (Hillman, 1991). Washing machines have taken much of the labour out of laundering but have also led to households doing more washing. It is now common for garments to be washed after being worn just once. Electric cleaners have made it easier to remove dust from carpets but nowadays this chore is likely to be performed several times a week. Meanwhile, as home and car ownership have become more widespread, more time has been devoted to odd jobs on the owners' dwellings, cars and gardens.

The historical benchmark

Leisure is most likely to appear to be on a long-term upward course when the early industrial period is adopted as the starting point for history. There were no time budget studies in pre-modern times but we know that in the countryside the burden of work was not consistently oppressive. People worked by 'natural rhythms'. At certain times such as harvests there was much that had to be done quickly but this did not apply week in, week out throughout the year, and the calendar was sprinkled with saints' and feast days. During the take-off into industrialism, working time was increased in the face of considerable workforce resistance, and it has been argued that since the 19th century the containment of working time has achieved no more than a recovery of the free time that was lost during the previous century (Wilenski, 1963). With a longer historical perspective, the early stages of industrialism stand out as the exceptional period when the demands of work were raised to a peak. Since then, it can be argued, the free time that was lost has been reclaimed and working time has returned to its historically normal level, but, even in the most economically advanced countries, people today are not enjoying more free time than in any earlier era or compared with many present-day people whose ways of life remain pre-modern.

The slowing pace of the decline in working time

In Britain the steepest decline in working time occurred between 1850 and the Second World War. Since then there have been reductions in the number of weeks worked per year and in the number of years in the typical (male) working life, but there has been little change in daily or weekly working hours. Benjamin Hunnicutt (1988) has argued that around the time of the Second World War the labour movements in Western countries changed their objectives. Formerly, he argues, they were inspired by a vision of a society in which people would work less and more time would be their own. Subsequently organized labour has demanded full employment, the right to earn and spend.

Some writers claim that some economically advanced countries have begun experiencing net increases in the weekly hours worked by full-time employees (see Fajertag, 1996; Holliday, 1996; and see also Chapter 3, pp. 76–85). In the mid-1990s Zuzanek and his colleagues (1998) found that, although average hours of work had continued to decline as the number of part-time jobs, filled mainly by women, had risen, if these occupations were excluded from or properly taken into account in the calculations, the hours worked by both men and women in the USA, Canada and the Netherlands were seen to have either increased or settled on a plateau.

However, it should be noted that working time is a topic on which it is very difficult to obtain highly trustworthy information. Where there are collective agreements between employers and trade unions, it is fairly easy to gather information on standard hours of work but these can be very different from hours actually worked. This also applies to hours set out (if any) in individuals' contracts of employment. Information on real hours of work has to be obtained by asking people, and when this is done we know that exactly how long they claim to work varies according to the precise wording of the question. A comparison of the UK figures in Tables 2.2 and 2.3 shows that, overall, workers claim that they 'usually' work more hours than on average they say that they 'actually' worked last week. Robinson and Godbey (1999) have argued that, in the USA (and probably elsewhere), both claims are overestimates: that people tend to say (and possibly believe) that they work more hours than is really the case (as estimated from time budgets). However, provided the propensity to exaggerate or otherwise distort the truth is constant, comparisons can be made over time and between countries.

In 1998 Martin and Mason found that since the 1970s both the total time worked by the entire UK workforce and the average per full-time worker had declined, but that in the latter case most of the decline had occurred in the 1970s, since when there had been little change (see Table 2.1). Table 2.2 indicates that during the 1990s and early 2000s the hours worked by full-time UK employees fluctuated trendlessly while part-timers' hours edged upwards marginally. There are no signs in any of this evidence of an all-round lengthening of typical hours of work in Britain, but rather of the earlier downward trend having ended and typical working time having settled on a new post-1970s plateau.

There are known to be substantial variations in average hours of work, and also in recent trends, between countries at similar levels of economic development. Table 2.3 shows that UK employees work longer on average than workers in virtually every other European country. Table 2.4 confines its comparisons to production workers in manufacturing and in terms of both annual hours worked and holiday entitlement the UK appears more akin to the USA and Japan than to mainland Europe. In this table the USA is the only country where there appears

Table 2.1.   Hours worked in Britain.

	Total hours of work (billions)	Annual hours worked per full-time worker
1971	45.5	1999
1981	40.5	1844
1991	42.1	1829
1996	40.9	1832

Source: Martin and Mason (1998).

Table 2.2.   Average actual hours of work, Great Britain.

	Full-time males	Full-time females	Part-time males	Part-time females
Spring 1992	40.0	34.4	14.3	14.9
Spring 1993	40.0	34.2	14.4	14.8
Spring 1994	40.4	34.5	14.9	15.0
Spring 1995	40.8	34.4	14.7	15.2
Spring 1996	40.7	34.5	14.8	15.1
Spring 1997	40.7	34.7	14.9	15.3
Spring 1998	40.7	34.6	15.0	15.3
Spring 1999	40.1	34.5	15.0	15.3
Spring 2000	39.8	34.1	15.1	15.4
Spring 2001	39.9	34.4	15.6	15.7
Spring 2002	39.7	34.4	15.0	15.7
Spring 2003	39.1	34.1	15.4	15.7
Spring 2004	39.2	33.7	15.7	15.6

Source: Labour Force Survey.

Table 2.3. Usual hours worked per week: full-time
employees 2002.

	Females	Males
Latvia	42.5	44.8
UK	40.6	44.9
Romania	41.4	42.1
Slovakia	41.4	42.1
Poland	39.9	43.1
Slovenia	41.0	42.0
Czech Republic	40.4	41.9
Bulgaria	40.8	41.4
Estonia	40.4	41.8
Greece	39.7	41.9
Hungary	40.3	41.5
Malta	38.7	41.1
Spain	39.5	41.0
Portugal	39.2	41.1
Austria	39.9	40.1
Cyprus	39.6	40.4
Germany	39.2	40.3
Sweden	39.6	40.1
Ireland	37.7	40.7
Lithuania	38.5	40.5
Luxembourg	37.9	40.3
Belgium	38.3	39.7
Finland	38.2	40.0
Denmark	37.7	40.1
Netherlands	38.1	39.1
Italy	36.4	39.8
Norway	37.6	39.0
France	36.9	38.2
EU 15	38.6	40.8
Acceding countries	40.2	42.4

Source: Eurostat Labour Force Survey.

Table 2.4a. Annual total hours actually worked (production
workers in manufacturing industry).

	1980	1990	1999
Japan	2162	2214	1942
USA	1893	1948	1991
France	1759	1683	1650
Germany	1719	1598	1525
UK	1883	1953	1902

Table 2.4b.   Annual leave plus public holidays.

UK	32.5
EU average	36.5
Japan	33.0
USA	26.9

Source: European Industrial Relations Observatory Online,
Industrial Relations in the EU, Japan and USA, 2001,
www.eiro.eurofound.eu.int/2002/12/feature/TN0212101F.html

to be a clear upward trend in hours of work. The clear trend continues to be downwards in France and Germany. Japan and the UK (again) display trendless fluctuations.

We should note here that an overall trend throughout a workforce (or the absence of any trend) can be a product of entirely different trends in different sections of a population and in different occupations. Chapter 3 will explain that there is evidence that certain groups of UK employees are working longer than formerly. That said, on the basis of all the evidence at hand, it cannot be claimed that throughout the economically advanced countries working time is increasing, or even that the long-term downward historical trend has ended everywhere. However, it appears that, for the present at any rate, the former decline in typical working time has ended in some countries, and that Britain is among this group. A long-term increase in working time seems improbable, even in the USA. It seems more likely that, having recovered the time that was lost during the take-off into industrialism, working time has returned to the historical plateau that human beings, maybe as a result of their earlier biological evolution, experience as normal and no longer feel needs further reductions. It is also likely that, with the progressive commercialization of leisure, workers' desire for higher earnings has taken precedence over their interest in still more free time. These possibilities are considered fully in the following chapter. At present it is sufficient to reinforce the grounds for doubting whether we really live in an era in which leisure has been and is still growing and will continue to do so inexorably in the absence of unforeseen developments.

However, it could be equally unwise to assume that the former decline in working time has ended permanently. In some countries (such as France and Germany) the long-term decline in working time appears to have continued into the 21st century, and historians have shown that reductions in hours of work, when they occurred, were not simply delivered by economic progress but had to be won through collective bargaining (Bienefeld, 1972; Rosenweig, 1983; Jones, 1986). If organized labour's will to achieve still shorter hours has weakened or if broader trends have undermined the power of organized labour, there seems little reason to predict further reductions in working time, but this is a topic on which prediction is hazardous. It is possible that, before long, organized labour may take the view that the only way to prevent an otherwise inexorable spread of mass unemployment is to reduce working time. In some European countries the trade unions have not only adopted this view but have persuaded their 'social partners', governments and employers, that normal working hours must be trimmed in the interests of social cohesion (*see* Blyton and Trinczek, 1996). Between 1998 and 2000 France introduced new laws which made 35 h the standard working week throughout the workforce (*see* Fagnani and Letablier, 2004). Up to now this has not led to a substantial all-round drop in working time in France, and additional exemptions to the 35-h rule were introduced in 2005, but it is impossible to rule out completely a future downward lurch in any country.

We should note here that an end to the decline in paid hours of work will not necessarily mean that the long-term growth of leisure has ended. Here time budget data are the better guide. In these data sets it is possible to include people without any jobs (housewives, the retired, students and the unemployed, for example) when calculating average hours of work. It is possible for there to be a decline in the proportion of all lifetime being spent in paid employment without any trimming of the working time of people within the paid workforce. However, the relevant calculations show that, although leisure time is still increasing in the UK, the current pace of increase is very modest. Between 1961 and 1995 average paid working time declined from 296 to 246 min/day (and nearly all the decline occurred before 1985). Average unpaid working time increased from 191 to 218 min as a result of increases in shopping, travel and childcare, offset partly by reductions in time spent cooking and on domestic work. Overall leisure time increased by just 20 min/day over the 35-year period (Gershuny and Fisher, 1999). The contrast with the pace at which leisure spending has increased is dramatic (*see* Table 1.5, p. 17).

The quality of the new leisure

A final set of reservations concerns the quality of any new leisure that has been created. First, people may be spending more money on their holidays, by going abroad instead of to domestic resorts, for example, but does this make their holidays better? Is it misleading to assume that the value of leisure can be weighed by the amounts of money that people spend? People may be cramming more leisure activities into roughly the same amount of leisure time. Does this indicate an overall improvement in their leisure?

Secondly, some of the apparent growth arises from the commodification of activities that were formerly self-organized. Music in the home today is most likely to be from tapes, the radio or compact discs. People undoubtedly spend more money on music and possess more leisure equipment that allows music to be heard than in the days when families made their own music and sang along, but can this be equated with growth?

Thirdly, Fred Hirsch (1977) has drawn attention to the fact that there is a 'positional element' in much personal consumption, meaning that the satisfactions that people derive do not depend wholly on their being able to have or to do something themselves, but also on other people being excluded. The satisfactions that arise from driving the latest-model motor car or being able to wear the most fashionable clothes or go on exclusive holidays are examples. Hirsch argues that, as standards of living rise, the positional element in consumption grows in importance, and the end result can be likened to a crowd where everyone stands on tiptoe but no one sees further. Everyone may be doing and spending more and yet no one is more satisfied than formerly. This will be part of the explanation of why the growth of leisure over the last 50 years has failed to make people feel more satisfied with life in the economically advanced countries.

A fourth argument draws attention to the spread of time pressure. Staffen Linder noted in 1970 that leisure time was growing more slowly than personal incomes and spending, and the end result, he argued, would be a 'harried leisure class'. Rather than the growth of leisure leading to more relaxed ways of life, he forecast that people would encounter increasing difficulties in 'finding the time'. There certainly seems to have been a trend in this direction, judged by the popularity of fast foods and fast sports such as squash, rather than cricket matches, which can last all day. Geoff Godbey (1975) has argued that, rather than a long-term growth of leisure, the condition that has recently spread is better described as 'anti-leisure'. This set of arguments does not dispute that, overall, people today have more leisure time and spend more money on and engage in more leisure activities than formerly, but simply points out that the end result may not be exactly what would have been expected, given the ordinary meanings of leisure. Godbey claims that in fact life has become less leisurely. Garhammer (1998) claims that pressure, not leisure, is on the rise in Germany. The causes, according to Garhammer, are wealth increasing more rapidly than spare time (Linder's argument) and also the speed-ups and demands for greater flexibility at work, with the outcome, we are told, that in Germany (where average working time has continued to decline) people are devoting less time to personal care and sleep and eating fewer family meals at home.

Current Trends and Future Prospects

The qualifications and reservations do not completely demolish the historical tale of leisure's growth. The fact remains that work-free time, leisure spending and leisure activity have all grown and are continuing to grow, and the following chapters confirm that social divisions have been and are still being blurred by these trends and that individuals are developing and expressing more personal interests through leisure and doing so in more civilized ways than a century ago. Nevertheless, in recent years a new set of additional trends has operated.

The distribution of leisure

Time, spending power and levels of activity have continued to grow as rapidly as ever before, but these different components of leisure have been distributed to entirely different sections of the population. Instead of most people experiencing marginal gains in leisure time, spending power and levels of activity, the population appears to be dividing into separate leisure classes. One class is working longer and earning more and can afford to participate in more activities but is experiencing mounting time pressure. A second class is time-rich but money-poor and has spare time rather than leisure as commonly understood. It is also possible to distinguish a third leisure class composed of people who work in the leisure and other consumer industries, generally in low-status, low-paid, seasonal or otherwise temporary, often part-time, jobs that require unsocial hours of work. Many of these jobs involve 'aesthetic labour', in which the employees' appearances and demeanour must be to the customers' satisfaction (see Nickson *et al.*, 1998; Tyler and Abbott, 1998). There is more work to be found in leisure nowadays but the downside of this picture is that most of the jobs are of poor quality. Across the entire economy, there are more jobs than formerly in the management and professional grades. In this sense employment is being upgraded, but this process is not affecting all occupations. There is still plenty of menial work in the world's most prosperous countries, and much of this work is in leisure (see Seabrook, 1988). The Victorian class of domestic servants has not been socially promoted so much as transferred into the new leisure industries.

Optimists and pessimists

It is possible to construct a highly pessimistic picture of the direction in which the so-called leisured society is heading. Forecasts of a leisure society used to be optimistic. They anticipated life becoming less pressured and that people would be able to do more things for the sheer enjoyment. This vision is consistent with the Inglehart thesis (see Box 2.1).

Much recent writing on trends in leisure expresses disillusionment and cynicism rather than optimism (see in particular Seabrook, 1988). One point of

---

Box 2.1. The Inglehart thesis (1997).

Richard Inglehart claims that a silent revolution is in process throughout the entire world: a decline in materialist and the spread of post-materialist values.

People today are said to be less interested than in the past in gaining higher and higher incomes and more and more goods. We are said to be becoming more concerned with 'quality' – in our experiences, relationships and time. Politics that appeal to people's material self-interests are said to be in decline. New social movements concerned with the environment and civil rights are said to be examples of the influence of post-materialist values.

Inglehart's own research, in many different countries, suggests that successive cohorts of young people have been less materialist than their predecessors. According to Inglehart, economic security in childhood and youth is the crucial condition leading to a decline of materialism.

However, other researchers' evidence indicates that the trends may be more complicated. For example, Helena Helve's (1998) studies of young people in Finland suggest that the same individuals are quite capable of subscribing to both materialist and so-called post-materialist values. For example, it is possible to support equality between the sexes and, simultaneously, to be interested in making plenty of money.

agreement between the older story of leisure's remorseless growth and the 'revised version' is their regard of the values fostered by leisure as important ingredients in the 'cement' that locks the population into the present-day socio-economic system. However, the 'revised version' warns that the 'cement' may eventually crumble. We shall see in Chapter 3 that those who are able to do so are tending to work as long and as hard as possible so as to earn and spend as much as they can, but at some point their motivation could slacken. Fred Hirsch (1977), who drew attention to the positional element in personal consumption, has insisted that there are social as well as physical limits to economic growth. At some point he believes that people will tire of standing on tiptoe and seeing no further. Frustration is at least equally likely among those who are time-rich but whose consumer aspirations are thwarted. Some argue that recent trends simply cannot continue indefinitely and that leisure research and theory should be seeking routes out of the impending impasse.

Time pioneers?

In Germany Karl Horning and his colleagues (1995) studied a small group of employees, described as 'time pioneers', who had voluntarily reduced their weekly hours of work to 20–32. No claim is made that these 'time pioneers' represent a trend, yet. They were contacted through publicity in national and regional newspapers and radio programmes. Among the 36 cases studied, half were considered 'time conventionalists'. They had reduced their hours of work for a specific reason, such as becoming a single parent, and had not challenged normal time structures but had filled their additional non-working time with housework, childcare or leisure activities. The true 'time pioneers', in contrast, had changed their ways of life because they wanted more time for themselves rather than to do anything in particular. They had calculated how much money they needed to support a basic lifestyle and had learnt to live within it. For some this had not been difficult; their lifestyles had always been frugal and their aspirations non-materialistic. The others had revised their consumer habits and had consciously rejected goods-intensive lifestyles. All the 'time pioneers' valued their temporal affluence and treated this as a key criterion of well-being. They appreciated life's slower pace and leisureliness, being able to pace and plan their own time and being able to create time buffers so as to prevent pressure building up.

According to their own reports, the 'time pioneers' were regarded as odd by their work colleagues. They were, in fact, highly committed to their work but to the tasks rather than the status, career prospects, income maximization and other aspects of the general employment culture. This is probably why they were experiencing mixtures of resentment, envy, confrontation and aggression from colleagues and supervisors. Nevertheless, all the 'time pioneers' stressed their good fortune. They regarded themselves as privileged. They had experienced full-time work as too stressful, exacting and costly, and spoke of how their changed schedules had transformed their lives: how they had started to live and taken a qualitative leap forward. Having taken this leap none wanted to turn back.

Horning and his colleagues realize that their 'time pioneers' are exceptional but demand that they be recognized as people who are pioneering a radically different and viable way of living. There are no signs as yet of widespread demands for such radical reductions in both hours of work and incomes, but there are signs of people who have 'made it' in terms of earnings and status querying the meaning of success. Ray Pahl (1995) studied ten such people in Britain, eight men and two women. One person had made his money and cut back to an extremely short working week. Others were continuing on arduous work schedules. But in some way or another they were all confronting problems in managing their commitments and investments in economic and personal life and in deciding exactly what success was. These issues reappear in the following chapter on work and leisure and in Chapter 7 on consumerism and consumer culture.

Summary

The long-term growth of leisure, described in some detail in this chapter, is undisputed. Although less widely recognized, it is difficult to dispute the extent to which modern leisure's basic forms were cast very early in industrial history: our main leisure occasions, the main types of leisure providers and what remain our main leisure activities. There is also little scope for disagreement that, during its long-term growth, leisure has become more commercial, less violent and more individualized and that age, sex and social class differences in uses of leisure have been blurred.

However, close inspection of recent trends opens vast areas of debate. It places question marks against whether leisure is continuing to grow and, if so, whether the outcome will continue to be more of basically the same. The extent to which leisure has grown, even over the long term, since the 19th century in the case of Britain, has been questioned. It is only male manual workers for whom the growth of leisure, in all its dimensions – time available, money to spend in it and levels of leisure activity – is unequivocal. For some people, any gains in time released from paid work will have been cancelled out by longer journeys to and from work and/or heavier domestic workloads. All told, the gains in free time since the early industrial era have amounted to no more, or little more, than a recovery of what was lost during the take-off into industrialism. In recent decades, in some countries, the rollback in average hours of work has ended or at least faltered. There are question marks against whether some of the ways in which leisure has grown recently mean that we really have 'more' or 'better' leisure: the commercialization of what was formerly do-it-yourself entertainment, spending more money on our holidays and evenings out and cramming more leisure activities into each unit of leisure time than formerly. The question marks against the extent and ways in which leisure has grown during the last 50 years provide possible clues as to why there has been no parallel improvement in life satisfaction.

We have seen that recent gains in leisure time and spending have benefited entirely different sections of the population, and that there are grounds for arguing that, in the long run, these trends are unsustainable: hence the possible long-term historical significance of the minorities who are currently pioneering alternative ways of living.

The next three chapters explore in detail how the growth of leisure has affected people in different kinds of employment, men and women and members of different age groups.

Further Reading

On leisure in Britain before the Second World War

Davies, A. (1992) *Leisure, Gender and Poverty.* Open University Press, Buckingham, UK.

For analyses of how gains in work-free time were won

Hunnicutt, B.K. (1988) *Work Without End.* Temple University Press, Philadelphia, Pennsylvania.
Rosenweig, R. (1983) *Eight Hours For What We Will.* Cambridge University Press, New York.

For critiques of the extent to which leisure has grown

Hirsch, F. (1977) *The Social Limits to Growth.* Routledge, London.
Wilenski, H.L. (1963) The uneven distribution of leisure: the impact of economic growth on free time. In: Smigel, E.O. (ed.) *Work and Leisure.* College and University Press, New Haven, Connecticut.

For a detailed examination of recent trends in leisure in America

Robinson, J.P. and Godbey, G. (1999) *Time for Life: the Surprising Ways Americans Use Their Time,* 2nd edn. Pennsylvania State University Press, Penn State, Pennsylvania.

For an example of alternative lifestyles

Horning, K.H., Gerhard, A. and Michailow, M. (1995) *Time Pioneers: Flexible Working Time and New Lifestyles.* Polity Press, Cambridge, UK.

3   Work and Leisure

Introduction

This couplet has always been prominent in the sociology of leisure. The work–leisure relationship was in fact among the subject's original issues. In Britain the sociology of leisure emerged in the 1960s largely as an offshoot from the sociology of work. When sociologists then studied leisure the chances were that their core interests really lay in the long arm of the job.

Researchers have emphasized that many features of individuals' jobs can influence their leisure. Hours of work and pay are obvious examples. The containment of working time and the growth in incomes have always been recognized as two of the long-term trends responsible for the growth of leisure. Indeed, pay and hours of work have been responsible for some of the clearest and most consistent findings in work–leisure research. From the beginnings of such enquiries it has been found repeatedly that the higher strata do more of most things, the main exception being television viewing (see, for example, Havighurst and Feigenbaum, 1959; Dawson, 1988a, b). Maybe this particular work–leisure relationship has never received the attention, measured by the number of dedicated enquiries or pages of reporting, that its importance merits. Part of the explanation is that researchers cannot repeatedly earn acclaim for the rediscovery, and there are limited ways of saying, that the higher socio-economic strata do more. One reason for the relationship is quite obvious – money – and there are no prizes for repeatedly confirming the obvious.

An upshot has been that researchers have always stressed that the implications of the pay they receive and the number and scheduling of the hours that people work do not exhaust work's leisure effects. In the 1950s and 1960s they were equally, if not more, concerned to investigate how work-based social relationships, interests and states of mind could pervade people's leisure. Subsequently, in the late 1970s and 1980s, this entire stream of research encountered criticism. In focusing upon paid work the research was accused of concentrating on men's work and leisure and neglecting the leisure implications of other types of work, such as housework and caring, typically unpaid and performed mainly by women. During the 1980s gender challenged work as the leading issue in the study of leisure. A consequence is that there is little danger today of anyone neglecting the implications of the unpaid work that is done mainly by women and, to a lesser extent, by men. The implications of unpaid work are considered in detail in Chapter 4, which deals with leisure and gender, while the present chapter concentrates on the implications of paid employment. This continues to merit detailed attention if only because it accounts for a substantial chunk of most people's time – women's as well as men's – nowadays because by the mid-1990s women were just over 49% of all paid workers in Britain, and in many regions the majority of the workforce was then female (Noon and Blyton, 1997). Today most men and women are in paid jobs for the greater part of their adult lives and work supplies most of the income that most people spend on leisure activities.

Work–leisure research is currently emerging from a hiatus. The slackening of research in the 1980s was not because the relationship was no longer considered important. Nor had its investigation fallen out of fashion. Rather, the hiatus was due to the work–leisure issues of the 1960s and 1970s receding in importance, partly because the questions of that era were answered satisfactorily, but also because work was changing and the research issues needed to be redefined. With hindsight, we can now see that former social and psychological work–leisure links were being undermined by broader social and economic trends. The problems of working non-standard hours (another popular research issue earlier on) were being transformed by the spread of flexibility throughout the economy and labour market. Another change is that research into work and leisure until the 1970s was conducted in a context where hours of work were in long-term decline and there was a corresponding growth in leisure time. Subsequently, as the previous chapter explained, in the UK (and in some other countries) these trends have stalled. A further change is that the significance of being employed in different kinds of occupations has been partly eclipsed by the spread of unemployment and the re-creation of an older division – between people in jobs of all types and the unemployed.

This chapter proceeds by discussing the research, which is now rapidly fading into the historical background, into socio-psychological work–leisure relationships. This research remains important if only because we need to understand why these issues have ceased to be prominent in the work–leisure research agenda.

This is followed by an overview of the main differences in uses of leisure between occupational groups. We shall see that there is one difference that overshadows all others – the higher strata do more – and money is a principal reason.

The remaining sections discuss issues that have risen to the forefront of work–leisure research during the last 20 years. An older stream of research into the leisure effects of shift systems, or unsocial hours, has broadened in response to an all-round destandardization of working time. The leisure implications of reduced hours of work have been replaced as a research issue by questions as to why some groups still work long hours and why, in some occupations, working time appears to be lengthening rather than contracting. Finally, the chapter considers the leisure implications of unemployment.

Spillover and Compensation

The long arm of the job

In the 1960s and 1970s there was much research, and even more debate, about the socio-psychological processes whereby the long arm of the job governed people's leisure. Investigators paid attention to how particular occupations induced characteristic states of mind, surrounded workers with work-based social relationships and gave them interests and social identities, and a social standing, which they carried into the rest of their lives. Just as, at a macro-level, leisure time had been created by the modern organization of paid work, so, it was argued, at a micro-level, the particular kinds of employment that individuals practised shaped their particular orientations towards and uses of leisure.

Two main kinds of work–leisure relationship were identified, usually from a mixture of anecdotal and case-study evidence. The first was spillover, where work-based relationships, interests and social and technical skills spread into leisure. A common example given was white-collar workers who were able to use occupational skills in running voluntary associations. A less attractive example of spillover was said to be the workers with routine, mundane, mind-numbing jobs, whose mentalities were so stunted that they were content to spend most of their leisure being passively entertained. The second type of work–leisure relationship was compensation, where individuals used their free time to seek experiences they could not obtain at work. An example frequently offered was the desk-bound executive who played sport in the evenings and at weekends. Another was individuals who were denied opportunities to display initiative at work who used their leisure to demonstrate their autonomy ostentatiously.

Opposition, extension and neutrality

It proved embarrassingly easy to find a theory – spillover or compensation – to fit virtually every case and an obvious problem was to explain what triggered the kind of influence that would operate. A major intervention in this debate was by Stanley Parker (1971, 1983), who affirmed the need for a 'holistic' approach, in which work and leisure were viewed as a totality, and proposed that whether spillover or compensation operated depended mainly on the nature of the job. Parker argued that compensation, which he retitled the 'opposition pattern', was most likely when people's jobs were experienced as hard and painful and aroused negative feelings. Under these circumstances Parker suggested that individuals would tend to draw a clear boundary between their work and their leisure. They would look forward to the end of each working day and week. On leaving the workplace they would experience feelings of release and freedom and would celebrate the opportunity to express their true selves. Parker did not actually study a group of workers in which this opposition pattern prevailed, but he was able to refer to evidence from other studies of occupational groups, such as deep-sea trawlermen who came onshore and indulged in binges, during which they enjoyed drink and heterosexual company and sought hedonistic pleasures that were unavailable at sea.

Parker argued that spillover, which he retitled the 'extension pattern', tended to occur when people liked their jobs and became absorbed in their work, when occupations fostered amicable and cooperative relationships among colleagues and when individuals were required to represent their professions and organizations to the wider public. Under these circumstances, Parker argued that employees would sometimes find it difficult to decide where their work ended and their leisure commenced. They would spend some of their free time reading professional literature and thinking about work tasks, often in the company of workplace colleagues. Parker found that this type of leisure was more common among the youth employment officers and childcare officers that he studied (the predecessors of present-day career guidance officers and social workers) than among a sample of bank clerks.

Between extension and opposition Parker identified a midway 'neutrality pattern', which seemed to apply among many of the bank clerks. He argued that, when people were neither enthusiastic about nor hated their jobs, they were likely to treat their work and leisure as just different, complementary parts of their lives. Work would not extend into leisure, but neither would individuals feel a need to compensate for the deprivations endured each working day.

Criticisms

A problem that soon became apparent with Parker's typology and explanations was that there were too many exceptions. Work might extend into leisure because individuals were highly involved in their jobs and identified with their occupations. But it was noted that occupational communities, which carried workplace social relationships and interests into leisure time, could also arise because the nature or locations of their jobs separated employees from the wider community, as was observed among coal miners, the police, prison officers and railwaymen (see, for example Salaman, 1974). It was also apparent that people who liked their jobs could still use some of their leisure to gain complementary experiences, like exercise-seeking executives.

It was also noted that Parker's theory was not explaining what people did with their leisure so much as who they spent their time with and how they felt about their leisure activities and relationships. It was observed that some leisure interests were popular among groups with very different occupations. For example, Mott (1973) noted that pigeon fancying was popular among some groups of skilled weavers and also in some coal-mining communities, where most of the jobs required physical strength and endurance rather than delicate hand skills.

A third problem was that work–leisure relationships that could be illustrated persuasively in case studies proved difficult to identify in sample surveys that covered people in a variety of occupations. In the data sets such studies

produced, it was sometimes difficult to discern any powerful spillover or compensatory relationships. Such studies have found rather more evidence of
spillover than of compensation, but all the relationships discovered, between
interest in work and uses of leisure, for example, have been rather weak
(Champoux, 1978; Miller and Kohn, 1983; Zuzanek and Mannell, 1983). Some
uses of leisure are found to be popular in virtually all occupational groups –
watching television, taking holidays and visiting family members – for example.
A study of coal miners, steelworkers, factory employees and white-collar staff in
South Wales in the early 1980s found common features such as these, alongside
clear age and sex differences, in uses of leisure within all the occupational
groups, but no distinctive occupational patterns except among the coal miners
(Lloyd, 1986).

Occupational change

This entire genre of research has subsequently become almost extinct. Maybe
the theorists were always mistaken or overstated the strength of spillover and
compensatory relationships. However, it is likely that such relationships as may
have existed in the past will have weakened. The distinctive work–leisure relationships that were noted in case studies tended to be in occupations practised
mainly by one sex (invariably men), usually for their entire working lives, and
were located in towns and villages dominated by major industries, where work-
mates tended to be neighbours and work and community influences on leisure
were reinforcing. Recent economic and social trends have broken up these social
formations. There are now fewer towns and cities dominated by single firms and
industries. The pace of economic and technological change means that occupations can no longer be relied on to last for an entire working life. The private
motor car enables firms' workforces to be drawn from wider catchment areas
than in the past, and the residents in most districts are now employed in many
different occupations. Trends towards home-centred lifestyles will also have
weakened former work effects. So will affluence, which gives some individuals
and households wider choices over what to buy and what to do, whether in their
homes or outside.

   This does not mean that work will no longer have important leisure effects;
rather that the types of effects will have changed due to changes in the nature of
both work and leisure. Spillover and compensation have probably become less
powerful. This has thrown the long-standing tendency for the more privileged
socio-economic strata to do more of most things into even greater prominence
than formerly.

Leisure and Social Class

The striking feature of this tendency is its omnipresence. We shall see in later
chapters that there are clear links between uses of leisure, on the one hand, and
gender and age, on the other. Men tend to do more of some things while women

do more of others. A particular age group (young adults) is the most active in out-of-home leisure but not in all out-of-home activities. To the social class–leisure participation relationship there are very few exceptions.

Table 3.1 shows that the higher social classes have higher participation rates in all the more popular sports and other forms of physically active leisure. The relationship between social class and sport participation does not appear to have weakened over time and this relationship is certainly not confined to the UK. In Flanders, Scheerder and his colleagues (2002) have charted an overall rise in sport participation between 1969 and 1999, and have simultaneously emphasized the unchanged width of the gap between the participation rates of the different social classes. It is true that when sport is unpacked – when specific sports are examined and when where people play is taken into account – we find that the social class–sport participation relationship is more nuanced that it might at first appear. The working class in Flanders (and no doubt elsewhere) is least represented in sports that require expensive outlays on equipment and membership fees (golf and horse riding, for example). The working class is best represented in body-contact sports. It is also the case in Flanders that the middle classes are the most likely to play in private (voluntary sector) clubs and also to use commercial facilities whereas public sport facilities have more working-class users, but all

Table 3.1. Sport participation by occupational class: percentages taking part in 4 weeks prior to interviews (2002).

	1a	1b	2	3	4	5	6	7	8
Walking	46	48	43	34	31	29	29	25	22
Swimming	24	20	17	13	12	11	9	8	8
Keep fit/yoga	20	18	15	15	11	9	7	6	4
Snooker/pool/billiards	9	9	10	10	9	9	8	7	6
Cycling	12	13	11	7	8	7	6	7	8
Weight training	11	9	7	7	5	4	4	3	3
Running	10	9	6	5	4	3	2	2	3
Soccer	6	6	6	4	5	5	3	4	4
At least one activity	75	75	68	58	57	54	46	44	38
At least one activity, excluding walking	59	59	51	43	43	38	31	30	26

Occupational groups:
1a. Large employers and higher managerial.
1b. Higher professional.
2. Lower managerial and professional.
3. Intermediate.
4. Small employers and own-account workers.
5. Lower supervisory, technical and skilled.
6. Semi-routine.
7. Routine.
8. Never worked and long-term unemployed.
Source: Fox and Rickards (2004).

these nuances are within the overall powerful tendency for the middle classes to do more.

This tendency is not specific to sport. With the exception of activities that are near-universal (such as watching television), the middle classes in Britain have the highest participation rates in all the main forms of home-based leisure (see Table 3.2). They are also the most likely to go away on holidays and to visit theatres, libraries, museums and other cultural facilities and they also drink more alcohol (Table 3.3). Sturgis and Jackson (2003b) have noted that a powerful and generalized class-based participation effect is operating. The present-day middle and working classes do more and less than each other rather than entirely different things.

The reason why the middle classes do more cannot be that they have more leisure time. In fact, exactly the reverse applies (see Table 3.4). Nowadays the middle classes have the longest paid-work schedules. Despite this, the middle classes spend at least as much and often more time than the working class on most leisure activities. There is just one big exception – watching television. The middle classes also spend slightly less time asleep, doing housework and on general social life and resting.

So why do the middle classes do more? There are several contributing reasons. These include childhood socialization and education, but the principal

Table 3.2. Participation in selected leisure activities by occupational class: percentages participating in 4 weeks preceding interviews (2002).

	1a	1b	2	3	4	5	6	7	8
TV	99	99	99	99	99	99	99	99	96
Radio	94	93	92	89	88	86	84	81	80
Records or tapes	92	90	88	82	81	80	78	75	72
Reading books	81	81	74	68	56	59	56	52	57
Singing or playing an instrument	12	14	15	10	10	9	8	6	8
Dancing	10	10	12	12	11	11	9	7	7
Painting	10	10	11	10	11	9	7	6	12
Writing stories or poetry	5	5	5	4	3	3	3	3	6
Running arts events	3	5	5	3	2	2	1	1	3
Performing in a play	2	2	3	2	2	1	1	1	3

Occupational classes:
1a. Large employers and higher managerial.
1b. Higher professional.
3. Lower managerial and professional.
4. Intermediate.
5. Small employers and own-account workers.
6. Lower supervisory, technical and skilled.
6. Semi-routine.
7. Routine.
8. Never worked and long-term unemployed.
Source: Fox and Rickards (2004).

Table 3.3. Percentages who drank during the last week: persons aged 16 and over. Great Britain 2000.

	Professional	Employers and managers	Intermediate non-manual	Junior non-manual	Skilled and own-account non-professional	Semi-skilled and personal service	Unskilled	Total
Men	84	82	80	77	71	65	61	75
Women	74	70	65	58	58	48	41	60

Source: www.statistics.gov.uk

Table 3.4. Average time (in minutes per day) spent in different main activities by socio-economic class.

Main activity	Managerial and professional	Intermediate	Manual and routine	Long-term unemployed/ never worked
Sleeping	491	503	513	533
Eating and drinking	88	85	84	105
Personal care	45	47	47	52
Employment	225	198	173	8
Study	5	4	5	7
Housework	163	184	179	239
Childcare (own-household children)	22	24	19	19
Voluntary work and meetings	17	17	15	24
Social life and resting	73	76	79	96
Entertainment and culture	7	6	5	5
Sport and outdoor activities	16	13	13	13
Hobbies and games	24	20	17	26
Reading	32	27	25	40
TV and video	122	137	168	187
Radio and music	6	7	8	11
Travel	95	83	79	64
Other	8	10	10	12

Source: UK 2000 Time Use Survey.

reason, the permitting reason, is money. The middle classes have much more of this than the working class and since the 1970s in Britain the gap between the higher and lower income groups has widened. Even when the social classes spend time and money on the same things, there are usually differences in exactly how they are taking part. Take motoring, for example:

> In one world of enabling consumption, for the 40% of households in the upper part of the income distribution, choice is the major factor with new or nearly new cars consumed as branded product which provides the use value of unproblematic mobility for work and leisure. Further down the income scale, middle income households in a different world of enforced consumption are constrained by petrol costs and must sacrifice non-motoring consumption; while at the bottom end of the income distribution, household mobility is risky as the fourth hand 'banger' may not start tomorrow morning and cannot easily be replaced.
>
> (Froud *et al.*, 2005, pp. 97–98)

Social class is not solely about money. Sociologists (many of us, at any rate) say that social classes are formed among people with common labour-market and work situations. The strength of an occupational group's labour-market situation is indicated by the rewards that people typically receive from work – the pay, of course, but also any fringe benefits (pension rights, health insurance, company cars and so on) – and also their security of employment (their risks of losing their jobs and becoming unemployed or having to accept inferior jobs) and their prospects of career progression. 'Work situation' refers to the social relationships in which people are involved at work – how much autonomy they enjoy, how closely they are supervised and whether they have control of and are responsible for the work of others. In all these respects the middle and working classes are polar opposites, the former is advantaged and the latter is disadvantaged.

Now, since people tend to spend their entire working lives doing similar kinds of jobs (if not exactly the same jobs with the same employers), since work accounts for such a large chunk of most people's lives and because people with similar occupations tend to live in similar neighbourhoods and have similar amounts of money to spend, it is normally anticipated (in sociology) that occupation-based classes will tend to develop into social and cultural entities. This means that members of a class will be more likely to interact with one another than with outsiders and that they will tend to develop common outlooks on life, preoccupations and political proclivities and similar uses of free time. When people argue seriously, as some do in present-day sociology (for example, Pakulski and Waters, 1996), that social class has declined in importance, they are not alleging that differences (inequalities) between the classes' work and market situations have lessened. The middle classes today (managers and professionals) are just as, and usually more, advantaged in every respect than ever before. The argument is that the social and cultural spin-offs have become less powerful, and in practice this argument is always about what has happened to the working class (skilled, semi-routine and routine manual workers). In Britain the working class has certainly become weaker in just about every possible sense (see Roberts, 2001). At the beginning of the 20th century the working class comprised around three-quarters of the population. It is now a minority – well under 40%. In recent decades the working class has also been weakened by a deterioration in the typical quality of the manual jobs that remain and higher risks of unemployment. Former workplace- and neighbourhood-based cultures and ways of life have been undermined in various ways by rehousing, television keeping people indoors and the motor car enabling them to go out in private.

In the USA Putnam (2000) has argued that over time there has been a general decline in 'social capital' (trust relationships among citizens) and that this is indicated, among other things, by a decline in memberships of voluntary associations. Throughout Europe there is no clear evidence of an all-round decline (see Harper, 2001). In Britain there has been an overall decline but this has occurred wholly in memberships of those organizations where the working class was once best represented, namely, trade unions and working men's clubs (see Table 3.5).

Voluntary association memberships are useful indicators of the extent to which the members of different occupation-based classes are knit together. Over time, in Britain, voluntary association memberships have become more concentrated within the middle classes. Simultaneously, what were formerly predominantly working-class organizations, most notably the trade unions and the

Table 3.5. Voluntary association membership, Great Britain, 1972–1999 (percentages).

	Men 1972	Men 1992	Men 1999	Women 1992	Women 1999
Sports/hobby club	25	26	26	11	14
Trade union	40	26	22	16	16
Professional association	11	–	14	–	8
Social/working men's club	28	21	18	8	7
Tenants'/residents' group	4	7	7	8	9
Political party	7	4	2	3	2
Environmental group	–	5	4	4	3
Voluntary services group	–	3	3	5	5
Parents'/school association	5	4	2	7	7
Religious/church group	10	8	7	12	11
Other community/civic groups	–	3	2	3	2
Women's institutes/groups	–	–	–	4	4
Scouts/guides organizations	–	–	1	–	2
Pensioners' group	–	–	1	–	–
Other organizations	15	12	8	9	7
At least one membership	77	64	59	53	51

Source: Li *et al.* (2002).

Labour Party, have undergone gentrification, meaning that the middle classes have moved in and have often taken over the running of these bodies. There have been similar trends in friendship patterns. Middle-class friendships have become more endogamous (confined within the middle classes). Meanwhile, working-class friendships have become less endogamous (Li *et al.*, 2002, 2003). These trends are wholly explicable in terms of the changes that have taken place in the proportions of the population in the different social classes and the inevitable implications, among other things, for absolute rates of social mobility. All told, the working class has become a weaker social formation while the middle class has grown stronger. When trends in the middle class are taken fully into account, it becomes difficult to argue that there has been an all-round decline in the importance of social class.

These are the background and the underlying reason why the main social class difference in leisure today is that the middle classes simply do more and this applies in virtually every type of leisure. The working class has become less distinctive in its leisure preferences and practices. The middle classes are now better represented than the working class in virtually all kinds of leisure. The different classes do not do different things so much as more and less of the same things.

Class-based and class-related leisure

It is more accurate to speak of present-day leisure as class-related than class-based. By far the strongest class relationship nowadays is that the higher strata do more of virtually everything that has a cash price (and many other things as well). It has become more difficult than in the past to identify qualitatively distinct leisure patterns that are typical of entire social classes or even specific occupations. The main differences are now quantitative and are maintained primarily through financial inequalities.

This has not always been the case. As explained in Chapter 2, historians have stressed the strength and persistence of qualitatively distinct class-based leisure patterns throughout the 19th and well into the 20th century (Howkins and Lowerson, 1979; Davies, 1992; Mason, 1994). In Victorian Britain the middle and working classes lived in different districts, dressed differently and spent their leisure in entirely different places, and this continued until the Second World War. There were changes in the leisure of all social classes related to rising standards of living, shorter working hours (for manual workers) and new leisure opportunities (flying, driving, dancing, holidaymaking, radio and the cinema, for example), but without breaking down the divisions between the classes.

According to Victoria de Grazia (1992) these social class differences persisted in the rural parts of Western Europe until the 1950s. Until then, leisure in Europe's rural villages was typically communal. Different classes had their separate ways of life, which came together, but were not fused, on days of national and religious celebration. The leisure ideal that the authorities (whether fascist, communist or liberal) promoted was of loyal citizens, members of different classes, each of which contributed to the strength of the society. Victoria de Grazia then explains how, from the 1950s onwards, communal forms of leisure began to be undermined as affluence and consumerism spread from the industrial classes and urban areas into Western Europe's countryside. She argues that leisure has subsequently become a sphere of choice for individuals and households, who spend their time and money in a variety of very different ways. In the Italian village whose history de Grazia traces in detail, the old communal festivities were being preserved primarily as tourist attractions.

Privileged omnivores

In overwhelmingly urban Britain the social and economic trends described earlier in this chapter will have diluted spillover and compensatory work–leisure relationships.

Trends towards home-centred lifestyles, prosperity, which has given some households a wider range of options, unemployment, which has impoverished others, and the normalization of non-standard work schedules (see below) will have conspired to undermine ways of working and playing that once character-ized entire communities and even social classes. Of course, there are still pockets where traditional working-class communities survive. Sections of the super-rich maintain exclusive uses of leisure. The development of distinctive lifestyles has been noted among sections of the new upper middle classes, and these develop-ments are discussed in Chapter 6. But the main class difference today is simply that economically advantaged groups have wider opportunities and do more. Mass affluence has reduced the number of leisure activities that are exclusive to privileged elites. Meanwhile, elite groups have been embracing popular culture. There was a time when the economically privileged tended to have distinctly highbrow tastes. They could be regarded as 'snobs' insofar as enjoyment of the popular arts could lead to a loss of status within the groups in question. Those days have gone, partly as a result of the volume of upward mobility – the number of people who now rise into the higher socio-economic strata, typically bringing lowbrow tastes with them (see van Eijck and van Rees, 1998; van Eijck, 1999). Today the economically privileged strata tend to be cultural omnivores (see Peterson and Kern, 1996; Sintas and Alvarez, 2002). It is true that they pur-chase much more classical music than the working class, but the economically privileged spend more on popular music than on classics (see Longhurst, 1996). In fact, they spend more on popular music than the working class. The higher strata are not distinguished by their exclusive tastes so much as by the sheer variety of their tastes (see Erickson, 1996). They not only dine out more frequently than the less affluent, but do so in a wider variety of restaurants (Warde *et al.*, 1999). Middle-class omnivorousness appears to be spreading worldwide, and basically the same reasons will apply everywhere. The working classes are hardly represented in the audiences for high culture, but this is not because they have their own equally rich alternatives. The less well off simply have a narrower range of tastes and activities. Money is not the sole reason. The upper strata's breadth of interests owes something to their education and their increasingly endogamous social networks. However, expressing their tastes involves spending money and a reason why poorer sections of the population cannot widen their tastes and interests to a similar extent is that they cannot afford to do so.

An outcome of all this is a leisure democracy in the sense that members of all social strata do similar things in their leisure, but democracy is not the same as equality: the privileged classes are distinguished by their ability to do more, which they exercise in virtually all areas of out-of-home leisure. At all occupa-tional levels, uses of leisure no longer integrate most individuals into culturally distinct social classes, which may then either celebrate or challenge the wider socio-economic–political order. Leisure, like many other areas of social experi-ence, is being individualized. Money is now at the root of the main differences between uses of leisure in different social strata, and nowadays the leisure differences between them are basically and blatantly inequalities rather than alternative ways of life.

Working Time: Destandardization

The development of shift systems

Shift systems are virtually as old as modern industry. Nineteenth-century manufacturers experimented with shifts as a way of maintaining output and keeping their expensive machines running for the maximum possible hours and, particularly important, as a way of coping with fluctuations in demand. Night shifts and double days have been worked for well over a century. Both world wars led to a rise in shift working. The disadvantages (for workers) have always been recognized. Workers and their trade unions have always demanded premium rates of pay to compensate for the disadvantages, employers have usually accepted the need to offer a financial incentive and workers on normal hours have considered those on shifts to be entitled to special recompense.

Insofar as the effects of shift working were investigated systematically prior to the Second World War, the principal interest was nearly always in output and productivity. Subsequently the effects on the workers' lives and well-being became a research area. This was related to the more widespread adoption of shifts during the so-called 30 glorious years of full employment and economic growth that followed the Second World War, when some firms could find markets for virtually everything they could produce. An additional incentive was that industry was becoming more capital-intensive and technological cycles were accelerating and employers were therefore keen to gain maximum output before each generation of equipment became obsolete.

The effects of shifts on leisure

Between the 1950s and 1980s the effects of shifts on workers' health, family and social lives were investigated in a series of studies (Brown, 1959; Mott *et al.*, 1965; Marsh, 1979; European Foundation, 1980; Brown and Charles, 1982; Carter and Corlett, 1982; Lloyd, 1986). The findings were crystal-clear and consistent. Investigators noted that the effects of shifts, or unsocial hours as they came to be described, depended on the particular shift and on the age and sex of the employee. For example, young people's lifestyles were particularly vulnerable. That said, all the studies found that shift systems were disliked: workers accepted the consequences only for the extra pay, and sometimes because the only alternative appeared to be unemployment. A common feeling was that rotating shifts were preferable to enduring permanently the inconveniences of any one unsocial schedule. Many employees accepted shifts only for a part of their working lives, when they had the greatest need to maximize their earnings.

Shifts have been found to damage employees' health. Sleep patterns are usually disrupted. Shift workers complain that they are unable to gain their normal hours of rest. Eating disorders are also common. However, shift workers have been equally vociferous in complaining about the effects on family relationships and leisure activities. Shifts desynchronize the time schedules of family members.

Individuals on shifts may be unavailable to sleep with their partners and share family mealtimes. They may have to miss evenings in pubs with their friends and weekend trips to sports events. Rotating shifts make it difficult for individuals to plan ahead or accept any regular social commitments: they cannot rely on being free at any particular time. Irrespective of whether their amounts of leisure time and overall levels of leisure activity are reduced, all the studies have found that shift workers complain about the lack of regularity and predictability in their daily and weekly routines and their problems in coordinating their own time schedules with those of friends and other family members.

Exceptions

Researchers have noted some leisure advantages in working unorthodox hours. Individuals can be left with expanses of private time to pursue personal interests and hobbies when other members of their households are at work or school. However, shift workers sometimes find that such time becomes accounted for by new social obligations. For example, men can find that they are expected to care for young children during the daytime. A further advantage appreciated by some shift workers is their ability to pursue leisure activities at off-peak, less congested and sometimes cheaper times.

Shift workers in better-paid, higher-status jobs have been the least likely to complain about their work schedules (Roberts and Chambers, 1985). Nearly all the early investigations were among manual employees. Up to and including now, these are the employees who have been the most likely to work shifts. However, there are some professions where unsocial hours are customary. In professions such as medicine the practitioners have probably accepted the occupational hours as part of the package. Money can ameliorate, if not solve, a host of leisure problems. Individuals with high incomes are the most able to take advantage of having private time to pursue personal interests. The relevant studies have found that the groups most vulnerable to the disadvantages of shifts are employees who are already disadvantaged, such as women in low-paid jobs, who have to juggle the requirements of their paid occupations and domestic responsibilities (see Roberts and Chambers, 1985). Middle-class couples have longer joint (paid) working weeks than working-class couples, but the latter are more likely to be on different work schedules (unsocial hours are still most common in manual jobs) and therefore spend less time together (Warren, 2003).

The normalization of non-standard hours

Non-standard working hours have now become sufficiently common to be described as normal, at least in a statistical sense. This has been due to the spread of flexibility throughout work organizations and labour markets. There are numerous signs of this trend. During the 1980s in Britain there were declines in the proportions of male and female employees in full-time permanent jobs (Brown, 1990). By the early 1990s the proportion of part-time employees had risen to approximately a quarter of all workers and nearly half of all women employees. In 1995 Will Hutton described the 30–30–40 society, Britain, where just 40% of the working-age population had permanent full-time jobs, 30% had no paid employment and the other 30% were in jobs with non-standard terms or conditions. Hours of work are more dispersed than formerly in terms of how many hours people work per week and their scheduling. In Britain there are more staff on part-time hours and there are probably more working 50-plus h per week (see below). In the early 1990s two-fifths of all British managers were working more than 50 h, and over a half were taking work home at least once a week (Institute of Management, 1993). Self-employment has also become more common. The number of self-employed in Britain doubled from roughly 1.5 to over 3 million between the mid-1970s and the mid-1990s. By then 11% of all firms had some home-based staff. These amounted to only 2.5% of the entire workforce but their numbers are expected to rise with the spread of teleworking (Huws, 1993). By the early 2000s 13% of Britain's workforce either usually worked at home on at least one day per week or normally worked away from home but from a home base (Felstead *et al.*, 2005b). Homeworkers and the self-employed can rarely separate work from the rest of their lives, as is possible when employees have separate workplaces, and the self-employed are renowned for working as long as and whenever is necessary. The decline of the standard working week can be seen in that, by the early 1990s, fewer than 20% of all work establishments in Britain required no Sunday working of any kind (Bosworth, 1994) and only 34% of all employees worked 'normal' full-time hours, that is, between 8.00 a.m. and 6.00 p.m., Monday to Friday (Hewitt, 1993).

It is fair to point out that employers have always sought flexibility (Pollert, 1991). They have always wanted their staff to learn new skills when necessary and to extend their working hours during upturns in demand, and have trimmed their workforces during recessions. However, since the 1970s, firms have become even more flexible and this has applied in every European Union country (Beatson, 1995). Total hours and work patterns have become more varied. There are more people working 4 days on and then 4 days off and on other schedules that obliterate the customary 7-day cycle. The ways in which flexibility is achieved vary from firm to firm, according to the type of business, and from country to country, but the trend has been noted everywhere. The conditions requiring flexibility are not new but have intensified and become more widespread. Businesses are increasingly capital-intensive and want maximum output before their investments cease to be 'state-of-the-art'. During recent decades additional developments have contributed to the spread of shift systems. The proportion of employment in consumer services, including leisure services, which must be produced and delivered when people want to spend and consume, has risen. The growth of leisure is among the causes of more people working at odd hours. Then there is the increasingly intense, often global, competition. More and more firms have reason to feel that they must be open for business whenever customers or suppliers in Korea or wherever are in their offices. International competition in manufacturing and in financial and other business services is increasingly fierce. Technological and product cycles continue to accelerate. Firms feel that they need to be flexible in order to cope with these turbulent conditions, and this means demanding flexibility of their employees. This may mean requiring permanent core staff to be adaptable, accepting continuing education and retraining simply in order to keep abreast, and being able to change the size and shape of establishments' workforces from year to year, month to month, week to week, day to day, and sometimes from time to time during each working day. So more full-time and part-time staff are expected to work overtime, paid or unpaid, or to take work home, as and when required. Evenings and weekends have ceased to be sacrosanct leisure occasions. Finally, information technology, specifically the mobile phone, the laptop computer and the Internet have made it easier for some employees to take work home or to work from home and to be on call at any time, and what becomes possible easily becomes an expectation:

> The emerging new landscape of employment is one in which spaces and times of work and non-work are not clearly separated, work time is spent in a variety of locations, many of which are not set aside specifically for job-related tasks, workers are required to construct their own sequences and sites of activities, and personal space in the labour process is absent, problematic or contested. We no longer go to the office but, instead, the office comes with us, every where and every when.
>
> (Felstead *et al.*, 2005a, p. 2)

In the 1960s and 1970s there was a trend towards flexitime, which allows employees to select their own hours of work around a compulsory core. Such practices continue. Indeed, by the mid-1990s one in eight employees in Britain was on some type of flexitime system (Noon and Blyton, 1997). However, since the 1970s it has become more common for employers to stipulate when and for how long their staff will work. Labour market conditions, with high levels of unemployment, have enabled employers to enforce these conditions, and many have felt that there has been no alternative if they have wanted to keep abreast or ahead of competitors. So it has become more common for employees to have contracts that guarantee only part-time, if any, hours but which expect the staff to be available (on call) or to work longer as and when required. In 1981 Stanley Parker argued that 'pure leisure' was most likely when institutions were flexible while individuals could be self-determining, but this is not how the economy has subsequently developed. Rather, it is the employing organizations that have been deciding how employees will be flexible.

Post-Fordism and the portfolio worker

These trends are sometimes seen as an aspect of the transition from a Fordist to a post-Fordist era. Under Fordism large firms and their occupational structures were among the reliabilities. Large firms survived recessions and could offer secure jobs and progressive careers. Post-Fordist flexibility changes this. Another manifestation of the new flexibility is that career ladders have been either disappearing completely or have become shorter and less secure, and fewer blue-collar and white-collar workers, skilled and other employees are able to regard their occupations as secure for their working lives. This applies in firms of all sizes. An upshot is that working life has become discontinuous. In this respect, what was once the norm for women only has now spread throughout the workforce. Up to now women have been at the centre of the 'revolution' in working patterns. They have been the most flexible workers. Male biographies and day-to-day ways of life remained perhaps remarkably stable alongside the changing experiences of women during the 20th century (see Hinrichs *et al.*, 1991; van der Lippe, 1996). However, men's jobs are being affected by the current changes.

It is essential to point out here that job changing has not become more frequent. Indeed, in Britain the average time spent in a job has actually lengthened (Taylor, 2002). The changes involved in the flexibilization of the workforce have been more subtle than an increased rate of job terminations. It is likely that, in the past, job moves were typically voluntary and in order to obtain a better job, whereas nowadays moves are more often enforced (though still voluntary, at least nominally, in most cases) and lateral or downwards. Opportunities for career progression will not have diminished but have probably become less reliable and predictable. More to the present point, firms can achieve flexibility not by speeding up their hiring and firing but by doing more training and retraining and by varying their employees' hours of work. Satisfaction with hours of work has declined steeply in Britain among men and women at all occupational levels (Taylor, 2002). The most likely reason is the destandardization of working time, and the fact that it is employees, not their employers, who are expected to be flexible.

One school of thought argues that the destandardization of working time, the increased variation in total hours of work and all the other manifestations of post-Fordist flexibility mean that the future will belong to the portfolio worker. These individuals will work for many employers (though the workers may be legally self-employed) consecutively and sometimes simultaneously. No organization will offer security and career progression. However, optimists argue that individuals will be able to find security and a sense of career development in their forever expanding portfolios of skills, which ensure a demand for their labour (Bridges, 1995). Like other trends, portfolio work is likely to mean different things at different occupational levels. It is common for the same individuals to occupy several company directorships and seats in the UK parliament as well in some cases. Some professionals do well as consultants. For other people, however, portfolio working is likely to mean a succession of temporary, often part-time, jobs, interspersed with periods of unemployment, as individuals try to generate sufficient income to maintain their lifestyles through combinations of office cleaning, waiting, supermarket and similar jobs.

Koen Breedveld (1996a) has argued that other writers have exaggerated the pace and extent of change. He has analysed Netherlands time budget data in order to measure the extent to which working time has been destandardized. The proportion of all work performed outside normal hours rose from 12.7% in 1975 to 14.2% in 1995. The proportion of workers who did some work at abnormal hours in a typical week rose from 49% to 56%. Breedveld concludes that 'Flexibilisation is definitely a hype . . . Figures that underline this hype are all too greedily welcomed and too cheerfully reproduced by those who, for their fortune and status, depend on them' (p. 15). However, working time in the Netherlands is more regulated by law than in most European Union countries (Britain is the least regulated), and in the Netherlands these regulations were relaxed slightly only in the 1990s. Breedveld's own figures show that by the mid-1990s more than half of employees in the Netherlands were doing some work at non-standard times.

Adjusting or tolerating the new flexibility?

Leisure research needs to catch up with these trends. There are diametrically opposed views on the likely leisure implications, but agreement that the implications will be profound. After all, the normal patterns of home life and leisure that developed after the Second World War depended on economic security and standard leisure occasions – evenings, weekends and holidays – which nearly everyone could enjoy. However, one possibility is that we are witnessing the advent of postmodern modes of time organization, which, in time, will become just as acceptable as modern, industrial time. The early factory owners had difficulty in disciplining labour to accept the new industrial work rhythms. Previously most people had lived according to so-called natural or cyclical time. Things were then done when they just had to be done or could be done. This was replaced by linear, industrial time, clock time, a key feature being that there were proper times, and places as well, for most things – work, education, play and worship. The first generation of factory workers was resistant, whereas by the late 19th century industrial time schedules had been accepted as simply normal.

Could we be witnessing the birth of new, postmodern patterns of time organization, which, when bedded in, will be just as acceptable as linear, industrial time? Under postmodern time it is said to become acceptable to do anything at any time. So working non-customary hours could be less of a problem than in the industrial past. Television entertainment and some cinemas, shops, restaurants and bars are now open around the clock. Telephone banks never close. Cities have been developing night-time economies and are becoming 24-h places – leisure places for some and workplaces for others. Video and DVD recorders enable people to record and watch any kind of entertainment at any time. In the future people may routinely bank time just as they have learnt to bank cash, thereby enabling themselves to reconcile the spending and leisure patterns that they personally prefer with the ups and downs of portfolio careers. For example, by working long hours while they are economically active, employees may earn sabbaticals. Average earnings and spending are now considerably higher than in the 1970s, so more workers should be able to take advantage of the opportunities and cope with the synchronization problems hitherto associated with non-standard working hours. Some couples deliberately seek different non-standard work schedules in order to maximize both the households' incomes and the time when at least one adult will be available to care for children (Corcoran-Nantes and Roberts, 1995). This optimistic train of thought on the broader social impact of the spread of non-standard work schedules is able to regard female workers as skilled time managers from whom others must now learn (Hewitt, 1993).

The contrary and, in my opinion, more realistic viewpoint is that most people will be unable to adjust their lives to the bewildering array of work schedules and career uncertainties in which they now find themselves enmeshed, and that, rather than dissolving, the problems associated with shift work will simply become more widespread. Insofar as they are able to do so, most people continue to cling to familiar routines (see also Breedveld, 1994). The 7-day cycle and occasions such as the weekend have a long-standing sociocultural appeal that may not easily be set aside. Willy Fache (1996) has deplored the spread of Sunday working in Belgium. He argues that the quality of life is impaired when there are no dependable leisure occasions when family members, together with work colleagues and neighbours, can rely on experiencing leisure at the same times. Many employees may see little point in complaining. Those coping with the problems, if this is what they are doing, are no longer a victimized minority. The problems associated with unsocial hours may have become normal without ceasing to be problems for individuals and families. Mulgan and Wilkinson (1995) have called upon the UK government to establish new time reliabilities to counterbalance the new flexibilities. They have in mind statutory rights to educational leave, parental leave and sabbaticals. If enacted, these new rights could be experienced as poor recompense for the loss of the right to work full-time in a secure job and to enjoy evenings and weekends as family and communal leisure occasions.

Individualization and the social organization of time

Greater variety in work schedules will be contributing to the individualization of leisure (see Box 3.1). Individualization is a broader social trend. As explained in Chapter 2, it arises from the national and international marketing of leisure goods and services and also from the decline in family stability, the weakening of neighbourhood and religious communities, the decline in the large firms and industries that once dominated many local labour markets, the spread of private transport, the accelerating pace of economic and occupational change and the more varied experiences of young and older people in post-compulsory education, part-time and full-time employment and periods of unemployment.

In the 1950s and 1960s there was much discussion about the spread of privatism – home- and family-centredness. This is not the same thing as individualization. Home- and family-centred lifestyles are vulnerable in the face of the kind of individualization that is now spreading. Family-centredness will be disrupted if more families have members with different work schedules. This does not mean that there will be no shared family leisure. It simply means that this will not always be as possible or as predictable and reliable as in the past. How many 'partners' nowadays have to consult diaries to discover when they will be able to spend a full weekend together? People may not spend the rest of their leisure time alone. They may be gregarious and go out frequently, but not reliably with the same people at the same times each week, year in, year out. Leisure companions

---

Box 3.1. Working time and collective rhythms and routines.

The greater the amounts of time that people spend at work and the greater the variety in their work schedules, the less likely they are to be able to spend their leisure doing things together at the same times each day, week or month. Thus it becomes more difficult for individuals to match their own leisure interests with those of other people who are free to do the same things (play sport, attend sport fixtures, rehearse a play for example) at the same times (see Jenkins and Osberg, 2003).

This applies within families. When both partners work, and especially when one or both work at odd hours, collective household rhythms and routines (like shared mealtimes) are disrupted (see van den Broek *et al.*, 2002).

The UK 2000 Time Use Survey found that married and cohabiting couples spent on average just 2½ h/weekday and 3½ h/weekend day doing the same things together at the same times. Most shared time was spent watching television, eating and doing housework. Couples rarely shared leisure activities: just 21% of all time devoted to entertainment, 10% of time devoted to sport and 10% of time spent on games and hobbies (Gatenby, 2004).

Trends in labour markets are individualizing leisure within families and are making it increasingly difficult to sustain leisure routines that require large numbers of people (sport teams, orchestras, theatre casts, etc.) to be available regularly at the same times. This is likely to be one reason for the increasing popularity of individual exercise in gyms rather than playing traditional team sports.

Weekend 11-a-side football in England has been suffering an exodus of players (Jackson, 2004). Clubs have folded. Entire leagues have vanished. Almost a million men are estimated to have given up playing between 1997 and 2004. In 2003–4 alone, around 100,000 men, roughly a fifth of all players, gave up playing park football. Demand for pitches has declined. At Hackney Marshes in East London there were once over 100 football pitches; by 2004 there were just 66. Commentators have suggested various reasons for the decline of 11-a-side weekend football:

- More games on TV.
- The poor state of pitches and changing facilities.
- Players switching to midweek five-a-side.
- Separated parents who need to spend weekends with their children.
- Opening up Sundays to virtually any activities and competing demands on players' time (such as shopping).

We should note that many of these alleged causes operate through wider trends making it more difficult for the same 11 players to play together every week at the same time.

---

will become temporary. Every individual will have a unique, individualized leisure career and social network, albeit based on experiences all of which are shared with many other people. Leisure will cease to be based on stable groups, times and places. Maybe people will be able to adjust to such situations but up to now those who have been able to work hitherto normal hours and to enjoy normal leisure appear to have remained grateful for the opportunity.

Work–Life Balance

Up to the 1970s working hours were in long-term decline in all the, by then, older industrial societies. The reason was obvious, or so it appeared; the working populations were taking some of the benefits of economic growth by enjoying more free time. This trend was expected to continue indefinitely. The 3-day weekend and the 3-day and even the 2-day working week were forecast. The question was not so much whether as when. Automation was to reduce the need for human labour. As well as shorter working weeks people were expected to enjoy longer holidays and even sabbaticals. How wrong can you be?

Longer hours for some and intensified work for all

As we saw in Chapter 2 (pp. 45–47), there is no evidence of a general extension of working time in Britain. Since the 1970s the overall picture has been one of overall stability with minor ups and downs from year to year. However, it is possible that hours of work have lengthened for some groups of workers, namely, those in the management and professional grades. We also saw in Chapter 2 (pp. 45–46) that it is very difficult to obtain completely trustworthy information on hours worked, especially for groups that do not clock or sign on and off and who are likely to take some work home. We have to rely on self-reports, which Robinson and Godbey (1999) regard as untrustworthy. That said, we know that in Britain the management and professional grades have the longest working weeks (Table 3.4, p. 63). Substantial proportions claim total working weeks in excess of 48 h. We also know that a growing proportion of all jobs are in these grades. The self-employed, among whom long hours have been customary, have also grown in number since the 1970s. It is mainly males who say that they are spending 48 or more h per week in their paid occupations. A quarter of all UK males, and half of all male non-manual workers, say that they work this long, and 10% say that they work for 60 h or more (Hogarth *et al.*, 2001; Reeves, 2002). An increasing number of females have been joining men in these long work schedules. In the late 1980s the number of full-time female employees began to rise (Hakim, 1993). They are still very much a minority in the higher-level professional and management grades and among the self-employed, but growing numbers of women have been joining men in these career grades, where working time is longest.

There is little doubt that people in employment have been working harder as the downsizing and delayering that began in the manual grades have spread up the occupational structure. The lunch hour appears to be a thing of the past: the average time now taken is just half an hour and more managers and professional staff spend breaks at their desks catching up with reading and paperwork. Only a third of UK workers say that they take a full hour for lunch (Reeves, 2002).

Long business lunches are out. Working breakfasts have joined business dinners in extending the working day. Work has become fashionable even among the super-rich (Seabrook, 1988; see Rojek, 2000b). Individuals who appear to have no financial need to do so become appointed to numerous boards of directors. Having plenty of spare time and making this visible no longer confer status. Nowadays it seems to earn far more respect to have a full diary into which it is difficult to fit any further engagement. The 'time pioneers' studied by Karl Horning and his colleagues (1995), the German employees who had voluntarily made drastic reductions in their hours of work (see Chapter 2, pp. 52–53), have not yet become trendsetters in Britain (or in Germany or any other country). The trend has not been towards people who succeed in easing up on employment. Quite the reverse: they have been working even longer. What happens to them upon retirement is discussed in Chapter 5.

The pace of life

Their longer working weeks (if some people really are working longer) will be only part of the reason why many people feel that life has become more stressful and hectic (Holliday, 1996). People certainly feel busier but work pressures are not the entire explanation (see Box 3.2). People are spending more time shopping and travelling. We have more money to spend and this takes time. Between the 1960s and 1990s in Britain the average daily time spent shopping rose from approximately 40 to 70 min and the traditional gender gap narrowed. Of course, shopping itself may be regarded as a leisure activity (see Chapter 7), but shopping still takes time, which ceases to be available for other purposes. Time spent on routine housework has declined and there has been some redistribution from women to men but people are spending more time on 'odd jobs' connected with their homes, cars and gardens. More women are in employment. Parents are

---

Box 3.2. The time squeeze.

- In the 1980s real consumer spending on leisure (excluding alcohol) rose by 50%. Leisure time expanded by just 2%.
- Since the 1960s time spent shopping and on related travelling has risen from an average of 40 to 70 min/day.
- The lunch hour is a thing of the past: the average time is now just half an hour.
- Managers say that their workloads have increased in recent years. Two-fifths claim to work more than 50 h a week. Two-thirds complain that their jobs are a source of stress.
- Between 1971 and 1991 the proportion of 7-year-old children going to school unaccompanied declined from 70% to 7%.

Sources: Hillman (1991); Institute of Management (1993); *Demos Quarterly* 5 (1995).

spending more time supervising their children or paying others for childcare, partly because the streets are now considered dangerous (Hillman, 1991). This owes something to increased traffic and also to the demise of neighbourhood communities, in which people knew each other and felt secure. Nowadays the territories outside people's gardens are typically perceived as full of strangers who cannot be trusted. We are also devoting more time to personal hygiene – cleaning and adorning our bodies. How have we found the time? Partly by sleeping less but also, it appears, by doing things faster and (probably) sacrificing literally spare time.

International comparisons

There are huge disparities in the number of hours worked per week and year in countries at similar levels of economic development (see Tables 2.3 and 2.4, pp. 47–48). In a European Union (EU) context, Britain is an extreme case (see Fajertag, 1996; Rosducher and Seifert, 1996). The average working week of Britain's full-time employees is roughly 3 h longer than the EU average (Noon and Blyton, 1997). However, Britain has a higher proportion of part-time employees than any other European country except the Netherlands and, when all employees are counted, the average hours in a working week in Britain, around 32, are not particularly long by international standards (Bonney, 2005). Unlike in Britain, the general pressure on hours of work elsewhere in the EU in recent years has been downwards, but this has been in a context where neither organized labour, employers nor governments have been able to identify an alternative solution to unemployment (much higher in most other EU countries than in the UK throughout the 1990s and early 2000s). In some countries, including Germany, employers have favoured reductions in standard working hours as an alternative to more expensive redundancies and compensation payments to workers placed on short time (see Blyton and Trinczek, 1996).

However, there is no EU country in which this downward pressure has led to a sharp all-round decline in hours actually worked. Nor have cutbacks in working time, when achieved, led immediately to increases in the number of jobs. France's 35-h laws, passed between 1998 and 2000, failed to have this effect and have subsequently been relaxed. When modest reductions in working time have been achieved this has usually been a defensive strategy, to prevent job losses rather than to create additional jobs, and it has normally been in exchange for greater flexibility (for the employers) over the scheduling of working time, plus an intensification of work. Volkswagen, where the standard working week for blue-collar and office staff was slashed to 28.8 h in 1994, remains a very exceptional case. Its workforce accepted a 16% cut in earnings in exchange for a guarantee of no redundancies. Polls of the Volkswagen workforce found the majority expressing satisfaction with the shortened working week, which created more time for leisure and their families. However, at Volkswagen it was possible to account for the greater part of the 16% drop in earnings by eliminating the former 'thirteenth month' (Blyton and Trinczek, 1996) and, early in the

21st century, citing the need to regain its competitiveness, Volkswagen extended its employees' working weeks towards the former level.

There are some signs that continental Europe may be moving towards the UK's, North America's and the so-called Asian tigers' generally longer hours of full-time work. In the Netherlands there has been an overall decline in average hours of work, but Zuzanek *et al.* (1998) have shown that this is entirely due to an increase in the proportion of part-time workers. When only full-time employees are considered, the same slight upward trend in working time noted in America becomes apparent.

The Japanese have made more recent progress than European countries in reducing their (previously comparatively long) hours of work, with encouragement from their government, which has wanted to improve the quality of life and to stimulate domestic consumption. However, employees in Japan and other Pacific rim 'tigers' still work more hours per year than employees in other economically advanced countries. In Japan it is still considered bad form to leave work promptly at the official end of the working day. Salarymen who do not wish to raise questions about their career and company commitment would not dream of using all their holiday entitlement (Koseki, 1989; Harada, 1994). Working time in Japan has declined since the 1960s but leisure participation has risen more rapidly, so daily life has become more hectic and time budget data show that, as in Europe and North America, the Japanese have found the extra time partly by sleeping less (see Steger, 1996). This is the context in which public sleeping – on trains, during breaks at work, in libraries and other such places – has become acceptable conduct in Japan. Apart from allowing individuals to recuperate, public sleep enables them to signal their exhaustion and, sometimes, to create private space and imply a lack of interest in whatever else is going on.

Ruthless economy or workers' preferences?

Has the ruthless economy become a threat to leisure? Juliette Schor (1991) has complained that Americans are overworked and blames, first, pressure from employers, who have been able to make heavier demands in a business climate where staff have feared for their jobs and careers, and, secondly, the 'addictive power of consumption'. Schor believes that leisure time is becoming a conspicuous casualty of prosperity. She has urged a search for 'new strategies', social progress beyond 'work and spend' and advocates an all-round reduction in working time, which, she believes, will lead to more satisfying and environment-friendly lifestyles and less inequality (Schor, 1998). This clarion call has been taken up around the world under the banner of work–life balance. The complaint is that too many people are living to work instead of working to live. Long working weeks have been regarded as a threat to the quality of life in general, and to family life and leisure in particular. Mothers of young children who also hold paid jobs are under the greatest (objectively measured and perceived) time pressure (Garhammer, 1998; Zuzanek, 2004). Women have been at the forefront of calls for a better work–life balance. This is not only because they are the main victims of time pressure. They also realize that mothers will never gain genuine equal opportunities in the workforce as long as success means long hours at work. However, it is not only women who have been complaining. One study has found that in Britain and the Netherlands men are more likely than women to report work–family conflicts (Cousins and Ning Tang, 2004). However, before deploring the pressures that induce male and female workers to sacrifice their leisure time, there are several points to bear in mind.

First, the fact that most workers say they would prefer shorter hours needs to be treated with caution. There are numerous studies that report people saying they would like to spend less time at work. In Britain less than a third of all employees work 40 h a week or less, whereas over two-thirds say that they would like to do so. Only 7% claim to want to work in excess of 50 h per week, whereas nearly a quarter do just this. On average, men say that they would like to work 37 h per week and women say that they would like to work 30 h (Fagan, 2002). Across the EU (pre-2004 15), on average, couples say that they would like a combined reduction of 12 h in their weekly working time and greater gender equality (Viasanen and Natti, 2002). When faced with so simple a question, it is hardly surprising that most people express a preference for working less. It would be no greater surprise to find that most workers would like higher pay. In practice, it is often necessary to trade one value against another. Three-quarters of Britain's employees say that they would prefer an extra day off to a 20% pay rise (Reeves, 2002). Maybe they would prefer this, but could they afford to act on the preference? Approximately two-thirds of British managers complain that their organizations confuse working long hours with commitment. Less than half say that they are happy with their current work–life balance. However, only a quarter say that they personally want to work fewer hours (Oliver, 1998). Very few people explain job changes in terms of, or say that they are trying to change their jobs to achieve, shorter hours of work (Bonney, 2005). Lewis (2003) found that nearly all the 50 UK chartered accountants she interviewed explained their long hours of work in terms of choice and enjoying their jobs. There is a class difference in the reasons typically given by workers who put in long hours. The higher paid are the most likely to name job satisfaction. The lower paid are more likely to say that they need the money (Taylor, 2002). As Lewis points out, even accountants and other higher-paid employees make their lifestyle choices in constrained career situations, but can there be any escape from such constraints? Maybe money and career advancement are now the stronger demands, and maybe this is due to the genuine attractions rather than the 'addictive power' of consumption.

Secondly, the same caution must be exercised in the face of evidence that long hours are stressful and, it may be inferred, bad for people's well-being. It is the case that around two-thirds of managers say that their jobs are a source of stress (Inkson and Coe, 1993). What must be borne in mind is that pressure is not necessarily damaging. It can sometimes be stimulating and challenging, even health-promoting. Length of working time is not related to reported stress (Schneider *et al.*, 2004; Zuzanek, 2004). The occupational groups with the longest hours of work score relatively well on all the standard health indicators. Having nothing to do, when unemployed, for example (see below), appears to be more corrosive than too much work. The threat of unemployment may be just as, if not more, debilitating as pressure to take on more tasks. In their Canadian research, Zuzanek and Mannell (1998) found that exceptionally heavy and exceptionally light workloads were both related to reported stress, but that long hours of work created stress only when the work schedules led to conflict with social and emotional aspirations, and that good physical health and good marriages were offsetting factors (see also Schneider *et al.*, 2004). Up to now, leisure researchers have failed to identify any leisure activities that buffer or otherwise alleviate other sources of stress (Zuzanek, 2004).

Thirdly, long working weeks, relative to the current average, do not appear to depress overall levels of leisure activity (Holliday, 1996; Robinson and Godbey, 1996). The UK Time Use Survey has shown that people who work 50–59 h per week spend no less time overall than people who work 30–39 h on entertainment and culture, sport and outdoor activities, reading and travel (see Table 3.6). Actually the occupational groups with the longest working hours have the highest participation rates across leisure activities in general. This applies when one compares the employed with the unemployed, housewives with part-time and the latter with full-time female employees, and workers on average with those on well above-average full-time schedules. The higher socio-economic strata still 'do more' at leisure, even though, on average, they

Table 3.6. Average minutes per day spent in different activities by number of hours (reported) usually worked per week (respondents with jobs).

Main activity	0–19 h	20–29 h	30–39 h	40–49 h	50–59 h	60 h and more
Sleeping	516	501	502	496	481	478
Eating and drinking	81	77	75	74	75	74
Personal care	47	50	47	44	41	40
Employment	128	194	284	323	357	408
Study	40	12	4	5	3	2
Housework	191	200	143	115	111	97
Childcare (own-household children)	30	39	19	15	17	15
Voluntary work and meetings	18	14	12	10	8	8
Social life and resting	78	78	69	65	60	58
Entertainment and culture	6	7	6	7	7	6
Sport and outdoor activities	14	10	12	15	12	12
Hobbies and games	21	15	19	17	17	17
Reading	20	22	18	19	20	15
TV and video	132	119	123	129	123	104
Radio and music	7	5	5	5	5	4
Travel	98	88	94	95	96	95
Other	12	10	7	7	7	5

Source: UK 2000 Time Use Survey.

are also doing more work. This phenomenon has been described as 'time elasticity' (van Ophem and de Hoog, 1998).

Of course, there has to be a point at which increased working time would suppress leisure activity. However, there are few such signs in Table 3.6, even among people working in excess of 60 h per week. If individuals worked so long that they had neither the time nor the energy to do more than work, eat and sleep, their leisure participation would be zero. The fact is that most people with relatively long work schedules today do not work that long, and one reason why they can have high rates of leisure participation is that the longer hours tend to be worked by the higher earners. They have the money to indulge their tastes in the leisure time that remains. Money can buy time. With sufficient cash people can do virtually whatever they want at the times that they choose. They can afford meals out, which makes it unnecessary to return home prior to evenings out. They can afford to have their cars repaired and serviced at garages and to hire paid help with their homes and gardens. It is also relevant that the self-employed, managers and professionals often have considerable 'time sovereignty', that is, scope to decide exactly when they will work. They tend to work their 'odd hours' at home. When work is taken home, it can usually be done at the employed or self-employed person's discretion (see Breedveld, 1996b). Interestingly, Smith and Carroll (2002), in a survey of around 900 local authority employees in north-west England, found that greater control over working time was a more widespread aspiration than shorter hours. How people respond in surveys always depends on the particular questions asked! Being able to control one's work schedule is a huge advantage for ensuring one's availability for preferred leisure occasions and activities. Housework and doing nothing in particular (just resting) are the uses of time that tend to be squeezed when people work relatively long hours. Participation in out-of-home recreation is unscathed and, indeed, appears to benefit from individuals' relatively high earnings. It is not clear that those involved are sacrificing their leisure. It is equally plausible to interpret their behaviour as maximizing their preferred leisure opportunities.

Fourthly, as the population's earnings, spending power and leisure time increase, one would expect a shift in people's preferences away from yet more leisure time and towards higher incomes. Additional earnings and additional free time will both be subject to diminishing marginal utility, meaning that the more people possess the less an extra unit of either will be valued. Hence the need to 'incentivize' senior managers and traders in financial markets with what appear, to workers in ordinary jobs, to be astronomical bonuses and pay rises. These occupations are extreme examples of a more general trend: as labour productivity and therefore earnings rise, the income sacrificed by a given reduction in working time or effort will increase. In relatively prosperous societies where there are omnipresent opportunities and invitations to consume, it is to be expected that appetites for further reductions in working hours will subside in preference for higher earnings. It is also likely that employers will become increasingly resistant to further reductions in hours of work and keener to obtain as much input as is possible, especially from their more skilled employees, who are the most expensive to train. In former times, when workers were at their jobs for 12 h or more each working day, it is likely that trimming their hours of work had such beneficial effects on the employees' attentiveness and energy when on the job that output declined far less steeply than working time (see Chapter 2). Diminishing returns will also apply in this area. Once relatively short hours have become standard, the improvements in employee performance that accrue from further reductions are likely to be negligible. Gratton and Taylor (2004) have explained the long hours worked by employees who say that they would prefer to work less in terms of a 'constrained labour market', in which the only options available are long hours or no hours, which chimes with Haworth and Veal's (2004) proposition that the balance between work and leisure is dictated by what maximizes profits rather than workers' preferences. However, this is surely too simplistic. Some employees in all grades work moderate hours. Clearly, this option is available. The real constraint is the potential career rewards that are sacrificed by an unwillingness to work long hours, and those opting for the career rewards obviously find these more attractive than the shorter work schedules they would prefer if only all other things could remain equal.

Petolka (1996) has noted some important exceptions in Finland in firms where shift lengths were reduced to 6 h and the standard working week to 30 h in government-backed attempts to create more jobs and reduce unemployment. In six companies that were studied, productivity rose to a sufficient extent to justify maintaining the employees' previous earnings. However, this was in a context where the workers feared both unemployment and significant reductions in their normal earnings. Also, there had obviously been sufficient slack in the earlier work regimes for the employees to speed up when given an incentive. Given the work intensification that has occurred in most Western companies in recent years, there must be many workers who would feel unable to raise their productivity as a way of paying for shorter working hours. This will mean that someone, the employer or the employee, will have to sacrifice income pro rata. The more highly paid the employees, the more someone will stand to lose. Employers who have invested heavily in training skilled labour are likely to treat such employees like expensive machines and want to keep them working for as long as is consistent with the required quality of work. If the employees have to pay for their own education and training, this will intensify their desire, and need, to maximize their earnings in order to obtain returns that justify their investments in human capital.

Fifthly, there are some jobs, generally higher-level management and professional positions, in which, provided all other things remain equal, practitioners become more knowledgeable and effective by reading as much as they can and discussing ideas with as many colleagues as possible. Senior managers are best able to run their organizations if they have frequent contact and communication with colleagues and subordinates. Politicians can stay on top of their jobs only by talking constantly to each other and being available to constituents. It is not necessarily workaholism – it is just as likely to be rational assessments of what the jobs require and the cost–benefit of increases and reductions in working time – that keeps the people concerned working for over 50 h a week. Given all this, the 'time pioneers' studied by Horning and his colleagues (1995) in Germany (see Chapter 2, pp. 52–53) seem more likely to remain deviants than to become trendsetters.

An uneven trend

A final set of points to consider stems from the lengthening of working time affecting only some occupational groups, and some of the workers within the groups in question. Working time is not expanding or contracting throughout the entire labour force in any country (Gershuny, 1986, 1992, 2000). There is no general, mounting, leisure-time famine. Gershuny has argued that people's ability to choose and control their hours of work will be sufficient to check any trends towards unwanted feasts or famines of leisure time. Across Europe the total amounts of time spent in paid and unpaid work have been fairly stable in recent decades (Mogenson, 1990). The main general change has been a narrowing of gender differences in time spent in both paid and unpaid work. Moreover, the recent rise in hours worked by some occupational groups in some countries is not the radical break with former trends that it might at first appear. As noted in Chapter 2, in the early 1960s Wilenski (1963) observed that most of the time released from paid work during the previous century had been used to enable some groups (mainly the young and the old) to withdraw from the workforce altogether, rather than to reduce the working time of those who remained in employment. The decline in hours worked up to the 1970s occurred mainly in the manual grades, who were then the majority of all employees. In many professions there has been no decline in working time since the 19th century. Staffen Linder's seminal book, *The Harried Leisure Class*, was first published in 1970. The main reason why life is becoming more hectic for many people is not that they are working longer but because their leisure time is increasing more slowly than their spending power and the things that they want, and can afford, to do.

The recent lengthening of working time among certain occupational groups in certain countries is probably less of a threat to leisure than the destandardization of work schedules, especially when employees have little discretion over exactly when they will work and for how many hours, if they have jobs at all. Under these circumstances the destandardization of working time is likely to play havoc with people's preferred leisure schedules. Moreover, job insecurity has many of the same disastrous consequences for personal well-being as unemployment (see below and also Gallie *et al.*, 1994).

The current trends in working time are certainly helping to create a more differentiated society. The growth of leisure has ceased to mean marginal gains in free time and spending power and more opportunities to participate in leisure activities for all sections of the population. Some people are working longer and harder and may have less leisure time than formerly but have the incomes that enable them to be highly active in the leisure time that they retain. Their leisure may adjust rather than suffer if more shops, banks, cinemas, restaurants, government offices and so on can be persuaded to stay open for business 24 h a day, 7 days a week. However, members of this section of the population are likely to suffer from a shortage of genuine 'spare time': private personal time when they can respond positively to any opportunities or invitations that arise in either their work or their leisure. Literally free time is a likely casualty of trends among the hard-working high earners.

Other sections of the population are working unsocial, though not necessarily long, hours in the generally low-paid occupations that supply leisure goods and services sought by the affluent. Hours of work do not need to be long in order to be oppressive. Studies of manual workers have consistently found that work typically dominates their lives – doing it, preparing for it and recovering from it. Extremely privatized, home-centred lifestyles have been more likely to arise from lacking the money, time or energy to go out than from free choice (Pearson, 1977; Devine, 1992). Even though their working hours are now shorter on average, the routines of manual employees, especially those in families where husbands and wives both work in arduous jobs, either or both on shifts, and where most of the household income is accounted for by rent or mortgage repayments and other routine expenses, are probably less compatible with satisfying leisure than the longer working weeks of managers and the self-employed. As explained below, one section of the population has no paid work. These individuals may have plenty of spare time but are usually poor and have lower rates of participation than all other sections of the population in virtually all forms of out-of-home recreation that cost money.

Unemployment

The return of unemployment

All capitalist economies have unemployment but the 30 years that followed 1945 are commonly referred to as an era of full employment. This is because, outside particularly depressed regions and especially vulnerable groups, such as the severely disabled, unemployment was usually short-term. Some individuals left school or jobs and had spells of unemployment before they gained or regained work but these brief jobless episodes seemed unlikely to make a lasting impression on the individuals' minds or lifestyles. In contrast, since the 1970s levels of unemployment have risen in virtually all modern societies, and, as this has happened, long-term and repeated unemployment have become increasingly common. This affects not only the people without jobs; as mentioned earlier, feelings of insecurity spread to those in employment (see Gallie *et al.*, 1994).

The reasons why unemployment has risen are strictly beyond the scope of this book. However, we should note that some writers, for over a century, have predicted a long-term decline in employment as machines take over more and more tasks. Up to now, such prophecies have appeared at loggerheads with the fact that all over the world the number of jobs has been rising. In Britain unemployment rates declined consistently throughout the 1990s (see Table 3.7), and by the early 21st century the return of full employment was being celebrated. We should note, however, that the UK has one of the lowest unemployment rates in the EU. Some writers argue passionately that the need for humans to work is in fact contracting and that contrary appearances, where these exist, are in fact a mirage, sustained by enrolling people in technically superfluous education and training, creating large numbers of part-time and other low-paid and low-productivity jobs, while also classifying huge numbers of the workless as sick

Table 3.7.   Unemployment rates, UK, Labour Force
Survey.

April–June	All persons 16–59/64
1992	9.8
1993	10.4
1994	9.7
1995	8.8
1996	8.4
1997	7.3
1998	6.4
1999	6.1
2000	5.6
2001	5.1
2002	5.3
2003	5.1

Source: Office for National Statistics.

Table 3.8.   Proportions of working-age households
where no one was in employment.

1984	16.2
1985	17.0
1986	17.3
1987	17.5
1988	16.3
1989	14.9
1990	14.8
1991	15.9
1992	17.3
1993	18.4
1994	18.7
1995	18.7
1996	18.9
1997	17.9
1998	17.5
1999	17.0
2000	16.4

Source: Office for National Statistics.

or retired rather than unemployed (Bowring, 1999; Forrester, 1999; Gorz,
1999). In the UK, throughout the 1990s, over a sixth of households that contained adults of working age had no one in employment (Table 3.8), and there
was a difficult-to-explain rise in the number of men officially classified as unfit for
work (Table 3.9)

Table 3.9. Males by age groups: sickness, invalidity and incapacity benefit; days of certified incapacity (in millions).

	20–29	30–39	40–49	50–59
1990	16.9	28.1	49.2	100.8
1995	43.7	72.3	98.5	172.0
2000	38.9	81.3	103.9	165.9

Source: Department for Work and Pensions.

The reasons why certain groups are particularly vulnerable to unemployment are also strictly beyond this book's scope, though it is relevant to note that, in most countries, unemployment, and therefore whatever the leisure effects might be, is highest among the age groups at each end of normal working life and among the least qualified and skilled.

The wider academic and policymaking communities have displayed considerable interest in what leisure research may reveal about the social and psychological consequences of unemployment and whether these could be changed by leisure activities and provisions. These are issues on which leisure researchers can command substantial audiences. Leisure research certainly has much to contribute to debates on whether persistent unemployment is creating an underclass or swelling the size of excluded groups. If such a stratum or strata exist, they will be distinguished not just by their unemployment and relative poverty but also by distinctive cultures – behaviour patterns and attitudes which in themselves would impede the members' integration into the workforce even if other obstacles were removed. Actually leisure research can make important contributions to all debates about the reproduction of old and the formation of new social classes at all levels in the social hierarchy.

Questions for leisure research

In studying unemployment leisure research has addressed two main questions. The first concerns the leisure effects, where it quickly becomes apparent that it is necessary to distinguish between the effects of unemployment and the effects of non-employment. The unemployed are individuals who want work, are seeking it and expect to be, and are expected by others to be, in employment, but who are unable to find jobs that they are able and wish to enter. Their situations and problems are different from those of other non-employed groups, such as children, students, housewives and the retired. The second question has been whether leisure activities and provisions can solve or ameliorate any of the problems that otherwise arise from unemployment.

Both of these questions have been answered unequivocally. These are not matters on which the evidence is ambiguous. All the research evidence points clearly to the same answers. First, unemployment is bad for people's leisure. In fact, unemployment seems to be disastrous for most things that people value – their physical and mental health and their family lives, for example. Divorce and separation rates are twice as high in UK households where someone is unemployed as throughout the population in general.

The functions of employment

A good way of grasping the implications of unemployment is through the functions that their jobs normally perform for people who are in work. First, employment provides income. This is both obvious and extremely important. On average, the incomes of the unemployed in the UK are less than 60% of their normal earnings. A minority are little better off when they are in employment but these are the working poor rather than people who live well on welfare. Redundancy payments and savings may cushion the impact of short-term unemployment, but if joblessness drags on savings are exhausted and households have to rely entirely on social security. This usually means doing without things that are taken for granted by the working population, such as buying Christmas and birthday presents, being able to share rounds of drinks and coping with the incidental expenses that are involved in attending most meetings of clubs and societies. Long-term unemployment invariably means long-term poverty.

A second function of employment is to supply what psychologists call 'categories of experience' that are good for mental well-being (see Jahoda, 1982). Jobs give people something to do. Irrespective of whether people claim to like their jobs, research suggests that almost any activity is preferable to idleness. Going to work also supplies social contact, which, once again, is conducive to well-being. Their occupations also set individuals goals and enable them to experience a sense of individual and group achievement. Of course, jobs differ in the degree to which these benefits are conferred, but all the research evidence suggests that almost any occupation is better than none.

Thirdly, employment creates a structure for workers' lives. It imposes a pattern on the day, week, year and lifetime. Emile Durkheim (1858–1917) was the founding father in sociology who recognized that individuals need structure and that total freedom is not a recipe for happiness. Durkheim argued that, in structureless situations, individuals experience anomie, a state of normlessness. They feel restless and an indication of their distress is a rise in the rate of suicide. A common complaint by the unemployed is that their time 'hangs'. Their lives can be so bereft of structure that signing on at the employment exchange may be experienced as a major highlight. It is necessary to have a job to experience the Friday night feeling. Without a working week the weekend becomes meaningless. Without working weeks there can be no holidays.

A fourth function of employment is to supply status and identity. Needless to say, occupations differ in status, but any job gives an individual a position in society. We place people by their occupations. Age, sex and marital status are other major social markers, but the everyday getting-acquainted question, 'What do you do?' is ordinarily taken to mean, 'What work?' The public at large may agree when questioned in surveys that the level of unemployment is due to economic conditions and maybe government policies and that the unemployed themselves should not be blamed. Nevertheless, in everyday social interaction the unemployed are made to feel responsible for their situations. Other people have jobs despite the economic situation and government. Encounters with acquaintances usually lead to enquiries as to whether a person has found work yet. Having to admit failure is painful. The unemployed complain that their self-respect is undermined, that they are made to feel non-persons and that they do not count. To avoid these injuries, the unemployed have been known to conceal their predicament from neighbours and even members of their own families by continuing to leave home every morning as if they had jobs to go to. For many people their occupations are not just things that they 'do' but also who they feel they 'are' – teachers, local government officers, salespersons, secretaries, etc. Our occupations become part of our self-concepts and their loss can remove one of the props that keep our personalities intact. The many functions that employment performs mean that unemployment usually inflicts psychological and social as well as economic damage.

Simply thinking carefully about the nature of leisure, on the one hand, and the functions of employment, on the other, suggests that leisure activities will not be satisfactory substitutes for jobs. Leisure activities, if the unemployed participate, may provide some valuable categories of experience – keeping busy, social contact and achieving goals. However, leisure activities are usually no substitutes, or extremely poor substitutes, in respect of all the other functions of employment. First, leisure activities are not income-generating. It may be possible for some of the unemployed to turn hobbies – gardening, sport or music – into paid occupations, but in such cases the activities become work rather than leisure. Leisure activities cannot normally structure time in the same way as paid occupations. All leisure activities are voluntary, or at least not obligatory: it is not absolutely necessary to do them. Some individuals may use leisure activities to give their lives a structure but this requires considerable self-discipline, whereas paid jobs 'have' to be done. For some individuals leisure activities may be developed into satisfactory bases for social and personal identities. Some international sports players use unemployment benefit in lieu of sports scholarships. Outstanding performers can use leisure activities to create socially esteemed roles and identities for themselves. But this is possible only for a minority. Leisure 'work' is usually valued only by members of the relevant interest groups. Becoming a competent golfer does not command the same general social recognition as having a paid occupation. Pay is important for the standard of living that it permits and also for signifying that one's contribution is valued by the wider society.

Bauman (1998b) pointed out that the present-day unemployed have an additional problem due to living in societies in which high levels of spending on leisure have become the norm. The unemployed are said to be 'flawed consumers'. They are deprived not only of work roles but also the ability to use their free time in ways that command respect.

Unemployment careers

The full deprivations of unemployment do not take effect the instant a jobless episode commences. Stages in unemployed careers have been identified. In the early days and weeks of being unemployed, individuals' morale can remain high. People typically retain their normal time structures and regard themselves as 'looking for work' rather than 'out of work'. They may have savings that allow normal patterns of spending to be preserved. They often keep themselves busy by doing outstanding jobs around their homes. For a time the unemployed may make an occupation out of job searching.

Many escape from unemployment quickly, but those who fail to do so tend to become frustrated. They become bitter when their job applications receive only formal acknowledgements, if that. Once homes have been redecorated and gardens tidied up and as their savings are exhausted, people begin to question what they had formerly taken for granted. They are likely to question their job search tactics, the advice that they may have been given and whether they really have any future chances of employment, and eventually they are likely to question their own worth.

At a later point, if their unemployment continues, they are likely to become resigned to the situation. Their job searching then becomes nominal. They become afraid to apply for jobs because repeated rejections are painful. The poverty and the stigma of unemployment inhibit social interaction. Daily routines geared to employment collapse. Individuals cease trying to keep up appearances. They become broken – economically, socially and psychologically.

The leisure of the unemployed

Rather than compensating for their lack of work by ploughing their time and energies into leisure activities, the unemployed tend to reduce their levels of leisure participation. Some have responded to leisure researchers' questions by replying, 'What leisure?' (Hendry et al., 1984). Many find the concept completely inapplicable to their own lives.

The unemployed may protect their leisure by maintaining the range of their activities while reducing their frequency of participation, or they may maintain the frequency while narrowing the range, or they may do things more cheaply than when they were earning a wage. Holidays away, nights out and new outfits can be purchased at relatively low cost. However, all the studies show that in some way or another unemployment depresses leisure participation (Stokes, 1983; Kelvin et al., 1984; Raymond, 1984; Roberts et al., 1987, 1991b; Kelly and Pesavento-Raymond, 1988; Lobo, 1993, 1999; Havitz et al., 2004). This occurs through a combination of financial constraints, the tendency for the unemployed's social networks to narrow as they lose contact with working friends, and their lack of status, which can make any social exposure threatening and distressing. Inevitably, it is leisure that costs money that tends to be trimmed or eliminated. Compared with the working population's leisure, the unemployed's is more home-based. They spend more time looking for work, doing household chores, in bed, reading, resting, watching television, listening to the radio and gardening. Television and other mass media feature prominently, though not necessarily as sources of immense satisfaction, in the unemployed's daily routines. Going out is inhibited by their inability to afford the costs of transport and incidental expenses associated even with nominally free out-of-home activities. This is how the unemployed lose contact with former friends and sometimes make excuses for non-attendance at family celebrations due to their lack of appropriate clothing and the other indignities connected with exposing their impoverished unemployed selves.

Leisure provisions for the unemployed

In virtually all parts of the UK and in all other Western countries, there have been leisure policies and programmes targeted at the unemployed. These can take the form of special sessions, reduced charges or even free admission (usually at off-peak times) to sports centres and other facilities. The impact of these measures has been studied systematically and two conclusions can be drawn.

First, the programmes do not reach the majority of the unemployed, and most of those who attend do not become regulars (Glyptis, 1989). The unemployed are notoriously difficult to mobilize, whether for political or recreational purposes. This is partly because the unemployed are a stream rather than a static group. Individuals who have recently joined the stream may not wish to identify themselves, or to be identified, with 'the unemployed'. Their aims and efforts are geared to seeking personal escapes, rather than joining others who share their unemployment problem. Those who fail to escape tend to become resigned, apathetic and fatalistic. The difficulties in tempting the unemployed into recreational activity are compounded by the fact that unemployment is highest among the least qualified and least skilled strata, where, as we have already seen, normal levels of recreational activity are relatively low. Individuals are more likely to continue to practise an activity during unemployment than to try something new, and the unemployed typically enter this situation with modest reserves of 'leisure capital' (Roberts and Brodie, 1992).

The second conclusion from studies of the unemployed's leisure participation, within and outside special programmes, is that high levels of activity, when maintained or generated, improve individuals' well-being but not to the level normal among the employed (Roberts *et al.*, 1982, 1989b; Kilpatrick and Trew, 1985; Kay, 1987; Evans and Haworth, 1991; Haworth and Drucker, 1991; Haworth, 1993). Participation in recreation improves the unemployed's leisure, and this is appreciated, but it is rarely considered an adequate substitute for employment. The clear message from research is that the unemployed want jobs and wages, not leisure opportunities. It is possible to compare leisure programmes for the unemployed with 'bread and circuses'. The label and the implied criticism have some foundation. Leisure, it appears, can be a palliative but not a solution to the unemployed's main problems. Leisure programmes, insofar as they succeed, may 'keep the lid on' without addressing the root sources of the unemployed's discontents. Successful programmes may suppress rage and adjust the unemployed to their situations, thereby reinforcing their social separation and exclusion.

Fear of civil unrest certainly seems to have been a factor in public spending on leisure facilities. The UK's 1981 riots were followed by the building of new sports centres in Brixton and Toxteth, and it is difficult to believe that Belfast would be the UK's, and possibly Europe's, best-provided city in terms of indoor sports facilities had there been no 'troubles' (see Roberts *et al.*, 1989a).

An underclass?

The leisure evidence does not suggest that, as yet, the unemployed, or even just the long-term unemployed, are becoming an underclass in the senses defined earlier, namely, possessing a different way of life and values that perpetuate their separation from the working population. This is not to say that minorities within these larger aggregates might not constitute an underclass. However, the leisure evidence does not indicate a general tendency for the unemployed to adopt values, attitudes and behaviour patterns that not only set and keep them apart, but make them want to remain apart from mainstream society. The leisure of the unemployed is impoverished, rather than qualitatively different. There are no signs in the leisure evidence of even a substantial minority of the longer-term unemployed having alternative sources of income or developing a preference for lifestyles that set them outside the wider society's legal and moral frameworks. When given the opportunity to become employed, most of the unemployed respond enthusiastically (Marsden, 1982). This is hardly surprising. The account of the unemployed's leisure presented above is unlikely to have persuaded any-one that unemployment is an attractive condition. It is true that some of the young unemployed 'work for a bit in order to do nothing for a while' and regard this way of life as preferable to continuous 'slave labour' (see Roberts *et al.*, 1982). However, the number one choice of most such individuals would be good jobs and their next best way of life is based on sub-employment, working intermittently, not long-term unemployment. Their way of life is only viable in conditions of near full employment, when the individuals know that they can return to work if they seek jobs actively and lower their standards as regards the types of employment they are prepared to accept.

A future leisure solution?

Up to now leisure may not have been a solution to the unemployed's problems. Even so, some argue that leisure could become a solution. Some insist that lei-sure must become a solution. At any rate, they demand that we continue to search for ways in which leisure might solve the unemployed's problems, since all other proposed solutions look at least equally frail.

Those who believe that leisure could or might be a solution to unemploy-ment point out that there are exceptions to the general 'rule' that joblessness damages people's leisure. The same applies with health. Some people's health improves when they escape from injurious work environments. In general, work may be good for people's well-being, but there are exceptions, when jobs are extremely stressful or demeaning, for example. Tony Walter (1985) has presented himself as an exception. He used his unemployment to complete an academic thesis and claims to have been content with his circumstances.

Furthermore, he claims that he was part of a significant minority, who are surrounded by a conspiracy of silence. Walter accuses politicians of all conventional ideological persuasions of finding it impossible to concede that unemployment might be beneficial for some people. He also accuses researchers of ignoring the exceptions instead of examining these cases in detail and discovering how they might be made more common. Fryer and Payne (1984) have been exceptions to this 'rule'. They identified and studied a small sample of 11 exceptional individuals in Sheffield who had approached unemployment proactively, meaning that they had planned ahead and taken charge of their lives instead of just reacting to events. Most of the individuals Fryer and Payne studied appeared to be putting their unemployment to good use by taking educational courses, training for new careers or undertaking voluntary community work, for example. Could such currently exceptional cases become more common? It is necessary to bear in mind that there are exceptions to all generalizations in social science, and there is usually no simple and practical formula for transforming the exceptions into the rule. It is perhaps noteworthy that Fryer and Payne admit that it was very difficult to locate their 11 cases. It is perhaps equally pertinent to the present discussion that most of the individuals who had found ways of coping during unemployment were involving themselves in other forms of work rather than leisure activities.

It is sometimes argued that people would find leisure a satisfying alternative to employment if only they would abandon the work ethic and adopt leisure values. 'If only' really makes such an exercise sound far too simple. We have seen that it can be their leisure interests that motivate people to work and earn as much as possible. Furthermore, in a study in Israel, Boas Shamir (1985) found that the work ethic tended to be an asset rather than a handicap in coping with unemployment: it kept people busy, searching for jobs among other things, and therefore assisted both their psychological survival during unemployment and their eventual escapes.

Clive Jenkins and Barrie Sherman (1981) have offered one of the more plausible leisure solutions. They believe that we are facing a long-term collapse of work due to the latest technological revolution (which, as we have seen above, may indeed be the case) and that the result will be a 'leisure shock' unless we devise an attractive leisure alternative. The Jenkins and Sherman alternative would involve a greater emphasis on leisure interests and activities in education and increased public investment in high-quality leisure services that would be cheap to users. Under these conditions, they believe that individuals would seek to reduce their hours of work in order to benefit from the new opportunities to express their leisure interests, and that paid work could therefore be spread around a larger number of employees, thereby soaking up unemployment.

One might query the political realism of these ideas, given the recent willingness of the more highly qualified, skilled and better-paid sections of the UK and North American workforces to extend their working time. However, a lifetime perspective on hours of work opens up a wider range of ways in which working time might be reduced – via education and training sabbaticals, parental leave and early retirement, for example – as well as by trimming the standard working week (Hoffman, 1996). We have already seen that in most EU countries the overt pressure on working time remains downward. Britain is the EU's odd case. It is exceptional, American rather than European, in the extent to which bargaining between trade unions and employers has shifted from national to firm and plant levels, and in the absence of a legally fixed floor on pay (until the minimum wage was introduced in 1998) and a ceiling on hours of work (the EU 48-h ceiling is simply not enforced in the UK – firms and individuals are routinely allowed to opt out). The UK also has a distinctive vision of Europe as a common market within which, as in other world markets, the separate sovereign states compete for shares. Other EU countries recoil at the prospect of such competition driving down wage levels, intensifying workloads and driving up hours of work. They are not attracted by the British model, which produces the widest income inequalities and the longest working weeks in the EU. Britain's reply has been that its own is the only course that will enable Europe to compete with the rest of the world, that acceptable hours of work and rates of pay are best judged by separate employers and employees, given their market situations, and that even poor-quality jobs are preferable to no jobs, not least in the former being able to act as stepping stones to something better. These arguments are likely to run for many more years.

Even in Britain and North America, despite their current implausible appearances, leisure solutions to unemployment look no more difficult than proposals to solve the problem through economic growth and job generation. Maybe leisure solutions will not work for all those currently unemployed but could operate satisfactorily among specific sections of the population. For example, Robert Stebbins (1992) has argued that people with serious leisure interests (see Chapter 1, pp. 8–9) are likely to be able to cope with, and may welcome, temporary or even permanent respites from paid work. Some sections of the population appear better able than others to cope with joblessness. Some individuals take early retirement voluntarily when given the opportunity (see Chapter 5, pp. 153–154). Women with young children are less likely to suffer socio-psychological damage during unemployment than most other sections of the population since they have alternative roles as housewives and mothers, which can structure their time and confer a social position and acceptable identities, and unemployed women's social networks prove less vulnerable than men's on account of the former's being less work-based and more reliant on kin and neighbours (Russell, 1999). Young people appear to suffer less damage from unemployment than older age groups. School leavers have no established occupational identities to shatter, they can be optimistic for their long-term prospects, their families often cushion the financial deprivations and alternative statuses are available in education and training. Leisure solutions, and other solutions for that matter, will not need to work with everyone in order to contribute to the elimination of involuntary, painful unemployment.

Eastern Europe

Like other conclusions in this and other chapters, the conclusions about the damaging effects of unemployment and the inability of leisure to offer solutions

Table 3.10. Unemployment and the maintenance of normal leisure in Poland, 1993.

	22–24-year-olds	
	Employed (%)	Unemployed (%)
Have use of		
Car	48	40
Video	61	56
Record/cassette/disc player	90	93
Satellite dish	26	24
Take part at least once a week		
Youth club or group	10	11
Play sport	27	27
Pubs, cafes	16	15
Cinema	–	1
Watch sport	3	2
Church	26	26
Last 12 months		
Holiday	59	46

Source: Roberts and Jung (1995).

are likely to be specific to Western countries with their particular kinds of work and leisure. There is evidence that the impact of unemployment was rather different in East–Central Europe in the immediate aftermath of the collapse of communism. A 1993 study of young adults in three regions of Poland found little difference between the leisure possessions and activities (except holidays) of the unemployed and individuals in jobs (see Table 3.10). It was possible to compare the findings from this Polish research with similar evidence from studies of young people in Britain in the late 1980s. Compared with British patterns, the leisure of young adults in Poland was less commercial and more family-centred and communal. This seemed to be why unemployment in Poland was not exerting the negative leisure effects that have been recorded in all the relevant studies in Western countries. However, at the time of the Polish research, the country's economy and its people's ways of life were experiencing rapid commercialization. The likelihood is that by now the effects of unemployment in East–Central Europe will have become Western.

Summary

Lack of income is one deprivation of unemployment. It is one reason, probably the main reason, though it is not the sole reason, why the unemployed's leisure tends to be impoverished. As Collins (2003) insists, poverty – crude financial hardship – is the principal reason for the low participation rates in sport and other leisure activities among so-called excluded groups. This is an example of an effect being overdetermined – several sufficient causes are operative. Even if unemployment created no additional barriers, the drop in income that usually follows would require the victims to cut back, at least on those forms of leisure that cost money.

Income inequalities are an important direct source, and an easily under-stood source, of the leisure inequalities between the unemployed and the employed and within the working population. As noted earlier in this chapter, income is a major, long-established and persistent source of work effects on lei-sure. Occupations differ from one another in numerous ways, but some of the most glaring inequalities are in remuneration. Pay has always been the most plausible explanation of why the higher occupational strata do more. Income is the source of the clearest, widest and most consistent leisure contrasts through-out the population. Income effects are so powerful that they override what, all other things being equal, would presumably be the negative leisure effects of managers' and professionals' relatively long hours of work.

Moving from the base to the top of the socio-economic hierarchy, we have seen how levels of leisure participation rise progressively. The better-paid groups take part in more activities, participate in them the most frequently and/or spend the most money on each occasion. This applies in sport, the arts and tourism, and indeed in all the main types of leisure activity that normally cost money. The main exception, and the source of the extra time that the better paid need in order to lead their busy leisure lives, is television viewing. The long arm of the job exerts some of its most powerful leisure effects via pay. These effects are long-standing and show no sign of diminishing. Changes in the nature of work and other social trends may have blurred some former socio-psychological work–leisure links, but this is not the case with income inequalities. Poor peo-ple's leisure tends to be uniform. It is dominated by low-cost, time-consuming, home-based activities, most notably watching television. The better off are able to do more of everything that costs money, and there is much more variety in their leisure. They are able to build on their particular interests, often related to age and gender, in ways that are simply impossible when people are poor (see van Ophem and de Hoog, 1998). Bauman (1998a) has observed that the eco-nomically advanced societies are being polarized into well-paid and mobile elites (the new tourists) and deprived groups, who are confined to their home areas by low-paid, insecure jobs or unemployment.

The class effect of individuals' types of employment or lack of any (the higher-paid middle classes tending to do more of everything than the lower-paid working classes) mediates all other types of work–leisure relationships. We have seen that working non-standard hours disrupts what have hitherto been normal leisure patterns and practices, but leisure can adjust, and adjustments are most likely when people have the resources, mainly money but also time sovereignty, to make the adjustments. The same applies to working relatively long hours. The middle classes appear to find that the benefits outweigh the disadvantages, and their leisure appears to benefit (from their higher incomes) rather than suffer.

When members of the working class work long hours this is usually explained in terms of needing the money and the need is more likely to be for essentials than for luxuries.

Further Reading

On present-day class differences

Erickson, B.H. (1996) Culture, class and connections. *American Journal of Sociology* 102, 217–251.

Peterson, R.A. and Kern, R.M. (1996) Changing highbrow taste: from snob to omnivore. *American Sociological Review* 61, 900–907.

Seabrook, J. (1988) *The Leisure Society*. Blackwell, Oxford, UK.

On the destandardization of working time

van den Broek, A., Breedveld, K. and Knulst, W. (2002) Roles, rhythms and routines: towards a new script of daily life in the Netherlands? In: Crow, G. and Heath, S. (eds) *Social Conceptions of Time: Structure and Process in Work and Everyday Life*. Palgrave, Basingstoke, UK, pp. 195–214.

On the long-hours culture, work–life balance and time pressure

Schneider, B., Ainbinder, A.M. and Csikszentmihalyi, M. (2004) Stress and working parents. In: Haworth, J.T. and Veal, A.J. (eds) *Work and Leisure*. Routledge, London, pp. 145–167.

Schor, J.B. (1991) *The Overworked American*. Basic Books, New York.

Zuzanek, J. (2004) Work, leisure, time-pressure and stress. In: Haworth, J.T. and Veal, A.J. (eds) *Work and Leisure*. Routledge, London, pp. 123–144.

On unemployment and leisure

Collins, M.F. with Kay, T. (2003) *Sport and Social Exclusion*. Routledge, London.

Havitz, M.E., Morden, P.A. and Samdahl, D.M. (2004) *The Diverse Worlds of Unemployed Adults: Consequences for Leisure, Lifestyle and Well-being*. Wilfrid Laurier University Press, Waterloo, Ontario.

Hendry, L.B., Raymond, M. and Stewart, C. (1984) Unemployment, school and leisure: an adolescent study. *Leisure Studies* 3, 175–187.

4 Gender

Introduction

This chapter opens by discussing the feminist critique of 'malestream' leisure research. What have been the reasons for the critique and do they apply any longer? We then consider the statistical evidence on gender differences in time use and patterns of leisure activity. We shall see that this 'hard evidence' does not, in itself, suggest that either sex is clearly the more advantaged. However, the following section introduces the arguments of writers who believe that women are less able than men to act on their leisure inclinations due to a combination of their generally lower incomes, heavier domestic responsibilities, cultural norms and the preponderance of men in power positions in the leisure industries. The chapter then proceeds to consider whether times are changing in all these respects, whether women's former disadvantages are disappearing and then whether the remaining differences in the sexes' uses of leisure are purely differences rather than evidence of advantage and disadvantage. The chapter concludes by discussing the possibilities of leisure acting as a site of empowerment where men and women can challenge and sometimes change conventional gender roles and divisions.

Critiques of the 'Malestream'

The neglect of gender and women

During the last 25 years gender and leisure has been a fast-moving, high-output research area. Things were not always so. Until the 1980s gender differences in general, and women's lives in particular, were neglected in leisure research. Textbooks dealt with these topics briefly, often as a sub-area within leisure and the family. In 1977 Liz Stanley's review of leisure research abstracts found that only 3% referred to sex differences. Why was gender neglected? It was simply not an issue for most researchers. Leisure research shared a tacit assumption with most other social sciences that women had already been emancipated and that the remaining differences in males' and females' lives were either natural or socially inevitable. Until the 1970s there were few dissenting voices.

Normalizing the masculine

By the mid-1980s a formidable critique of conventional 'malestream' leisure research had been mounted. The neglect of women was the starting point but not the sole telling criticism. Large-scale surveys of the public's leisure had always gathered information from and about both women and men. The bias (now admitted by everyone) had arisen when researchers studied trends in working time and leisure (see Chapter 2, pp. 42–43) and the leisure effects of different kinds of employment or not having any job and when they explored youth cultures, for example. In all these areas the focus was far more likely to have been on males than on females. There were many more studies of young men's than young women's leisure. Part of the explanation was that young males were considered the main problem – the main perpetrators of thefts, vandalism and other antisocial acts. It was also relatively easy for (usually male) fieldworkers to establish contact with young male peer groups on the streets. Young women were more likely to be at home. They were less visible. The public spheres of work, politics and leisure were all dominated by men. Their lives obviously appeared the more interesting, judged by the research attention they attracted. Women were often glimpsed in research reports from youth (and other) scenes solely through the eyes and lives of the principal male subjects. Males and females received equal attention only in studies of leisure and the family, which tended to reinforce the impression that the family was a woman's proper place.

However, what the critics, who became increasingly numerous from the 1970s onwards, really resented was that research findings from male subjects were typically presented as if they were gender-neutral. Males were treated as straightforward normal people rather than specifically masculine creatures. The leisure (and other) effects of particular types of education, employment, levels of income, unemployment and so on were rarely interpreted as mediated by the subjects' masculinity. Male behaviour and responses to particular situations were treated as just normal. So when women were studied any peculiarities in their behaviour seemed to require a special gender explanation.

A male concept of leisure?

It was also argued that researchers were operating with a male concept of leisure, which was difficult to map on to women's lives. The residual concept, the definition adopted in this book, which roughly equates leisure with time that is left over when other things have been done, may more or less correspond with the realities of life for most men. Critics argue that the concept looks far less reasonable when confronted by women with childcare and other domestic responsibilities.

Do they have any genuinely free time? The titles of the books that have asked rhetorical questions, such as *What Leisure?* (Green et al., 1990) and *All Work and No Play?* (Deem, 1986), arise from the reactions of women who have been unable to recognize the researchers' concept of leisure in their own lives.

Critics of the 'malestream' argue that it is more difficult with women than with men to measure their amounts of leisure time. Researchers (see below) have now shown that women's leisure activities and experiences are often entwined with or derived from paid and unpaid work. There are similar problems when trying to measure women's leisure participation with the standard checklists of activities. When males have visited sports centres and cinemas, it may be reasonable to assume that they will have gone to pursue their own leisure interests. Women are more likely to have been accompanying other family members. Holidays, especially self-catering holidays, are not exactly the same experience for women and men (see Deem, 1996). Research has now shown that women's own pleasures are often extracted from sharing the activities and experiences of male partners and children. Critics of conventional approaches in leisure research have urged the adoption of concepts and methods more in keeping with the realities of women's lives.

The feminist response

The criticisms continue despite the fact that since the 1970s gender differences, and women's leisure in particular, have developed into probably the leading area in leisure research. There is now a massive and still fast-growing literature. Much of the impetus, needless to say, has arisen outside leisure research itself. The impetus has been supplied by second-wave feminism – by the women's movements that have made gender a live, and a lively, issue not only in the study of leisure but also in research into education, labour markets, politics and so on. The leading contributors in the research and debates on leisure and gender have been women, most of whom, I think, will accept their description as (various types of) feminists. Their efforts make it impossible today to claim that gender differences or women are neglected in the study of leisure. There is no longer a crude information deficit. This has been a field in which research has not merely collected more and more facts but where there has been clear conceptual and theoretical progress in response to the original criticisms (of the neglect of gender) and also to perceived inadequacies in the initial responses to these criticisms. The issues have been reconceptualized repeatedly as research into successive sets of questions has led to the questions themselves being reappraised or enlarged.

A prominent theme in the early studies, those conducted up to the mid-1980s, which were able to fulminate against the previous neglect of women and gender in leisure research, was that women were the disadvantaged sex. Women were portrayed as being heavily disadvantaged in their leisure and these disadvantages were often seen as just one set of manifestations of patriarchy (male power), which had pervaded all historical and existing societies. The leading issues in this research were the ways in which women's leisure was disadvantaged (by the availability of time and the range and frequency of their activities, for example), the sources of these disadvantages and the kinds of leisure policies and provisions that would promote gender equity. Subsequently, as this chapter explains, these alleged disadvantages have been queried. Some writers argue that times have now changed and, indeed, that second-wave feminism has been responsible for many of the changes that have improved the positions and opportunities of women in all spheres of life, including leisure. As we shall see, the extent of the changes, the proportion of women who have been able to benefit and the depth of the changes have all been contested. Other critics of the continued portrayal of women at leisure as disadvantaged have argued that gender differences (which everyone recognizes) are not necessarily inequalities and that there may well be distinctive strengths rather than just deficiencies in women's leisure. Masculinity has come under the spotlight. Maybe male leisure is subject to constraints that are equivalent to those experienced by women. Finally, amid these discussions, researchers have appraised leisure as a site of empowerment where women (and men) can examine, question and sometimes enlarge their 'selves', contest the gender roles that have been scripted for them and then spread their liberation into other areas of their lives.

Disadvantaged Women?

The first thing that has to be said is that it is not obvious from the available statistics derived from nationally representative samples that women are disadvantaged in leisure. Nor is it obvious that men are disadvantaged. It is crystal-clear that the sexes use leisure in rather different ways but not that either men or women have or do more than the other.

Overall, men in Britain (and everywhere else from where we have evidence) have the higher participation rates in sports and physically active recreation (see Table 4.1). Men are more likely to cycle, to run and to play football and cue

Table 4.1. Sport and gender: percentages participating in previous 4 weeks (2002).

	Men	Women
Walking	36	34
Swimming	12	15
Keep-fit/yoga	7	16
Snooker/pool/billiards	15	4
Cycling	12	6
Weight training	9	3
Running	7	3
Soccer	16	0
At least one activity	65	53
At least one activity excluding walking	51	36

Source: Fox and Rickards (2004).

sports. However, women are the more likely to attend keep-fit and yoga sessions and to swim, while there is little difference in the frequency with which the sexes take long recreational walks. Men in Britain are the more likely to stake (and lose) money by gambling. In 1999, the occasion of Britain's comprehensive Gambling Prevalence Survey, 76% of men compared with 68% of women gambled at least once. Bingo was then the only form of gambling in Britain where women were the majority of the gamblers. Men drink more alcohol – a lot more – an average of 17.2 units per week against a mere 7.6 by women in 2002. In recent years, young (16–24-year-old) women have increased their intakes considerably but they are still well behind their male peers (see Table 4.2).

There are certainly areas in leisure in which men definitely do more – a lot more drinking, a little more gambling, with sport in a midway position (see also Sturgis and Jackson, 2003a). However, if we examine the list of additional leisure activities covered in the 2002 General Household Survey (see Table 4.3), we find either no gender differences or women ahead of men (in reading books and dancing). There are either no differences or only minor differences in the sexes' likelihood of taking holidays away from home and visiting the cinema and parks, and this list could run and run. Since men and women live together as couples, married or cohabiting, for so much of their lives, huge similarities in their uses of leisure are probably only to be expected.

The impression of rough gender parity, with men doing rather more of some things and women rather more of others, is confirmed by the findings from the UK 2000 Time Use Survey (see Table 4.4). Here men were spending an average of 380 min/day while women were spending 386 min (a tiny difference) in paid

Table 4.2. Average mean alcohol consumption by gender (units per week).

	1992	1994	1996	1998	1998*	2000*	2001*	2002*
Men								
16–24	19.1	17.4	20.3	23.6	25.5	25.9	24.8	21.5
25–44	18.2	17.5	17.6	16.5	17.1	17.7	18.4	18.7
45–64	15.6	15.5	15.6	17.3	17.4	16.8	16.1	17.5
65 and over	9.7	10.0	11.0	10.7	10.6	11.0	10.8	10.7
Total	15.9	15.4	16.0	16.4	17.1	17.4	17.2	17.2
Women								
16–24	7.3	7.7	9.5	10.6	11.0	12.6	14.1	14.1
25–44	6.3	6.2	7.2	7.1	7.1	8.1	8.3	8.4
45–64	5.3	5.3	5.9	6.4	6.4	6.2	6.8	6.7
65 and over	2.7	3.2	3.5	3.3	3.2	3.5	3.6	3.8
Total	5.4	5.4	6.3	6.4	6.5	7.1	7.5	7.6

*Weighted.
Source: Office for National Statistics.

Table 4.3. Percentages participating in selected leisure activities (4 weeks preceding interviews) by gender (2002).

	Men	Women
TV	99	99
Radio	89	87
Records or tapes	83	83
Reading books	57	72
Singing or playing an instrument	12	10
Dancing	8	13
Painting	8	10
Writing stories or poetry	4	4
Running arts events	2	3
Performing in a play	2	2

Source: Fox and Rickards (2004).

Table 4.4. Average time spent in different main activities (in minutes per day) by gender.

Main activity	Males	Females
Sleeping	503	513
Eating and drinking	86	88
Personal care	41	52
Employment	228	127
Study	15	16
Housework	126	215
Childcare (own-household children)	11	28
Voluntary work and meetings	14	19
Social life and resting	70	87
Entertainment and culture	6	6
Sport and outdoor activities	18	11
Hobbies and games	26	16
Reading	28	28
TV and video	161	137
Radio and music	8	7
Travel	88	81
Other	9	10

Source: UK 2000 Time Use Survey.

work, study, housework and childcare combined. Men were spending more of their time on sport and outdoor activities, hobbies and games, watching TV and videos and travel. Meanwhile, women were spending more time sleeping, on social life and resting, on personal care and on voluntary work and meetings. This evidence indicates some interesting lifestyle differences but not that either sex has more leisure or does more in its leisure than the other. The time-use picture from the UK in the year 2000 is far from extraordinary. Bittman and Wajcman (1999) have shown that, in every time budget study conducted throughout the world since the 1960s, men and women have been devoting roughly the same amounts of time to the various forms of work on the one hand and leisure on the other.

In order to argue that women at leisure are disadvantaged, it is necessary to claim that the above statistics are misleading and this is exactly what feminist critics of the leisure scene have argued. They have claimed that in various ways women's leisure is less 'pure', that women's scope for choice, their ability to act on their own preferences, is more restricted, and that participation rates and time-use data (derived from 'malestream' research) fail to record any of this. Women's leisure is said to be less pure and more restricted than men's for four reasons: women's generally lower incomes, their greater responsibilities for housework and childcare, cultural norms that prescribe what is 'proper' for men and women and the under-representation of women in power positions in the leisure industries.

Income

The evidence speaks clearly: men earn more money than women and have more money to spend on their own leisure. Within both sex groups levels of leisure activity rise when people have jobs and when their jobs are well paid as opposed to poorly paid (see Deem, 1986). Even though women's labour market participation has risen steadily since the Second World War, there are still far more full-time housewives than house husbands, and women workers are far more likely than men to be in part-time, low-status and low-paid jobs. Having money and, just as important, earning money are important for the spending power that is conferred and for additional reasons. Going out to work widens people's social networks beyond their kin and immediate neighbours. Moreover, individuals who are earning are likely to feel, and to be regarded by others, as having earned the right to spend on their own pleasures.

It may be argued that personal earnings become irrelevant, or at any rate far less relevant, when men and women live in the same households within which financial resources are pooled, and it is the case that, in general, women's standards of living benefit when they gain a share in a male income (Taylor-Goodby, 1985, 1986). However, the allocation of resources within households is more likely to leave men than women with money on which there is no claim apart from their own pleasures (Dale, 1986; McGlone and Pudney, 1986; Pahl, 1990; Nyman, 1999). In most families women are responsible for day-to-day and week-to-week household spending, which, it is said, makes it far more difficult for women than for men to identify and set aside their 'own' money. Kay (1998) has pointed out that, with the arrival of children, mothers usually 'contain' their hours of paid work whereas men do not. As explained below, men are more likely to feel that they have the right to indulge their leisure interests, particularly when they have earned the money to do so. Women have been more likely to attract censure for squandering family resources when attending bingo and visiting pubs than males who watch and play sport.

Leisure equality is most likely in conditions of economic equality. When husbands and wives both work full-time, and have similar earnings, housework is distributed more equally than in other households and the sexes are likely to retain similar amounts of money to spend on themselves. Male and female higher-education students have similar sources and levels of income and similar levels and patterns of leisure participation and are most likely to engage in joint leisure on equal terms, sharing expenses, for example (Furlong *et al.*, 1990). When higher-education graduates (and younger school leavers) commence employment they earn similar amounts, but males tend to receive more training and have better career prospects (Roberts and Parsell, 1991). With the arrival of children, it is still nearly always the mother who interrupts her career. This is why it is still usually the male's earnings that are decisive in the size of mortgage that a couple can obtain, and therefore the type of house and district where they can live and their standard of living more generally. This is the context in which the male's career tends to be given precedence in deciding whether a family will stay put or move to another part of the country, for example. This is the context in which the male's leisure interests take precedence.

The division of domestic labour

Women do more housework – a lot more – than men. Times are said to be changing in this respect. In the 1970s there was much discussion about dual-career families and the emergence of a symmetrical family type in which males and females participated more or less equally in both paid and domestic work (Young and Willmott, 1973). It was argued that in such families males and females would engage in leisure on equal terms (Bell and Healey, 1973). There are certainly more women in employment today than in the past but on average they work for fewer hours, for less money per hour, less continuously and less progressively and in lower-status occupations than men. The sexes are still a long way from symmetry in employment. Time budget studies show that there has been a trend towards housework being shared more equally (Gershuny, 1992). However, Warde and Hetherington (1993) concluded from their study of 325 Greater Manchester households that the remaining gender differences were so wide that any equalization must have been minor. McMahon (1999) has echoed this observation: time budget data show that men still do far less housework than women, despite the widespread belief that nowadays these tasks are shared out more equally. Gender role attitudes have become less traditional (more so among women than among men), but this has made little impact on the distribution of domestic tasks (see Crompton *et al.*, 2005). This is an instance where there is a glaring difference between what most people say and what they actually do. When wives take paid jobs, husbands usually increase their participation in housework but it is the women's total workloads that expand most substantially. The burden of ensuring that family members with different work schedules are all fed and have laundered clothing ready for their work and play tends to fall on the housewife (Hantrais, 1985).

It has been pointed out that men and women usually do different kinds of household chores. Men take responsibility for particular things – the garden, the car, decorating and maybe the washing-up, for example. Men's housework is 'contained'. Women's housework, in contrast, is typically unbounded. Women may never be unequivocally off duty, especially when they have young children to care for. Hence the 'What leisure?' question that women often address to researchers and which features in the title of Green *et al.*'s (1990) book. Women's leisure tends to be fragmented and contaminated, as they try to watch television or read while attending to the cleaning, the ironing and their children. Bittman and Wajcman (1999) have shown from time budget data that, while women may not be disadvantaged in having less leisure time, they are far more likely than men to combine leisure with something else (watching TV while ironing, for example). The same time budget data also show that women spend less time than men in adult-only situations and are less likely than men to enjoy long, unbroken periods of leisure: hence Kay's (2003) conclusion that women are still heavily disadvantaged in access to independent leisure.

Men are the more likely to have, or to claim, the time to do their own things. Barrell and his colleagues (1989) interviewed 24 distance runners and their partners to discover how the participants found the time for their sport. This research encountered many examples of male power as time was bought, taken or somehow made available. Males tend to assume that they have a right to time in which to indulge their own interests, certainly masculine interests such as sport. They assume that their children will be cared for and their meals prepared and sometimes that their kit will be washed and ironed. Shona Thompson (1990) has observed that women have been incorporated into sport largely by servicing male players and Margaret Talbot (1979) has argued that servicing the play of other family members and deriving their own pleasures vicariously by watching and otherwise helping their children and male partners to play are general features of females' leisure. Girls have often been prepared for such futures during childhood when they have been more likely than their brothers to be expected to assist with housework, in school sport when girls have sat on the sidelines and watched the boys play (Leaman, 1984) and in their own time, so much of which has been devoted to cultivating feminine identities. This has commonly taken a great deal of teenage girls' time and money. Once a girl's feminine attractions have caught a male, this relationship has often become her main leisure activity and any incompatible or inconvenient personal leisure interests and friendships have been dropped (Sharpe, 1977; Griffin, 1985).

As a result of their leisure socialization when young, females may internalize the servicing role. They may feel that they ought to put their children's and husbands' interests ahead of their own and feel guilty and selfish when spending time and money on themselves (see Samuel, 1996). Some women seem unable even to express, let alone act on the basis of, their personal desires. So, with the arrival of children, it is usually the woman's career and leisure interests that are sacrificed. Large-scale survey evidence shows that, with the birth of children, both mothers and fathers reduce their personal leisure activities, but women change much more than men (Smith, 1987). This is illustrated vividly in Betsy Wearing's (1993) study of 60 Sydney mothers with young babies. They all reported some loss of personal leisure, whereas their husbands were said to be preserving their own leisure time, spending and activities.

New technology seems to have been absorbed within existing patriarchal relationships at work and in the home. Vacuum cleaners, washing machines and so on have permitted higher standards and expectations of home care instead of decimating women's domestic work time. Bittman *et al.* (2004) have used Australian time budget data to show that increasing the number of domestic appliances in a home does not reduce the total amount of time that women devote to housework. Appliances were reducing men's housework time, but not women's! Second cars (the first nearly always being claimed by the male) may expand women's mobility but may also be accompanied by the expectation that they will ferry children to school and for leisure.

Sociocultural regulation

Critics of the 'malestream' have drawn attention to social norms, widely shared views and feelings, about the kinds of leisure activities that are appropriate and unsuitable for either men or women, and have argued that women are the sex whose lives tend to be the most restricted by these processes. In their study of over 700 Sheffield women, Eileen Green and her colleagues (1990) were repeatedly told that it would not be right or, at any rate, it would not be considered proper and would damage a woman's reputation if she visited a public house unescorted or, if she was married, if she went for an evening's dancing with a group of female friends. Noel Parry and Daphne Johnson's 1970s study of 352 18–32-year-olds in Hatfield emphasized just how limited women's leisure options could be, especially married working-class women's. For some, television was virtually their only leisure activity. Their opportunities to go out were extremely limited. When they went out, this was usually as a family or to visit other family members (Parry and Johnson, 1974). It has been considered OK for women in groups or singly to go to church, to evening classes or to bingo, but to very few other leisure destinations. In pubs, sports centres and cinemas, unescorted females have been assumed to be available for the attention of predatory men. Any who have looked attractive have been deemed to be 'asking for it'.

This is one respect in which times are supposed to be changing. However, Sue Lees (1986) has described how girls in comprehensive schools can be subjected to daily verbal and even physical abuse by male pupils. Male sexuality continues to control unprotected, that is, unescorted women by harassment and abuse in many public situations (see Coveney *et al.*, 1984). Women can now seek legal redress for sexual harassment at work but not usually when they are at leisure. Yorganci's (1993) analysis of 149 returned questionnaires from female sports players found that 54% had experienced harassment or knew someone who had been harassed by a (usually male) coach, and 57% of these incidents were considered sexual. In a questionnaire study of 553 elite female Norwegian athletes, 51% reported some experience of sexual harassment (Fasting *et al.*, 2004).

No one claims that all males are personally guilty of sexual harassment. Rather, the claim is that masculine norms tacitly condone the conduct and protect the perpetrators from censure. It does not need all or even most men to be harassers to make most women feel vulnerable. Fear of being out of the home alone, especially at night, was mentioned time and again by the women in the Sheffield study (Green *et al.*, 1990). Males can visit cinemas and public houses and play sport without fearing similar harassment (though they are actually more likely than women to become victims of male violence), and it is not only young women who feel vulnerable. Mason's (1988) study of 50–70-year-old women found that their leisure was restricted by lack of free time and money and fear of harassment. It may not be so much males' attitudes and behaviour that have changed in recent years as women's former acquiescence. The older women in Alan Tomlinson's (1979) study explained that they had willingly given up the lei-sure of childhood and youth in exchange for different ways of life that were filled by family and community work. Dorothy Hobson's (1979) study of young, working-class, married women, conducted at roughly the same time as Alan Tomlinson's, found that these younger subjects had misgivings about the passing of the period between leaving school and settling down when they had been able to see their own friends regularly and enjoy a good night out.

A further aspect of the cultural regulation of women's leisure is that their interests and activities tend to be devalued. Anything done mainly by women, playing bingo, for example, is likely to be dismissed as frivolous. This is an example of male cultural power. O'Connor and Boyle (1993) have argued that television soap operas and sport offer very similar gratifications to their audiences – gender role models, emotional expression and material for small talk. Yet sport is treated as the more worthy, serious business. The tastes of its followers are legitimized by the daily treatment of sport in the media. The sums of money that men spend in following their teams are not condemned. The cash that women are said to fritter away on bingo and their alleged naivety in becoming hooked on soaps probably say more about male cultural power than the respective motivations and gratifications of sport and bingo players and the followers of television light entertainment.

Leisure provisions

Most leisure providers are male. They occupy most of the power positions in the public authorities, voluntary organizations and private-sector businesses that cater for leisure. Insofar as these are run mainly by men, it is possibly only to be expected that the providers will cater primarily for men. As yet there is no hard evidence that women in power positions act differently in politics, leisure or other businesses. Maybe the exceptional women who have 'got on' have needed to become 'one of the boys'. However, it is difficult to believe that magazine and video shops would continue to display pornography, that women's sports and women-only sessions in sports centres would not find it easier to claim prime time, that sportswomen would remain as vulnerable to harassment or that the current bar-room cultures would continue to be tolerated if most of the power positions in all the relevant organizations were occupied by females.

Sheila Scraton (1987, 1992) has argued that girls are eased out of sport not so much because they are unable to enjoy the activities themselves as by the surrounding masculine culture that conflicts with girls' preferred feminine identities. Would this culture remain so pervasive if most of the power in sport was wielded by women? Would the portrayal of women in the media remain unchanged if most television stations, newspapers and magazines were run by women? It is possible to ask these questions only rhetorically because it is impossible to experiment. Universities, colleges and schools have maintained acres of playing fields and other expensive sports facilities that have been used mainly by male pupils and students. Would this have happened with so little controversy if women had been spending the money? Or would there have been steps towards equivalent spending on the interests of female pupils and students?

In this and other respects (see below), change is said to be under way, with more and more women breaking through former glass ceilings and with public- and private-sector leisure providers becoming more sensitive to women's tastes, aspirations and spending power. However, in the public sector, there have been signs of such changes grinding to a halt. Feminist demands may have been most influential in the 1970s, when welfare and community development ideologies were fashionable (Yule, 1997a,b). In the 1990s, market-oriented thinking became ascendant. Local authority leisure services departments reduced the number of women's officers and special provisions for women in sports centres were cut back (Aitchison, 1997).

Female writers have warned of the dangers of requesting better leisure provisions for women while these demands have to be addressed to powerful men (see Green *et al.*, 1990). They fear that any targeted provisions will be on the basis of men's conceptions of women's needs and entitlements – mother- and-toddler sessions and women's sports at off-peak times, for example. Women players often value sport because it provides them with time and space away from their homes, husbands and children (Roberts and Brodie, 1992). It has been argued that the preconditions for equitable leisure provision include women organizing to express and press their own demands and filling power positions in leisure provision organizations, thereby becoming the decision takers. These preconditions, needless to say, could arise only if the other causes of woman's alleged leisure disadvantages were removed – their second-class status in employment, their domestic workloads and the less tangible social and cultural obstacles to equal leisure opportunities.

Different Today?

Changing times

There are two replies to claims that, despite what the statistics appear to say, women are disadvantaged leisure-wise. One is to argue that, even if this was true in the past, times have now changed. Many of the citations in the preceding section were from the 1970s and 1980s. Maybe you thought that some passages felt dated.

There have certainly been major changes in women's lives. Since the mid-1980s in Britain, girls have overtaken boys at all levels in education – in their performances in the 16-plus examinations, then at 18-plus, then by entering universities in greater numbers and then by gaining better degrees. Nowadays girls outperform boys in education in all the economically advanced countries. The proportions of adult women in the workforce and the proportions of the workforce that are female have risen. More and more mothers have been taking maternity leave instead of terminating their employment. The dual-earning couple is now the most common form of partnership. In Britain in 1970, when the Equal Pay Act was passed, women were earning on average approximately 70% of the hourly earnings of men in similar jobs. Subsequently this gender gap has narrowed – women's hourly earnings are now less than 20% down on those of comparable males. Young adults have been delaying marriage and parenthood. Divorce and separation rates have risen. One outcome is more single-person households. It is expected that by 2010 the single person will be the UK's most common household type (Scase, 1999). In these households it is impossible for one sex to do more of the housework. Some of women's alleged leisure disadvantages have arisen from their childcare responsibilities. These disadvantages include spending less leisure time than men in adult-only situations. However, the main difference here depends on both sexes, depending on whether there is a child aged under 10 in the household (Bittman and Wajcman, 1999), and most women do not spend the greater part of their lives caring for under-10s.

More and more young women are using their leisure in ways that were once (allegedly) considered unfeminine. Nowadays they are just as likely as young males to use indoor sports facilities (Department for Education, 1995). Neither sports centres nor licensed premises are male enclaves any longer. Differences between young men's and young women's drinking habits have narrowed. Between 1987 and 1999 15-year-old girls in Glasgow caught up with or overtook male peers in their levels of smoking, drinking and drug use (see Table 4.5). Teenage girls no longer (if they ever really did) subordinate their own friendships and leisure preferences to the requirements of boyfriends. The 13–14-year-old girls studied by Morris and Fuller (1999) were far from passive in their social lives. They 'handled' getting and having boyfriends, defined the boundaries of acceptable behaviour and ensured that friendships with other girls remained intact.

Vivienne Griffiths (1995) has argued that nowadays teenage girls' leisure is not devoted primarily to making themselves attractive to boys and that they do not always sacrifice their own interests and existing friends for the sake of a mere male. Her 1990s study of 12–16-year-olds confirmed the restrictions to which girls in this age group are usually subject by their parents and the general threat of male harassment. Yet Griffiths found that the girls she studied were succeeding in constructing busy leisure lives. They were finding time and space for themselves in clubs, bedrooms and elsewhere in their homes. Griffiths also emphasizes that the popularity of disco dancing among teenage girls is not solely

Table 4.5. Smoking, drinking and drug use by 15-year-olds in Glasgow.

	Males (%)	Females (%)
Currently smoke		
1987	14	16
1999	22	29
Current drinking (monthly or more frequently)		
1987	22	15
1999	61	66
Ever used drugs		
1987	11	6
1999	42	39

Source: Sweeting and West (2003).

on account of the opportunity to display themselves to male audiences. Many teenage girls prefer to stay and dance with girlfriends. Dancing ability can be a source of self-esteem and peer-group admiration and straightforward sensual pleasure, with or without male admirers (see also Brennan, 1993). Pini (2001) argues that disco-club cultures, where young women dance and socialize according to their own inclinations, have been important in giving them a taste of independence. Carr (1998) found hardly any differences in young males' and young females' behaviour – in the places they visited and the things they did – while on holiday in Torquay (southwest England). A Dutch panel study of young people and their parents in the 1990s found that young males and females alike wanted different lives and relationships from those of their parents (du Bois-Reymond *et al.*, 1995). The young people of both sexes in this study wanted to combine labour-market careers with participant parenthood. In searching for new roles, the Dutch young people had the support and encouragement of their parents, especially their mothers.

Dating adverts provide further indications of how times have changed. Men used to advertise their jobs and financial resources while women advertised their physical attractions. Nowadays women also advertise their professional status while men also advertise their lifestyle interests and bodily attributes (Jagger, 2001). Looks still matter! Irrespective of gender, we are most willing to cooperate with others we regard as good-looking (Mulford *et al.*, 1998). Girls and boys alike are still under social pressure to 'do looks' (Frost, 2003).

There have been changes in gender relationships among young singles, and these appear to be followed through when some couples cohabit or marry. Lia Karsten's (1995) study of 40 20–45-year-old Dutch women offers some good examples of this trend. She used diaries, interviews and questionnaires to distinguish three types of women in her sample. First there were 'traditional' females (a declining group). They did not have paid jobs and therefore had ample free time but did not claim this as their own. Rather, they entwined virtually all their leisure with caring and servicing. Two growing types of women were also identified. One was 'modern' women, who were usually well educated and had paid jobs, but these were more likely to be part-time than full-time. However, what identified these women as a leisure group was that, despite earning their own money, they behaved like traditional women in subordinating their leisure to the needs of their families. Karsten's third group was composed of 'individual-ized' women. Some were single and had full-time jobs. Others were married and, if they had jobs, these were usually part-time. Full-time and part-time employ-ment and living singly and being married were all proving compatible with indi-vidualized leisure, when women were determined to demarcate their own free time. Another Dutch study (see Te Kloeze, 1998) has identified similar changes to those discussed by Karsten. This second study was conducted over a 20-year period in two Dutch villages and noted a movement from traditional, to modern, to postmodern family patterns. Traditional families were embedded in neigh-bourhood and kinship relationships, which presented and enforced different ways of life for the sexes. Modern families escaped from these communal con-straints and emphasized conjugal togetherness and sharing (of paid work, childcare and leisure). In the latest type of postmodern family the partners had greater respect for each other's individual rights, including the right to pursue independent leisure interests. However, there were limits to how far even postmodern couples were prepared to pursue individualization. For example, they were nearly all opposed to separate holidays.

The changes outlined above will have owed much to the successes of second-wave feminism in the 1960s–1980s. It is probably due to these breakthroughs that our present age can be described as post-feminist, with young women being less inclined to join women's groups and movements to campaign for further liberation and more intent on using the opportunities that are now available.

The extent of change

It becomes difficult to measure the extent of change in gender divisions when some of the protagonists insist that it is impossible to quantify women's leisure. However, many would argue that the conditions for genuine equality include equal paid work and equal domestic work. We are still a very long way from equality in these respects. The UK 2000 Time Use Survey found that men were spending an average of 228 min per day in employment against women's 127. Meanwhile, women were devoting 243 min to housework and childcare com-pared with men's 137 min.

It is easy to illustrate how, under conditions of economic equality and equal freedom from unbounded domestic responsibilities, other inequalities are likely to wither. Taylor (2001) interviewed 240 English-speaking female tourists who were travelling without partners in Jamaica and the Dominican Republic. The women were approached on beaches and the response rate was 92.5%. A third of the women said that they had experienced one or more sexual relationships with local men during the course of their holidays. These women tended to be on their second or subsequent visits to their holiday destinations. The women did not regard their sexual partners as prostitutes, though 60% acknowledged an economic element in their relationships. They had given cash or gifts or bought meals. Only 3% described their relationships as purely physical. Even so, Taylor argues that there is an overlap with men's sex tourism. Jeffreys (2003) has disputed the extent of this overlap. She argues that the local men are best described as romance entrepreneurs: maybe, but the fact remains that, if women have the dollars, they are able to command the kinds of relationships they want, when they want.

There is still a long way to travel if the goal is total sex equality in paid work and housework, but we appear to be journeying in this direction, albeit slowly, with men doing a few minutes more housework per day each passing year (Robinson and Godbey, 1999; Sullivan, 2000; Sullivan and Gershuny, 2001). Women are doing less housework (in terms of time spent) than in the past (Gershuny, 2004). However, there can be no guarantee that these trends will run and run; many women (and maybe men as well) will not be satisfied with the assurance that their male and female grandchildren may be able to enjoy leisure on equal terms.

The depth of change

Another claim is that many of the changes in women's leisure have been superficial. Elsden (2001) studied a group of Watford ladettes, female fans who expressed their support for their football team in hitherto masculine ways. They wore the colours, drank pints before matches and behaved raucously around and inside the football ground. However, the ladettes were not accepted as 'just like us' by the male fans. They were subjected to traditional sexual banter. More to the point, following their Saturday afternoon fun, the ladettes reappeared in conventional feminine roles and garb for their nights out.

Harris (2001) studied the women's football eleven at a UK university. These women were clearly breaking into formerly male territory. They took their own matches very seriously. Before, during and after the matches in the club bar, their behaviour resembled that of male players. But were these women acting as pioneers for their sex? They disparaged female 'softies' who played netball and other women's sports, and insisted that men's football was the real game and that the men's eleven was the real standard-bearer for their university.

The breadth of change

Finally, questions have been raised about the number and proportion of women for whom life has changed. Much of the evidence of change is from young childless women. Life will be different for the fifth of teenage girls who become mothers, usually single mothers nowadays. The adult women who live singly following divorce or separation include lone parents, whose leisure (see Chapter 5, p. 146) is extremely restricted. How many of today's young female singles will continue to enjoy leisure on equal terms with their male partners following marriage and parenthood? Kay (1996) has argued that it is mainly well-educated women and their partners with professional and management jobs who are able to adopt so-called postmodern lifestyles. Kay also argues that there is little likelihood of trickle-down because the number of good jobs is limited and it will be impossible, however long we are prepared to wait, for most women to share the lifestyles that are options in households that are flush because of two middle-class salaries, which enable them to pay for help with housework and childcare.

Critics of post-feminism argue that only a minority of females have been able to benefit from any of the new opportunities to evade former constraints in education, the labour market and leisure. Sheila Scraton (1994) insists that women as a group are still heavily disadvantaged in the labour market, in the domestic division of labour and by the threat of male violence. Women's opportunities, she argues, are still governed primarily by their gendered life chances rather than their own lifestyle choices. Coppock and her co-authors (1995) have queried whether women's positions have changed fundamentally in any way in recent decades. They argue that the liberal reform agenda has patently failed and that male power is still firmly in place, and construe post-feminism as a male-inspired backlash against feminism's very limited achievements.

Just Different?

Irrespective of whether things really are very different today, sceptics have an additional reply to claims that women at leisure are disadvantaged. They argue that differences may not indicate inequalities, advantages and disadvantages, but may simply be differences, akin to some people preferring Chinese cuisine while others prefer Greek. Exactly how and why the differences have arisen – biology, socialization, different aspirations, different constraints – may be irrelevant to the value that men and women derive from their particular uses of leisure. Neither party may wish to be like, or feel advantaged or handicapped compared with the other. In Australia Baxter (2000) has shown that, while both parties acknowledge that women do more housework than men, men and women alike are most likely to regard this division of labour as fair (given that men usually do more paid work and whatever other considerations are deemed to be relevant).

In 1982 Sarah Gregory urged greater attention to women's leisure achievements instead of repeatedly deploring their failure to escape from male oppression. She praised women's ability to make full use of time (often doing two or more things simultaneously), their resourcefulness in deriving leisure experiences from unpromising situations, their ability to adapt to change and their interpersonal skills, which, Gregory pointed out, allow women to confide their own feelings to others and facilitate others in expressing theirs (Gregory, 1982). Duncombe and Marsden's (1993) highly original study of couples draws attention to how men and women tend to talk and think emotionally in quite different ways. Women are taught to express their feelings, whereas men have been expected to maintain stiff upper lips. So women complain about their partners' limited emotional participation, while their men, who do not want to burden anyone else with their feelings, either cannot understand or, even if they do, are incapable of response. In some ways, Western forms of masculinity and femininity appear to make men and women emotionally incompatible (Nare, 1996). The strengths of women's leisure encompass features that are said to make women the skilled time-managers men will need to emulate to adjust to ongoing changes in the world of work (see Chapter 3, p. 73). Instead of trying to overcome their barriers to male leisure, it has been argued that truly woman-friendly leisure policies and provisions will take their lead from women's existing wants (Gregory, 1982).

Other writers, having noted that the conventional male concept of leisure fails to match the realities of many women's lives, have embarked upon alternative conceptualizations and have reached conclusions similar to Gregory's. For example, Lenskyj (1988) has argued that there are three major contrasts between men's and women's leisure orientations. First, she argues that women tend to be task- rather than time-oriented: that women's ways of life lead them to associate leisure with enjoying particular tasks rather than discrete periods of time. Secondly, she argues that women tend to be altruistic rather than self-centred and derive genuine satisfaction by contributing to the well-being of others. Thirdly, she argues that women are less concerned with the quantity than the quality of their leisure activities and experiences. The sexes' different approaches to leisure appear to be rooted in broader feminine and masculine value orientations. In Western cultures women tend to be the more compassionate sex (more sensitive to the well-being of others), more concerned to identify inner meaning and purpose in their own lives and generally less materialist and competitive than men (see Beutel and Marini, 1995). Lenskyj's contrasts between men's and women's leisure make the former's priorities – grabbing as much time as possible for themselves and filling this time with as many activities as possible – appear distinctly unattractive.

Additional writers have echoed many of Lenskyj's points about the characteristics of women's leisure. For example, Betsy and Stephen Wearing (1988) also suggest that women are less likely than men to associate leisure with given times, and more likely to describe any times and activities as leisure if they are freely chosen and yield self-actualization (self-development and expression). Approaching women's leisure in these terms is said to allow their portrayal as enterprising and enabling rather than passive victims. Karla Henderson and her colleagues (1989) have also noted the importance of choice and enjoyment (the type of experience) in women's ideas about leisure, an implication being that leisure may be experienced within, and need not be separate from, other areas of women's lives, including their paid and unpaid work. Hence the case for a feminist concept of leisure or, at any rate, one that is equally applicable to men's and women's experiences. The 24 women in rural Australia who were interviewed by Penny Davidson (1996) had varied views on holidays. Some viewed them as work whereas others regarded going away as an opportunity to spend 'quality time' with their families. Davidson uses this evidence to query the validity of defining leisure as a part of life. She argues that leisure is 'an experience that is defined as much by relationship and contribution to self-identity as it is to reduced pressure and pleasure' (p. 102).

Box 4.1 lists the characteristics of women's leisure identified by Lenskyj and the other writers whose work has just been mentioned, together with the masculine opposites. It is doubtful whether anyone would conclude from the characteristics listed that males are clearly leisure advantaged.

Now, the fact that household chores and even paid work can be a source of satisfying and productive leisure experiences does not necessarily mean that women should remain reconciled to deriving leisure experiences in this way. Rosemary Deem (1982) has argued forcefully that most of the alleged strengths of women's leisure arise from making the best of heavily constrained and basically disadvantaged situations. She argues that the main beneficiaries of most of the differences between men's and women's leisure are in fact men. Deem does not want to force anyone to be masculine but insists that women should have the same range of leisure options as males. This, she argues, will only become possible when women have jobs, economic independence, self-confidence and private transport, when they themselves and others recognize that they have a legitimate right to pursue personal leisure interests and when women have their own support networks, friends who may be either male or female, who are able to assist individual women in doing just this (Deem, 1986).

However, as noted above, the fact that some of the features that distinguish women's leisure may well have developed in response to constraints will not of itself prevent their leisure being a source of satisfactions that are just as valuable as those experienced by men. Box 4.2 lists activities that are likely to be practised by adult men and women who live singly. It is not obvious here, any more than in Box 4.1, that men are the advantaged sex. Maybe as a response to the greater constraints that they face (due to their lower incomes and spending power, for example), women's leisure is the more likely to create and nurture mutually supportive relationships with others, and also to permit the development of serious leisure careers and maybe offer 'flow' and other experiences that boost well-being and the quality of life the actors experience. Could it be that, in qualitative terms, men's leisure is the more impoverished – dominated by sport, alcohol and sometimes gambling and spent amid emotionally sterile social relationships?

Box 4.1.   Stereotypes of feminine and masculine leisure.

Feminine	Masculine
A kind of experience	A type of time and/or activity
Embedded in other activities	Separate part of life
Task-oriented	Time-oriented
Relationship-based	Activity-based
Seek quality experience	Seek maximum activity
Cooperative	Competitive
Self-generate	Purchase

Box 4.2. Leisure activities of male and female adult singles.	
Single man, 30–50	**Single woman, 30–50**
Terminator IV at home	Book club with friends
Take-away Chinese	Organic pasta
Surfing the Net	Stretching at yoga class
One-night stands	Serial monogamy
Five-a-side	Feng shui
Strip club	Shakespeare play
Playstation	Meditation
BMW	Renault
Next, The Gap	Agnes B, French Connection

Derived from Scase (1999).

Vulnerable males

Interest in all gender differences, rather than just women's lives and restrictions, forces recognition that masculinity is imposed upon males just as females are socialized into femininity. Many males have always submitted to conventional masculinity with reluctance. Some have not enjoyed tough and competitive sports, having to play the hunter–aggressor in heterosexual encounters or suppressing any inclination to display their emotions in public. The desire of some males to explore alternatives has helped to usher in the 'new men's studies' (see Morgan, 1992; Nardi, 1992).

Several recent studies have drawn attention to the frustrations and vulnerability created for some males by the social expectation that they should be conventionally masculine. Wright's (1994) interviews and observations among 58 14–16-year-old working-class males in Glasgow found that, although their group talk objectified females and treated them primarily as vehicles for male gratification, privately many of the teenage boys expressed frustration with the passive role to which girls were expected to conform and with which, in the boys' experience, they usually did conform. Valerie Hey's (1986) analysis of the two sexes' experiences and behaviour in public houses underlines the harassment to which female customers and staff have been routinely subjected. However, she argues that much of this stems from male vulnerability. Hey notes the importance that men attach to their reputations among other male regulars. Some men feel that they need to go out with their mates regularly and drink freely in order to prove that they are not 'under the thumb'. Relationships within these male groups are not emotionally intimate. The men talk about sport and cars but not about their private lives, except in jocular or otherwise superficial terms. This is the world of male small talk, with which women can find it impossible to engage in either leisure or work situations. But, because so little of their private, emotional lives become known to their male friends, individuals' public identities are liable to be shattered in any face-to-face encounters with women: hence, Hey argues, the men's need to police females into well-defined subordinate roles.

Researchers have illustrated that there can be different kinds of both femininity and masculinity. More men than in the past, albeit still a small minority, are taking career breaks and opting for reduced hours of work so that they can play a larger role in childcare and, they hope, lead more balanced, better-quality lives (Walton, 1996). The variety is not entirely new, but some long-standing variations are now receiving closer attention because they are posing new problems. For example, Mac an Ghail (1996) has emphasized how young middle- and working-class males have always expressed masculinity in rather different ways, but then goes on to explain how working-class masculinity is currently in crisis due to the disappearance of so many of the manual jobs that males formerly entered. In this situation, males may either devise alternative ways of expressing and confirming traditional working-class masculinity or redefine what it means to be masculine. Tony Blackshaw (2003) has written an insightful and partly autobiographical account of how a group of males in Leeds who grew up together on one of the city's council estates had stuck together, sharing at least occasional nights out, until they were into their 30s. The story is about how nights out in pubs, especially in the city centre, were occasions when the men could reaffirm, enact, experience and express what they regarded as real masculine identities. This was despite the economic and occupational changes, and the changes in women's behaviour, that had taken away the jobs in which the men's masculinity had been an asset and undermined their role as breadwinners. In their mid-adulthood, leisure had become the only site where the males could gain assurance from each other that they were real men.

Maybe the injured male should not be writ too large. Rosemary Deem (1982, 1986) insists that men have been the net beneficiaries of gender differences in employment, the family and leisure. There has been much more servicing of men's leisure by women than vice versa. Men have been able to walk the streets and parks without fear of predatory females. Even so, both sexes could benefit from change.

Empowerment

> I seek to maintain the balance between the power of structures such as class, gender, race and ethnicity and institutions such as the media, to constrain individual leisure experience and the power of the individual and group to see, resist and move beyond these constraints through leisure.
>
> (Wearing, 1998, p. 178)

> No woman is entirely powerless. In the view being constructed here, leisure spaces provide relative freedom for women to move beyond situations in which power is a zero-sum game where men always appear superior and women inferior, in which men always dominate and women are subordinate and in which women appear as the victims of structured and/or discursive oppression.
>
> (Wearing, 1998, p. 59)

Despite Betsy Wearing's claims, it is probably very much the exception rather than the rule when leisure is used to challenge gender roles and divisions. However, there are plenty of examples in recent times of young and older women using leisure to contest patriarchy. This is said to happen in disco night-clubs (see Pini, 2001) and in sports facilities. Margaret Talbot (1990) and Sheila Scraton (1992) have both drawn attention to how sportswomen can challenge orthodox views of femininity. Women can use sport to prove to themselves and others that they can be strong, independent and competitive. Eileen Green (1998) claims that leisure contexts are important for women, especially those contexts that create space in which women can talk to one another. She argues that through leisure talk women can develop and consolidate preferred identities with which to challenge conventional stereotypes. Maybe this is how women have developed the confidence to claim formerly male public space in sports centres, pubs and city precincts. Leisure can be used to defy gender stereotypes without the risk of personal costs comparable to losing a job or being unable to obtain employment. This follows from the basic character of modern leisure – its separation from the rest of life (see Chapter 1, pp. 6–7).

It is not only existing gender divisions that can be challenged during leisure. This is where most young people first break out of childhood. It is largely through play that young people initially learn to act and to feel masculine and feminine. A great deal of teenage girls' leisure is devoted to experiments in the construction of femininity. Likewise teenage boys spend a great deal of time playing at being men. Among girls, choosing the appropriate clothes and hairstyles, preparing for a night out and then discussing what happened afterwards can take a great deal of time, effort and money (Sharpe, 1977; Griffin, 1985). We shall see in Chapter 5 (p. 152) that senior citizens are equally capable of using leisure to challenge oppressive stereotypes of their age group and to construct new identities for themselves.

All that said, there are several points to bear in mind before applauding how leisure affords opportunities that enable people to become whatever they wish. First, people may choose to use their leisure to consolidate rather than to challenge existing roles (including gender roles). Jennifer Hargreaves (1994) points out that some female athletes do just this when surrounded by sexualized imagery. This may benefit event sponsors and promoters but the female athletes are not necessarily being exploited reluctantly. Some use their sexuality deliber-ately and actively to promote their own careers. The same is no doubt true of many actresses and actors, as well as men and women in relatively mundane occupations.

Secondly, the empowering potential of leisure varies, depending on the resources that people are able to bring into their leisure from other areas of their lives. These resources differ depending on many things, but most basically and pervasively by social class. As we have seen above (pp. 113–114), Tess Kay (1996) has argued that recent changes, the new opportunities for 'liberation', have benefited mainly a highly educated minority of women who enter manage-ment and professional jobs. These women's male partners, if they have any, are most likely to have similar occupations. There has been a trend towards such women working full-time and continuously and, if they have children, paying for childcare. Such woman's lifestyles are now resembling those of their male partners. However, Kay shows that this trend has been confined to the upper socio-economic groups. Women with children aged under 5 in Registrar General's Social Class I are 30 times more likely to work full-time than women in Social Class V (unskilled manual). Kay argues that the lifestyles of the higher socio-economic groups cannot spread downwards because there are only a limited number of top jobs, and gender segmentation remains strong, generally to women's disadvantage, in lower-level employment. The net result is a narrowing of gender differences at the top of the socio-economic hierarchy alongside a widening of social class differences within each sex. Within the working class there has been no coming together of the sexes' opportunities and lifestyles. Indeed, in some parts of the country, traditional gender differences are likely to have strengthened as youth unemployment has prevented males becoming providers while among females it is associated with early (usually single) motherhood (see Roberts *et al.*, 1990).

Thirdly, it is not only women who can actively challenge or reinforce gender roles through leisure. Boys and men can play the same game. Boys do this daily in playgrounds and on sports fields, where they demonstrate their masculine abilities (see Martino, 1999; Swain, 2000). Tony Blackshaw's mates (see above, p. 118) were reinforcing (or rescuing) traditional working-class masculinity through their chosen leisure practices. There can be occasions when the challenges mounted by different groups – men and women – are zero-sum: both sides cannot win.

Fourthly, leisure empowers adults to socialize children, through the latter's play, in the adults' preferred ways. One person's or one group's empowerment is another's subjugation. Girls are still being given dolls and prams and are instructed to be neat and tidy. Boys are still being sent to play with footballs and soldiers and are excused if they are rough and dirty. Inappropriate play by either sex is discouraged by most parents. Teenage boys are given the freedom to roam neighbourhood streets and city centres, where they learn to claim public space. Girls are more likely to be required to do housework and are generally more protected. Parents often insist on escorting their daughters to and from leisure destinations and want to know where they are going and precisely when they will be back. The consequences of these leisure practices are likely to extend well beyond leisure itself. Eileen Green and her colleagues (1990) have stressed the importance of leisure as a site where patriarchal relationships are reproduced and hegemonized, meaning that they are made to appear 'just natural'. If people behave in masculine and feminine ways during their leisure, when they have the maximum scope for choice, the apparent implication is that they are expressing their basic natures rather than playing roles imposed on them by the wider society. An interesting tendency for present purposes is the frequency with which and the ways in which conventional masculinity and femininity are used to assert their independence from adults by teenage boys and girls, respectively. Paul Willis's *Learning to Labour* (1977) describes graphically how lower-stream working-class boys reject the 'sissy' aims their teachers urge upon them and insist that they intend to become real men who do real work. Girls often transform school into social life by using toilets and other spaces to create their own time to talk, put on make-up and so on (Griffiths, 1995). Young people thereby commit themselves, ostensibly entirely voluntarily, to conventional male and female roles in their future family and working lives.

Finally, the separation of leisure from the rest of life, which makes it possible for individuals and groups to experiment, to take risks and to mount challenges, simultaneously makes it likely that the consequences of this behaviour will be confined to leisure. The unfeminine conduct of Elsden's Watford ladettes (see above, p. 113) was confined to their roles as football fans. In the next chapter we shall see that much the same applies to most participants in the more spectacular youth subcultures.

Summary

This chapter opened with the critique of 'malestream' leisure research that was mounted in the 1970s and 1980s and with its tirades against the neglect of gender and women and the normalization of male questions and perspectives. Over time we have become aware that the nature of the critique creates serious problems in addressing some of the charges and questions raised. If there are major qualitative differences between men's and women's leisure, then it becomes difficult, perhaps impossible, to quantify alleged advantages and disadvantages.

We have seen that the 'hard data' reveal some clear gender differences, but they do not show that either sex has more leisure time or engages in more leisure activities. Arguments that women's leisure is disadvantaged are not based on men doing more or women feeling particularly restricted. Rather, it is argued that women's leisure must be the more constrained on account of their generally lower incomes, the boundless character of their domestic responsibilities, a patriarchal culture and men occupying most of the power positions in the leisure industries. Even so, it is difficult to reconcile complaints that women's leisure is deficient with the failure of the growth of 'malestream leisure' to improve the quality of people's lives (men's lives and women's lives) over the last 50 years (see Chapter 1, pp. 19–21).

We have also reviewed the evidence on the extent and ways in which gender differences in uses of leisure have been changing. There have been noteworthy changes over the period (the last 30 years) during which nearly all the literature on leisure and gender has been written. As part of second-wave feminism, the literature itself will have contributed to some of the changes. Gender is the topic in this book on which everything written has been at greatest risk of early obsolescence. However, we have seen that the changes have been limited. There is evidence of some convergence in men's and women's leisure behaviour – in rates of sport participation and alcohol consumption, for example. Yet even in these areas the changes are not obliterating gender differences insofar as men and women continue to play different sports, drink different beverages, and so on. We have also noted that there are huge differences in uses of leisure among men and among women, often related to age and social class, and that there are limits to the spread of the relatively genderless leisure and other practices that have been adopted by certain age and social class groups.

This chapter has also noted that there are (arguably) distinctive strengths in women's leisure and that conventional masculinity is experienced as a constraint by some men.

The possibility of leisure acting as a site of empowerment, where men and women can appraise and change their selves (if they wish), their lives and sometimes their societies, has also been assessed. Here we have seen that the possibility of leisure being empowering depends on the resources that actors are able to carry into their leisure, that the empowerment efforts of different groups may neutralize each other and that leisure is just as (probably more) likely to be used to affirm as to challenge conventional gender roles and divisions.

Gender and leisure is this book's hottest topic and the one where the debates have led to few agreed and clear conclusions, save to confirm that leisure is heavily context-dependent. The questions originally posed have proved more complex than was originally thought, but the difficulties in extracting any clear and agreed answers probably owe just as much to the fact that there are huge overlaps in men's and women's uses of leisure. The differences, around which all the arguments pivot, are by no means as glaring or as consistent as those associated with social class (see Chapter 3) and life stages (see the next chapter).

Further Reading

The following are widely acknowledged and cited interventions in the debate on women's leisure

Deem, R. (1986) *All Work and No Play?* Open University Press, Milton Keynes, UK.

Green, E., Hebron, S. and Woodward, D. (1990) *Women's Leisure, What Leisure?* Macmillan, London.

Lenskyj, H. (1988) Measured time, women, sport and leisure. *Leisure Studies* 7, 233–240.

For an elegant critique of theories about leisure from a feminist perspective

Wearing, B. (1998) *Leisure and Feminist Theory.* Sage, London.

On men and masculine leisure

Blackshaw, T. (2003) *Leisure Life: Myth, Masculinity and Modernity.* Routledge, London.

5   The Life Course

Introduction

This chapter begins with the basic data on how leisure behaviour changes over the life course. This is followed by a discussion of how, in the advanced industrial societies, the life course Itself has changed since the mid-20th century: how links between key life events and age have loosened and how paths through life have become less standardized and more individualized.

This is followed by sections on the uses of leisure that are characteristic of successive life stages – youth, adulthood and later life. There are, of course, leisure differences related to social class and gender within each life stage. Over time, there have been major changes in people's experiences of work and family life within each life stage and some corresponding changes in uses of leisure. Yet, as we shall see, some basic features of leisure during each life stage and the changes associated with life stage transitions have remained constant.

The chapter concludes by examining individuals' leisure careers: the changes and continuities in the leisure tastes and behaviour of the same individuals as they move through life.

Life Course Trends

Tables 5.1, 5.2, 5.3 and 5.4 present some basic raw facts about how uses of leisure and time more generally change during the life course. It is possible from this evidence to divide our uses of time into five broad groups:

1. Youthful uses of time where participation declines throughout the life course from youth onwards:

- Sleeping.
- Studying.

Table 5.1. Average time per day (in minutes) in different main activities by age.

Main activity	8–15	16–24	25–44	45–64	65 and older
Sleeping	609	547	504	491	516
Eating and drinking	67	72	74	91	114
Personal care	48	50	44	45	51
Employment	5	180	246	191	11
Study	229	84	8	3	1
Housework	45	74	151	198	244
Childcare (own-household children)	1	14	43	5	0
Voluntary work and meetings	9	9	11	23	23
Social life and resting	52	90	68	76	97
Entertainment and culture	9	8	7	6	5
Sport and outdoor activities	29	20	13	15	13
Hobbies and games	94	26	18	19	25
Reading	10	10	16	32	58
TV and video	139	141	129	145	196
Radio and music	8	11	5	6	13
Travel	76	96	94	85	58
Other	12	6	8	10	14

Source: UK 2000 Time Use Survey.

Table 5.2. Sport and age: percentages participating in 4 weeks before interview (2002).

	16–19	20–24	25–29	30–44	45–59	60–69	70 and over
Walking	29	31	33	39	40	37	22
Swimming	19	17	17	20	13	7	3
Keep-fit/yoga	15	16	19	16	11	7	4
Snooker/pool/billiards	31	26	17	9	5	3	2
Cycling	18	12	12	13	8	4	2
Weight training	11	13	12	8	3	1	0
Running	11	9	11	8	3	1	0
Soccer	24	13	11	6	1	0	0
At least one activity	77	69	70	67	59	50	30
At least one activity excluding walking	72	61	61	54	39	27	14

Source: Fox and Rickards (2004).

Table 5.3. Percentages participating in selected leisure activities (4 weeks preceding interviews) by age groups (2002).

	16–19	20–24	25–29	30–44	45–59	60–69	70 and over
Watching TV	100	99	99	99	99	99	99
Listening to radio	92	93	93	92	89	82	76
Listening to records/tapes	98	97	95	91	83	71	57
Reading books	63	67	66	65	67	64	64
Singing/playing an instrument	21	15	12	12	10	7	7
Dancing	21	23	14	11	8	9	5
Painting	24	13	11	11	7	8	5
Writing stories/poetry	12	5	4	4	3	2	2
Running arts events	4	2	2	2	3	4	2
Performing in a play	8	3	3	2	2	1	0

Source: Fox and Rickards (2004).

Table 5.4. Average mean alcohol consumption by age (units per week).

	1992	1994	1996	1998	1998*	2000*	2001*	2002*
Men								
16–24	19.1	17.4	20.3	23.6	25.5	25.9	24.8	21.5
25–44	18.2	17.5	17.6	16.5	17.1	17.7	18.4	18.7
45–64	15.6	15.5	15.6	17.3	17.4	16.8	16.1	17.5
65 and over	9.7	10.0	11.0	10.7	10.6	11.0	10.8	10.7
Total	15.9	15.4	16.0	16.4	17.1	17.4	17.2	17.2
Women								
16–24	7.3	7.7	9.5	10.6	11.0	12.6	14.1	14.1
25–44	6.3	6.2	7.2	7.1	7.1	8.1	8.3	8.4
45–64	5.3	5.3	5.9	6.4	6.4	6.2	6.8	6.7
65 and over	2.7	3.2	3.5	3.3	3.2	3.5	3.6	3.8
Total	5.4	5.4	6.3	6.4	6.5	7.1	7.5	7.6

*Weighted.
Source: Office for National Statistics.

- Entertainment and culture.
- Sport and outdoor activities.
- Travel.
- Alcohol consumption.

2. Where the participation graph is 'U-shaped' with a dip during adulthood and then recovery in later life:

- Social life and resting.
- Hobbies and games.
- Listening to music and the radio.

3. Where the participation graph is 'hump-shaped', with participation peaking in adulthood:

- Employment.
- Childcare.

4. Older people's uses of time, where participation and time spent peak in later life:

- Eating and drinking.
- Housework.
- Reading.
- Watching television and videos.
- Voluntary work.

5. Steady: fluctuations but without any overall life course trend:

- Personal care.

How are we to explain these life course patterns? Identifying the patterns is relatively straightforward: their explanation proves far more difficult. It is necessary to disentangle several influences, all related to age: physical capacities, positions in education and/or employment, family and housing circumstances and individuals' stocks of leisure tastes, interests and skills.

From Life Cycle to Life Course

The life cycle

Rhona and Robert Rapoport's (1975) solution to some of these problems was to adopt the life cycle as their central concept. Following extended interviews with a sample of London families, they argued that during their lifetimes most individuals were experiencing three main careers – work careers, family careers and leisure careers. The Rapoports illustrated how these careers typically interacted to create successive life stages, each with its own preoccupations, usually arising from the actors' work and family situations, which gave rise to particular interests, which, in turn, led to characteristic uses of leisure. They argued that adolescents were typically preoccupied with identity problems. 'Who am I?' was said to be the preoccupation characteristic of this age group, and in order to discover themselves young people were said to seek a variety of leisure experiences: hence their high participation rates in most forms of out-of-home recreation. Young adults, in contrast, were said to be preoccupied with embarking upon work careers and family formation, so their leisure became more focused around particular partners and, subsequently, more home-centred. Afterwards individuals were said to become preoccupied with establishing themselves in their careers and families, and their leisure became even more home- and family-centred, usually in ways that strengthened family bonds. The Rapoports argued that life cycle transitions associated with starting employment, getting married and becoming a parent, for example, were important moments for leisure because it was at these points in life that patterns of day-to-day living were likely to unfreeze and become available for reconstruction, and larger-scale statistical evidence has now confirmed that this is indeed the case (see Gershuny, 2003).

Needless to say, the Rapoports recognized that each life cycle stage had a rather different significance for males and females, and that there were important social class differences throughout. However, it appeared that most people were joining particular social class and gender groups early in life and then following the life cycles characteristic of their groups. It was as if the members of each group were being herded into public transport vehicles when young, after which each group would travel through successive life stages together, sharing typical experiences throughout (see Berger *et al.*, 1993). The members of any age group could look ahead, see what had happened to the cohorts who had been in their own situations some years previously and thereby glimpse how their own lives were most likely to unfold in employment, the family and leisure. In 1975 the Rapoports' use of the life cycle concept was uncontroversial. Its introduction to leisure research was generally applauded. At that time, family relationships usually lasted for life, and there were clear and firm links between age and most other social positions.

Destandardization

Since then, life seems to have stopped going round and round in cycles. The social sciences are now littered with references to the life course being destandardized. This is another example of the recent loosening of older structures. Labour markets are said to have become more flexible and occupational careers less secure, risks of unemployment certainly have risen and work schedules have become more varied. Alongside these economic trends, neighbourhoods have become less close-knit than they once were, families have become less stable and researchers now recognize a variety of masculinities and femininities. Major life events are no longer as closely linked to given ages as in the past. People today often retire from their main occupations when, in other respects, they are at the peak of adulthood. People in midlife have been restarting careers, sometimes by returning to full-time education or training. More people in their 30s and 40s are experiencing the dissolution of their domestic partnerships and rejoining the singles scene.

An upshot is that there is greater variety within all age groups. It has become more hazardous to try to generalize about the circumstances and behaviour of people of any given age. Among women aged 25–40, for example, there are still some traditional housewives, but more than formerly are in dual-career partnerships, more than formerly are single parents and more than formerly also are single and childless. Age has become a less useful predictor. By age 25 many young adults have established themselves in good jobs, but many others have poor jobs, many have obtained most of their labour-market experience in schemes and unemployment and more than in the past are still full-time students. Some writers regard the all-round destandardization and flexibilization that have been spreading as features of a new postmodern condition (see Chapter 6).

The life course

There is still a life course. Age has not become socially meaningless. It remains a powerful basis for social discrimination in situations ranging from labour markets to discos. People's behaviour and experiences early in life still have profound implications for their subsequent opportunities. For example, it remains as important as ever to become as well educated and qualified as possible when young in order to maximize one's chances of a high-rising career in management or the professions. The change is that educational success when young no longer guarantees entry to such a career, and entry no longer guarantees that the career will last for life. It is still as necessary as ever to have children to stand any chance of becoming a grandparent and receiving economic and social support from one's descendants in later life. However, parents have become less able to rely on their family links remaining strong.

It is worth stressing that the destandardization of the life course is a trend, not an absolute state. The trend explains and justifies the growth of interest in groups such as single parents rather than all parents, and the early-retired rather than all older people. Researchers have become more sensitive to variations within all age groups (as is the case with gender). But the full effects of the recent destandardization of the life course will become evident only during the lifetimes of current and future generations of young adults. They have been exposed immediately and directly to the full force of the trends, and it is they who will experience marriage dissolution levels of 40% or more if current rates continue. Up to now no cohort has gone through life and experienced this degree of family flexibility. However, youth has already become a different kind of life stage from what it was in the recent past for the majority of young people. As yet, the same cannot be said for later life stages. This is now an additional consideration to those that have inspired special interest in young people's lives in the past. There are some obvious continuities. Young people are still the age group that is most receptive to the latest sounds and fashions. They still have the highest participation rates across out-of-home leisure in general. But to what extent are these continuities basic as opposed to superficial?

Youth Cultures

Youth's new condition

For present purposes 'new' means post-1970s. There are several stark contrasts with young people's earlier situations. First, the life stage has been prolonged. Perhaps it is more accurate to say that its length has become more varied. There are still some young people entering employment at age 16. Some teenagers still marry and become parents. But the typical ages at which young adults cross these thresholds have risen. This is partly because jobs have become more difficult to obtain amidst the higher levels of unemployment that have followed the 30 glorious post-war years. Simultaneously, young people have become keener to remain in education so as to become as well qualified as possible. A desire for qualifications was once considered middle-class whereas nowadays parents and young people from all social classes recognize the advantages, especially in tough labour markets, of entering as well qualified as possible. Family transitions have slowed down, partly as a result of transitions into employment being delayed. However, young women's control of their own fertility, their improved labour-market opportunities, some parents' greater ability to support their children through prolonged transitions and young people's own worries that their partnerships may dissolve have all contributed to this slowdown (Hobcraft and Kiernan, 1995; Irwin, 1995).

There has been no upward movement in the characteristic ages at which youth commences. Sixteen has remained the statutory school-leaving age in Britain since 1972. By age 16 the majority of young people have adopted some adult leisure practices. For example, the majority are drinking alcohol regularly. The age of first full sexual intercourse is probably as good as any other single indicator of how slowly or quickly young people are establishing independent lifestyles, and this age, typically 16 nowadays, has been falling. Nor has there been an all-round upward movement in the ages at which young people first leave their parents' homes to live independently. The mean age has actually fallen in Britain as more young people have progressed into higher education (Jones, 1995). Most young people now experience an intermediate stage between leaving their parents' homes and marrying. Until the 1960s, for most young people, these transitions occurred simultaneously (see Leonard, 1980), whereas nowadays most marrying couples are already living at the same address. Cohabitation has been normalized. Travelling is another way in which some young adults fill the life space created by the prolonging of their transitions.

Secondly, young people's biographies have been individualized. This trend has already been mentioned in earlier chapters. Among young people it has spread partly due to the variety of courses in post-compulsory education, training schemes, part-time and temporary jobs and periods of unemployment that they now experience. It is also due to the contraction of the major firms and industries that once dominated many local labour markets. There was never a town where absolutely every boy went down the pit or every girl into the cotton mill, but in many parts of the country there used to be main types of employment into which most males or females, with specific educational backgrounds, would progress. Individualization is also a product of the break-up of neighbour-hoods that were once knit together by their residents' lifelong acquaintance. These trends have made it more difficult to conduct youth ethnography in the traditional ways. It was once possible for fieldworkers to make contact with (usually male) peer groups in given localities and to emerge with portraits of their typical backgrounds, attitudes, lifestyles and futures. These groups are no longer present in most districts. The places where young people congregate nowadays, in clubs and pubs, for example, tend to draw customers from a variety of backgrounds and they remain part of the scenes for only brief periods and then disperse to different futures. Individualization does not mean that young people's family origins and achievements in secondary education have become unrelated to their future life chances. These old predictors remain in excellent working order (see Roberts and Parsell, 1992). The old predictors are proving resilient but nowadays operate in a variety of configurations. This means that young people themselves are less likely to be aware of all they share in common with other members of any social category. They are more likely to feel personally res-ponsible for their current circumstances and for building their own futures.

Thirdly, young people's futures have become uncertain. It is more difficult than formerly for young people to know the types of adults they will become. This is partly a straightforward consequence of individualization. When large numbers from a cohort travelled into adulthood together, following a predictable life cycle, it was relatively easy for them to look ahead at what had happened to earlier cohorts of young people like themselves and to glimpse their most likely futures. Uncer-tainty is also a consequence of the substantial numbers of young people who enter recently introduced educational courses and training schemes with no track records. Equally, it arises from the larger numbers on longer-established routes, in higher education, for example. Nowadays there are so many university students that their qualifications cannot unlock as attractive career prospects for them all as rewarded earlier generations of graduates. Perhaps most basically, uncertainty is a consequence of the sheer pace of economic and social change, which means that the adult roles that many of today's children will play are still unknown. This is a different situation from that confronting young people in the 1960s and before. By age 19 the few who remained in full-time education were an academic elite, who could be confident of entering commensurate employment. Others were completing apprenticeships and could expect to be skilled for life. Others knew that they were unlikely to obtain anything better than ordinary jobs. For young people today, basing their self-concepts on what they hope to become is hazard-ous. Rebelling and dropping out from predictable futures have not become unfashionable so much as impossible.

Fourthly, a corollary of their uncertain futures is that all the steps that young people can take have become risky. They cannot avoid risk-taking. Higher edu-cation may lead to an excellent career but a university entrant today would be unwise to rely on this. Employer-based training may lead to a skilled job. If so, the occupation may last for a long time, but there is simply no way of being sure. Personal relationships have become equally risky. Marriage may lead to lifetime domestic security or to despair. Young people have lost much of their former security. Individuals have to take risks nowadays and the stakes are their own future lives. They have to travel towards adulthood without reliable maps, as if in private motor vehicles, albeit with differently powered engines since some have already accumulated advantages, rather than the metaphorical public transport vehicles in which entire cohorts used to embark on the life course. Their new situation can appear threatening but some members of earlier generations felt stifled by their predictable futures. Uncertainty and risk-taking can be liberating experiences. An indeterminate future can be more attractive than knowing the limitations of one's prospects. Today's young people would not all love to exchange places with their counterparts of the 1950s and 1960s, if they were able to do so. Needless to say, this is not among their options. Facing uncertain futures and taking risks are just normal parts of life for today's youth, and the majority appear fully prepared to take charge of their own lives. Their futures are not scripted for them, or so it appears to them. Many of the old 'rules' have simply disappeared. This forces young people to be reflexive – to reflect upon their circumstances and then decide how to act. They know that they need to be able to give their reasons for quitting or remaining in full-time education. Irrespective of whether they can explain their own behaviour convincingly, they know that they must face the consequences.

Fifthly, young people's dependence on their families has been prolonged. Needless to say, families differ in their ability and willingness to discharge their prolonged responsibilities. The parents in a recent Dutch study of 120 young people (see Chapter 4, pp. 111–112) were nearly all extremely supportive. They did not try to exercise authority but advised and negotiated with their grown-up children and tried to prepare them for 'choice biographies' (du Bois-Reymond *et al.*, 1995). Young people without families on whom they are able or wish to depend are at a heavy disadvantage. Family support is often crucial in enabling young people to complete their full-time studies and to make the transition into independent households (Coles, 1995; Jones, 1995). Remaining in an intact family is a huge advantage (see Spruijt and de Goede, 1995). The young people who are still making quick transitions – leaving education and seeking employment as soon as they are legally able to do so, and becoming teenage parents – are mostly from heavily disadvantaged family and educational backgrounds (Kiernan, 1995).

Constant functions

It would be amazing if the above changes in young people's situations had not affected their leisure, given that leisure is so highly context-dependent, and we shall see that there have indeed been changes but these have occurred alongside strong continuities. Leisure performs some functions for all age groups. Chapter 1 explained that the standard functions of leisure include allowing individuals to recuperate, to express themselves (to let off steam) and to acquire skills that may subsequently prove useful in other domains, and bonding participants into groups. Young people's leisure has always kept them apart, and continues to set them apart from adults because, being young and therefore having no deeply ingrained tastes, they are receptive to the latest fashions. There are additional functions that young people's leisure has performed in all modern (and some pre-modern) societies. It enables them to assert their independence from adults, typically with the blessing of their elders, and acts as a milieu in which they can learn to play sexualized roles and acquire the associated feelings and self-identities.

Children's play is not really leisure insofar as it is normally organized and supervised by adults. Children have to be taught to play in approved ways and to enjoy the experience. This teaching occurs daily in most families and schools. Children learn that there are correct times for play and correct things to do in these times and that playtimes should be enjoyed. They are given equipment to play with (toys), taught how to use them and earn adult approval by playing correctly, which includes expressing enjoyment. The ways in which children are taught to play vary by sex, by social class and among ethnic groups. Child's (1981) study of the behaviour of 22–55-month-old Birmingham children on play buses found that those from Asian families were less active and more respectful towards their play leaders. Children learn to play in ways that are appropriate for their age and they earn adult approval, which is amplified in peer groups, by playing in ways that demonstrate they are growing up.

Individuals begin to leave childhood behind when they start to play independently, usually with the approval of their parents and teachers, who know that the young must learn to make their own ways into adulthood. Leisure is the arena in which most young people first learn to act independently. During youth there is a gradual trend away from spending leisure in settings such as youth clubs, which are organized and supervised by adults, towards spending time with groups of friends in unsupervised situations and then, later on, towards using commercial facilities (Hendry et al., 1993, 2002a). Young people assert independence simply by having their own friends with whom they develop their own tastes and decide what to do with their time and money. Friends become key figures in young people's leisure. Simply being with their friends is extremely important to most young people. So are friends' opinions, but usually only on leisure matters, such as which music to listen to, which hairstyle to adopt and which clothing to wear. In peer groups young people learn to deal with social equals without close supervision by anyone in authority – a skill they will need in their future family and working lives. In developing such skills, young people learn to claim their own space in streets and parks, within their homes (in their own rooms) and later on in settings such as sports centres, pubs and clubs. They learn to play the consumer role and to expect to be treated with the respect normally commanded by paying customers.

Establishing independence does not require young people to defy adults. Overtly defiant behaviour usually has some additional significance, connected with class-related attitudes towards authority, for example (see Willis, 1977). Parents are usually delighted rather than offended when their children show that they are growing up. Activities such as smoking and drinking, which are forbidden for children but permitted for adults, usually have special attractions. Breaking the law is exciting for anyone, but simply establishing independence does not require everyone to commit 'proving offences'. Nor is young people's need to assert their independence a sufficient explanation of the now widespread use of illegal drugs (see Parker et al., 2002). Young people's willingness to experiment and try out new things is relevant, but the main appeal of leisure drugs among young people is based on the elementary fact that they make the users feel good (*see* below, pp. 142–144).

The second function that makes young people's leisure different is that it is the arena where sexual roles are learnt and sexualized identities acquired. Societal expectations are not just transmitted but amplified in peer groups. Young people are under enormous pressure to prove to others and to themselves that they are sexually normal. This involves displaying the correct attitudes towards one's own and the other sex, and learning to treat members of each sex in the appropriate ways. Social pressures interact with biology to teach males and females not just to behave but also to feel masculine and feminine. Young people learn to display their emotions in gender-appropriate ways. Girls learn to confide in same-sexed friends. Boys normally learn to be independent and self-contained. It has been argued that male socio-emotional norms matched the kinds of conduct required in the more powerful occupations in the past, thereby disadvantaging women, whereas, in present-day occupations, which require more intricate interpersonal skills when dealing with colleagues and clients, femininity is more likely to prove advantageous (Halford and Savage, 1995; Nare, 1996).

Young people learn sexually appropriate conduct initially among same-sexed peers and then in mixed-sex crowds, and then subsequently practise their skills in couple relationships. This is one of the processes that make youth cultures finely age-graded. Young people are acutely sensitive to age distinctions. 'Mature' 16-year-olds do not want to be confused with 14-year-old 'kids'. Successive age groups claim space in different settings or have ways of keeping themselves apart in the same places. As they become sexualized, young people develop and adopt their own norms for regulating sexual conduct. They decide whether it is OK to have sex in a casual relationship and judge each other accordingly. They also decide how to recognize if a relationship is steady. Relationships are usually so regarded if they are sexually exclusive and the partners communicate with each other (*see* du Bois-Reymond *et al.*, 1995). Within such relationships young people may feel that it is unnecessary to practise 'safe sex', though they learn rapidly that steady does not always mean permanent. Serial monogamy appears to have become the norm throughout modern societies, and this norm is initially established among young people.

Its special functions give young people's leisure a different significance even when they take part in the same leisure activities as adults, such as going out for a drink or staying in to watch television or to listen to music and converse. The crucial differences – the independence that young people find it necessary to assert and their sexual expressiveness – often alarm adult observers. Young people have always been regarded as a threat, liable to overturn normal patterns of family life and commit offences. Adults tend to regard themselves as potential victims but from the standpoint of the young it is they who are the vulnerable, harassed, victimized age group. Sheila Brown's (1995) questionnaire study of over 1000 11–16-year-olds and interviews with 200 found that 30% of this age group could recall being followed by an adult on foot and 18% recalled being followed by an adult in a car. Over a fifth had been physically assaulted by other young people. The young people's main defence strategy was to stay with their own groups. Another such strategy in recent years has been to carry a weapon of some description. Most young people are telling the truth when they explain this behaviour, which most adults find offensive, as a defensive precaution.

The continuities in young people's leisure can easily beguile all age groups into believing that nothing has changed. Parents who were shocked by the rave culture and body piercing in the 1980s and 1990s could very probably recall that they themselves provoked similar outrage with their football hooliganism or punk styles in the 1970s or as mods or hippies earlier on. While expressing horror at today's youth, adults can comfort themselves with the belief that they understand present-day young people's behaviour and problems. Adults have always been able to respond to the latest youth scenes with such ambivalence. However, in the recent past, alongside the continuities, there have been major transformations in the character of youth cultures. One such transformation occurred after the Second World War, and in the late 20th century an equally important shift began.

Post-war youth cultures

In the early 1950s Teddy boys were being sighted all over Britain. No one seemed to know where they had come from or what they wanted. The Teddy boys were named after the way they dressed; their long draped jackets were parodies of the formal Edwardian frock coat. Teds wore their long jackets over drainpipe trousers and thick-soled footwear – crêpe, not heavy industrial boots. They favoured bootlace ties and looked fearsome when they congregated in town and city centres. There were press reports that some carried cut-throat razors and bicycle chains, which were used in fights between rival groups late at night in urban parks. Around the same time, young people were being excited by a particular kind of music. An American group, Bill Haley and his Comets, had recorded 'Rock Around the Clock'. This number had made little impact when first released but was subsequently incorporated in a film, *Blackboard Jungle.* Teenagers all over Britain (and elsewhere) flocked to see the movie. They jived in the aisles and sometimes ripped up cinema seats, and there were reports of riots in the streets outside. Some local authorities banned the film, which appeared to increase teenagers' eagerness to see it. Bill Haley had a brief reign as a teenage idol. In the USA he was soon eclipsed by Elvis. Britain produced Tommy Steele, Marty Wilde, Adam Faith and, the most outrageous of all at that time, Cliff Richard. In the 1960s most of these solo performers gave way to groups – the Rolling Stones, etc. and, the biggest of all the groups at that time, the Beatles. Teenage fashions changed as rapidly as pop stars. By the end of the 1950s Teddy boys were all but extinct. They were then being replaced by mods and rockers. The latter wore leather or denim (and grease) and drove motorbikes, while the mods dressed more conventionally and adopted the scooter. On summer weekends and bank holidays, hundreds of these riders converged on seaside resorts, where they drove and wandered around, confronted each other, engaged in occasional scuffles and thereby triggered a media-fed moral panic

(Cohen, 1972). By this time additional youth types were appearing. Beatniks were scruffy – long hair and long woolly jumpers – but they gradually metamorphosed into hippies, the flower people, who also had long hair but were clean, wore beads and loved each other. Skinheads also surfaced initially in the 1960s. They, together with other young males, adopted football grounds as alternatives to town centres as places to gather on Saturday afternoons, and thus a new kind of football hooliganism was born. Punks appeared in the 1970s.

By then, the wider society's reactions were calmer. The new generations of parents had been Teds, mods or rockers, had very probably screamed at the Beatles and felt that they understood when their own teenage children came home with green hair or went out wearing deliberately ripped jeans. In the 1950s and 1960s, adults were usually at a loss to understand. Established youth organizations and leaders were manifestly out of touch (Albermarle Report, 1960). Commentators said that civilization was threatened by a new generation war. The new youth cultures were linked in media discourse to the rising rates of juvenile delinquency and teenage sexual activity. It is only in retrospect that the youth cultures of that era look rather tame. Drugs were unknown among young people. Alcohol was not part of the youth scenes. The first jukeboxes imported into Britain were installed in milk bars, soon to be restyled as coffee bars – just one example of Americanization. These were the places where skiffle groups – aspiring rock performers of the era – developed their skills and made their first live performances. The Liverpool Cavern, where the Beatles played before they were famous, was 'dry'.

By the 1960s, links were being formed between some of these new youth cultures and more serious political movements. This began in Britain on the Easter marches organized by the Campaign for Nuclear Disarmament (CND) and in the USA with the civil rights movement, which was protesting at the persistence, a century after the legal abolition of slavery, of formal racial segregation in much of the country and the persistence everywhere of racial discrimination to the disadvantage of coloured people (subsequently described as blacks or African Americans). By the beginning of the 1960s, students of all races from all over America were flocking into the segregated southern states to participate in demonstrations and acts of mass civil disobedience. This was the era of Martin Luther King and also Bob Dylan, Joan Baez and 'We Shall Overcome'. During the 1960s, these youth protest movements (and CND in Britain) embraced opposition to America's war in Vietnam. These protests spread to Europe, where the issues were extended to opposition to the allegedly oppressive capitalist system. In spring 1968, student demonstrators in Paris were joined by workers and their trade unions and threatened the rule of the French government. In the USA there were instances of student protesters being shot and killed by the security forces. It appeared that generations really were at war with one another. Then suddenly the war in Vietnam was over and all the protests ended.

Another kind of event pioneered by young people in the 1960s has enjoyed greater longevity. The first widely publicized pop festival, an inspiration for all that followed, was held at Woodstock in New York State in 1969. An estimated 450,000 turned up. The site organization was overwhelmed. Catering and everything else was insufficient. It was a cold, damp weekend. Those who attended recall the cold and the empty stomachs, but also how they enjoyed the music and the joints, and the atmosphere of peacefulness amid so many happy, smiley people. In Britain the first Glastonbury was held in 1970. Just 1500 turned up, paid £1 and in return could obtain free milk from the farm as well as enjoy the entertainment. A more successful (in terms of attendance) event was held at Knebworth in 1975, when the 70,000 or so who tried to attend blocked all the approach roads and lanes for miles around with their VW Beetles and camper vans. It is Glastonbury that has continued, but today it is a different kind of event, with audiences of 100,000 paying over £100 per head. The significance of the early pop festivals was primarily cultural. Nowadays they are more commercial.

By the 1960s, social scientists believed that they understood what the new post-war youth cultures signified. They had arisen in the new post-war economic conditions, in which full employment had eradicated low-paid juvenile jobs and youth unemployment. School leavers were able to advance rapidly to full adult earnings. Their new economic power had transformed young people's status within their families. They were paying 'board' from the start of their working lives and keeping the rest of their earnings, which were available for their own discretionary spending. Commerce thus targeted the teenage consumer with types of music, clothing and transport that had a manifest appeal to the age group (Abrams, 1961). Participation in the new youth cultures was clearly not a sign that those concerned were dropping out. Actually they were making accelerated transitions to adulthood – achieving adult-type jobs and adult-level earnings earlier, and also getting married and becoming parents at younger ages than formerly, usually following just one serious relationship (Leonard, 1980). Following marriage, participation in the youth scenes soon ended. Youth was indeed a 'brief flowering period'. Pop stars of that era were told that to remain in the business they had to continue to be (or at least to appear) young, single and available. The era of Posh, Becks, Brooklyn *et al.* lay decades ahead.

Were the post-war youth cultures really new? Teenagers had always formed strong peer relationships and developed lives of their own (see Davies, 1992). In earlier times some teenage groups (gangs) had achieved local and occasional wider recognition (notoriety), usually for their toughness and delinquency. The difference in the post-war era was that, by virtue of how they dressed and the music that they listened to, young people could align themselves and be identified by others as members of national and sometimes transnational 'types', which thereby were able to appear 'from nowhere' in any part of a country and, indeed, all over the world.

It was never the case that most young people became Teds, mods or rockers. From then right up to now, most young people have insisted that they are just 'normal' or 'ordinary' (see Hendry *et al.*, 2002b; Shildrick, 2002). However, even normal and ordinary young people have been able to enjoy temporary and partial affiliations to particular 'types' by attending a particular demo, concert or club. None of the post-war 'types' have been real groups with definite memberships. They are better described as 'reputational crowds' – reputational because they may never congregate en masse but exist primarily as cultural formations. This is the character of the culture-rich world in which all age groups now live, but young people's cultural environments are especially complicated. In any school or college there will be 'types', such as computer geeks, designer-label crowds and sporting types (see Kenvyn, 2000), sometimes regarded as part of wider forma-tions, all liable to classification into hierarchies, such as cool, bad and sad (see Hendry *et al.*, 2002b). These are the contexts in which all generations of post-war youth have needed to develop and manage preferred identities.

During the 1970s, sociologists based at or connected with Birmingham University's Centre for Contemporary Cultural Studies (CCCS) made a series of interventions in the ongoing debates about post-war youth (see Hall and Jefferson, 1976; Mungham and Pearson, 1976; Willis, 1977; Hebdige, 1979), and their arguments have acted as a point of reference, if not departure, for nearly all sub-sequent work on youth cultures. Two of the arguments with which the CCCS was and remains closely associated are well worth summarizing here. First, these writers insisted that the participants in the new youth scenes were not moronic, mindless yobs; rather, their cultural creativity and artistry deserved admiration and applause. The CCCS writers argued that the young people were not gullible dupes, exploited by commercial operators. Quite the reverse: the young people were credited collectively with creating 'types' or 'styles' that commerce had to follow and service. In a similar way, pop stars were said to be made by their audi-ences, not foisted on teenagers by the record companies. The CCCS writers mar-velled at how young people had taken everyday objects such as blue jeans and industrial boots and, in the case of the skinheads, endowed these with original meanings. Secondly, the CCCS writers argued that the post-war youth cultures were really subcultures, meaning that they had developed within pre-existing cul-tures, specifically class cultures. They drew attention to how the new youth cultures attracted young people from specific social class backgrounds and trajectories. For instance, the Teddy boys, rockers and skinheads were said to be empathically working class whereas the mods were said to be actually or aspirationally upwardly mobile. The emphatically working-class youth subcultures were said to incorporate, rework and express in novel ways elements of their parent culture – the tough masculinity, patriotism/racism, recognition of the need for group loy-alty and a willingness to defy and resist authorities. The CCCS writers claimed that the participants in these subcultures were making important statements – politically significant statements – about their feelings towards their wider society and their own positions within it. The dress and postures (all told, the 'styles') of Teds and skinheads were said to disturb the wider society precisely because they were intended to have this effect. So the mere presence of these youthful actors in neighbourhoods or in town and city centres could trouble adult observers. The CCCS writers applauded the skill of their subjects in expressing contempt simply by how they dressed and their demeanour. On a cultural plane, they were said to be engaging in class struggle, albeit a struggle they would quit on returning to their homes and mundane jobs after a weekend of excitement. The political sig-nificance of working-class youth cultures became apparent only when decons-tructed by academic analysts (such as the CCCS group), whereas the political links of campus-based hippie cultures were explicit and unmistakable.

Girls were peripheral in the CCCS writers' accounts of post-war youth cul-tures. Girls were glimpsed only as companions of the principal actors, as girlfriends and sometimes sisters, for example. Female youth researchers subsequently con-firmed that girls' representation as marginal was in fact realistic. The early post-war youth cultures were male-centred. Girls who accompanied mods and rockers sat on the pillions. At that time, girls' own social lives were culturally more home- and bedroom-based (see Sharpe, 1977; Griffin, 1985; McRobbie, 2000).

There are ongoing debates about whether the CCCS writers were right at the time (see Smith, 1981; Muggleton, 2000). These debates could be, but have not yet been, resolved by gathering oral histories from now ageing ex-Teds, mods, rockers and so on. However, there is unanimity among present-day writers that current youth cultures differ in important ways from those described in the CCCS classics, but disagreement about the significance of the differences.

Another transformation?

It is always important not to lose sight of continuities, but there have been a number of trends, all related to youth's new condition (see above, pp. 129–131), which make present-day youth cultures different from their counterparts of the 1950s and 1960s. First, a wider age group is involved in today's youth scenes. This is a result of transitions to adulthood being prolonged or, at any rate, becoming more variable in length. Today's 30-somethings are often still mingling with the young singles, while some of their age peers are parents of teenage children. When he interviewed a sample of young adults who were visiting the night scene in Newcastle upon Tyne city centre, Robert Hollands (1995) found that his respondents were aged up to 31. There has been speculation about whether youth cultures are disappearing (see Wallace and Kovatcheva, 1998). If so, youth unemployment will not be the reason. Young people without jobs face similar leisure problems to the unemployed in other age groups in Western countries. They have subnormal rates of participation in virtually all types of recreation that cost money. However, most students and youth trainees, and many of the young unemployed, manage to participate in a wide range of leisure activities with the cash that they raise from parents, grants, loans and part-time jobs (see Roberts and Parsell, 1991). In 1999–2000, Carr (2002) found that students in UK higher education were willing to sink deeper into debt in order to enjoy holidays away. The students who were interviewed in this study were taking an average of two holidays per year, lasting 16.7 days on average. There are huge inequalities in young people's incomes and spending levels, but their spending patterns prove that it is possible to participate in most youth scenes at different levels of expense. Nights out, holidays and new outfits can cost a lot or can be managed much more cheaply. If youth cultures disappear, this will not be a consequence of young people's poverty. It is more likely to be a consequence of pre-teen children being introduced to youth fashions in dress and becoming an important market for pop music, individuals staying young into their 30s and the spread of popular consumer cultures into adult age groups. At present, we lack a word to convey the (variable) length of this life stage. Nowadays the main age division in musical tastes, above which the appeal of pop and rock dips, is not between teenagers and adults but above and below the 50-somethings (Longhurst, 1996). Unlike in the 1950s, it is no longer only, or even mainly, young people who purchase leisurewear and recorded music. In 2002 the

12–19 age group accounted for just 16.4% of all album sales in the UK, whereas 40–59-year-olds accounted for 33.4% (de Lisle, 2004). Consumer values and their associated culture have ceased to be as age-specific as formerly. However, it seems unlikely that youth cultures will become indistinguishable from other popular consumer cultures, if only because young people remain particularly susceptible to the latest trends, their leisure still performs some age-specific functions and also (see below) becoming a parent continues to make a substantial difference to day-to-day and week-to-week leisure.

A second post-1970s trend has been that gender and social class divisions within youth cultures have become less clear-cut. This is not to say that either type of difference has disappeared. Despite unisex fashions and the gay villages in some cities, most young (and older) people succeed in looking unmistakably male or female, and heterosexual masculinity and femininity are expected, if not demanded, in most informal social settings. One change is simply that most youth cultures are not as male-dominated as formerly. Young women have broken out from the bedroom culture. As we saw in Chapter 4 (pp. 110–111), since the 1980s, teenage girls in Glasgow have caught up with or overtaken boys in their rates of drinking alcohol, smoking and drug use. Meanwhile, boys' leisure has become more home-based: they are spending more time at home watching TV sport and playing computer games (Sweeting and West, 2003). The recent changes in their leisure behaviour are certain to be related to young women making more headway in education (outperforming males at all levels) and in the labour market, and gaining effective control over their own fertility. Nowadays young women are as likely as young men to use indoor sports facilities (Department for Education, 1995). They have been claiming space in other public places also – city centres, wine bars and throughout the club scenes (see Chapter 4, pp. 110–112).

There has been a similar blurring of social class divisions. Since the 1960s popular culture has been adopted by young people on middle-class trajectories in secondary schools' academic streams and in higher education. This has not driven out high culture; it is more a case of young (and older) people now feeling able to enjoy both classics and pop. There is more intermingling of the social classes in comprehensive secondary schools and in post-compulsory education. This, along with the less certain futures of all young people, has made them harder for researchers and one another to classify. An outcome is that there are no longer any clear social class differences in the kinds of music young people listen to, the fashions they wear or the leisure places they go to. Robert Hollands (1995) found that Newcastle city centre nightlife was equally popular among university students and local young people. That said, young people still tend to stick with their 'own kind', people like themselves in terms of social class and educational backgrounds (see MacRae, 2004). Also, those from middle-class home backgrounds who are educationally successful still tend to do more leisure activities, even if the 'more' is of the same kinds of things in which working-class youth are also involved. Middle-class youth, and males more so than females, are more likely to become committed participants and to play leadership roles in all kinds of leisure. For example, they are the most likely to be involved in running sports clubs and playing popular music, but the activities themselves are not restricted to, or even ostensibly associated with, any sex or social class (see Roberts and Parsell, 1994).

A third trend has been the splintering of youth cultures. Needless to say, there are still many things that most young people do. The majority go on nights out and consume alcohol, listen to popular music, watch television and play sport (see Roberts, 1996). However, there are no longer any particular musical genres or fashions that can claim to be the dominant style. No present-day artists seem able to exert the mass appeal of the Beatles and Elvis. New technology is part of the explanation. The music production and distribution industries have more players. There are more radio stations, all trying to appeal to specific taste publics. But technology is not the reason why it is now equally fashionable to have short-cropped or long hair or why there is no 'uniform' worn as widely as blue denim in the 1960s and 1970s. Young people's tastes do not map neatly on to either social class, gender or geographical divisions (see Roberts and Parsell, 1994). There is simply more variety within all social groups, which will somehow be related to the broader processes of individualization. Young people use leisure to develop and express their individuality but can only do this via their specific subcultural affiliations.

A fourth trend is that young people's leisure has become more commercial. This has happened as teenagers' and young singles' scenes have merged, and as younger children (not to mention teenagers) have been enabled to spend more money. The art of passing time without spending money appears to be dying. Nowadays young people are less likely to go out simply to hang about; now they go somewhere or do something that involves spending money (Sweeting and West, 2003). Pop festivals are more expensive than in the 1970s, when there was no such thing as late-night clubbing on which to spend money.

A fifth trend has been towards young people's subcultures acting as a base for 'proto-communities' (Willis, 1990) or 'new tribes' (Maffesoli, 1994), rather than expressing membership of pre-existent groups. The groups of young people (and adults) who become fans of specific sports teams and who attend raves and similar scenes where their preferred types of music are played can experience intense camaraderie. Much of the appeal of these occasions is that they are incredibly social. Everyone is friendly. Individuals find that they are accepted. None of this is completely new. The change over time has been that the young people who play together nowadays have rarely grown up together in the same districts and attended the same local schools. Their participation in the 'new tribes' is usually temporary. Participants are always drifting off to other scenes. Sometimes the subcultures simply disappear:

> Club cultures are taste cultures. Club crowds generally congregate on the basis of their shared taste in music . . . Taking part in club cultures builds, in turn, further affinities . . . Clubs and raves, therefore, house ad hoc communities with fluid boundaries which may come together and dissolve within a single summer or endure for a few years.
>
> (Thornton, 1995, p. 3)

However, some youth cultures, skinheads and goths, for example, have survived for decades and acquired collective memories that are passed on to new participants (see Hodkinson, 2002), and being part of even the most temporary scenes can be extremely important to young people. Those studied by

Robert Hollands (1995), who were part of Newcastle's downtown nightlife, were going to the city centre 2.7 times a week on average and spending £16–£18 per occasion, which amounted to 38% of their total incomes. They nearly all said that they would feel unacceptably restricted if they were unable to experience these nights out.

It is plausible to argue, though difficult to prove, that through their subcultural affiliations today's young people do not so much express as acquire social identities and self-concepts. If education, occupations and gender no longer confer the clear identities they offered in the past, if today's young people cannot be sure about the kinds of adults they will become, if they cannot know what their occupational or social class destinations will be, they may need to become immersed in specific subcultures in order to define who they are. Young people could be the vanguard age group in this respect. In the 1950s and 1960s, the new youth scenes signalled the spread of consumer cultures. Maybe today's young people are similar pioneers, using lifestyles that incorporate their pre-ferred uses of leisure to create their most significant, identity-conferring social positions. Some say that this is the future of leisure, which will become more widespread as current cohorts of young people carry their styles into adulthood (see Chapter 6). This suggests that leisure is now acquiring a role that extends beyond the economic, psychological, social and political grounds for treating it seriously that were itemized in Chapter 1.

A sixth trend is that post-1970s youth cultures have been less political. Not-withstanding 'rock against racism' and Band Aid and despite Andy Bennett's (2001) claim that all post-Second World War music-based popular cultures have conveyed some political message, broadly defined, none have mobilized young people in ways comparable to those witnessed in the 1960s. This is not because young people today are less interested in political and public issues. Most young people have never been very interested in politics. Most young people in the 1950s and 1960s took no part in demonstrations. Nevertheless, there was a sense in which those who did take part were speaking for their entire age group. In the 1930s Karl Mannheim (1936) coined the term 'political generation'. He argued that people's lifetime social and political outlooks were always liable to be affected profoundly by their experiences while becoming adults, and that in times of major upheaval the upcoming generations would acquire outlooks that set them apart from their elders. Mannheim was seeking to understand the rise of fascist and communist movements in the 1920s and 1930s, especially in those countries that had suffered defeat in the First World War. Inglehart (1977, 1997; see Box 2.1, p. 51) has subsequently built on these ideas. He argues that adults who came of age in the 1950s and 1960s in Western countries had been reared in conditions of unprecedented prosperity and, as a result, were less materialist than their elders and more likely to subscribe to post-materialist values, such as peace and equality between all peoples. Inglehart claims that the 'baby boomers', as they became adults, felt unrepresented by the age groups that, at the time, were in positions of power. Since the 1950s and 1960s, there appear to have been no further new political generations in the West, though in post-communist lands the situation is rather different. In the absence of really new political gener-ations in the West, it has been impossible for anyone to speak for the younger age groups against the holders of power. Young people have usually been divided in their opinions in much the same ways as adults, and it has become impossible to read anyone's politics from the way they dress or the music they listen to.

Lives at risk?

Some of the above trends, not the lengthening of childhood to adulthood transitions and the commercialization of leisure in the life stage in themselves, but the uses to which this new life space is being put, are said to pose short-term and long-term risks to young people's and, indeed, the upcoming adult population's health and welfare. The British Medical Association (2003) has warned that unless young people change their ways we must expect a rise in involuntary infertility and a decline in life expectancy (see Box 5.1).

The British Medical Association's views have a firm basis in fact. Around three-quarters of Britain's young people use an illegal drug at some time (see Table 5.5). It is no longer the norm for young couples to marry as a sequel to

---

Box 5.1.   Adolescent health.

The British Medical Association claims that:

Adolescents in the UK are not eating optimal diets. Girls in particular fail to meet recommendations for exercise. As a result, in common with the rest of the population, overweight and obesity is increasingly prevalent among adolescents. (p. 13)

Adolescents in the UK are increasingly likely to experiment with smoking and use recreational drugs. Over time they have begun to drink greater quantities of alcohol and now have one of the highest levels of alcohol use and binge drinking in Europe. (p. 26)

There are further warnings about 'the growing prevalence of STIs [sexually transmitted infections] among this age group' (p. 42). Screening surveys find that around 10% of women aged 16–25 are infected with chlamydia.

Source: British Medical Association (2003).

Table 5.5.   Drug use by young people in northwest England: 22-year-olds in 1999 (percentages).

	Ever	Last year	Last month
Been offered drugs	93		
Drugs used by at least one close friend	94		
Used personally	76	52	31

Source: Parker *et al.* (2002).

their first serious relationship. Nowadays men claim an average of six and women an average of four sexual partners prior to cohabiting or marrying (National Centre for Social Research, 2003). Over a fifth of the UK's men and women are now clinically obese and another 47% of men and 33% of women are over-weight (Department for Health, 2001). Nutrition is believed to be part of the explanation: eating too much and eating unhealthily. Lack of exercise is another culprit. The foundations for inactive lifestyles are laid in present-day childhood. In their free time, when they are not at school or work, the UK's 8–19-year-olds are less active overall than the over-65s (Fisher, 2002). Low sport participation is not responsible. Children and young people play a lot of sport. Sport participa-tion among schoolchildren has been rising. They play a lot of sports in school and in 2002 were devoting an average of 8.1 h each week to sport and exercise outside school lessons (see Table 5.6). The problem is lack of exercise in the rest of their free time, a result of being driven to school and to leisure activities and then taking over the driving themselves, and spending many hours watching television and video movies, playing computer games, and so on.

However, it was UK youth's so-called binge drinking that inspired a moral panic in early 21st-century Britain. Again, the raw facts appear to suggest that the concern was justified. Twenty-seven per cent of Britain's 11–16-year-olds drink at least once a week. Ninety per cent of young people aged 16 and above drink alcohol, and over 80% visit pubs and over 50% go clubbing at least once a month. Thirty-seven per cent of 16–24-year-old males and 23% of females drink in excess of the recommended safe limits of 21 units per week for men and 14 units for women. Nowadays Britain's teenagers top the European drinking league (Alcohol Concern, 2002; Boseley, 2002; Hollands and Chatterton, 2002), though across all age groups the British are not Europe's heaviest drinkers. Britain's lead among young people is probably related to their growing up more rapidly than their continental peers in other respects – doing part-time jobs, finishing education, entering full-time jobs, having sex and incurring debt. Also, although alcohol consumption by Britain's young females has risen substantially in recent years, there has been a slight decline in males' (much higher) rates of consumption (see Table 5.4, p. 125).

Since the 1970s, moral panics over the state of the nation's youth have been spasmodic rather than ongoing. Their fashions and music have ceased

Table 5.6. Young people and sport.

	1994	1999	2002
Mean number of sports done at least once in school lessons (years 2–11)	8.3	8.4	8.9
Mean number of sports done at least once out of lessons (years 2–11)	10.0	10.3	11.2
Mean time (in hours per week) spent taking part in sport and exercise out of school lessons (11–16-year-olds)		7.5	8.1

Source: Sport England (2003).

to shock. Too many adults were one-time drug users to be outraged that so many of today's young people are acting likewise. Rising crime (actual and alleged) is old news. Gun crime is different, but only a tiny minority of Britain's young people have ever carried firearms. It takes something widespread and apparently new to provoke panic nowadays, and 'binge drinking' has been one such recent scare. This particular 'cause for concern' was actually part of the solution to an earlier moral panic. 'Raving' was the cause of the earlier panic. This occurred in the late 1980s, when experiences of all-night mass partying in Ibiza and other Mediterranean holiday resorts began to be replicated at home at impromptu events announced by flyers posted on lamp posts and distributed outside colleges, which drew hundreds of ravers to country sites and disused industrial premises. This outbreak subsided only when new laws were passed that made such impromptu events illegal and when, simultaneously, the rave scene was allowed to move indoors by permitting town and city centre clubs to remain open well past midnight (see Critcher, 2000). Thus Britain's towns and cities developed booming night-time economies and their streets became teeming and lively in the weekend wee small hours. Respectable adults remained unaware until television crews and newspaper photographers publicized images of what was happening in the cities after daytime users were at home and in bed.

These 'dangerous' levels of drinking, and also drug use and smoking, continue partly because young people have their own theories and hierarchies of risk, and these differ profoundly from what most adults appear to believe is dangerous for young people. The latter accept that drugs can be dangerous but do not feel the same way about alcohol, tobacco or X-rated movies. Young motorcyclists believe that the risks can be overridden by road skills. Some drugs are considered safe provided they are used responsibly and the users remain 'in control', which most young drug users (like most drinkers) believe applies to them. In any case, young people say that risk is a part of life and that risk-taking can be exciting (Green *et al.*, 2000; Abbott-Chapman and Denholm, 2001; Bellaby and Lawrenson, 2001). In many young people's minds, real danger is associated with encountering groups of young males when alone, and sometimes specific members of their own families and residents in their own neighbourhoods. They believe that the best way to safeguard themselves against all risks is to stay among their own friends and to follow their advice.

However, the reason why few young lives are really threatened either short-term or long-term is that the relevant lifestyle features remain prominent only during the youth life stage. The exceptions are nutrition and exercise levels, which are resulting in not just young people but children and adults also becoming fatter than is good for them (see Table 1.7, pp. 20–21). Risks are greatly reduced when practices are life stage-specific. Most young people's allegedly and actually risky practices, and much that is benign as well, are all liable to eradication or substantial downscaling during the 'life-cycle squeeze'.

Adult Leisure

Adulthood has been affected by the destandardization of the life course. The impact may have been less dramatic than among young people up to now, but, while young people's futures have become uncertain, adults' actual lives have become less stable in many cases and less secure for the majority. Adulthood today is at greater risk of disruption due to occupational restructuring and the dissolution of domestic partnerships. There is also more variety in the pace and order in which people make the transitions normally involved in becoming adult – marrying and having children, living independently from one's parents and becoming self-supporting financially through one's own or a partner's employment. Individuals need not make any of these transitions in order to gain social recognition as adults. However, despite the transitions tending to occur at later ages, more 30-somethings remaining part of the singles scene and more women in this age group remaining childless, the vast majority of the population are still making all these transitions at some point or another. As regards the leisure implications, the crucial transitions are to living with an opposite-sexed partner and the arrival of children. The biggest shake-ups in leisure behaviour from year to year coincide with these life events (see Gershuny, 2003), and the effects seem little changed from when there was a more reliable life cycle.

The squeeze

Estes and Wilenski (1978) coined the term 'life-cycle squeeze' to describe the consequences of marriage and parenthood. Their vocabulary is still the best available. The squeeze occurs as constraints increase – mortgages to pay off, households to run and more dependents to support. These constraints make new demands on time and money. An outcome is that adults' leisure is vulnerable, especially women's since up to now men have been the more skilled at protecting or maybe just more able to protect their own pastimes (see Chapter 4, pp. 105–107). Nevertheless, living with an opposite-sexed partner, and even more so the arrival of children, leads to an all-round reduction in out-of-home leisure for both women and men. Spare time, such as remains, tends to become home-based. When adults go out, this tends to be as a family, on holidays and day trips, for example. Once again, this is especially true for women. Younger people's leisure-based lifestyles and their alleged identities seem unlikely to survive this squeeze. The squeeze is not slackening. The total working time (paid and unpaid) of parents of dependent children is not only longer than in any other section of the population but has been lengthening rather than diminishing, due mainly to more mothers being in paid employment without any compensatory reduction in the time that fathers spend in their paid jobs. With the birth of children, total workloads tend to rise more steeply nowadays than was the case in the past (see Zuzanek *et al.*, 1998).

There is more variation than in the past in the ages at which the squeeze begins. Nowadays it can be at any point from the teens to beyond 40, though the longer childbearing is postponed the more unlikely it becomes. Voluntary infertility seems less likely to occur from a firm decision early on never to have any children than from a series of decisions not to have one 'now' until a point is reached when aspirant parents may realize that reproduction will be difficult and it is too late to do anything about the problem, or adults have reached career and income levels where they feel they have too much to lose (Hobcraft and Kiernan, 1995). Nevertheless, some adults begin their careers as parents when aged 35 plus, a time of life when some of their age peers are relinquishing their main child-rearing responsibilities. Children today remain dependent for longer, so it is by no means exceptional for these responsibilities to extend beyond age 60, by which time the adults may have become substantially responsible for the care of their own ageing parents – an implication of older people living longer (see below).

Family instability

The instability of adults' lives nowadays does not alleviate but intensifies the squeeze. A mother's own leisure may be more vulnerable than her male partner's, but lone parenthood is no solution. Lone parents, who are nearly always women, tend to have extremely home-based leisure lives. They are more likely than other women to ask, 'What leisure?' (Streather, 1979; Hardey, 1990). This domesticity is enforced rather than the mothers' preference in most cases; it is a product of lacking the time and money to spend on their own pleasures. When adults embark on serial partnerships, this is likely to intensify and prolong the squeeze. Absent parents (usually fathers) can find their time and money drained by having to contribute to the support of two households and by their desire to retain contact with their children. When second partnerships yield more children, the squeeze is extended. All the evidence points to the leisure benefits of the conventional intact family. Young people benefit from the support that such families can provide during their prolonged life stage transitions and this is evident in the young adults' physical and mental health and relatively low risks of unemployment (see Spruijt and de Goede, 1995). Adults' leisure, men's and women's, also benefits more often than not from an intact relationship.

Time and money pressures

Washing machines and other items of domestic technology should have reduced the time squeeze and higher rates of employment among mothers should have alleviated the financial squeeze if all other things had remained equal. In practice, however, financial pressures tend to be exchanged for time pressures or vice versa. As Chapter 2 explained, expected standards of home and childcare have risen. Moreover, in certain respects, present-day societies have become child-unfriendly. Parents are more reluctant than in the past to simply send their children out to play. Streets and parks are often considered dangerous. Parents often feel that it is necessary to escort or transport their children to and from school and to and from leisure activities. Needless to say, not all parents are willing and able to be so dedicated. Sometimes an outcome is that children are expected to amuse themselves with televisions and other items of leisure equipment. Parents who are willing and able to take their children out may find the occasions stressful. They are likely to find that young children are unwelcome in many adult leisure settings. McKeever's (1993) study of catering establishments in the Oxford area found that few made any special provisions for young children; their parents often complained of being made to feel like second-class citizens.

Social class differences

There are social class differences in the severity of the squeeze. The middle classes' advantages are based more on money than on time. As observed when discussing work–leisure relationships, money can alleviate, if not solve, many leisure problems. Better-off parents are better placed to spend on childcare and to preserve their own nights out and maintain existing leisure interests. They are also more able to take their children out for leisure, coping with the stresses. A child in a household tends to reduce the adults' participation in cultural activities while increasing their sports participation (see Sturgis and Jackson, 2003b), but this latter trend is class-related. This has been illustrated vividly in Fishwick and Hayes's (1989) study of 401 Illinois adults. The arrival of children was associated with increased sports activity among the wealthier respondents; children were an additional reason for going to sports centres. In contrast, poorer parents' sports participation declined with the presence of children. Allan and Crowe (1991) have pointed out that home-centredness need not be at the expense of wider sociability. Acute privatism is more likely to be an outcome of constraint than of preference (see also Devine, 1992). Children are nearly always an additional constraint on their parents' leisure, but more so in working-class than in middle-class households and most of all when the parent is single.

The most representative life stage

Adult leisure inevitably displays most of the general features of leisure in present-day societies. It is normal leisure writ large in the amounts of time spent at home, with the family and watching television. The normal gender and social class differences become more pronounced than in earlier life stages. Holidays are a major item of leisure spending, and the adults' own out-of-home leisure, when they have the opportunity to devote occasions to themselves, is most likely to involve going out to eat and/or drink.

Despite the current level of marital breakdowns, one of the main pleasures that most married partners experience is the other's company. Oriel Sullivan's (1996) research, which involved 380 couples keeping time diaries for a 5-day period, found that activities were most enjoyed when undertaken jointly. This was particularly true of leisure activities, and most of all when the leisure involved socializing with other people. The couples in this research appeared to be trying to coordinate their schedules so as to increase the amounts of time they spent together. Even so, the proportions of their activities done simultaneously were only slightly higher than for pseudo-couples (males and females paired at random). Pseudo-couples do many things at the same times because, despite the destandardization that is in process, most people still work during weekdays, watch television in the evenings, and so on. Insofar as individuals deviate from such normal schedules, as a result of working odd hours, for example, it seems to be difficult for couples to coordinate their activities and offset the disruption of their togetherness even when they wish to do so: hence the finding from the UK 2000 Time Use Survey that married and cohabiting couples were averaging just 2½ h per weekday and 3½ h per weekend day doing things jointly, and their joint activities were usually eating, chores and watching television. Togetherness was exceptional in other kinds of leisure (see Gatenby, 2004; see also Chapter 3, pp. 74–76).

Leisure at home

The compensation for the squeeze is supposed to be that adults obtain homes of their own in which they can savour each other's and their children's company. Some of this is just hopeful idealism. We know that homes are sometimes places of stress, violence and abuse. However, we have seen that most couples do in fact value each other's company.

In 1982 Sue Glyptis and Deborah Chambers drew attention to how little is known about leisure in the home. This remains the case, despite occasional forays such as Sullivan's and despite it being long-standing knowledge that the home is where most leisure time is spent. Part of the explanation for the gaps in our knowledge is that home life is private, impossible for outsiders to observe unobtrusively. Researchers have to rely on what their informants show and tell them. However, when they conducted a study of leisure and the home among an east Midlands sample, Glyptis and Chambers found that nearly all their subjects were extremely cooperative (Glyptis *et al.*, 1987). Home-based leisure remains rather mysterious, not so much because people are unwilling to say what they do but because unless sexual and other intimate details are revealed the picture is unremarkable. Home life appears to be composed of chores, television and small talk. Can it really be as mundane as the reporting makes it appear? When we stand back, try to detach ourselves and adopt an external view of our home lives, the banality can be difficult to explain.

Glyptis and her colleagues conducted a time–space analysis of their subjects' daily lives. They investigated what their subjects did, with whom and where, measuring not just how much of their time was spent at home but also how the space in the dwellings was used. Their evidence, which can be made to sound either unremarkable or surprising, showed that day-to-day activity tended to be concentrated within a communal living area in most households. The residents were not making the fullest possible use of all the space they had at their disposal. There were few examples of cellular living, despite the electricity, central heating, studies and garage workshops that some of the dwellings contained.

Spending leisure alone at home seems to be common only when no one else is in. At least part of the explanation will be that family members really do enjoy each other's company. But another part of the explanation could be that a principal function of much home-based leisure is straightforward recuperation – or maybe we are slaves to tradition and addicted to television. The evidence from Glyptis and Chambers's study is difficult to square with Gordon Cherry's (1984) portrait of homes bulging with leisure equipment the occupants lack both the time and the space to use. Most homes appear to contain a great deal of both underused space and underused leisure equipment, and the occupants, when at home, devote a great of time to just resting, relaxing and watching television.

Patterns of family life in Britain appear little different from those in eastern Europe, where the typical dwelling has just two or three rooms, shared by two or three generations, and all the rooms are used for both living and sleeping (see Roberts and Jung, 1995). The hours the typical adult devotes to television do not suggest that time scarcity prevents the audio equipment, computers and sports gear in Western homes being used more frequently. It could be that the owners derive satisfaction from leisure equipment simply being available if and when they wish to use it. It could be that there are advantages in upstairs rooms often being used only for sleeping so that household members do not have to go to bed simultaneously or interrupt each other's leisure when they do so. Maybe these returns are considered sufficient to justify our investments in our homes. Or do the types of dwellings we buy and the ways we equip them reflect our aspirations and the images we prefer to present to visitors and the rest of the outside world, rather than how we actually live?

Maybe the Chinese are more realistic. Freysinger and Chen (1993) report that the family is not a preferred leisure milieu in China. They attribute this to Confucianism, the family being regarded as the primary cell of society and properly ruled by authority and obedience rather than free expression and affection. In Britain, as in China, for young people and adults alike, real leisure appears to mean going out. Young people willingly sacrifice this leisure, maybe having learnt its limitations, and then have little option but to lead more home-centred lives due to a combination of financial necessity and their obligations to dependents.

Leisure in Later Life

Change and continuity

The recent literature on growing older in later life (the ageing process begins at birth) is as brimful as youth research with references to the life course being destandardized and deinstitutionalized and chronological milestones being removed (Laczko and Phillipson, 1992; Young and Schuller, 1991; Kohli *et al.*, 1992). Whether the changes in later life justify the discourse is debatable. The change in older people's circumstances that has prompted the references is that more men have been terminating their employment careers, or having their careers terminated for them, at younger ages than in the past. More men have been taking voluntary retirement, have been compulsorily retired early or have been losing their jobs and then been unable to regain work before age 65. This milestone, or millstone, has not so much been removed as changed in significance. Sixty-five is still the age at which full state retirement pensions become available on demand (though a possible change to age 70 is currently being debated). Sixty-five is also the UK's 'default age' at which, provided the employees consent, they can be retired by their employers. Most occupational pension schemes have always operated on the assumption that people will pay contributions, or have these paid on their behalf, for 40 years in order to qualify for full pensions. The change is that in the past most men knew that they would have to work, or be able to continue working, depending on how they felt about their jobs, up to age 65. At this age they knew that their main careers would end. Since the 1970s most adult men have wondered how close to 65 they will be when their working lives terminate. Some have feared being cast on the scrap heap. Others have wondered whether they will be lucky enough to be offered enhanced early-retirement packages. In the past some men resented having to work up to age 65. Others resented being compulsorily retired merely because they had become 65 years old. However, up to the 1970s, in the decades of full employment, it was not uncommon for men to continue working either full-time or part-time, in their existing jobs or in other occupations, well beyond age 65. This has become much rarer. Things may change in the future if, on the one hand, labour shortages make employers keener to retain or hire the over-65s and, on the other hand, if employees seek to extend their working lives and enhance their eventual pensions. However, between the 1970s and the turn of the millennium, flexibility in retirement shifted into the pre-65 age group. The age 65 milestone did not disappear but changed in significance. Men's reactions have differed. As we shall see, some have welcomed the change while others have felt victimized.

There have been other changes affecting the population's experiences in later life. More people are now retiring with occupational in addition to state pensions. More women are accumulating pension entitlements in their own right and there has not been a decline in the proportion of women working beyond age 55. People are now living longer; old age lasts longer on average than in the past. This is the main reason why many governments want workers to carry on for longer. However, lower mortality among the over-60s means that many younger old people, in their 60s, for example, are helping to support even older relatives. Many of the costs of supporting the ageing population have been transferred from the state welfare budget, the National Health Service and local authority social services departments to the 'customers' and, to some extent, their younger relatives.

However, the process of ageing in later life has always been lengthy. It begins, in a sociological sense, when people begin to disengage from what have been their main lifetime roles. One such disengagement is from child-rearing. This usually occurs gradually, rather than abruptly, as children grow older and more independent and leave the parental home one by one, but at some stage there has normally been an 'empty nest'. Another disengagement is from employment. This has sometimes occurred abruptly but it has often been gradual via part-time, temporary and voluntary work, and this remains the case today, though the transitions tend to occur earlier in men's lives.

Other life events happen inevitably at some stage – bereavement and the loss of physical and mental capacities.

Growing old involves a series of transitions and changes. There has never been just one big abrupt step. Compared with young people's transitions, those in later life normally occur over a longer time period and involve relinquishing rather than taking on new roles, and the individuals concerned have rather less control over their life events. Whereas young people have some say over when to terminate their education, when to marry and whether to become parents, older persons have less control over when their children leave home and when their own physical and mental capacities decline. Some have no choice over when to terminate their main lifetime employment. Even when they have some say over 'when', there is an inevitability about the events happening at some time or another.

Disengagement and engagement

A theme in the literature on leisure in later life is that disengagement from the major roles of adulthood can be an opportunity to engage in other things. This is the 'Third age' or 'Golden years' perspective, which emphasizes that disengagement from family and work obligations can open opportunities for a leisure renaissance in which people do things they really value. Most of the 60 recently retired or employees who were approaching retirement in Vickerstaff and Cox's (2005) case studies of retirement policies and practices in a UK local authority and a large private transport company had looked forward or were looking forward to retirement. They saw retirement as an opportunity to do things they really wanted to do. However, for others it was a step into the unknown. There were some 'deniers' who simply avoided thinking about retirement, and others who had been 'blown off course' by changes in company policy, in their own health or in their domestic circumstances.

Most people may have positive expectations of retirement, but the hard evidence suggests that the hopes of many are disappointed and that talk of the 'Third age' contains more advocacy than description. It is more about what ageing could be like rather than what it currently is like for most people. We are living and staying healthy for longer. Many of us relinquish family responsibilities and retire from employment with decades of active life ahead. With mortgages paid off and no dependents, some households have unprecedented cash, which can be spent on holidays, theatres, meals out and so forth. It is not difficult to find people acting in precisely the way that the engagement theory prescribes. The 'woopies' (well-off older persons) have become a major segment in several leisure markets, especially holidays. Thousands spend the winter months in warm climates. This age group provides most of the customers on ocean cruises. At any holiday resort, coastal or countryside attraction, they can be seen alighting from or boarding their coaches and filling the hotels throughout the year. Some become leisure connoisseurs, experts on what the holiday trade, stately homes, art galleries and museums have to offer. Max Kaplan, a one-time leading American writer on leisure, has been among the advocates of the engagement view of ageing. His main book on this topic (Kaplan, 1979) was prompted by his own official retirement. In it Kaplan drew attention to how ageing and leisure, in combination, offered opportunities for commitment, company, service and aesthetic and tourist experiences.

Many obstacles have been identified to making later life a leisure renaissance for everyone. Ill health and poverty restrict many, but other obstacles might be removed more easily. One is ageism, which views the elderly as lacking capabilities and even appetites. This societal perspective may even influence the ways in which ageing persons view themselves. Another obstacle is said to be the low regard that many people still have for leisure. However, Betsy Wearing (1995) has argued that leisure offers alternative discourses with which ageing people can prevent their devaluation. A leisure perspective, she argues, can highlight the many things that ageing people are able to do, and she offers examples of older persons using leisure to enrich their lives and to demonstrate to others that older people should be targets for envy not pity, and that the 'Third age' is something that everyone can anticipate eagerly. Robert Stebbins (1998) argues that serious leisure, when people have such interests, can be the basis for fulfilment during retirement, and there is mounting evidence to support this view. Long-term leisure interests, especially serious leisure interests that are a source of intrinsic satisfaction, are known to boost well-being, to smooth out life stage transitions and to contribute to successful ageing (see Carpenter and Patterson, 2004; Siegenthaler and O'Dell, 2003; Hawkins *et al.*, 2004).

Leisure trends in later life

The aggregate picture is well known, does not appear to have changed over time and bears little resemblance to the engagement perspective. As people grow older, the general tendency is for them to reduce their leisure activities. Specifically, the range is reduced, especially in out-of-home recreation. But, as previously explained, ageing takes a long time and older people rarely make major changes in their leisure from year to year. Their leisure is more stable than in any other age group. Young people are far more likely than their elders both to adopt new activities and to drop existing interests (see Mihalik *et al.*, 1989). Older people tend to have very fixed routines. It is tempting, but maybe unfair, to describe them as being stuck in ruts.

In the early 1980s, Jonathan Long and Erica Wimbush studied a sample of men in Scotland shortly before and just after they retired from employment (Long and Wimbush, 1985). This study recorded very few examples of retirement being seized as an opportunity to develop new leisure interests. Nor were there many examples of sudden disengagement. Overall, there was a slight decline in leisure activity. In some ways retirement was having similar effects to unemployment – people were having to adjust to lower incomes and the loss of work-based social relationships. Very few of the men in this study had received or made careful preparations for retirement. Most simply carried on and adjusted as best they could; the momentum of their lives seemed to carry them along. Their leisure resembled the unemployed's in that they spent most of their time at home and, compared with the general population and their own lives prior to retirement, they watched more television and did more reading, gardening and listening to the radio.

The overall tendency among the ageing is for life events such as retirement from employment and declining health to be accompanied by a reduction in leisure activity. However, the aggregate is made up of many different experiences. It is known that, at some points in later life, some people increase their involvement in certain kinds of leisure, taking holidays, for instance. It is also known that the elderly are over-represented in some forms of out-of-home leisure – voluntary work, using parks, going to bingo and to churches and playing bowls, for example. Later life lasts a long time and covers a huge variety of circumstances. The population experiencing later life varies widely in age and physical and mental capacities. There are wide differences in health within all age groups, and there are equally stark contrasts in social and economic circumstances. In later life, some people retain strong family connections. In some cases these act as a support system, though it is often the ageing who are the supporters of grown-up children and grandchildren and more elderly relatives. Inequalities of wealth and income are wider among the elderly than among people of working age (Abrams, 1980). Some older people retain the use of their cars, whereas others find their mobility restricted by their lack of private transport, poor public transport, declining physical capacities and lack of income.

The stability of older people's routines is actually a short-term phenomenon. Very few change their habits abruptly in any year but, as already stressed, later life can last a long time, longer than adulthood (the period when they are established in their main lifetime roles) for some people. In Germany Walter Tokarski's (1991) research among a sample initially of 222 older men and women, declining to 52 over 15 years, recorded a great deal of lifestyle change. People were changing their ways of life as their economic, domestic and health circumstances changed. Over the 15-year period major change was normal, indeed inevitable in many cases, as people grew older, lost partners, saw their savings exhausted, and so on.

Early retirement

There have been several studies of early retirees, mainly men. There has been the same gender imbalance in research into leisure in later life as in other fields. Retirement from full-time long-term employment careers, a momentous transition for more men than women, has attracted more attention than changes in domestic roles, including bereavement, which is more likely to affect women since men tend to die at younger ages. The studies of early retirees are none the less interesting because of their conflicting evidence.

On the one hand, there have been studies such as Young and Schuller's (1991) research among mainly working-class men in London who lost their jobs well ahead of the normal retirement age. These men are portrayed as in a limbo; too old to have any real hope of regaining decent jobs but too young to consider themselves, or to be regarded by others as, properly retired. Most of these men were bitter and disillusioned by the tattered and undignified endings to their working lives. Platman's (2004) research among older free-lance workers in the UK media industries produced many similar stories. All the freelancers were searching for freedom and flexibility in the latter stages of their working lives, but they were finding that they were acutely vulnerable and insecure. They were easily slipping into downward spirals of diminishing work portfolios, shrinking professional networks and lack of up-to-date skills. Most of the 'voluntary' early retirements in Vickerstaff and Cox's (2005) study had really been enforced. These authors argue that, while the opportunity to retire early was enlarging the options for some, it was also enlarging the risks that the entire age group needed to address as individuals. However, there are studies such as Elizabeth McGoldrick's (1983). She encountered little bitterness in her questionnaire survey of around 1800, and interviews with over 100, early retirees. Most of McGoldrick's sample had volunteered to retire early and only 6.5% expressed regret at having done so. These retirees were healthier and wealthier than the retired population in general. Few had taken early retirement on account of failing health. Nor had many been inhibited by serious financial worries; most had quit with attractive severance packages. Some had volunteered for early retirement in order to escape from negative aspects of their jobs – the pressure, the other people or the constant travel, or whatever else was irking the individuals concerned. However, most had been at least equally, if not more, motivated by the prospect of new lives, sometimes involving new jobs, but often based on hobbies or being able to spend more time with friends and families.

Jackson and Taylor's (1994) study of 175 unemployed men, all aged over 51, who were followed up from 1982 to 1983, offers some pointers into what separates the winners from the losers when working lives are shortened. They found that individuals with the financial and other resources to build lives and identities outside the labour market gained psychological benefits, including a feeling of being in greater control of their own lives, by considering themselves retired. Those who could not opt or had not opted for this solution to their unemployment were mostly struggling unsuccessfully to regain work.

Leisure may be hopeless as a general solution to unemployment (see Chapter 3, pp. 92–94) but this will not prevent it being part of the solution for some members of specific sections of the population. People who end their working lives ahead of or at the normal retirement age can retain the status and identities associated with their former careers. They become retired professors, plumbers or whatever. If individuals can be guaranteed pensions that secure their standards of living and if they have leisure interests to which they wish to devote more time, these may well perform some of the functions normally associated with employment – structuring time, providing activity, goals and social contact. Needless to say, when early or normal-age retirement occurs on the basis of who volunteers, it is likely that those who take the step will be those who are able to benefit by doing so. It is perhaps noteworthy that one exceptional use of free time that peaks in the older age groups is voluntary work (see p. 126), perhaps indicating that one need that other forms of leisure cannot easily meet is a need to be needed.

Leisure and later-life satisfaction

All the relevant studies show that high levels of leisure activity in later life are related to life satisfaction as self-assessed in questionnaire studies (see Box 5.2). Leisure is related to expressed life satisfaction in all age groups (see Chapter 1), but this relationship is especially strong among the elderly. It is never easy to prove whether a statistical relationship is spurious or causal and, if the latter, in which direction. It is likely that people who suffer chronic health problems will be generally less active and satisfied with life simply on account of their ailments. However, it is no less likely, and consistent with all the evidence, that older people with leisure interests that keep them busy and provide social contact will find their lives more satisfying than those who spend nearly all their time at home, watching television for 50 h or more per week. Since elderly people are less likely than other age groups to have paid jobs and heavy family responsibilities that nevertheless supply satisfying experiences, leisure differences can be expected to discriminate their general life satisfaction more powerfully than in other sections of the population.

Questions about why people differ so considerably in their levels of leisure activity in later life and why some rather than others have sufficiently strong leisure interests to tempt them into early retirement are of practical as well as academic importance. Satisfactory health and income are important for well-being in later life. These advantages will facilitate leisure activity, but they are not the whole explanation of why some of the elderly are far more leisure-active than others.

Box 5.2.   Leisure and the quality of later life.

Strong relationships between leisure participation and satisfaction with later life have been recorded in all the countries where such studies have been conducted.

In a study of 360 retired people in Puerto Rico, Nelson Melendez (1992) found that leisure activity was more strongly related to satisfaction with life than any other variables, including health and income.

A US study of 1649 over-55-year-olds found that their leisure activities were satisfying needs normally met by paid work in younger age groups (Tinsley *et al.*, 1987). Leisure was supplying companionship, opportunities for self-expression and social recognition. It was also supplying some of the sample with a sense of power since their leisure interests gave them a chance to run things. Among the over-55s, leisure could confer these benefits without individuals being niggled by the feeling that they really ought to be in paid employment.

Siegenthaler and O'Dell's (2003) study of 19 67–87-year-old golfers concluded that their serious leisure activity (playing golf) was contributing to their successful ageing.

Carpenter and Patterson's (2004) case studies of selected couples illustrate how long-term leisure interests can contribute to smooth transitions in later life.

Hawkins *et al.*'s (2004) study of 50–90-year-olds in Australia and the USA found that leisure participation (provided the activities were satisfying to those concerned) was boosting self-assessed well-being.

Leisure Careers

Most research on leisure and the life course has compared the leisure patterns and activities of different age groups and explored how these change during youth, family formation and up to and then in later life, but there is a complementary way in which life course trends in leisure can be analysed, which is to examine changes and continuities over time in the behaviour of the same individuals. Such research is not easy. Panels can be studied longitudinally, as in Walter Tokarski's (1991) study (see above, p. 153), but this type of research takes a long time before it yields longitudinal data. Fortunately, with the more structured leisure activities it has been shown that most people have sufficient powers of recall to reconstruct their leisure biographies (see Hedges, 1986). At any rate, their accounts look realistic in terms of the sex and social class differences that emerge and the overall participation rates that are indicated. This kind of research can produce quick results and it has greatly enlarged our ability to study long-term leisure careers. However, it shares one major limitation with panel studies, namely, that the social contexts may have changed considerably since people currently in later life were young, so their leisure biographies in youth and the factors that shaped them could be poor guides to what is happening today.

Massive continuities

Nevertheless, the findings from research that has traced individuals' leisure biographies are startling in the strong continuities that are revealed. In the USA, Scott and Willits (1989) restudied in later life a sample that had been surveyed initially when young, 37 years earlier, when information was collected about their uses of leisure. This research showed that the people who were involved in voluntary organizations, those who had wide circles of friends and those with intellectual and artistic interests in later life were nearly always the same individuals who had been doing these things when they were young. The exceptional people who were taking up new leisure activities in later life usually turned out to be following a lifelong pattern. Likewise those who were reducing their leisure participation following retirement had mostly been narrowing their leisure interests throughout adulthood (see also McGuire *et al.*, 1987).

The best predictor of any individual's future uses of leisure is that same person's past behaviour. This is a far better predictor than the individual's current circumstances – type of occupation, employed or unemployed, for example. An individual's past leisure behaviour usually proves an excellent predictor from day to day, week to week and, indeed, across the life span. Most of us use the relative freedom of leisure to stick to our routines. In our leisure most of us are basically conservative and become more so as we grow older. We tend to stick to familiar routines and do tried, tested and trusted things. Taking risks at play may be safe compared with the potential losses at work and in family life, but, once youth has been left behind, very little leisure behaviour is experimental.

Early leisure socialization

Personality factors can account for some of the continuities over time. Sociable people will tend to make friends throughout their lives. However, early leisure socialization appears to be extremely influential. This has been demonstrated in the arts and sport. In every country high culture is a minority interest. Everywhere nearly all the members of this minority become involved in the arts early in their lives, usually in their families, but sometimes in education. Individuals who attend classical concerts or visit art galleries regularly when they are young are very likely to continue doing these things throughout their entire lives, whereas the rest of the population is most unlikely to take to high culture during adulthood. The crucial role of early socialization into the arts and the importance of the family as a socializing milieu led the coordinators of the international study that collated the information to express pessimism about the prospects of enlarging substantially the audience for high culture (Hantrais and Kamphorst, 1987). Early exposure to the arts also appears to have further benefits that extend beyond leisure. With all other potentially influential factors controlled, Robson (2003) has shown, using data from the UK's 1970 birth cohort study, that 16-year-olds who visit libraries and museums and who take part in music-making and other cultural pursuits go on to achieve higher standards in education and subsequently achieve higher earnings and also have higher rates of civic participation in adulthood, compared with young people who are similar in all other respects except their uses of leisure.

Sport is not exactly the same. Most children play sport fairly regularly but in most cases this does not lead to lifelong sports careers or, as far as we know, to a wider range of long-term benefits. Two factors appear crucial to whether people will remain sports-active into adulthood. The first is the richness of their early sports socialization – not the sheer amount so much as the number of different sports that individuals learn to play. Young males whose skills and enthusiasm are confined to football are unlikely to have long-term sports careers. The second crucial factor is whether individuals remain in sport during their transitions from education into the labour market, marriage and parenthood. Individuals who stay in sport through these life events are likely to remain sports-active for the remainder of their adult lives. In contrast, individuals who drop out before their mid-20s are unlikely to return to sport on a permanent basis. If their sports careers are restarted, they run high risks of lapsing again. It proves much easier to keep the committed in sport than to convert 'couch potatoes' (see Roberts and Brodie, 1992). Health and fitness gyms are skilled at recruiting new members who pay upfront fees and then fail to continue attending after just a few weeks (Hickman, 2003).

The extremely low rates of participation in physically active recreation within the present-day older age groups are not due solely to their having dropped out of sport during their adult lives but also to the poverty of their childhood sports socialization and the limited opportunities that were available for them to continuing playing sport after leaving school (see Boothby *et al.*, 1981). This is a case where there have been major changes since people currently retired were young. Schoolchildren are now being introduced to a much wider range of sports than in the past, and indoor sports centres have been opened throughout the country, so young people have become much more likely to continue playing after completing their full-time education (see Roberts, 1996), though, as we saw earlier (Chapter 1, pp. 14–15), since 1996 there has been an unexpected and so far unexplained downturn in sport participation among young people.

Career development

Careers in different types of leisure may develop through a series of similar stages, but this is a topic on which far more research is required. Linda Heuser (2005) found that the bowling careers of the older women members of a Perth (Australia) bowling club had typically developed through five stages (albeit with zigzags in individual cases). The stages were:

- Introduction to the sport.
- Becoming hooked.
- Playing regularly, and probably becoming 'serious' about it (in Stebbins's sense; see Chapter 1, pp. 8–9).
- Taking on organizational roles.
- Retiring, but retaining the sport as a base for social life and the experience of belonging to a community.

Gary Crawford's (2003) research among supporters of the Manchester Storm (a UK ice hockey team) found that the fans' careers typically developed through broadly similar stages:

- Becoming interested.
- Becoming engaged.
- Becoming enthusiastic.
- Possibly becoming a 'professional' supporter by writing about the sport or taking on a role in a supporters' association.

Implications for leisure providers

Promoters of particular forms of leisure appear well advised when they target the young, but the contrasts between the arts (where rich childhood socialization alone appears to be a sufficient foundation for long-term interest) and sport (where breadth is necessary and dropout during young adulthood remains common) suggest that the details of a success strategy will depend on the type of leisure. Since it is impossible for every adult to be a frequent participant in every kind of leisure, different promoters may partly cancel out each other's efforts. However, some adults succeed in doing more than others with similar resources. Many older persons lead limited leisure lives partly because they have few interests on which to draw. The findings from research into long-term leisure careers suggest that this situation can be changed, but the bad news is that achieving major changes in the population's leisure habits is more likely to take decades than months or years.

The best recipe for spreading any use of leisure and maintaining participation at a high level appears to be, first, to ensure that children are introduced to the skills and the satisfactions that are available and then, secondly, to ensure that they remain active for long enough to become locked in not just by routine but through organizational memberships and social commitments and a desire to continue to benefit from what they know are reliable sources of satisfying experiences (see Roberts *et al.*, 1991a). This same recipe seems likely to work equally well in religion and politics.

The reasons for the higher socio-economic strata's general tendency to do more include their early leisure socialization. Middle-class homes where the parents have wide-ranging leisure interests are rich learning environments. Higher education can be particularly valuable in extending young adults' leisure interests and skills and maintaining their involvement into their 20s. The unemployed have low rates of participation in out-of-home leisure not just on account of their immediate circumstances but also because the sections of the workforce at the greatest risk of unemployment (the least qualified and least skilled) have the lowest levels of leisure activity. Retired professionals are active in more forms of leisure than retired manual workers partly because the former were already doing more prior to retirement.

Up to now, childhood and youth have been the main life stages for leisure capital formation. This is not to suggest that leisure learning ceases once individuals become adult. Skills and interests may continue to be acquired throughout life, but in adulthood, as opposed to childhood, the learning is likely to be deliberate and conscious (see Erickson, 1996). The key point is that adults do not learn haphazardly but incrementally, on the basis of existing skills and interests. This is why childhood and youth leisure socialization are crucial. Most people base the rest of their leisure lives on interests, which may subsequently be built upon, to which they were initially introduced when young. This would change if the life course were totally destandardized. Leisure learning would then become equally likely at any age. In practice, however, destandardization is not being, and cannot be, pushed this far. Marriage and parenthood continue to trigger a leisure squeeze. The general tendency in later life is still for people to narrow down their existing leisure interests and activities. Wider social and economic trends have not shattered any of the main leisure patterns – the gender differences, the tendency for the economically privileged to do more of most things, or childhood and youth being the life stages where the foundations are laid for long-term leisure careers. As with financial arrangements, the best time to begin preparing for leisure in later life appears to be as young as possible.

The evidence from long-term sports and arts careers may foster pessimism about the prospect of policy initiatives or anything else achieving quick changes in the population's leisure patterns, but the long-term prospects are far more encouraging. In the future it is likely that leisure will supply many people's most dependable threads throughout the life course – social relationships, activities and satisfactions on which they know they can rely in societies where so many other things have ceased to be reliable. People's leisure is affected by life events, but in turn their leisure habits affect individuals' ability to cope. We have seen (see Chapter 3, pp. 91–92) that, if leisure activities are maintained during unemployment, this is good for the well-being of those concerned and that the unemployed are far more likely to persist with existing uses of leisure than to start anything from scratch. Likewise, later life satisfaction depends largely on the leisure skills and interests that individuals carry with them from earlier life stages. The leisure careers evidence points to the counterproductivity of seeking quick results from policy interventions. It shows that secure and lasting effects need a long-term strategy. Whether we wish to use the findings is a different matter, but leisure research tells us how to widen the entire population's leisure repertoires and, in the long term, boost overall levels of leisure activity in all social categories.

Summary

This chapter began by noting the main trends in leisure behaviour over the life course. We saw that youth is the time of peak participation in many leisure activities – entertainment and culture, sport and outdoor activities, travel and alcohol consumption. New household and family formation triggers a leisure squeeze. In later life, participation recovers somewhat, but only in a fairly narrow range of activities – hobbies and games, listening to music and to the radio, watching television and videos/DVDs, reading, resting, socializing and voluntary work.

We then saw how, over time, life courses have become less orderly, less standardized and less predictable for individuals, and how most major steps in life have become more risk-laden. Youth has been prolonged overall, and it has also become more variable in length and youth biographies have been individualized. It is hardly surprising, therefore, that present-day youth cultures differ in important ways from their counterparts of the 1950s and 1960s. Yet, despite this, there are some massive continuities, especially in the distinctive functions that leisure performs in young people's lives – enabling them to establish adult-like independence, and learning how to play sexualized roles, express sexual feelings and develop sexual identities. Also, during youth there is still the same progression as 50 years ago from adult-led to peer-group-based leisure, then towards developing and spending time in personal networks of friends, and from leisure based in the family, through voluntary associations, to commercial provisions. Young people's leisure continues to trigger adult panics. Parenthood and new household formation have not ceased to squeeze the time and money that are available for adults' own leisure interests. During adulthood, uses of leisure become home- and family-centred. Family instability usually intensifies and prolongs 'the squeeze'. Most people appear to look forward to later life for the expected opportunities to do things that they really want to do, and in later life leisure activity becomes a major influence on overall life satisfaction. Unfortunately, most of the kinds of leisure where older people begin to do more are home-based and informal, and the overall trend is still for leisure participation to decline as people move into and then through later life. Historical changes in the character of the life course – destandardization, individualization, etc. – do not appear to have undermined any of the long-standing life stage features of leisure.

The chapter concluded by examining individuals' leisure careers. It explained how most of us build incrementally upon, while progressively discarding and narrowing down, skills and tastes first acquired when we were young. Childhood and youth are the critical life stages for building up lifetime stocks of leisure capital. Some people develop long-term careers – serious careers – in particular uses of leisure. However, once interests have been dropped, they are rarely revived. In adulthood we are much more likely to continue practising existing life interests than to try something completely new or even to restart an activity that was dropped earlier in life. The reasons why so many older people's leisure is so limited include the narrow stocks of leisure capital they built up when young and the loss of some of this capital during the adulthood squeeze. There are answers here as to why, despite the now well-established ability of leisure activity to enhance well-being, the general growth of leisure in recent decades has not made people any happier in the world's wealthiest countries.

Further Reading

The classic book, still well worth reading, on leisure throughout the life cycle

Rapoport, R. and Rapoport, R.N. (1975) *Leisure and the Family Life-Cycle*. Routledge, London.

On contemporary youth cultures

Hollands, R.G. (1995) *Friday Night, Saturday Night.* Department of Social Policy, University of Newcastle, Newcastle upon Tyne, UK.

MacRae, R. (2004) Notions of 'us' and 'them': markers of stratification in clubbing lifestyles. *Journal of Youth Studies* 7, 55–71.

Sweeting, H. and West, P. (2003) Young people's leisure and risk-taking behaviours: change in gender patterning in the west of Scotland during the 1990s. *Journal of Youth Studies* 6, 391–412.

Thornton, S. (1995) *Club Cultures: Music, Media and Subcultural Capital.* Polity Press, Cambridge, UK.

On changes in leisure and typical patterns and problems during adulthood

Smith, J. (1987) Women at play: gender, the life cycle and leisure. In: Horne, J., Jary, D. and Tomlinson, A. (eds) *Sport, Leisure and Social Relations.* Routledge, London.

Sullivan, O. (1996) Time co-ordination, the domestic division of labour and affective relations: time use and the enjoyment of activities within couples. *Sociology*, 30, 79–100.

On leisure in later life

Hawkins, B., Foose, A.K. and Binkley, A.L. (2004) Contribution of leisure to the life satisfaction of older adults in Australia and the United States. *World Leisure Journal*
46(2), 4–12.

Wearing, B. (1995) Leisure and resistance in an ageing society. *Leisure Studies* 14,
263–279.

On long-term leisure careers

Heuser, L. (2005) We're not too old to play sports: the career of women lawn bowlers.
Leisure Studies 24, 45–60.

Roberts, K., Minten, J.H., Chadwick, C., Lamb, K.L. and Brodie, D.A. (1991a) Sporting
lives: a case study of leisure careers. *Society and Leisure* 14, 261–284.

Scott, D. and Willits, F.K. (1989) Adolescent and adult leisure patterns: a 37 year follow-up
study. *Leisure Sciences* 11, 323–335.

6   Lifestyles and Identities

Introduction

The development of leisure-based lifestyles that act as a source of identities, which in turn are capable of igniting 'political' action, is the latest version of the 'society of leisure' thesis (for older versions see Dumazedier, 1967, 1974, 1989). Growth has always been a theme in texts on leisure, and rightly so; this book is no exception in this respect. The uncontested sense in which leisure has grown is that we now have more of the same – more leisure time, rising participation rates in leisure activities and more money being spent on them – all easily measured and the growth is easy to demonstrate. Beyond this, however, it has been argued recurrently that leisure is also expanding qualitatively by taking on new functions. This has always been much more difficult to prove. The senses in which leisure was supposed to become not just larger but also more central, pivotal, in our lives, have changed over time. One prediction was that an old work ethic would be replaced by a leisure ethic, meaning that, instead of valuing people according to their occupations, we would begin judging each other according to our leisure tastes and achievements. Unemployment would have ceased to be so destructive an experience and we would probably have witnessed a flight from paid work if such a trend really had occurred (see Chapter 3, pp. 85–95). Another forecast was that, instead of leisure time being residual, what remained after more important tasks had been completed, leisure time would become pivotal and that we would begin organizing our family lives and paid work schedules around our leisure interests and commitments: no sign yet of this version of the society of leisure! Another version envisaged leisure values – doing things for their own sake, for the intrinsic satisfaction – invading other areas of life. A recent variant of this argument suggests that 'game-ization' is under way, that we are turning work, shopping and virtually everything else into playful games (Kravchenko, 2004). However, the currently fashionable version of the emergent 'society of leisure' adopts a rather different line. It argues that lifestyles based upon or incorporating leisure activities are becoming principal sources of our identities – who we think we are and how we are identified by others. As we shall see, the stronger alleged role of leisure in identity formation may or may not be at the expense of older foundations – occupation, social class, sex/gender, place/ nationality/ethnicity and religion. This chapter assesses whether this particular version is more plausible than older visions of society of leisure. If true, we will have another possible explanation for the failure of the growth of leisure to make us more satisfied with our lives. Maybe we spend too much of our leisure constructing ourselves and too little simply being and enjoying ourselves.

This chapter proceeds by outlining different definitions and typologies of lifestyles. It then examines the so-called postmodern identity problem, to which identities arising from leisure-based lifestyles could be, but will not necessarily be, a solution. Next, the evidence for the existence of present-day lifestyle groups is presented, leading to a discussion of whether these are likely to replace or to be blended with older sources of identity.

Lifestyles: Definitions and Typologies

Max Weber, 1864–1920

An examination of leisure and lifestyles really has to begin with Max Weber. This is not merely because this founding father of modern sociology wrote a great deal about styles of life: his statement of the key issues has proved strikingly prescient of current claims about the role of leisure and lifestyles in constructing social positions and identities.

Much of Max Weber's work can only be understood as a debate with Marx: some say the ghost of Marx since it was the Marxism of the late 19th and early 20th centuries rather than Karl Marx's own works with which Weber was directly engaged. Marx was then regarded as having propounded a mono-dimensional view of social stratification, in which other inequalities, of political power, for example, were seen as arising from an economic class base. Weber, in contrast, argued that classes, status groups and political parties arose in separate domains of social stratification, which were interdependent but irreducible to one another (see Gerth and Wright Mills, 1948). He defined classes as economic formations. In Weber's view, classes were normally formed in marketplaces, in labour markets in the case of the classes to which the working population belonged, whereas status groups could be identified by the degrees of prestige or honour that were attached to their styles of life. Expressed rather crudely, but highlighting the main points, it might be said that Weber believed that their class positions depended on how people earned their money, while their status depended on how they spent it. Weber believed that the Indian caste system illustrated the processes of status group formation, but his main example from his own society (Germany) was the *Junkers*, the counterparts of the English aristocracy, whose way of life had a status that industrialists, whatever their fortunes, could never match.

Weber realized, of course, that class advantages could be converted into status, that some lifestyles required an outlay that set them beyond the means of many classes of people and that status could be used to advantage in economic markets. He did not claim that class and status were completely independent. However, he insisted that neither was wholly reducible to or arose directly and automatically from the other. Weber believed that the relative importance of classes and status groups could vary from time to time and place to place. So in periods of severe economic dislocation and change he suggested that class divisions and interests might become prominent whereas in periods of relative tranquillity status groups could become more important as sources of interests and political action.

Neo-Weberians

Subsequently even Weber's sociological admirers have not always remained strictly faithful to his original concept of status groups. The term neo-Weberian has often been applied loosely to any non-functionalist, non-Marxist sociology. Market, work and status situations have sometimes been treated as different components of occupational stratification. Such treatment is often described as neo-Weberian, and likewise when occupational classes are defined in terms of their prestige or social standing. American sociologists have commonly used such a concept of occupational class. The American 'leisure class', about which Thorstein Veblen (1857–1929) wrote caustically, was a status group in the Weberian sense, identified by its conspicuous consumption. Veblen (1925) was critical of this group's role and influence, but he was equally scathing about America's predatory and parasitic capitalist businesses. His hope was that the status of engineers would rise and that there would be a revival of the 'instinct of workmanship'. In Britain until 1981, the Registrar General's social classes were supposed to be based on occupations' social standing. Subsequently it was claimed (by the Registrar General's office, prompted by the government of the day) that the classes in fact represented skill levels. Academic sociologists had always been suspicious of this official class scheme because the groupings had never been based on comprehensive and systematic research into occupations' social standing or skill requirements, and in 1994 the Economic and Social Research Council accepted a brief to propose an alternative official scheme. The scheme proposed (see Rose and O'Reilly, 1997), and adopted as the UK's official class scheme in 1998, is a slightly modified version of a scheme originally developed by John Goldthorpe in the 1970s in the course of a large-scale study of social mobility. Each of the eight classes in the new official scheme is defined by its distinctive mix of work and (labour) market situations. Despite this, commentators often present the classes as if they represented a skill hierarchy (which they do not). Class has become unfashionable: present-day politicians and many other commentators prefer to avoid the word. Alongside the class scheme, Goldthorpe has identified, and developed procedures for measuring, a status order that proves to be related to but distinct from class positions (Chan and Goldthorpe, 2004).

Current debates on lifestyles have returned to the issues on which Weber himself wished to focus. Earlier chapters have identified a series of changes that have arguably weakened (though certainly not eradicated) the predictive power of types of employment, sex and age as regards people's uses of leisure. The expansion of leisure itself, the growth in the amounts of time and money that people have available for leisure, has enlarged their capacity to use these resources in a variety of ways. Hence the plausibility of claims that people are now able to use leisure, along with other resources, to construct styles of life that have to be compatible with but need not be closely or directly shaped by their types of jobs, ages or sex roles. Rather than age, sex and occupational groups each having a given 'way of life', some writers claim that members of all these groups now have greater scope to construct preferred 'styles of life', which may then become the most significant markers of their social positions and identities. Unlike in the neo-Marxist critique of consumer culture (see Chapter 7), this lifestyle theory puts 'the people' in charge of their own lives, using commercial and other goods and services for their own creative purposes. This is the attractive side of the lifestyle scenario. It is suggested that through the lifestyles they construct people can become almost whoever they want.

Clearly, lifestyle groups are not new. Weber wrote about them. There is a long history of dandies, flappers, bohemians and so on. The Victorian professional gentleman was recognized by his appearance and lifestyle rather than merely by knowledge of his occupation. Then there are the youth cultures, which now have a long history (see Chapter 5, pp. 134–142). However, it is claimed that, on the one hand, the growth of leisure means that more people have the time and money to fashion or adopt lifestyles if they so wish, and that, on the other, nowadays most of us are experiencing an unprecedented need to do so since older foundations of social identities are crumbling fast.

Definitions

Since Weber, numerous definitions of lifestyle have been offered, usually adding precision to Weber's concept but in a variety of different ways. Conceptual dissent is, of course, quite common in the social sciences. There are alternative definitions of politics, the family and social class, not to mention leisure (see Chapter 8). Tony Veal (1993) has reviewed the lifestyle literature and discovered numerous definitions – almost as many as there are authors. However, it is possible to identify a more limited number of axes of disagreement. One is whether lifestyles are to be treated as individual or group phenomena. Some authors have used the term to identify the ways of life that express different personalities, so extroverts are said to lead extroverted lifestyles, and so on. Other definitions treat lifestyles as properties of groups such as young upwardly mobile professional people (yuppies) and well-off older people (woopies). Another disagreement is whether lifestyles are to be identified solely in terms of how people behave or whether attitudes and values are to be included. A further disagreement is over what can be included in a lifestyle. Should lifestyles be defined to include everything that people do – their jobs, politics and religious affiliations, for example, as well as their family patterns, types of housing and leisure activities?

Conceptual dissensus does not always indicate disagreement on what exists 'out there' in society and people's everyday lives. Sociological and psychological concepts are tools for looking at and analysing real situations but are not usually intended to mirror everything or anything faithfully. They deliberately focus on particular features and processes, and the definitions selected always depend largely on the analysts' purposes. Social psychologists, who are interested in the relationships between personality traits and leisure behaviour, are likely to find it useful to define lifestyles as properties of individuals. Sociologists who propose alternative definitions are not necessarily disputing that some leisure differences arise from individual personality factors. For sociologists, however, it will usually be more appropriate to employ the lifestyle concept to identify uses of leisure that tend to 'go together' and characterize a particular social group (Gattas *et al.*, 1987). This is a sensible use of the lifestyle concept, given sociologists' purposes. Sue Glyptis (1981), for instance, has examined the extent to which the leisure of people who visit the countryside regularly differs in additional ways from the life-styles of the rest of the population. No one has absolute authority to assert how any term must be used. Concepts cannot be appropriated as the private property of sociologists, psychologists or anyone else. However, at some point, everyone has to justify their concepts by demonstrating that they lead to significant findings. This is how conceptual disputes are normally resolved.

Tony Veal (1993) has proposed a definition of lifestyle that will accommo-date most uses, which is both a strength and a weakness: 'Lifestyle is the distinc-tive pattern of personal or social behaviour characteristic of an individual or a group.' The problem with this and other common denominator definitions is that it is too bland to serve anyone's purposes. If, as in the current chapter, the issue is whether leisure today enables people to develop lifestyles that then act as bases for their identities – who they believe they are and how others see them – a particular kind of definition of lifestyle is required. Lifestyles that confer social identities will necessarily be group phenomena, a 'modern form of status group-ing,' according to David Chaney (1996, p. 14). Also, the meanings of behaviour, rather than just the behaviour itself, must be included in the definition. It will be sensible to define lifestyles as composed of meaningful behaviour over which individuals have some significant short-term choice, such as their leisure-time activities. So age, sex and occupation will not be recognized as possible bases for lifestyles in the following discussion, or as part of the definition, though this does not exclude the possibility of people adopting lifestyles that attribute specific meanings to their age, gender or type of employment. The yuppies, if they exist, identify themselves through the places where they congregate (wine bars, for example) and their clothing (smart business attire), from which their types of employment may be (correctly or incorrectly) inferred. The employment itself, however, is insufficient to offer membership of the lifestyle group. Similarly, woopies (well-off older people) are identified through their high levels of leisure spending and activities; chronological age and wealth alone do not confer the social identity. As Tony Veal (1993) has noted, this is the crucial difference between the 'ways of life' that have hitherto arisen among groups surrounded by

the distinctive constraints and opportunities associated with their types of employment, ages and sex roles, and the 'styles of life' or 'lifestyles' that some but probably not all members of such groups, and maybe individuals from several such
groups, are nowadays said to be able to construct or adopt through their own
choices.

Typologies

Seeking a definitive and comprehensive list of lifestyle groups would be setting
oneself or expecting someone else to accomplish an impossible task. First, if lifestyles are chosen or constructed by the actors, the lifestyle 'map' is likely to be
extremely fluid. One would expect some lifestyle groups always to be in the process of formation, some becoming more sharply defined and others fading away.
Any map is unlikely to remain reliable for long. Secondly, the chances are that
different groups will use different combinations of music, clothing, beverages,
sport, the arts and so on in constructing their lifestyles. So the lifestyle map at
any point in time is likely to be chaotic rather than tidy. Thirdly, it is unlikely that
all members of the public will identify themselves or be identified with any particular lifestyle groups. When young people have been invited to describe their
own subcultural affiliations the majority have always insisted that they are
just 'normal' or 'ordinary' (Brown, 1987; Willis *et al.*, 1988; and see Chapter 5,
pp. 136–137). This seems certain to apply among adults. One would expect lifestyles to appear almost haphazardly, some growing in prominence and others
fading on the sociocultural landscape, with many, probably most, members
of the public positioning themselves as detached, though possibly interested,
observers. However, if lifestyles are of increasing importance as sources of social
positions and identities, one would expect there to be a historical trend towards a
growing proportion of the population seeing themselves as belonging to such
groups and a related trend towards the groups becoming more stable, more
clearly defined and more easily identified.

There are lifestyle typologies – several have been developed and used – but
in most cases these do not identify specific lifestyles but lifestyle clusters. These
may be identified theoretically by analysts who guess that particular processes or
divisions are likely to be important and then use the typologies in their own
investigations or hope that someone else will do so. For example, Koch-Weser
(1990) has developed one lifestyle typology based on different mixtures of
choice and constraint and a second set of ad hoc types – media-dominated,
intellectual inner-directed, convivial tradition-directed, and restrained. However,
the value of these schemes has yet to be tested in research. Other typologies
have been constructed and used in market research. For instance, the ACORN
typology (a classification of residential neighbourhoods) is a British scheme that
groups districts according to their residents' socio-economic standing, types of
dwellings and tenure and age and household composition. This typology can be
used to predict the likely demand for and the use that is likely to be made of
leisure facilities ranging from sports centres to wine bars and arts centres. Tony
Veal (1989) describes this and several other market research typologies in the

course of advocating status and lifestyle as a pluralist alternative to Marxist class analysis in the investigation of leisure differences. The socio-economic classifications of UK market researchers that distinguish ABs, C1s, C2s and so on are useful for identifying the motivations and spending patterns of the sections of the population that should be able to afford given products and, therefore, how these should be designed and marketed so as to maximize their appeal within the relevant groups. These and other typologies have to be judged by whether they serve the intended purposes, but these do not include delineating lifestyle groups with which real people identify. There can be very few people, if any, who regard themselves or are identified by others as ABs or C2s. Market research has also identified general lifestyle trends, such as a recent concern for health and fitness. In the 1950s and 1960s sociologists noted a trend towards home-centredness. These trends are not lifestyle groups, though they may serve as a base for such groups' formation. Indeed, the identification of trends in how people live may be a useful first step towards investigating the development and adoption of and identification with particular lifestyles within specific sections of a population.

The Postmodern Identity Problem

The weakening of modern structures

The possibility of using leisure to formulate identities is said to have been extended through the growth of leisure. The need to use lifestyles in this way is said to have spread through the erosion of older traditional and modern sources of identity. Features of high, late or postmodernity (depending on the author's preferred terminology) are said to include a weakening of former structures and a blurring of older divisions. The globalization of economic relationships and cultural flows and the spread of information technology are usually held to be deeply implicated in these trends (see Featherstone, 1988, 1991; Hughes, 1993). Former fixtures in local and national social and economic landscapes are said to have become vulnerable. Flexibility, it is claimed, has become part of the price of survival for businesses, workers and, indeed, entire countries. It is argued that the basis of contemporary economic life is no longer the production of material goods by businesses embedded in specific industries and places but is best conceptualized in terms of 'flows', increasingly of goods and services whose value, like money, is primarily symbolic (Lash and Urry, 1994). In these circumstances, companies' sites, and workers' occupations and careers even more so, lose their former solidity. Work ceases to be something to be done reliably at particular times and places. Occupations can no longer be relied on. Alongside these trends in economic life, it can be argued that sex roles have become more diverse, and likewise age roles. A consequence, it is claimed, is that neither sex, age nor employment, even in combination, remain good predictors of how people will spend their leisure. Another consequence, it is argued, is that everyday life becomes fragile and the old social markers (age, sex and occupation) cease to supply 'given' identities (Giddens, 1991; Laermans, 1994). Likewise the expansion of international flows of people, goods, services and symbols and the rise of transnational companies and organizations such as the North Atlantic Treaty Organization (NATO), the EU, the International Monetary Fund (IMF) and the World Bank are said to be weakening nation states and undermining the certainties that national and kindred affiliations, such as ethnicity and religion, formerly offered. 'Fundamentalists' attempt to defend these heritages while others look elsewhere for answers to the fundamental identity questions: 'Who am I?' 'Who are we?' 'Which "we" do "I" belong to?' 'What are our interests?'

Modern social structures created deep divisions, advantages and disadvantages, but, it is currently argued, people knew their places and with whom they shared interests. An outcome could be fierce conflicts: wars between nations and, within countries, class conflicts in industry and politics. Individuals may have been discontented but they knew what they were discontented about and who their allies and enemies were. Nowadays it is claimed that these older certainties have disintegrated: that nationality, age, sex and occupation no longer give individuals clear positions, interests and identities.

How much credence to attach to this diagnosis of the current condition of (Western) humanity is open to debate. We have seen in previous chapters that there have been changes in employment, gender and age roles, all with implications for leisure, but to what extent have these roles become more fragile? Let us suppose, for present purposes, that the changes do create an identity problem. The need for a leisure solution depends on this supposition.

New options

Compared with the earlier industrial or modern age and times before, many people today have more money and some have more time at their disposal, and we are all surrounded by a plethora of consumer industries supplying goods and services rich with symbolic meanings as well as material uses. This, it is argued, presents possibilities for people to create identities according to what, where, when and how they consume (Featherstone, 1991). Numerous writers have made this claim in recent years (see Box 6.1).

This interpretation of consumer behaviour offers a more attractive picture of consumption and consumers than critiques of consumer culture that portray people as passive and manipulated (see Chapter 7). The identity construction interpretation credits people with the scope and capacity to choose, and portrays them as creative architects of identities that are assembled by making appropriate selections from the 'modules' of consumer goods and services that are available, or which can be generated in the voluntary, commercial or public sectors or privately.

The recent claims of some leisure scholars about the larger and stronger role that leisure now plays in identity formation are paralleled elsewhere in sociology by arguments about occupational classes being replaced by consumption cleavages as sources of collective interests and political partisanship. In political sociology it has been argued that there has been a process of class de-alignment (Crewe, 1989) when class is measured in the conventional way, by occupation,

---

Box 6.1. Consumption: the new structuring principle.

Pekka Sulkanen (1997), a Finnish social scientist, claims that consumption has now become the main process structuring or patterning people's lives. She claims that our actions are now governed primarily by a search for happiness, so behaviour is more likely to be expressive (of our feelings) rather than instrumental (geared to a more distant goal). She argues that nowadays we relate to one another primarily via the 'tribes' we choose to join by virtue of what, when and where we consume, and that the cohesion of these groups is essentially emotional rather than based on rational calculations of mutual interests.

David Chaney (1996) acknowledges that consumption-based lifestyles pre-date the 20th century, but argues that their development has accelerated with the spread of mass consumption.

According to Robert Bocock (1993, p. x), 'Consumption now affects the ways in which people build up, and maintain, a sense of who they are, and who they wish to be. It has become entwined with the processes surrounding the development of an identity.'

Alan Warde (1995) has pointed out that attributing such importance to consumption opens the possibility of individuals committing suicide (with their identities) every time they shop. By changing one's consumption style, it would appear possible to obliterate an old identity and acquire a replacement, though no one is obliged to be born again repeatedly.

---

and that the more significant social cleavages increasingly pivot around consumption factors such as housing (whether people own their own homes or rent) and whether people are able to purchase and actually purchase health care, education, transport and social security privately as opposed to relying on state services (Saunders, 1990).

These arguments provide a useful reminder that lifestyles are not based on leisure alone (unless a very broad definition of leisure is adopted). People can also make lifestyle choices by virtue of where they choose to live, their types of dwellings and the vehicles they drive. It is also important to recognize that occupations, age and sex are not necessarily or even likely to be eliminated totally from the processes of identity formation. No one has made so extreme a claim. Rather, one claim is that the trend is towards these statuses being given meanings by the actors' lifestyles rather than operating as determinants of each group's identity and therefore its members' uses of leisure. Frank Mort (1996) has claimed that when commerce targeted the young affluent male consumer in the 1950s the market was pre-structured in that the young males in question already possessed core identities and purchasing predispositions, arising from the neighbourhoods where they lived, the schools they attended, the jobs they entered and the peer groups in which they thereby became involved. By the 1980s, in contrast, Mort argues that advertisers and the media more generally were playing more active roles in actually constructing images of masculinity which, above all else, were associated with lifestyles based on particular sorts of clothing, leisure activities and places. As lifestyles become more important to people, the sociocultural value of goods and services, rather than their mundane uses, is said to become paramount, and symbolic capital and a particular kind of communicative competence are said to become vital assets (see Chaney, 1996).

A leisure solution?

There is a big problem with the suggestion that leisure (or consumption) can be a source of solutions to the problems posed by the destablization of older social markers. Writers on postmodernity who have identified forces that are destabilizing employment, gender and age roles have sometimes gone on to argue that leisure will be affected by the same new technologies and the same globalization that are transforming other life domains. In a world where everything else changes rapidly, leisure is unlikely to be an oasis of stability. There is a substantial but maybe healthy measure of conscious exaggeration in most portraits of a post-modern condition. Writers focus on and extrapolate specific trends and tenden-cies. This can still be useful for highlighting specific developments, provided no one forgets the distortions that are being introduced. This certainly applies when characteristics of postmodern leisure are listed. These should not be viewed as even near descriptions of what present-day leisure is actually like so much as characteristics that may grow in prominence alongside a broader postmodern condition. With this proviso, three features of postmodern leisure, all supposedly increasingly evident, have been identified by a series of writers (see, for example, Denzin, 1991; Laermans, 1994; Maffesoli, 1994; Rojek, 1995).

First, it is claimed that leisure places and experiences are becoming decontextualized. For example, it has become possible to enjoy simulated tro-pical holiday environments in cold-climate countries, while theme parks can cre-ate safari conditions or the Wild West in any place. The Internet allows us to communicate with others irrespective of their locations (provided they have the technology). Virtual reality technology may soon allow people to experience any situations, irrespective of their physical locations: hence the alleged appearance of the 'post-tourist' who finds actual travel tiresome, grows weary of being shown especially arranged spectacles and relies on TV travel programmes and suchlike to reveal places as they really are and what the live tourist will be and will not be allowed to see. In a similar way, so-called 'post-fans' may follow sports teams primarily 'on the box', whose presentations are regarded as 'the real thing', for which attending matches is a poor substitute. Distinctions between the real, imitation and fiction may thereby break down. Soap opera dramas and characters are reported in newspapers and discussed as if they were real. Another manifestation of the loss of 'grounding' is said to be that the (fictional) public images of celebrities, living and dead, exert a powerful hold on people's consciousness.

Secondly, in postmodern conditions it is claimed that cultural commodities and their meanings change constantly. Everything speeds up and leisure envi-ronments become discontinuous and fragmented. This, it is said, leaves people feeling insecure and that nothing can be relied on. In these circumstances people may see no reason to assume that things must remain or will remain as they are.

They are likely to feel at risk and to become sensitive to the harm that they might suffer from the foods they eat and the environments in which they work and play. Identities based on postmodern leisure are likely to be fragmented and chronically unstable. Indeed, the postmodern citizen at leisure has been portrayed as perpetually anxious, insecure, restless and unable to settle: a voyeur adrift in a sea of symbols (Denzin, 1991). Ulrich Beck and Elisabeth Beck-Gernsheim (1995) have described a similar situation as individualization and the weakening of older structures enable men and women to relate on more equal terms, to develop 'pure relationships' and to seek in each other love and warmth in an otherwise uncaring world. Meanwhile, it is argued, couples' individual commitments, in the labour market, for example, are pulling them apart like never before. It has been suggested that people can react to such conditions in several ways. One is social and emotional disengagement. Another is to escape into fantasy – to abandon oneself to postmodern experience. Another is to seek security and belonging in the 'new tribes' or 'proto-communities' that develop around cultural products such as sports teams and musical genres. As already mentioned, there is a measure of conscious exaggeration in all this. No one really believes that consumers are distressed and anxious every time they make a purchase, fearful that the lifestyle for which they are opting will disappear or be degraded. As Alan Warde (1994) has pointed out, consumers have an array of coping strategies such as relying on the judgements of close friends. The crucial point is that, if older social structures are being subjected to flexibilization, leisure may become an arena in which individuals try to restore order and stability to their lives, but, if so, these efforts are liable to be undermined by the same trends and conditions that prompted the attempts.

Thirdly, the collapse of modern structures is said to lead to people's concerns for beauty, appearance and pleasurable experience breaking out of leisure time and infiltrating their working lives, family lives, shopping expeditions and so forth (Lash and Urry, 1994). People thus become sensitive to the design of the furniture in their homes and offices, and even the cans and bottles in which they purchase all manner of commodities. David Chaney (1996) argues that, as lifestyles shape our selves and sensibilities and as everyday life is aestheticized, we find constant reasons to worry about our own surface appearances and about the meaning of other people's appearances, and constantly feel that our identities are at risk.

One might protest that the above sketches of postmodern leisure stray far beyond the bounds of useful exaggeration and bear little resemblance to most people's lives: that few people spend much time in virtual reality situations or theme parks, that most people know the difference between the real and the fictional and, in any case, that none of the features attributed to postmodern leisure are really novel. Earlier generations escaped into fantasy at circuses and fairgrounds, in music halls and cinemas. The appeal of Jesus shows that fascination with the dead pre-dates modernity. The crucial point is that, if postmodernizing trends really are undermining familiar sources of identities, leisure is unlikely to prove a safe refuge. The 'hyper-differentiation' that is a feature of some versions of our postmodern condition (see Box 6.2, p. 181) is said to leave individuals adrift without any stable, core identities, continuously reinventing themselves as they move from situation to situation and with the passage of time. However, there is another interpretation of our current transformed social condition – the reflexive modernization version (see Box 6.2, p. 181), which claims that people are still able to construct stable identities but must do this reflexively, that is, consciously and deliberately, from the various positions that they occupy and the resources at their disposal.

Plausible claims

We need to be realistic about the extent and ways in which leisure may have become more thoroughly implicated and possibly central in creating and maintaining our social identities. First, this will not involve all leisure behaviour (or consumption), much of which is private or has no generally agreed symbolic significance. Our purchases of motor fuel and car insurance, the food that we eat at home, the books and magazines we read and the television programmes we watch do not send out any clear signals to other people, in some cases, or any signals at all, in others, about the kinds of people we are. Colin Campbell (1995) has ridiculed some of the more extravagant claims about the significance of present-day consumption. He accuses writers of attributing symbolic meanings to behaviour that is really mundane. Campbell claims that most purchases do not have any definite meanings. Buying flowers for a woman is probably an exception. What, though, he asks, is the significance of wearing blue jeans to go shopping? Campbell shows that most members of the public are hopeless at judging even the prices of most things, let alone at reading some agreed symbolic significance into other people's and their own purchases and possessions.

Secondly, specific leisure interests and activities are unlikely to supply identities that are recognized in most social contexts. All social roles confer identities, but these can be specific to the times when we engage in the activities and among the people with whom we interact on these occasions. Being a fan of a sports team is an identity (see Crawford, 2004), but, even if one is a serious fan, how are one's neighbours and work colleagues to know this and, if they do, what significance are they supposed to attach to the knowledge? Lifestyle sports (otherwise known as extreme or alternative sports) confer identities (see Wheaton, 2004), but how widely do such identities travel? Some leisure identities are adopted vicariously, as weekend fun. This applied to the Dutch Death Metal fans who were studied by Wendy Eygendaal (1992). Even leisure about which the participants are serious may be meaningless in most social contexts. What difference is it supposed to make if I know that a neighbour or work colleague is a regular surfer or canoeist?

Thirdly, sections of the public will vary in their need and ability to develop identity-conferring uses of leisure. Graham Murdock (1994) has pointed out that minorities, but substantial minorities, of the present-day populations, even in the rich West, remain completely excluded from the consumer society. They are prevented by sheer poverty from developing preferred identities by purchasing appropriate clothing and being seen in the right places. Lunt and Livingstone (1992) conducted a detailed study of the shopping practices of 279 adults in southern England. This sample was questioned about their attitudes towards saving, borrowing, debt and possessions, on their ideas about what was a luxury and what was a necessity, as well as about where and when they shopped and what they bought. From their analysis of this evidence, Lunt and Livingstone concluded that no more than a quarter of the sample could be described as life-style shoppers. The rest were making nearly all their purchases in customary ways to meet their needs. This also applied to the Glasgow households on post-war private and council estates who were questioned about their home fur-nishings by Madigan and Munro (1996). Hardly any of these consumers had ever gone shopping for a style that would give their homes and themselves a dis-tinctive identity. Most had built up their stocks of furnishings over the years and possessed a mixture of styles. Rather than seeking homes that would align them with wider lifestyle groups, this sample invoked family values. Above all, they wanted homes that felt comfortable and yet looked tidy.

Fourthly and finally, meaningful and widely recognized social identities are more likely to be associated with clusters of uses of leisure rather than single activities, and, in identity construction, these are more likely to be blended with than to entirely replace identities associated with types of employment, gender and age. It is in the course of such blending that uses of leisure may (if indeed they are doing this) obliterate certain older divisions while creating new social cleavages and blocs that may be mobilized into political action.

Present-day Lifestyles

As argued above (pp. 168–169), it is impossible to offer and unrealistic to expect either an exhaustive typology of lifestyles or a comprehensive lifestyle map of contemporary society. However, the literature offers plenty of illustrations of lifestyle-based groups. These are mostly from two sections of the population – youth and young singles scenes and sections of the middle classes, specifically the professional, typically university-educated, sections.

Young singles

Youth cultures have already been examined and discussed in Chapter 5 (pp. 134–142). Here we just need to recapitulate some particularly relevant points. It is true that involvement in youth cultures and young singles scenes is life stage-specific; participation drops drastically during the life-cycle squeeze that most people still experience at some point before age 40 (see Chapter 5, pp. 145–146). However, youth has been extended, and many of the relevant scenes involve people of mixed ages up to 40-something and males and females participate on a more or less equal basis, as do individuals from all kinds of family and educational backgrounds, usually without knowing or enquiring what each others' backgrounds are. It is true that young people's closest friends tend to be people like themselves in terms of social origins and habituses (in Bourdieu's terminology; see below, pp. 177–178) (see MacRae, 2004). It is also true that young people's lifestyle clusters (uses of leisure that tend to go together) tend to form within middle- and working-class boundaries (Hendry *et al.*, 1993). It is equally true that young people on middle-class life trajectories tend to 'do more' – middle-class omnivorousness begins early in life (see Roberts and Parsell, 1994). Also, Robert Hollands (1995) tells us that, in the 1990s, Newcastle upon Tyne's students and young workers tended to favour different city-centre pubs, which played different kinds of music. However, it is unlikely that most of the participants are aware of any of the above social patterning. As far as the participants are concerned, it must appear that they congregate solely on the basis of shared enjoyment of the relevant scenes.

Nowadays youth cultural identities really do appear to be generated autonomously rather than expressing or embellishing identities originally anchored elsewhere (see Hollands, 1995). Steve Miles (2000) argues that contemporary youth cultures and young singles scenes provide temporary but, for the time being, secure identities for individuals who are in life stage transition and who have no settled employment or family roles with which they can identify or through which they can be identified by others. As such, lifestyle-based identities give young people anchorage points in their otherwise insecure lives. Admittedly, these identities appear to lack depth and make little impression on the individuals' social and political outlooks. This has been demonstrated by John Bynner and Sheena Ashford (1992), using evidence from the Economic and Social Research Council's 16–19 Initiative, a set of longitudinal investigations among representative samples of young people from four parts of Britain – Kirkcaldy, Liverpool, Sheffield and Swindon (see Banks *et al.*, 1992). This research found that the samples' social and political attitudes did not cohere neatly into a limited number of clusters. However, socio-political attitudes were more strongly related to the young people's family backgrounds, sex, past educational attainments and experiences in education and the labour market after age 16 than to their leisure activities. In fact, there were hardly any connections with leisure patterns. This suggests that their leisure activities were not among the principal sources of the young people's ideas about the kinds of adults they would become and where their long-term interests lay. Class trajectories and gender roles rather than leisure-based lifestyles were continuing to play this role, even if they were unable to supply as well-defined and powerful collective identities as in the past.

This squares with Lindsay's (2004) findings from a qualitative study of 31 young hairdressers in Melbourne, Australia. Hairdressing is a lifestyle-oriented occupation, but the young hairdressers who were interviewed by Lindsay regarded their work as serious rather than fun. Their lives were dominated by their long hours of work, the stress of dealing with customers all day long and the low pay. The young people's senses of who they were were dominated by work features rather than leisure features of their occupation. Of course, the young hairdressers did 'go out' and enjoy a good time, but even those who identified with 'spectacular' youth styles did not regard these as the most important parts of their lives. In the early 1960s, Ralph Turner (1964) found that young Americans' commitments to youth cultures were nearly always superficial, and there is absolutely no evidence that this has changed anywhere. Bynner and Ashford (1992) found that high levels of participation in leisure that brought young people into contact with others enhanced self-confidence and esteem. In other words, leisure was continuing to perform its 'modern' functions. Leisure activities can make people feel more satisfied, whatever their circumstances, but it is still not clear that leisure interests alone can tell people who or what they really are.

Middle-class lifestyles

Middle-class lifestyles are really the crucial test case for the proposition that leisure activities have become significant sources of social identities. There is no doubt that these groups exist but the conclusions that can be drawn from this evidence remain matters for debate. Most recent studies of the development of new lifestyles within sections of the upper middle classes, or the service class or salariat as these strata are now often described by sociologists, have acknowledged their debt to Pierre Bourdieu, a French sociologist who, among other things, studied the audience for high culture in France and related the findings to his broader interest in social stratification. Bourdieu (1984) has contended that, in France, cultural production and consumption are part of the class structure and serve simultaneously partly to conceal and partly to reinforce and reproduce economic and political class relationships (see also Bourdieu and Darbel, 1997). 'Habitus', 'field' and 'capital' are key concepts in Bourdieu's sociology. Habitus refers to subconscious, internalized dispositions, which, while not fixed rigidly for evermore, are acquired and deeply embedded during primary socialization. Habituses structure the phenomenal fields, the views of the world within which individuals operate and within which they feel 'at home'. Education, the labour market and the arts are examples of fields, which are constituted by actors who bring with them various types and amounts of economic, social and cultural capital. Actors within a field who share habituses are said to be able to interact comfortably and build up their social and cultural capital through mutual exchange. Only the right types of social and cultural capital have exchange value within particular fields. Members of 'in' crowds are thus said to be able to recognize each other instantly and, in subtle but effective ways, consciously or unconsciously, exclude outsiders. Thus groups such as social classes are said to be able to reproduce themselves over time and down the generations.

Bourdieu recognized and, indeed, stressed that there was not a perfect fit between France's economic, political and cultural elites. His argument was that their manifest separation was important for the reproduction of them all. Despite their manifest separateness, Bourdieu showed that the audiences for high culture – visitors to classical concerts, art galleries and so on – were heavily skewed, with the economically advantaged and politically powerful grossly over-represented. He argued that cultural taste was one way in which the members of privileged strata could instantly recognize one another and their children, and exclude other sections of the population from their circles. Moreover, when seen 'on stage', he argued that members of these strata were most likely to be displaying their cultural tastes, which thereby became prominent parts of their public identities. Those concerned were able to regard themselves, and hopefully be regarded by others, as persons of superior taste, sensibilities and abilities rather than self-interested wielders of economic and political power. Exploitative class relationships were thereby given a more acceptable veneer, which legitimized, consolidated and permitted the reproduction and perpetuation of these inequalities.

As a general theory of class structure and relationships (which is not what Bourdieu claimed to be offering), these arguments must be judged inadequate. Too few members of the present-day upper middle classes are sufficiently versed in high culture for this to be much use in enabling them to recognize each other or in seeking wider esteem for their social strata. Chapter 3 explained that, over time, class-based cultures and ways of life have weakened. The upper strata have become leisure omnivores (at least on a collective level), who have sufficient money to nurture and indulge their typically wide-ranging tastes. Moreover, Bourdieu's explanation of how social classes are reproduced inter-generationally cannot be easily harmonized with the volumes of upward and downward mobility that are known to occur or the processes whereby mobility is accomplished (see Goldthorpe, 1996). However, Bourdieu's ideas can be applied to status group formation within sections of the upper middle classes, which, in fact, is among the principal ways in which his ideas have been used.

George Hughes (1993) has offered a Bourdieu-inspired interpretation of super-yachting by the super-rich. Why do they spend so much money on vessels that they rarely sail personally, which cannot offer the comfort of five-star hotels but largely protect the passengers from, rather than expose them to, the challenges of the ocean elements? Hughes's explanation is that the actors are attracted by the social identities that super-yachting confers. The vessels advertise their owners' wealth while providing them with a public image as people who are basically interested in pleasure and challenge, with which the population at large can sympathize. Most of the wealth of the super-yacht owners may be employing workers on low wages in dangerous or unhealthy conditions, but on the public stage the super-rich are able to present and enjoy alternative identities.

Derek Wynne (1990, 1998) studied the construction of social position among the rather less prosperous, but still quite well-to-do residents of The Heath, an upmarket private housing development in northwest England. The prices of the dwellings excluded all but the solid middle class. All the households had members who were professionals, managers or self-employed. To outsiders with ordinary jobs, The Heath's residents must have appeared uniformly privileged. However, Derek Wynne explains how different groups of residents developed different lifestyles, involving different uses of neighbourhood and other facilities, and in this way The Heath became divided into different types of people. One lifestyle group was composed mainly of highly educated (graduate) professionals, who played sport, went to avant-garde theatre productions, and selected à la carte or self-constructed holidays. Their lifestyles and social identities were quite different from those of a group composed mainly of managers and the self-employed, who participated in a drinking culture and bought expensive home furnishings, meals in steakhouses, tickets to big shows in big cities and package holidays. Wynne claims that nowadays middle-class social identities are typically rooted not in the jobs people do but in their types of consumption and leisure practices, and that these processes are helping to fragment the middle class and outdating the view of this group as uniformly conservative, socially and politically.

A similar distinction between the lifestyles of professionals and managers was found by Mike Savage and his colleagues (1992) in their analysis of the spending and activity patterns of the upper middle classes, using data from large-scale market research surveys. Savage and his colleagues actually distinguished two lifestyle groups among highly educated professionals. One pursued health and fitness through their choices of food and regular exercise. Another was identifiable by its cultural proclivities – visits to the theatre and such-like – and a fondness for entertaining friends to dinner and drinking wine. The lifestyles of the managers in this study were relatively 'undistinguished'. It is not an entirely unfair caricature to say that their tastes were not very different from those of manual workers except that the managers were able to spend more money on them. Alan Warde's (1995) analysis of food consumption in Britain's upper middle classes reached a similar conclusion. The highly educated professionals had food-purchasing patterns that clearly distinguished them from manual workers – far less bread, potatoes and beer and more fresh fruit, wine and salads. Once again, however, the managers' diets seemed best described as 'undistinguished'.

Other recent studies of Britain's middle classes have suggested, or at least implied, that nowadays sections of these groups recognize each other and identify themselves as much by their consumer lifestyles as by their types of employment. For example, Butler and Savage's (1995) edited book on *Social Change and the Middle Classes* contains just three chapters on the middle classes' employment but six that deal with their housing, uses of the countryside, food consumption and urban gentrification (see also Thrift, 1989). The book argues that social classes need not be formed in workplaces and occupational associations but can be constructed in the districts where their members reside or which they visit for leisure in their green wellies or Range Rovers, for example, thereby signalling their group membership. Some believe that it is in such groups that we are increasingly likely to be mobilized for political action – to preserve traditional country sports, to defend the countryside against motorway construction or to have any further building sited so that quiet villages remain uncongested, for example.

Lifestyles and Other Divisions

A partial stumbling block for the lifestyle-based identities theory may appear to be that all the clear examples of adult lifestyle groups exist within a particular section of the upper middle-class. This stumbling block is only partial because it can be claimed that their present-day lifestyles are fragmenting a formerly more homogeneous middle class. These lifestyles do not rest squarely on the entire middle-class, but neither do they obliterate the middle–working-class divide. This is recognized by the investigators who have identified the groups in question.

They do not claim that all older social class divisions are being overwhelmed, only that the middle class is either being fragmented or arranged into different fragments from formerly. Scott Lash (1990) argues that, up to now, clearly defined lifestyles have developed primarily among people in new occupations or in old types of employment that have expanded and changed markedly in recent years to such an extent that they no longer confer customary identities. Jobs in finance, the law and especially the new communications industries fall into these categories. So do the student role and the role of the university 'don', given the recent expansion of higher education. Lash argues that lifestyle experimentation is most likely in groups who live and work in symbolically rich environments, the media and post-secondary education being obvious cases.

Adult middle-class lifestyles do not obliterate but add to and embellish older 'middle-class' markers. The relevant sections of the middle classes bring some preformed class-based meanings to gentrified inner-city districts and the country villages they visit at the weekend or where they choose to live. Present-day social classes are not formed exclusively through their practices of rural or inner-city living (see Cloke *et al.*, 1995; Urry, 1995a, b). Nowadays the middle classes are too mobile for places or even broad types of housing or housing tenure to supply the long-term interests and identities offered by occupational careers. There is a wealth of evidence of occupational class determining where people live and their types of housing, but no one has found the latter determining people's jobs or otherwise playing the lead role in class formation (Wait, 1996). Dale Southerton (2002) interviewed 48 individuals who were living in three different kinds of districts in new towns in southern England. The samples were asked a series of questions about, 'Who is like me?' and 'Who is not like me?' The respondents often used types of housing and districts as reference points for placing other people, but this placing was invariably into employment-based classes. The houses in which people live are public knowledge, more so than their jobs, and locals know that the types of housing that neighbours can afford depend on their occupations and incomes. Hence the value of housing in placing/classifying people. However, these formations are at least partly class- and employment-based rather than derived *sui generis* from consumer lifestyles – how people choose to spend their money.

Leisure scholars do not need to claim that, if uses of leisure have become important in identity formation, this must be at the expense of something else. Gender-, age- and occupation-based classes have clearly not receded to insignificance as social markers and dividers. If leisure today is playing an enhanced role, this is much more likely to be alongside and through blending with other social markers. Extreme claims about the decline of older sources of identity are all too easily discredited.

Some writers have proclaimed change even when there has been no hard evidence that anything has changed. Phillips and Western's evidence (see Box 6.2) covers only a limited time frame, from the late 1980s to the late 1990s, and Australia may be an atypical modern country. However, the fact that Australia is a recently formed country (and nation) compared with its European counterparts and the fact that much of Australia bypassed the industrial age suggest that postmodern and similar identities should be evident in Australia,

---

Box 6.2. Postmodernization and reflexive modernization.

Tim Phillips and Mark Western (2005) have conducted a secondary analysis of representative sample surveys conducted in Australia in 1986 and 1998. They use the evidence to test postmodernization and reflexive modernization theories. Respondents were asked a series of Likert-style questions about the importance (to them) of different sources of identity: 'The decline of traditional institutions and forms of social organization described by reflexive modernization, and the hyperdifferentiation of postmodernization both imply a declining significance of class, work and occupational identities' (p. 167).

The postmodernization theory suggests that identities have become fluid, disconnected from social structures, with no stable hierarchy or continuity. Rattansi and Phoenix (1997), for example, have queried whether people today possess any core, stable identities. They invite us to entertain the possibility that all roles and identities have become variable and fluid.

The reflexive modernization theory, in contrast, argues that identities are nowadays reflexively constructed but coherently organized.

However, Phillips and Western's evidence shows stability over time and between birth cohorts. Country-based and occupational identities remained strong in Australia. In both 1986 and 1998 and in all birth cohorts, the two most important identities named by the respondents were supplied by their country (Australia) and their occupations. Over time, there was a slight strengthening of gender identities and a weakening of class identities. Sports team (the one leisure option offered) was rated the least important source of identity: 'The evidence with respect to salience and patterning therefore does not suggest that the contemporary period is one in which social identity processes are distinctively different from earlier times' (p. 183).

---

if anywhere. In practice, Phillips and Western have been able to show that most Australians' identities remain firmly attached to place (Australia) and occupation, and there are no signs whatsoever that major changes are under way. Britain is probably unexceptional in the absence of any decline in the strength of employment- and class-based identities since the 1960s (when such survey questions were first asked) (see Marshall *et al.*, 1988). It is worth reiterating (from Chapter 3) that the clearest differences in consumption practices are still between, not within, occupation-based classes. Alan Warde (1995) has shown that, although there are differences in food consumption between managers and professionals, by far the widest differences are between both these groups, on the one hand, and the working class, on the other, and these differences have not narrowed since the 1960s. Some social class differences in leisure behaviour have become more pronounced, which is hardly surprising in countries where income inequalities have widened. Knulst (1992) has shown that in the Netherlands the audiences for high culture have become more exclusively middle-class than formerly due to price/income effects plus the ability of non-core audiences to satisfy their tastes from the radio and recorded music. Pierre Bourdieu always insisted, correctly, that cultural consumption was deeply entwined with economic and political stratification.

Summary

This chapter opened with definitions and typologies, and noted that since the time of Max Weber it has been commonplace in sociology to distinguish occupation-based classes from status groups based on particular styles of life.

We then saw how, according to some writers, the weakening of older social structures and divisions has created a need for individuals and groups to use other resources to construct identities. However, we also noted that the same historical trends that are said to be destabilizing employment, age and sex roles are likely to be wreaking similar havoc in leisure, which, therefore, is an unlikely safe haven in an otherwise stormy world. The chapter then emphasized the importance of not overstating and making implausible claims about the role of leisure.

We proceeded to note the existence of publicly recognizable lifestyle groups, typically involving clusters rather than single definitive leisure activities. We saw how all the groups in question have developed either among young singles or within a particular section of the middle class. It was suggested that, insofar as leisure now acts as a significant source of identity within the groups in question, this will be in combination with, rather than at the expense of, older social markers such as occupations, age and sex.

Further Reading

On the role of lifestyles in present-day society

Chaney, D. (2002) *Cultural Change and Everyday Life.* Palgrave, Basingstoke, UK.
Sulkanen, P. (1997) Introduction: the new consumer society – rethinking the social bond. In: Sulkanen, P., Holmwood, J., Radner, H. and Schulze, G. (eds) *Constructing the New Consumer Society.* Macmillan, London.

On the identification of leisure-based lifestyles

Veal, A.J. (1989) Leisure and life-style: a pluralist framework for analysis. *Leisure Studies* 8, 141–153.
Veal, A.J. (1993) The concept of lifestyle: a review. *Leisure Studies* 12, 233–252.

Studies of selected lifestyle groups

Miles, S. (2000) *Youth Lifestyles in a Changing World.* Open University Press, Buckingham, UK.
Wynne, D. (1998) *Leisure, Lifestyle and the New Middle Class.* Routledge, London.

7 Consumption and Consumerism

Introduction

An earlier generation of writers forecast that the mass media – the popular press, films, recorded music, radio and television (all of which were introduced during the first half of the 20th century) – would create a mass society in which the public was atomized into individual listeners, readers and viewers and rendered susceptible to thought control by whoever ran the media. Marxist writers drew attention to how not just the mass media but also other leisure industries were organized and run not only for immediate profit but also to produce submissive workers and consumers. For example, they argued that sports taught males to be self-disciplined, to subordinate themselves to a team and to follow instructions and that people who became accustomed to being passively entertained would be equally submissive at work and politically.

This is another set of arguments that, over the last 30 years or so, has metamorphosed. Nowadays it is McDonaldization, not the mass media, that is said to be standardizing people's everyday lives. It is said to be consumer culture that imprisons people in a soothing and warm but still basically exploitative and oppressive economic system. It is argued that consumer capitalism blurs the distinction between human needs and artificially created wants, thereby locking people into a work-and-spend regime, creating ever-expanding markets for profit-seeking businesses that sell consumer goods and services, which spread superficial contentment or, when people remain unhappy, persuade them that this must be their own fault. Here we have yet another explanation of why we use our leisure in suboptimal ways: our uses of leisure are said to be governed by the interests of commerce rather than by our own authentic needs.

This chapter considers whether these criticisms of modern consumption and consumerism are justified or whether, as orthodox economists have always claimed, the increase in the supply of consumer goods and services has extended people's scope to live as they please and thereby enlarged their freedom.

First, however, consumption is defined, the rise of consumerism during the 20th century is reviewed and then shopping is considered as arguably the quintessential leisure activity in a consumer society. We then see how public providers and voluntary associations have been affected by having to operate in a more commercial context. The concluding chapter sections present the critique of consumerism and then its defence, leading into a discussion of whether the end of the consumer society is now in sight.

Consumption

Debates about consumerism and consumer culture are relatively new, but consumption itself is an age-old process. It is as old as work. The two go hand in hand. By working on nature or on partly produced items, people produce goods and services for later consumption, and they have done this in all societies whose members have not simply lived off nature. Consumption is the complementary process. Work increases the value of whatever is worked on. This is why people work. In consumption, value is depleted and eventually used up. People can only consume if they, or others, also work, and an object of working is always to be able, later on, to consume the product of one's own or someone else's labour or to enable another person or persons to do so. Alternatively, nowadays people may consume prior to working. Credit permits this. The consumers thereby become indebted. But someone must have already worked for there to be anything to consume.

In some types of consumption, the value of a product is depleted quickly, as when a meal is eaten or a beverage drunk. Other goods' value is depleted more slowly. We expect our new cars to last for many years and to have retained some value when they are traded in. The same applies to houses. In fact, during some historical periods people have been able to regard their dwellings as investments. Some products can be 'consumed' without diminishing their future availability. A film can be viewed without depriving others of the opportunity. Indeed, the same person can watch a film over and over again. Some works, usually described as 'art', are able to command endless audiences. With most such products, however, individuals eventually tire of repeats, everyone who wishes to watch does so and the value of the products can then be considered exhausted. By then, of course, the producer or whoever has the property rights is likely to have recouped many times the value of the labour invested in the production. In some cases, like classical works of art, the returns may continue indefinitely. However, these are not exceptions to the rule so much as extreme cases. Normally people work only in the expectation that the value of whatever they produce, whether they are making something for their own use or for wages, will be greater than the value of the effort they expend.

Consumption is an age-old process, but there are three features that make modern consumption more prominent and important than in earlier times. First, production and consumption are usually, though not always, entirely separate. People still produce things they intend to use themselves in their homes and may consume them almost instantly, as when meals are cooked and eaten. Nevertheless, what most people, at any rate those in employment, regard as their main work is done for money. So life becomes divided into producing and consuming. People go to work to earn the money to spend in their non-working time. Production and consumption are separated temporally, and also in that people do not expect to consume what they themselves have produced or helped to produce. They use their earnings to claim shares in the products of other people's labour. Workers earn the money to spend and, in a sense, the time when they can spend it. No one defines the whole of non-working time as leisure. Nor do people spend all their non-working time consuming, except in the sense that they can be said to consume their free time. Nevertheless, in modern societies, for most people, there are times and places where they work and other times when they are able to consume.

Secondly, in market economies where people work for money wages, they are presented with a huge array of choices and constant invitations to spend and consume. Producers compete to sell their goods and services. Beyond the core value of their products, merchandisers attempt to increase their attractiveness through design, advertising and other marketing strategies. It is these processes that generate a consumer culture – all the images, sounds, smells and tactile sensations that become loaded with meanings and surround products and the processes of consuming them. Consumption may seem an odd umbrella term to describe what we are doing with all our purchases and the uses that we make of them. After all, we do not consume furniture and Mediterranean resorts in exactly the same way as pints of beer. But from the point of view of the merchandiser it is all basically the same. Holidays are packaged, furniture is manufactured and then these commodities disappear from the market. The products have left the hands of the producers or their agents and have been appropriated by consumers.

Thirdly, when most people have sufficient spending power to make consumer choices, consumer culture can become mass culture. The birth of mass consumerism is then possible, meaning that some of most people's hopes and aspirations become centred around consumption. Who people feel they are, their social identities and self-concepts, may depend, at least in part, on what they are able and choose to consume (see Chapter 6). Individuals' conceptions of the kinds of people they would like to be and try to become may be constructed in terms of consumption.

The Construction of Consumer Culture

Beginnings

Consumerism is a recently coined, post-Second World War term, but the phenomenon has attracted attention for much longer (see Box 7.1).

People's leisure opportunities expanded in the early years of the 20th century and especially between the world wars, when the radio and the cinema developed

> **Box 7.1.** The affluent worker in the 19th century.
>
> When John Goldthorpe and his colleagues (1969) conducted their study of affluent manual workers in Luton in the 1960s amidst a debate on the alleged embourgeoisement of the working class, they discovered that there had been a similar debate almost 100 years earlier.
>
> As Chapter 2 explained, in the closing decades of the 19th century workers were earning higher wages and enjoying higher standards of living. They were becoming better housed and taking holidays away from home at expanding seaside resorts such as Blackpool, and there were new forms of entertainment – spectator sports, music halls and theatres for those able to afford the admission prices.

rapidly as forms of mass entertainment (*see* Chapter 2, pp. 34–35). Driving and flying also became new leisure activities for the relatively well-to-do, but cycling was the mass pastime. Simultaneously, new forms of public transport enabled more people to take day trips and longer excursions to coastal resorts and the countryside. Rambling thus became another popular recreation. The holiday resorts continued to expand and professional football clubs built new, larger stadiums. Among young people, modern dancing became popular, but it was developments in the manufacture and purchase of consumer durables that may have had the greater long-term significance.

New forms of marketing

There was much excitement when department stores began to open from the mid-19th century onwards. These attracted the same kinds of attention as supermarkets in the 1960s and shopping malls and retail parks subsequently. It was noted when department stores first opened that these were often people's main targets during days out. There were much discussion and concern about shoppers, especially women, becoming bewildered, dazzled, seduced and tempted to spend beyond their means by the array of goods, all within their physical reach but usually beyond their immediate means. In the 19th century, the department stores catered almost exclusively for middle-class shoppers, but subsequently they targeted a wider market. During the 1920s and 1930s, mass markets were developed for a new range of consumer products, which were displayed prominently in the department stores and elsewhere. Some of the new products, or at least their mass marketing, became possible as more and more homes were connected to mains electricity. Irons, vacuum cleaners and lighting fixtures fell into this category. Gas-fired boilers and cookers, bicycles and radios and gramophones were other goods that sold in mass quantities. At that time, refrigerators remained luxury items and washing machines even more so. Mail-order catalogues and hire purchase were also introduced during the interwar years.

In retrospect, sociologists have traced the beginnings of home-centred, privatized lifestyles to this period. This was when manufacturers began to use advertising to create or structure mass markets for their particular products (Bowden, 1994). In America, Henry Ford and then numerous competitors had begun to mass-produce motor cars with the aim of bringing their price within the means of the average family. This was achieved by mechanization and mass production, which meant, for example, that customers could have any colour 'so long as it is black'. In Britain it was not until the 1960s that private motoring became a mass phenomenon.

Enduring divisions

The interwar years are best remembered for the recession, unemployment and hard times that blighted the economic and social landscapes, but, for people who remained in work, rates of pay and standards of living rose. The new types of consumption developed most strongly and spread most widely in southern England, rather than in regions where levels of unemployment were much higher. Even in the more prosperous parts of Britain, the majority of people were not part of the consumer boom. Until the Second World War, around a third of Britain's manual working class lived beneath or barely above the poverty level, meaning that their incomes were sufficient to purchase little more than necessities. The typical working-class family could expect to sink into poverty at vulnerable points in the life cycle, particularly when one wage earner was supporting a spouse and children and later on in old age. Layoffs and unemployment were likely to create financial crises at other times. Life was a constant struggle to maintain decent standards for most working-class households. Respectable working-class families might have placed themselves above the 'roughs', but they did not share middle-class lifestyles.

During the interwar years, working-class families began to be rehoused from inner-city slums to council housing estates. Meanwhile, middle-class families were purchasing the detached and semi-detached properties that were being built throughout the length and breadth of Britain. At that time, middle- and working-class children were educated at different schools – secondary schools for children whose parents could pay, while most working-class children received elementary education only. The middle classes worked in and dressed for office environments, and they had their own leisure tastes and activities. When the working and middle classes went to the same places for entertainment – to football grounds and music halls, for instance – they usually stood or sat in different areas (see Mason, 1994).

Within all social classes, men were the normal breadwinners and there were huge differences between males' and females' ways of life. There were also pronounced age differences. Successive cohorts of males and females followed the life-cycle sequences and patterns characteristic of their social classes. Consumption rose in all these groups but, prior to the Second World War, not sufficiently or widely enough to break down the characteristic group patterns (see Davies, 1992).

The breakthrough

Social historians trace consumer culture's decisive breakthrough to the period between the 1930s and 1950s. The Second World War, of course, bisected this period, but was more important as an accelerator than as a catalyst. In retrospect, it is possible to identify a set of interrelated key developments:

- First, a new economics associated with John Maynard Keynes explained how governments could spend their countries out of recessions and mass unemployment. The USA's New Deal programmes in the 1930s applied this prescription. European governments followed suit as they began to rearm. Needless to say, during the war itself, all labour was needed. By the end of the war, there was intergovernmental agreement that in the new world order mass unemployment should never be allowed to return. All Western governments adopted Keynesian economic policies and the countries experienced several decades of full employment and economic growth.
- Industrialists and their spokespersons endorsed this type of state intervention. They remained hostile to 'socialism' – meaning nationalization and high taxation – but not to 'sensible' macroeconomic management. Expanding economies that kept workers in jobs with progressively higher earnings meant larger and wider markets from which businesses could profit.
- Once full employment was seen to be a realizable goal, trade unions softened their demand for shorter hours of work. They demanded full employment policies from governments and, from employers, progressively higher earnings (see Hunnicutt, 1988).
- Finally, the population's ability to spend and consume grew, and people's appetites for still higher levels of consumption were stimulated. Married women began entering the labour force in increasing numbers from the 1940s onwards and, unlike during the two world wars, this time they were in the labour market and staying. At first, many explained that their earnings were for extras and that their husbands remained the real breadwinners. Everyone has subsequently learnt how one decade's luxuries become normal expectations in the next. Life today would be intolerable for many households without central heating, televisions, vacuum cleaners and telephones.

Consumerism as the dominant culture

Consumerism takes root as spending becomes increasingly central in people's life goals. Gary Cross (1993) has argued that this had happened by the 1950s throughout the Western world and that consumer culture has continued to reign since then. Likewise, Celia Lury (1996) presents consumer culture as the material culture that became dominant throughout Euro-America during the second half of the 20th century. People have been willing to work hard and long and, in recent years, in some cases, even harder and longer than previously, in order to satisfy their consumer aspirations. Simultaneously, more and more goods and services have become commodities, which are produced for and purchased by more and more people.

In consumer societies governments are judged primarily by their ability to maintain rising standards of living. Trade unionists judge their leaders by much the same yardstick. This has remained so despite the return of mass unemployment since the 1970s. Of course, politicians of all parties, and certainly the trade unions, want and demand a return to full employment, but in practice all these leaders are more responsive to the demands of the mainly employed voters and fee-paying trade union members, who continue to judge their leaders according to the trends in their pay packets. Even when opinion polls have suggested that voters regard unemployment as a leading issue, if not the leading issue, the 'feel-good factor' has continued to depend more on trends in the self-perceived prosperity of the majority, who are in jobs.

Since the 1970s the real earnings and living standards of most people in employment have continued to rise. They have been responsible for the rise in spending on VCRs, DVDs, cable and satellite television, long-haul major holidays, second breaks, and so on (see Martin and Mason, 1986, 1990, 1992). The interests of businesses, the earn-and-spend aspirations of the workforce and the electoral pressures, which all political parties that aspire to office must respect, have formed a self-sealing circle. However, Gary Cross (1993) has warned that we should not expect the consumer culture to reign indefinitely. It has been dominant in the West for only half a century and is unlikely to be the end of history. Whether the consumer culture is currently disintegrating or threatened is an issue to which we shall return shortly.

For the present, we should note that some sections of the population have remained outside the consumer society. In Britain around 40% of the population takes no holidays away from home. Just under a third is without private motor transport. But today when people talk about a two-thirds, one-third society, it is the two-thirds who are the alleged haves. This is unlike the 1930s and before, when poverty was a general working-class problem and the working class amounted to around two-thirds of the population. Today's have-nots are not necessarily suffering the same kinds of hardship as those in poverty before the Second World War, but today's poor are excluded from most of the consumption that is taken for granted by most members of their society. This is a different kind of deprivation, which, in its own way, may be just as painful as the poverty of earlier decades (see Bauman, 1998b).

Shopping and Leisure

The monetarization of leisure

In a consumer society one would expect shopping to be less of a chore than a core, if not the core, leisure activity, especially if shopping is defined broadly to include all kinds of looking at and for things to buy, preparing to purchase and subsequently not only using the purchases but also reflecting on the value of the deals and considering what to buy on the next occasion. All this can be expected to supply peak leisure experiences for people who are immersed in consumer culture. This should be reflected in the time that people devote to shopping and its position in their overall leisure schedules. Chapter 3 explained that leisure time has expanded much more slowly than people's spending power in recent decades. Consumer spending almost doubled in Britain in the 25 years up to 1996, whereas free time hardly increased at all (Martin and Mason, 1998). So merely purchasing, not to mention using the purchases, accounts for a growing proportion of people's non-working time. Time budgets have recorded the increase in the amount of time spent shopping in Britain: up by around 50% since the 1960s. More and more of our leisure time has become geared to purchasing.

Commodification

More and more goods and services – everything that people want or can be persuaded to want – are packaged as commodities to be acquired by anyone who will pay the price. Holidays are bought as packages. Excitement and exotic experiences can be bought by visiting the appropriate theme parks. Friends of a preferred type become available by joining the right contact club. Conversation is available for the cost of a telephone call. In societies where all this is possible, one would expect people's aspirations to become geared to spending. All types of experiences become things to buy. Everything has a price. So what most people want, above all else, and what they feel they really need, is money.

Ubiquitous marketing

Merchandisers have become extremely imaginative in marketing their wares so as to meet or preferably to structure the public's demands. Much of the Western world's most creative talent has been recruited into advertising. It is no longer sufficient to have a product stocked on shop shelves. Goods and services need to be designed, packaged and promoted to make people aware of their availability and what the purchases will do for them. Gas cookers, blue jeans and many additional otherwise mundane objects have been surrounded by all kinds of improbable imagery. Developing and disseminating the imagery has become a high-status, well-rewarded activity. Leading actors and other celebrities who once feared that appearing in adverts would damage their reputations are now keen to do voice-overs and other endorsements. The recipe obviously works. Consumers are said to acquire not just the material products but also the associated meanings. Being seen in the right restaurant, night club or holiday resort and wearing the right brand label on one's shirt or trousers advertise an individual's membership of 'people like that'. The sums now spent on consumer market research dwarf the budget for academic leisure studies. Nowadays consumers' motivations and attitudes are explored assiduously. Most of the findings never become public property. They belong to the commercial purchasers. Great expense is incurred in order to discover the brand name, the shape of car and so on that will result in marginal but often crucial increases in sales.

Marketing is ubiquitous. It is impossible to move through cities or the country-side, to open newspapers or to surf the television channels without being reminded of purchasing possibilities (*see* Wernick, 1991). In a consumer society the most sensitive indicators of trends in leisure, more sensitive than time budgets, are data on spending. These show, for example, that during the 1980s and 1990s the main growth areas in UK consumer spending were on overseas holidays and home entertainment equipment. Other leisure commodities, including alcohol, did not benefit to the same extent from the overall rise in consumption (*see* Martin and Mason, 1986, 1990). Irrespective of whether our self-concepts are now based primarily on what we buy and where we buy it (*see* Chapter 6), our uses of leisure are increasingly based on or at least geared to purchases.

Chore or leisure?

Nowadays it is difficult for leisure researchers to decide how to treat shopping. The customary practice in time budgets has been to classify shopping as one of the chores that simply have to be done, but this now seems at loggerheads with where, when and how people shop. Shopping might be used as a lead example of a postmodern condition in which modern divisions and categories are blurred. Work spills into what used to be leisure time as more people take work home or go to work in the evenings and at weekends, while people find leisure experiences in their paid jobs and in what were once unpaid chores. Times, places and activities become impossible to classify unambiguously as work, unpaid chores or leisure. The only sensible question may seem to be how people experience the times, situations and activities (*see* Box 7.2).

When people have days off work, shopping is often their core activity. The shopping is not done as quickly as possible and put aside so as to leave as much time as possible for other uses of leisure. Saturday is the week's main shopping day. When shopping itself is treated as a leisure activity, it becomes far and away the most common form of out-of-home leisure. The introduction of Sunday trading in Britain in the 1990s immediately transformed the 'sabbath' into another major shopping day. Sunday shopping quickly became so popular that stores

---

Box 7.2. Attitudes to shopping.

People's attitudes to shopping vary enormously, from love to hate.

People often explain how their feelings depend on the type of shopping. Whereas the weekly supermarket trip for groceries may be experienced as a chore, people often feel differently about shopping for a new outfit.

Men and women alike nowadays may spend considerable amounts of time shopping, but attitudes are still gender-divided. The people who love shopping are mostly women, while those who hate it are mostly men: hence the case for treating shopping as the female mode of consumption par excellence.

Source: Campbell (1997).

and car parks became congested and traffic jams extended for miles, despite the absence of much of the normal weekday work traffic.

The shopping environment

The retail trade knows full well that simply pricing goods down and making them available will not always maximize sales. Shoppers are attracted to complexes with numerous stores through which they can browse, and where there are places to relax and refresh themselves. Some complexes contain entertainment and play areas for children (and adults). Individuals, families and organized groups travel for miles to major shopping centres. US cities' shopping complexes are often central attractions in advertised weekend breaks, for which people travel in a variety of ways including by air. Of course, shopping has always been a part of the traditional holiday. The main resorts' attractions have always included their shopping facilities. Nowadays, it seems, the shops are often the main attraction. Hence the spate of recent enquiries into the types of facilities that tempt people to shop as a leisure activity (see Jansen-Verbeke, 1987; Roberts, 1987; Shields, 1992).

Purchasing has become time-demanding because, prior to spending their money, many shoppers like to view all the alternatives. Window-shopping is a normal prelude or accompaniment to actual purchases. Major and minor purchases may be surrounded by extensive sampling, often in the company of friends or family members who can offer authoritative advice. The occasions then supply much material for subsequent small talk. Friends and families discuss who has bought what, together with their future spending hopes and plans.

Major shopping developments are now consciously planned and designed so as to appeal to the leisure shopper. Pedestrianization is known to enhance the quality of the experience, judged by the effects on trade. Maximizing pulling power depends on having the right mixture of large and small stores offering different kinds of wares. More conventional leisure facilities – cinemas, gardens, pubs, restaurants and art galleries – can add to the appeal. Conventional tourist attractions are now used routinely to tempt shoppers. Some resorts have natural environments that would be blemished by overdevelopment. They need to strike the right balance but they can be sure that today's visitors will have cash to spend not just on accommodation and food but on virtually everything else that the stores can offer.

Sport spectacles are now sought by cities throughout the world. The value of the television rights is important but so are the visitors, who will pay admission prices and for many other things as well. However, the arts and heritage are unrivalled for attracting tourists. They can attract visitors throughout the year, year in, year out, and the same visitors will sometimes visit again and again. Moreover, the types of tourists attracted by the arts and heritage tend to be people with money. The core attractions can be made available free of charge. The cities profit from visitors' spending while in the vicinities. The modern tourist can be relied on to shop. In a consumer society all major leisure occasions – holidays, Christmas and family celebrations – become orgies of spending and consumption.

New forms of shopping

It is unnecessary to go out in order to shop. Daily and weekly reading matter is packed with adverts. So are most television channels. In fact, there are dedicated shopping channels on cable and satellite TV. The adverts on other channels and in the press do not seem to repel viewers and readers. They are probably an added attraction. However, it is not only the explicit adverts that persuade people to spend. Newspaper features and photographs and television programmes cannot help but display products that people decide they would like to possess, and the purchasable items are often shown alongside attractive role models. Ellis Cashmore (1994) has argued that a main effect of television has been to make people spend more. It may be unclear whether television sex and violence spread these phenomena into real everyday life, but there seems to be no doubt that exposure to television makes people spend. If they do not have cash in hand or in the bank, there is now a massive credit industry to take the waiting out of wanting.

For a long time it has been possible to shop by mail or telephone. Nowadays we are also able to call up demonstrations on our computer monitors and send orders 'down the line'. However, it seems unlikely that people will be lured from the attractions of live shopping. The new alternatives are most likely to be added to without replacing the traditional activity.

Even people who are unable to purchase cannot escape the consumer culture. According to Wernick (1991), we all now live amidst a promotional culture in which advertisers' clever techniques have to be copied by everyone – politicians and even academic authors – who wants to deliver a message. No serious political party would now face an election without its 'spin doctors'.

The Public and Voluntary Sectors in a Consumer Society

Commercial leisure, which provides goods and services for profit, has been the central force in the spread of consumer culture, but other kinds of leisure provision have inevitably been affected. The public and voluntary sectors now operate in a different context compared with when most of the services and many of the organizations had their origins.

The public sector will provide whatever politicians want, or are willing to endorse, subject only to normal political constraints, but until recently public providers usually claimed to be catering for people's 'needs' rather than their manifest 'wants', and it was usually the providers' conceptions of other people's needs that was decisive. Traditional public leisure provisions have been basically paternal. The providers have usually claimed to be making sport, the arts, the countryside and so on accessible to all, thereby widening their opportunities to engage in 'desirable' uses of leisure. They have often stressed their responsibilities towards disadvantaged groups – children and young people, the poor and, in more recent times, women and ethnic minorities. In practice, however, the provisions have never been used by everyone, and public provisions have rarely made much impression on social inequalities in participation. In sport, for instance, social class differences in participation remain as wide as ever and, despite the sustained promotion of classical music by the BBC since the 1920s, the audience has neither grown significantly nor become more representative in social composition. Sustaining traditional public leisure provisions has always depended most of all on the providers being able to satisfy key constituencies – the vocal and politically influential – rather than the public in general. For a long time most citizens were acquiescent but the spread of consumer culture has changed this.

There are several ways in which consumerism and related developments have undermined paternal public provisions. First, in the past, except when they went away on holiday, most people had little choice but to use local leisure facilities. Nowadays the public is more mobile, thanks mainly to the spread of private motor transport. So people have a wider choice of destinations when they go out for an evening or at the weekend. Local authority leisure facilities now need to compete with public and private providers in neighbouring areas if they are even to hold on to their local publics, and this usually means offering what people manifestly want rather than what they are believed to need. Secondly, in the early days of the modern public leisure services, there was simply no way in which most people could afford to play sport, visit museums and art galleries and use parks except by using free (at the point of use) or heavily subsidized public services. Nowadays, in contrast, more people can afford to pay for and are offered commercial options – theme parks, tennis centres and exhibitions of various types, for example. The effect, once again, has been to loosen the public sector's hold over its traditional markets. Thirdly, as people have become more accustomed to paying for leisure and as more and more opportunities have been made available by the private sector, citizens have inevitably begun to ask why they should pay for public provisions they do not use. So public providers find it becoming more and more difficult to increase their budgets from tax revenues. Politicians start to demand efficiency gains and suchlike and they start to demand clear objectives and measurable outcomes. Even to maintain their resource levels, public providers are likely to discover that they need to raise revenue in alternative ways – by seeking sponsors and charging users, for example. In other words, they experience pressures to become more commercial.

These are the developments that underlie recent changes in the ways in which public leisure services are administered. In 1992 in Britain local authorities became obliged to introduce competitive tendering for the management of most of their leisure services. Since then, it has been possible for commercial and voluntary organizations to take over the management of these facilities. Up to now, in most cases, the contracts have been awarded to 'in-house' bidders, but, even so, under the new regime (described as 'best value' since 1997) the providers have been under pressure to cut costs to a minimum and to maximize revenue from outside the public purse. This has usually meant catering for people's manifest wants: in other words, becoming more commercial. Whether these developments are applauded or deplored depends largely on commentators' assessments of the respective merits of traditional public and commercial leisure provisions. Some believe that the recent changes will leave the public better served (Coalter, 1998). Others deplore the further spread of consumer-based capitalism (Ravenscroft, 1998).

Voluntary associations have been able to continue in their customary ways, provided they have been able to attract sufficient members with sufficient enthusiasm. In practice, however, with present-day consumers having access to a wider range of easier attractions, many clubs and societies have experienced shortages of volunteers. This affects youth organizations, sports clubs and similar bodies. Simultaneously, some voluntary organizations have had the option of becoming more commercial. This has meant some combination of introducing commercial-type marketing, raising user or participant charges, seeking sponsorship and appointing paid staff, which is how segments of sport and the arts have been reshaped into commodities.

The Critique of Consumerism

Peter Taylor (1992) has complained about an anti-commercial bias in leisure research. He has a point. Taylor's charges are that commercial leisure has been either ignored, despite its obvious importance, or disparaged, despite its manifest popularity, without sufficient evidence to justify such treatment. It is certainly the case that there have been hundreds of academic studies of public-sector policies, provisions and participants, but very few equivalent enquiries into commercial leisure. It is also the case that most academic writing has been critical of the introduction of commercial pressures into local authority leisure services in Britain via the requirement, since 1992, that their management be opened up to competitive tendering or, since 1997, 'best value' criteria (see Ravenscroft, 1998). One reason for the neglect of commercial provision, of course, is that commercial providers are more likely to commission their own market research than to call on academics. The latter have found the public sector far more willing to consider their research findings and conclusions carefully. However, very few leisure researchers have displayed a desire to undertake sympathetic studies of the situations and problems of commercial operators. Writers on consumerism and consumer culture have often been powerfully influenced by Marxist perspectives.

Marxism and leisure

Marxists have always insisted on the basic role of economic processes and relationships but, even so, they have often had much to say about leisure. Marx himself did not write a theory of leisure as such but, as Rojek (1984) has pointed out, it is not difficult to extract a theory of leisure from Marx's works. In the first half of the 20th century, Marxists became embroiled in a series of heated debates about leisure. One set of arguments was about whether bourgeois arts and competitive sport could have any place in a socialist society. By the 1930s there was a clear Communist Party line on these matters: the socialist countries would do

these things even better than the bourgeois societies in which the activities origi-
nated. The authorities in the young Soviet Union displayed intense interest in
their people's ways of life. Time budgets were pioneered by Soviet researchers,
who hoped to chart the breakdown of older divisions, such as between town and
country and intelligentsia and workers, and the development of a socialist way of
life that would be superior to the folk cultures of the past and to the high culture
and popular cultures of capitalist countries (see Roberts, 1990).

From the 1930s onwards Western Marxists have been formulating elegant
critiques of leisure under capitalism. They have argued persistently that the
'relative freedom' that people possess in leisure is in fact extremely limited, that
much leisure time occurs in fragments when it is not possible to do much except
recover from work, and that most people have little money left for discretionary
spending once they have made all the purchases necessary to participate in their
societies' basic ways of life (see Clarke and Critcher, 1985). Marxists have also
drawn attention to the legal and moral prohibitions that have been built around
people's so-called free time, and how the capitalist state has promoted
non-subversive forms of recreation. Here much attention has been paid to the
state's enthusiasm to promote sports, which have taught young males the virtues
of teamwork, discipline and the need to submit to leadership (see Hargreaves,
1982; Hargreaves, 1986).

All the members of the original Frankfurt School (see Box 7.3) deplored
what they regarded as the overwhelmingly oppressive influence of the culture
industries. But some, including Walter Benjamin, believed that leisure time created
at least the possibility of workers reflecting on their situations, individually and
collectively, and becoming aware of and resistant to the restrictive character of
capitalism (see Rojek, 1997). Subsequently Marxists have often dwelt on these

---

Box 7.3.   The Frankfurt School.

From the 1930s onwards the Frankfurt School became renowned for its critical
analyses of how the capitalist culture industries (the press, the cinema, radio
and subsequently television) numbed people's political sensibilities while
applauding the Western way of life.

The leading members of this school (see Adorno and Horkheimer, 1977)
developed what many still regard as the most systematic, searing and challenging analysis of the culture industries that has ever been produced. It is the
original 'class domination' theory in the sociology of leisure.

Its core argument is that during the 20th century the culture industries
became pivotal in capitalist domination by creating and then satisfying false
needs. Adorno and Horkheimer argued that the culture industries produced
standardized commodities with only superficial variations (films and popular
songs, for example), which could be sold for profit. The products were designed
to command mass attention. Pleasure could be derived effortlessly. People
thereby became passive, obedient and uncritical, corrupted by immersion in
pleasures that were superficial and ultimately false.

contradictory features of leisure. On the one hand, people's minds and emotions are said to be vulnerable to control by capitalist industries. Simultaneously, Marxists have been interested in the working class's struggles to win its own time and space and to develop a culture based on its own organizations – social clubs, brass bands and suchlike. These have sometimes been linked to trade unions and political movements. David Rowe (1995) has argued that all popular cultures, created in space wherein people can pursue their own pleasures, contain elements of 'resistance' to the dominant social order. However, the success of the capitalist industries might be judged by the limited headway of allegedly more 'authentic' working-class leisure.

Within Marxism and beyond, the Frankfurt School's arguments have been incorporated within a broader critique of consumer culture. Since the 1950s Marxists have been obliged to attend to Western consumer cultures. It became obvious very early in the Cold War era that the leading capitalist societies were giving their working classes higher living standards than the socialist countries. Moreover, the Western working classes were evidently more interested in benefiting from the consumption opportunities offered by capitalism than in changing the system. Marxists were obliged to address these developments. Capitalist societies were not developing in the way that Marxism originally predicted. This required a Marxist explanation or the abandonment of the theory, and convincing explanations needed to treat consumption seriously (*see* Tomlinson, 1990).

The corruption of pure leisure?

The academic literature is littered with criticisms of consumer culture. In one way or another and to some extent or another, all the critiques draw upon Marxist thinking, as when consumerism is said to be defiling or deforming true leisure. Writers construct images of past times, sometimes invoking the ideas of Aristotle and Plato, when a superior kind of leisure is supposed to have existed. Classical contemplative leisure has been compared favourably with the hectic pace of modern consumption (*see* Dare *et al.*, 1987). Commercialism has been accused of filling people's free time with mere amusements and diversions (Hemingway, 1988), creating endless insatiable desires that leave people unfulfilled and restless (Goodale and Godbey, 1988; Wearing and Wearing, 1992), and turning people into passive receptacles of entertainment to which no critical response is possible (de Grazia, 1962). Steve Miles (1998) argues that consumerism is a product of capitalist production, that businesses and consumers alike have to operate within the constraints of markets and that genuine forms of individuality (which is different from individualization) are undermined.

An inescapable problem with commercial leisure, according to these arguments, is that it requires a division between the provider and the consumer. A consequence is said to be that the consumer's experience is inevitably more limited than when people create their own leisure either individually or in groups. The contrast here is between, for example, the family group, which might once have played music on a piano and sung along, and the modern audience for music, which is far more likely to listen to records, tapes or discs. It can be argued that there are special satisfactions in self-provisioning:

> We believe that involvement in such groups [voluntary organizations] offers people something probably unique in our society: the chance to come together with others to create or participate for collective benefit and enjoyment rather than for sale to an impersonal audience or producer.
>
> (Bishop and Hoggett, 1986, p. 3)

Harper (1997) has argued that leisure is only satisfying when it involves some work-like features – that true happiness really does have to be earned. He criticizes much contemporary provision for making leisure too easy and offering only hollow satisfactions. Jeremy Seabrook (1988) noted in his interviews exploring the experiences of people from several parts of Britain that their most meaningful activities did not usually include those purchased in the market. People who make their own leisure can be creative and experience growth in their skills and capabilities. Equally important, they remain in full control of the character and pace of their activities. Serious leisure (see Chapter 1, pp. 8–9) appears always to be based on the arts, crafts, hobbies or volunteering rather than purchases of commodities (Stebbins, 1992; Parker *et al.*, 1993).

Undermining alternatives

Commercialism is said by its critics to undermine or suppress other kinds of leisure. These are likely to be marginalized and devalued by the culture that surrounds consumption. Spending confers status. Moreover, provided people have money, it is very easy to spend to be entertained and amused. We are offered endless opportunities. Purchasing a holiday package is more straightforward than constructing one's own itinerary. Operating a CD player is easier than learning to play a guitar or to sing. People who are reared in consumer societies may lack the basic skills for or even an awareness that there are alternative ways of creating enjoyable leisure. They may feel unable to have holidays if they cannot afford a package. Withdrawal of television or telephone communication may be experienced as a crisis. Hence the argument that, wherever commercial forces are unleashed, other kinds of leisure become casualties.

Individualization

A related criticism is that consumerism tends to break up communities. The contrast here is between the bonds that develop among people who make their own leisure and between people who purchase similar goods and services. Victoria de Grazia (1992) has made this contrast:

> the old ideal, for better or worse, was the politically mobilised citizen occupied in uplifting activities, whereas the contemporary ideal has become the individual consumer, self-interestedly and occasionally occupied with others, choosing his or her leisure activities at will, almost invariably by commercial means and influenced by a commercial idiom . . . The new associationalism differs in several respects from the

conception and practice of organised leisure in the past. It caters to a wide spectrum of clienteles, defined less by class than by market segments formed around income, gender, age, ethnicity and taste.

Post-communism

In recent times there has been a unique opportunity to study the impact of commercialism on people's leisure as a result of the collapse of communism in the former Soviet Union and East–Central Europe. The pace of change has been rapid; the societies became open to Western observers in the early 1990s, when older ways of life were still available for study, as were new emerging life-styles, which involved the purchase of the consumer products that began to flood in from the West. Under communism there had always been chronic shortages. Most goods were in short supply. People were told that they were fortunate to be experiencing the development of a socialist culture, which offered superior satis-factions to the consumer role (Hidy, 1982), but this was probably insufficient compensation to people who were spending hours in queues. The queues dis-appeared as soon as market reforms were introduced. The city stores suddenly became stocked with the full range of Western products. It became possible for consumers to obtain whatever they wanted – cars, fashion clothing, video cassettes and so on – provided they could pay. What was being lost?

First, the lifestyles of the former intelligentsia were undermined. These strata disintegrated and their members lost their positions as high-status, high-profile role models. The lifestyles of the intelligentsia were based partly but crucially on the production and consumption of state-subsidized high culture. With the end of communism most of the subsidies were withdrawn. The incomes of most intelligentsia families were insufficient to pay market prices for their cultural tastes. So domestic cultural production declined and was replaced by imported Western culture, mainly the lowbrow varieties (see Jung, 1994).

The former ways of life of other strata were also at risk. Under communism people retained the art of spending time without spending money. They had no alternative because their incomes were low and, in any case, there was little to buy. Young people would spend afternoons and evenings with friends in each other's homes, on the streets or in local parks. At weekends, and sometimes for holidays, they would visit nearby lakes or mountain regions, taking not only tents but often sufficient food to meet their needs. All this would be done while spend-ing little money, if any. Young people in the West would probably find this impossible. It appears that they cannot go out, into town centres or even down their neighbourhood streets, without purchasing confectionery and drinks. West-ern youth believe that they need fashionable jeans, shirts and trainers before they can face their peers. They also feel that they need the latest recordings for their home entertainment. Nowadays they eagerly await the time when they will be able to drive and afford motor cars (see Carabine and Longhurst, 2002). Young people in the communist countries succeeded in appearing much the same as Western youth, but at a much lower cost. They were also skilled at keeping abreast of the latest sounds by making and exchanging pirated tapes.

These skills and the ways of life in which they were embedded were not lost as soon as market reforms began, but they were clearly at risk (see Roberts and Jung, 1995). A minority of families were able to benefit immediately from the new earning opportunities that became available in the expanding private economies of the former communist countries. They were able to consume conspicuously and become the new high-profile, high-status role models. The advertising that accompanied market reforms extolled the lifestyles in question. And the new capitalist businesses with Western links demanded the suppression of the pirating and copying of their products. By the mid-1990s, a visit to McDonald's had become far more attractive to young people in East–Central Europe than an evening in the local park. The kind of communalism that was sustained when people had to make their own leisure, and which 'insulated' young people from the effects of unemployment in the early 1990s (see Chapter 3, pp. 94–95), has been another casualty of the reforms.

Commercial manipulation

Another part of the critique argues that consumerism has not triumphed in response to the authentic demands of customers but through the power of commercial interests. As explained above, since the 1950s a variant of Marxism has switched its focus away from the relationships of production to the relationships of consumption in explaining how, in present-day circumstances, the non-capitalist classes become locked into the system. These critics of consumerism have noted that consumption is just as vital as production in sustaining a capitalist economy. People need to be induced to sell their labour power. Equally they must be persuaded to spend their earnings. A strike of consumers would be just as crippling to capitalism as a strike of producers. Needless to say, a consumers' strike is far less probable. Consumers are dispersed, whereas workers are drawn together in workplaces, which creates opportunities for them to form conceptions of common grievances and interests and to organize for collective action: hence, it is argued, the crucial role of consumption and consumer culture in sustaining capitalist systems. It may not always be easy to make people want to work. It is usually far simpler to make them want to consume, and once they want to consume they need to work and earn. Once consumer wants have been created, capitalist systems can operate with few overt controls. The systems become 'hegemonized'. Capitalism is made to appear a natural response to people's wants. Early capitalism succeeded by controlling labour, whereas under late or postmodern capitalism it is the control of consumption that is said to be crucial.

Marxists, needless to say, have remained critical of capitalism. They have insisted that workers get poor value by selling pieces of themselves when they work daily and then try to buy them back after hours in the form of fun (Wright-Mills, 1956). Marxists argue that, while consumers can choose which particular products to purchase, they cannot determine the range that is made available, which always confines them to the consumer role (Clarke and Critcher, 1985). Furthermore, they point out that the price of making consumer choices is acceptance of the ideology of consumption, which is how people become locked into a basically exploitative and oppressive system (Chambers, 1983). According to Baudrillard (1998), this lock-up is consolidated by the consumer industries surrounding the entire population with a profusion of goods, thereby creating an illusion of mass happiness and equality. Anyone who does not share these feelings is made to feel 'odd' rather than normal.

McDonaldization

The basic arguments in the critique of consumerism were originally formulated by the Frankfurt School (see Box 7.3, p. 196), but these arguments have now been extended from the original culture industries to the wider range of consumer industries and the marketing techniques that were developed during the second half of the 20th century. In addition to the original Marxist version, there is now a Weberian variant that highlights the progressive rationalization or 'McDonaldization' of leisure and society in general.

George Ritzer (1993, 1998, 2004) has argued that Max Weber was basically correct about modern societies being progressively rationalized but mistaken in believing that this would be principally through the spread of large bureaucracies. Ritzer argues that the form of rationalization that is becoming dominant is in fact best illustrated by McDonald's. This business operates on the rational principles of efficiency, calculability, predictability and control, and pushes them to their utmost. Every aspect of production and delivery is measured. All the burgers are a precise size and are cooked for a precise period. They are exactly the same wherever they are sold. The surroundings, the restaurants themselves, are almost as predictable. Ritzer argues that this kind of rational organization is spreading rapidly in education and medical care, as well as in sport and leisure activities in general. He argues, following Weber, that rational organization can produce irrational consequences, such as boring products, which consumers may desert for something more exciting. Nevertheless, on account of their efficiency and the predictability of what will be obtained and the cost, Ritzer believes that McDonald's has a decisive advantage: hence his prediction of a progressive McDonaldization of society.

Resisting commercialization

Some critics of consumerism have formulated a reform agenda aimed at rescuing consumption from capitalist market relationships and making it expressive, passionate and liberating (Tomlinson, 1990). There are pessimists who believe that consumerism is irresistible and will roll on remorselessly. Some consider parts of the modern consumer industries to be beyond reform. For example, Mander (1980) has advocated the elimination of television, and insists that this case be taken seriously because, in his view, no reforms could address television's basic flaws. In Mander's view these are to deny individuals immediate experience by virtue of the ease with which second-hand experience is made available, elite control, the creation of confusion and submission among viewers, who are bombarded with powerful but often contradictory messages and images, and the inability of the medium to convey anything except simple linear messages.

However, other writers have made a case for step-by-step reform of the consumer industries (see, for example, Tomlinson, 1990). They hope, first, that through exposing their ideological role the influence of the capitalist consumer industries will be weakened. Simultaneously, they advocate making as many of these industries as possible democratically accountable, meaning responsible to their workers or consumers. They also propose strengthening the voluntary associations through which people are able to generate and manage their own leisure opportunities. The intention is to provide more satisfying alternatives to capitalist consumption and to enable people to form relationships with one another and, hopefully, to acquire the skills with which to take the class struggle into other domains, such as work and politics. This, in fact, was the agenda of the Greater London Council (1986) in the early 1980s when it sought to redirect some of its leisure spending towards tenants', women's, gay and lesbian, ethnic minority and other community organizations. The extent to which the Council's leisure spending was shifted away from the usual (mainly middle-class) beneficiaries was in fact minimal, but this did not prevent the Council's policies being labelled 'loony left' and featuring prominently among the arguments that led to its abolition (Tomlinson and Walton, 1986).

The Defence of Consumerism

Is radical reform necessary? Is consumerism as hostile to satisfying leisure as its critics suggest? The big question here is whether commerce has seduced us into acting contrary to our true interests, or whether, when we use commercial wares and immerse ourselves in consumer culture, we do this knowing full well what the costs and benefits will be and prefer the commercial package to any of the alternatives. Personally I find the second viewpoint the more plausible but, obviously enough, there are plenty of well-informed people who take the contrary position. So how are commerce and consumer culture defended?

Leisure and consumption

First, they can be defended by disputing claims that consuming and consumer values now dominate people's leisure. No one disputes that commerce has become more important in leisure provision than in the past. It is true that nowadays most of us purchase our holidays, Christmas celebrations and evenings out, and that when we spend leisure time at home we typically use consumer goods such as televisions, telephones, soft furnishings and so forth. But does this mean that our leisure is being reduced to or dominated by consumption? Graham Murdock's (1994) reminder is pertinent once again: a substantial minority is excluded from most parts of the present-day consumer society. In the UK the numbers who are retired on state benefits or otherwise non-employed have risen in recent decades, and many members of these groups have experienced a decline, not a growth, in their consumer spending. The spending of many households is swallowed by essentials. They are adrift from the strata whose members are able to spend the winter months planning their summer holidays, who spend the preceding months spending towards the Christmas celebrations, who scan the colour supplements in search of purchasing suggestions and who can afford to go lifestyle shopping on occasional Sundays.

It is rather misleading to portray even the relatively affluent's entire leisure in terms of consumption. It may be the case that in most of our leisure time we are using consumer products, but this is not all we are doing. We can be simultaneously relaxing, thinking and talking and people do not simply consume but use most of the goods that they buy. Consumption has possibly become an overworked concept. Tim Dant (2000) argues that critics dwell too long on marketing and purchasing, and pay too little attention to uses, contexts and users' meanings. It may all be straightforward consumption to the suppliers but rather different from the purchasers' perspectives. John Kelly (1986, 1991) has pointed out that in all social strata the most popular leisure activities, in terms of time accounted for, are relatively low-cost and that most people's core activities revolve around social relationships rather than bought goods or services. Kelly has shown that, when people prioritize their own uses of leisure, they insist that the activities in which they participate with other people are more important than the commodities they acquire and possess. Leisure is broader than consumption conceptually (see Mullett, 1988) and in terms of the reality of people's everyday lives. There has been a growth in consumption and commercial leisure provision, but have these trends really squeezed other kinds of leisure? Much leisure time is still self-organized privately by individuals, families and groups of friends. The voluntary sector has not diminished but has actually grown, only parts of it have been commercialized, and the strata with the highest incomes and spending power are the most likely to belong to these organizations. Also, the public sector has played and still plays a major, not a residual, role in leisure provision and, although it is now subject to greater commercial pressures than in the past, its sustenance still depends primarily on political will, not market forces.

Consumer choice

Portraying consumers as passive victims whose purchases and leisure are governed by the skill of advertisers and other marketing specialists conflicts with much of what we know about how purchases are actually made and used. The evidence suggests that customers are usually discerning and discriminating, rather than gullible, and typically use the things they buy for their own purposes. People purchase motor cars so that they can then drive themselves to and for leisure, to places and at times of their own choice. They buy garden tools so that they can design and cultivate their plots according to their own tastes. They purchase standard houses and then paint, decorate and customize the dwellings according to their own aspirations. Are these choices trivial? Are they from a very limited range of options? Has the range been narrowed or has it been widened by the growth of the consumer industries? The development of commercial leisure during the 20th century in Western countries has arguably been a great liberating force that has done more than anything else to widen people's leisure options.

There is now a considerable literature showing that most media audiences are anything but passive. In addition to audience research that calculates the size and composition of the audiences for television and radio programmes and the readerships of newspapers and magazines, we now have studies of how people actually view and listen and what they do with their reading matter. This research shows, for example, that television viewers are not passive receptacles. Few can be described as hooked or addicts. Families discuss and sometimes quarrel over which channel to select. The action and talk on screen may lead to discussion and argument among the viewers (see Morley, 1986). This is in line with the findings from early research into the impact of the printed media, about a two-step flow of communication: from the media into primary groups, where information is sifted and opinions are accepted or rejected. Sometimes the output from the audio-visual media is used merely as background noise. The young Finns in Paivi Pontinen's (1996) study usually ate, talked or rested while they 'watched' television. It was the exception rather than the rule when they switched on to watch anything in particular. These young people had no loyalties to any particular channels or favourite programmes. Critics of the culture industries have always claimed to take proper account of consumers' choices. Ien Ang (1996) accepts, indeed stresses, that present-day television audiences are plural rather than monolithic, that they have a wider than ever choice of channels and programmes, that they are active meaning producers and that their meaning production is deeply embedded in the micro-politics of their everyday lives. Even so, she disputes that this is leading to the disempowerment of the television industry. Rather, she argues that a reconfiguration of the television industry's power is under way: that the 'hard-to-get audience' is being built into production systems, that viewer choice and self-determination are being developed as hegemonic ideas (accepted as simply factually true by everyone) and that this blinds audiences to the limits of the range from which they can choose. The contrary view is that most people have their own leisure priorities, which are responsive primarily to their economic, gender and age situations rather than implanted by leisure suppliers, that they use radio and television accordingly and that much the same applies when they are making other purchases.

Chapter 1 (pp. 8–9) introduced Robert Stebbins's (1992) concept of 'serious leisure'. In coining this concept Stebbins has drawn attention to how people can become seriously committed, highly knowledgeable and increasingly skilled in sports, breeding tropical fish, choral singing, wine tasting, astronomy, acting or whatever they are passionate about. Most leisure may be non-serious in Stebbins's sense, but all the indicators suggest that consumers are becoming increasingly knowledgeable and discriminating. Their tastes are not being progressively shaped, homogenized or McDonaldized by advertising and other marketing techniques. Chris Gratton (1992) has drawn attention to the rise of the skilled consumer. David Darton (1986) has highlighted the growth of leisure connoisseurs, who have discriminating tastes in wines, visits to stately homes, meals out and weekend breaks. Rather than becoming increasingly passive, consumers are becoming more active and keen to participate in structuring their activities. For example, the holiday purchasing public is becoming more mature. The 'standard package' is becoming less popular (see Henley Centre, 1993). A growing number of holidaymakers want something different, and often welcome the opportunity to construct parts of their itineraries, to pick their own hotels and where to eat. This applies in all product markets.

Hugo van der Poel (1994) has argued that the 'modularization' of leisure provision enables people to pick and mix their own lifestyles from the variety of goods and services that are available. This is not a particularly recent trend. In the 1970s, the work on post-war youth cultures at Birmingham University's Centre for Contemporary Cultural Studies (see Chapter 5, pp. 137–138) shattered the view that youth styles were constructed 'up there' and then 'sold' to young people. These researchers explained how young people themselves had created Teddy boy, mod, rocker, skinhead and other styles by blending products in their own ways and how the media and other merchandisers had to try to read and follow, but were unable to dictate, young people's leisure tastes and activities (see Hall and Jefferson, 1976; Hebdige, 1979).

Supply-side pluralism

Defenders of commerce and its consumer culture argue that the reason why consumers are able to make significant choices is that they have so many leisure goods and services to choose from. It is true that some leisure business sectors have large, sometimes multinational, operators, who strenuously attempt to shape consumer taste and demand. This applies in newspapers, broadcasting, holidays, drink manufacture and gambling. However, even the biggest businesses are not monopolies and, even if they were, they would not be marketing essentials such as fuel that people have to buy. Moreover, the big operators share all their product markets with hosts of smaller competitors. Most restaurants, holiday companies, sports goods suppliers and television programme makers are small businesses. They operate in markets where tastes are fickle, trade is often seasonal, competition intense and the business failure rate high. These businesses do their best to cater to consumers' demands; they cannot afford to try to dictate or even shape people's preferences (see Butler, 1978; Hodgson, 1988; Berrett et al., 1993). Many proprietors of small leisure businesses do it partly from interest. They were often involved in the markets as consumers prior to becoming suppliers, and depend for their success or survival on their inside knowledge, flair and initiative. Most leisure markets are intricately segmented. Market forces do not standardize tastes. Nor does commerce normally seek out, and cater exclusively for, a 'lowest common denominator'. The best recipe for success is normally to identify and cater for a specialist market segment. This applies whether the merchandise is printed matter, housing, sports clothing, prepared meals, holidays or fitness training. Most leisure products can be aimed realistically at only limited sections of the public, which is why enthusiasts with specialist knowledge can often find niches for their small businesses.

They realize that their viability depends on knowing their customers' preferences, and providing a 'quality' service that is at least a little better than or different
from everything else on the market (see Roberts *et al.*, 1988). Commerce will
cater for all, majority and minority, demands for which customers are willing to
pay the market price.

Anyone who is dissatisfied with the range of commercial provisions can look
to voluntary associations. These will do anything for which their members have
sufficient enthusiasm. This is the engine that drives the voluntary sector, the
equivalent to profit in commercial businesses (see Bishop and Hoggett, 1986).
Some voluntary organizations cater for their own members' interests. Others aim
to meet the needs of other groups. Any medium-sized town has hundreds of
voluntary bodies. These are based on hobbies, sports, the arts and anything else
that has enthusiasts. Commercial leisure has not wholly absorbed the voluntary
sector – and arguably cannot – because these are not functional equivalents or
alternatives. Each provides its own distinctive experiences and satisfactions.
Money is never likely to rule more than a small part of sport. Most teams and
clubs are still amateur and exist simply because their players and officers are
enthusiastic and want to express their enthusiasm. Voluntary effort not only
reduces the costs of participation but delivers special satisfactions.

Then there is the public sector. This will still provide anything that politicians
want to provide and pay for. The many reasons why central and local government inevitably becomes involved in leisure provisions were explained in
Chapter 1 (pp. 11–13). For present purposes, it is sufficient to note that the
public sector adds substantially to the range of leisure provision, and competitive
tendering for the management of Britain's local authority facilities is not reducing
the scope of the public sector. If they find nothing attractive on offer in any of
the 'sectors', people do not have to use any. They can spend their leisure
privately and do their own things, either in solitude or with friends or family
members.

Given the diversity of leisure supply, is it really possible for any provider, or
even one of the main sectors, to stamp a clear pattern on the public's leisure
behaviour? Public provision may make a difference at the margin but it cannot
force people to do what the providers might prefer. At any rate, public provision
cannot be this influential in market economies. Under state socialism, where
there was no voluntary sector and where commercial provision was minimal, it
was possible for the state to make a significant and noticeable difference,
though even under communism people at leisure could withdraw into private
life in their homes and with their families. In market economies, in countries
where people are able to self-organize, surely it is they who ultimately decide
what voluntary associations will do and which public sector and commercial
facilities will be used. Most people, needless to say, pick and mix, and the end
result is that the roles of public, voluntary and commercial provision become
thoroughly interwoven. Sport teams that run on voluntary effort often play in
publicly provided facilities and nearly always use clothing and equipment
supplied by commerce.

This book's position is that explanations of leisure behaviour have to start
with types of people – their circumstances, desires and opportunities – not types

of provision. It is different when explaining what people do at work or the education they receive. People's jobs are organized by businesses that have to meet market demands at market prices. The employers decide how work will be organized and then recruit workers to do the jobs. In school education, over 90% of all pupils are in publicly funded establishments and it is state policies that dictate what opportunities will be available. Explanations of the types of education that different groups receive have to begin with the system. Leisure is different. Exaggerating the force of consumerism and consumer culture is just one example of failing to recognize this.

Strengthening consumer sovereignty

There is another extreme, but possibly more realistic, view: that in present-day capitalism the balance of market power has swung decisively in favour of consumers (see Miller, 1995). This argument points out that consumers, who are mostly car drivers, have a variety of places where they can shop and numerous commodities on which they can spend their money. If they stay at home, there are many things they can do or watch. Their consumer choices are registered constantly in supermarket and other tills and are nowadays fed instantly by computers not just to shelf-fillers but also to the retailers' suppliers. The retailers have to stock what consumers want, at competitive prices, otherwise their market shares will contract, so they must pass on consumers' messages and pressures, ultimately to the producers. According to this argument, it is the pressure of Developed World consumers, now the supreme historical force, that is forcing down the incomes of Developing World producers and, increasingly, also pay levels in much of the Developed World. This adds another dimension to the picture (see Chapter 3) of people's own consumption aspirations subjecting them to heavier pressure in their roles as workers.

Nowadays consumers often act collectively in an organized way. Consumer associations, which test and compare products and recommend best buys, began in the USA in the 1920s and have since spread throughout the world (Hilton, 2005). Consumers normally use their consumer power, whether individually or collectively, to get best value for their money, but they can also act with socio-political objectives. This behaviour has become more common than many people suppose. In Sweden 52% of women and 43% of men can be described as 'political consumers', meaning that they have participated in boycotts or 'buy-cotts' during the last 12 months. These consumers tend to be in their 30s or older (not young people), well-educated high earners, interested in politics and with leftward orientations, but less trusting of mainstream politicians than other citizens (Stolle and Micheletti, 2005). Their aim may be to bring pressure on governments they wish to undermine (the white South African governments in the apartheid era, for example) or businesses that are judged to be threatening the environment or paying poverty wages in impoverished countries, or to promote what the purchasers regard as fair trade (fair prices for the producers). Political and otherwise organized consumer action has replaced consumer cooperatives as the main form of collective consumer behaviour. It became one of the new social movements of the 20th century, and it could become an even more powerful force during the 21st century.

The End of Consumerism?

Social historians such as Gary Cross (1993) have warned against treating modern consumer culture as a permanent fixture. This sociocultural form has been powerful only since the mid-20th century, and then only in the Western world, and it is most unlikely to endure or retain its current strength eternally. Marxists have drawn attention to the hegemonic tendencies of consumer capitalism while arguing that alternative ways of organizing and catering for leisure are possible and that there are at least signs of 'resistance' in popular cultures. Non-Marxist writers such as Gabriel and Lang (see Box 7.4) have speculated on how consumer cultures are most likely to end or be transformed. Actually Gabriel and Lang do not predict the end of consumerism so much as its transformation, or maybe just a gradual evolution from the kind of consumerism that was dominant in the mid-20th century.

Box 7.4. The unmanageable consumer.

Gabriel and Lang (1995) claim that the form of consumer culture that became dominant in the mid-20th century is already being eclipsed. They argue that the 1950s and 1960s were the golden decades of mass consumption. Its success then is said to have depended upon:

- The ascendancy of Fordist modes of economic organization. Big was best. Mass production created affordable products that could be mass-marketed.
- Keynesian economic management, which created secure jobs and incomes, which made people willing to spend and spend, often using credit.
- New types of goods were being produced, consumers were immature and were easily persuaded to purchase standardized articles.

Gabriel and Lang argue that subsequently the props on which mass consumption rested have been removed or gravely weakened:

- Jobs and incomes have become less secure.
- People are now experiencing spending fatigue. It has become more difficult to persuade people that yet another purchase will quench their appetites.
- More mature consumers have become fickle and discriminating. Their purchases tend to be opportunistic and spasmodic and, from the point of view of suppliers, chaotic and unmanageable.
- Businesses are now obliged, and are able, to respond because new technology has made small beautiful. Small-batch production can be as profitable as long runs. Small businesses can afford state-of-the-art technology. Firms are also able to make themselves flexible. This enables them to target market niches rather than the mass, and to respond to constant, unpredictable changes in the volume and types of consumer demand.

Transformed growth

Writers who claim that an end to consumer culture is actually in sight usually do so on the ground that 'things just cannot go on like this indefinitely'. Some of these arguments, critiques of the 'work and spend' society and the ongoing polarization into the money-rich, time-poor and the money-poor, time-rich, were encountered in Chapter 3. Martin and Mason (1998) have drawn these arguments together in a critique of social and economic policies that prioritize growth in output, employment and affluence and allow nothing to stand in the way. They argue that such policies simply create too many problems. Some of these problems have to do with the distribution of paid work and free time. They point to one section of the population having too much paid work and another section having too little income to use free time to maximum advantage. They claim that current policies and trends are depriving most people of 'quality' free time. They also argue that current trends are placing unsustainable pressure on space and other environmental resources. Hence their advocacy of transformed growth, which would redistribute paid work more evenly across the lifespan, allow employees to package their free time in more useful 'chunks' (such as sabbaticals) and simultaneously reduce the number of people outside the workforce completely. They advocate educating children and young people in purposeful, serious, self-developmental uses of leisure and locating more leisure facilities in local neighbourhoods so as to reduce travelling.

The weakness in the Martin and Mason scenario is that its achievement seems to depend on a government-led reorientation of education, coupled with public information and opinion-forming campaigns to change people's attitudes towards work and free time. It all seems as likely as Marxist prognoses that consumerism will one day be overthrown by working-class resistance. No doubt there will eventually be an end to consumer culture as currently known. In the immediate future, however, the most likely trends appear to be an intensification of the consumer processes highlighted by Miller (see above, p. 207), and the significant but subtle changes in the character of consumption described by Gabriel and Lang (Box 7.4, p. 208). What about the problems? It is most likely that in the first decades of the 21st century, as in the 20th century, people will simply cope with them.

Summary

This chapter's big, overarching questions have been:

- Is commerce, with its consumer culture, a Trojan horse that has risen with the growth of leisure while depressing the quality of people's leisure lives?
- Have commerce and consumer culture imprisoned us in a velvet cage, or have they enlarged people's options and enhanced the quality of their leisure?

The chapter opened by defining consumption, the counterpart of production, and explained how modern consumption differs from consumption in earlier societies – by its separation from production by space and time and on account of the extent to which money decouples most of what people produce from what they themselves consume. The chapter then reviewed the growth of commercial leisure and the spread of consumer culture, which had become the leading material culture in Euro-America by the mid-20th century. This happened as a result of a set of partly related and partly coincidental developments, principally the expansion of consumption, the development of new marketing strategies and Keynesian macroeconomic management. We saw how, over time, shopping (some of it, for some people) has ceased to be a chore and has become a leisure activity in its own right, or at least a leisure-like activity, and how public- and voluntary-sector leisure providers have been affected by needing to operate in consumerist contexts.

The chapter then moved to its truly controversial issues:

- Critiques of consumerism, typically scathing, mainly by Marxists, but with Weberian and other contributions.
- The defence of commerce and consumer culture, with free-market economists to the fore in these arguments, but with contributions from other social sciences.
- Are we currently glimpsing the end of the consumer society or its radical transformation into a new kind of consumer age?

Further Reading

On the historical rise of consumer culture

Cross, G. (1993) *Time and Money: The Making of Consumer Culture*. Routledge, London.

For critiques of the consumer society

Bauman, Z. (1998b) *Work, Consumerism and the New Poor*. Open University Press, Buckingham, UK.
Clarke, J. and Critcher, C. (1985) *The Devil Makes Work*. Macmillan, London.
Ritzer, G. (1993) *The McDonaldization of Society*. Pine Forge Press, Thousand Oaks, California.

For a relatively heavy theoretical neo-Marxist critique

Baudrillard, J. (1998) *The Consumer Society: Myths and Structures*. Sage, London.

On current trends and likely future developments

Gabriel, Y. and Lang, T. (1995) *The Unmanageable Consumer: Contemporary Consumption and its Fragmentation*. Sage, London.

8 The Transformation of Leisure?

Introduction

Modern societies have always been dynamic, continuously changing, and this remains the case today. Are the current changes so extensive and so fundamental as to change the character and to require a new concept of leisure? The preceding chapters have sometimes hit problems in applying the leisure concept adopted at the outset of this book to people's actual lives. Pristine concepts are always liable to grate on encountering a murkier real world. This applies with definitions of education, the family, religion, social class and work as well as leisure. Some degree of jarring when concepts meet reality has to be tolerated. However, critics allege that the amount of jarring when leisure is defined basically as 'time left over' (as throughout this book up to now) is simply too great to be tolerated, that the amount of jarring is increasing as the character of our societies changes and likewise the role played by and the character of our leisure.

This chapter proceeds by introducing the criticisms (there are many) of residual concepts of leisure. It then presents an alternative way of defining leisure – as a kind of experience – and the advantages claimed for such a definition. This leads on to a section on the weaknesses of experiential concepts and finally the case for building squarely on previous research and existing knowledge, which will mean continuing to study people's varied experiences within (residual) leisure.

Criticisms of Residual Concepts

What is wrong with defining leisure as time and money that are 'left over' and therefore 'free'? Everyone agrees that the definition leads to problems. First, there are problems in identifying the leisure of the non-employed. Some have commitments that can be treated as the equivalents of paid work – pupils and students who attend schools and colleges full-time, for example. But few of the unemployed and the retired have commitments or obligations that are close equivalents of paid work. In trying to study their leisure, questions arise such as whether they lead entire lives of leisure or have no leisure at all. Both propositions look ludicrous. And the non-employed are not a small insignificant minority. Less than half the populations in Western countries are in paid employment, and the non-employed sections are growing. There are more unemployed than in the 1950s and 1960s, and the numbers who are retired are not only higher than in the recent past but will grow steadily throughout the early decades of the 21st century. Roughly three-quarters of all free time is 'enjoyed' by people who are not in full-time jobs (Martin and Mason, 1998).

Secondly, it has always been difficult to apply the residual concept to women's lives, irrespective of whether they have paid jobs. This is due not just to the quantity, but also to the character, of women's domestic obligations. In women's lives these obligations are not normally time-bounded. Women, who are the principal, albeit unpaid, carers of dependent children and nowadays increasingly the elderly, have never had fixed hours of work. Hence the case for 'feminist' research methods and concepts that identify leisure as a feature of tasks, relationships or experiences rather than as blocks of time.

Thirdly, the residual concept has always done some violence to the lives of male employees. Just as some women have experienced going out to their paid jobs as an escape from domestic drudgery and tedium, so some, possibly most, men have obtained leisure-like experiences at and from their paid work. This becomes apparent as soon as investigators ask what people lose when they become unemployed. In most cases they miss the companionship of work colleagues and the interest, challenge and sense of accomplishment they found in their occupations.

Fourthly, it can be argued that current trends are fast outdating the residual concept of leisure and diminishing the merits it once possessed. Work time is being destandardized. Alongside this, the notion of there being set times for leisure interests and activities could also be rendered obsolete. Women still do most of the housework but men, albeit slowly, are becoming more involved. There is a pervasive process of individualization, which requires individuals to negotiate their own paths through life. In the case of leisure this means accumulating personal 'capital' from various sources, not just specifically leisure settings, during successive life stages, and finding ways to use this capital to advantage in situations subsequently encountered during the course of careers in family life, paid employment and leisure. Rob Lynch and Tony Veal (1996) distinguish modern leisure from several earlier varieties and also from postmodern leisure, which is said to be spreading. According to Lynch and Veal, in modern times work and leisure were clearly demarcated; leisure time was otherwise residual time, which could be used for rest, entertainment or self-development and was serviced by specialized leisure industries. They believe that, in present-day and increasingly postmodern conditions, the old boundaries between work and leisure have become fractured and fluid, that (for some) there has been an explosion of opportunities to spend money on 'stylized' goods, services and activities, whose main value lies in their culturally assigned meanings, and that leisure thereby becomes a component of broader lifestyles, whose significance extends well beyond the now traditional functions of modern leisure. It can be argued that some leisure pursuits, which used to be very occasional and therefore out of the ordinary, have now become so common as to break down the everyday/out-of-the-ordinary distinction. According to Rojek and Urry (1997), this applies to tourism. Nowadays many of us travel, and encounter visitors in our home areas, so frequently that all this may be regarded as mundane rather than an escape from routine. This is just one example of a blurring of the divisions that once made leisure a more easily recognized part of life. The mounting problems with residual concepts are exposed, some argue, by the growth of uses of time and money that cannot be clearly assigned to leisure or anything else. Time spent in education, especially post-compulsory education, is one example. Part-time students, whose numbers have risen, might be regarded as choosing to devote some of their free time to education, but many of the students would argue that their education is at least partly vocational and that they regard their time spent studying as work. Full-time students will usually regard their education in this way but they may also agree that the intrinsic satisfactions and general attractions of student life are among their reasons for being at college. Time spent shopping has risen. In the past, leisure researchers usually treated shopping as a chore. Nowadays it can be argued that much window-shopping and the subsequent purchasing ought to be classified as leisure. The sums that households spend on food (for home consumption as well as when eating out), transport, housing, clothes and telephones usually include a leisure element. None of these are minor items, but it is difficult, if not impossible, to decide how much of the costs of a motor vehicle, for example, should be regarded as leisure spending rather than as a domestic or work requirement. All these examples, it can be argued, illustrate the breakdown of 'modern' boundaries and the break-up of residual leisure.

Some leisure researchers have always seen advantages in defining leisure not as a type of time but as a kind of experience, and they are now able to claim that history is on their side. They can argue that the rise of modernity was accompanied by a dominant form of time organization, in which most things had proper times and places, whereas in the era that we are entering these links are more tenuous. Even some who doubt whether contemporary societies are really experiencing a postmodern transformation still welcome postmodernist thinking for rescuing social thought from the illusions of modernity under whose influence, it is claimed, we imagined that our 'grand narratives' could explain, or even change, a real world that was always far less orderly (Rojek, 1995).

It is worth noting that no one recommends defining leisure as a type of activity. It has always been just too obvious that any activity might be leisure or work. Gardening and playing sport are examples. Some people are paid to watch films and television to monitor the output. Simply observing behaviour has never been sufficient to establish whether the activity should be classified as paid work, unpaid work or leisure. The debate among leisure scholars has always been whether an activity should be regarded as leisure depending on when it occurs or whether the actor's experience should be the arbiter.

Leisure as Experience

Decentring leisure

Decentring, a little-used word except by the social theorists who are part of the 'postmodern turn', was introduced into leisure studies by Chris Rojek in his book *Decentring Leisure* (1995). Writers have different ways of describing what decentring means. Rojek himself explains that something is decentred when we realize that:

> meaning and reality are structured by language. What we take to be truthful and objective is merely an effect of language ... [Leisure] is part of the representational and symbolic machinery that we use in order to negotiate daily life. (p. 131)

This is said to be a radical view insofar as:

> most contributions to political economy assume that real needs can be identified and that effective policies can be formulated to address them. Decentring violates these assumptions. It treats needs and policies as links in a metonymic chain in which meaning is permanently unstable ... In the light of this critique leisure studies is reduced to the mere play of signs and symbols. (pp. 131–132)

In other words, if, when we develop theories about leisure, we believe we are making statements about a real world out there, we are gravely mistaken. In fact, what we take to be knowledge is simply a product of our use of language. Subsequently Rojek (2000a) has applied his reconceptualization in showing how leisure can be treated as a cultural product that people use to construct performances and to weave identities for themselves. Everyone who uses a language is likely to accept its view of the world as objective truth. This applies equally to the discourses of laypeople and scientists. Decentring (in Rojek's sense) makes everything relative. The pedestal of objectivity is kicked away. Truth becomes merely a discursive convention. Once scholars realize that there are always many possible ways in which things can be constituted discursively, they are expected to cease imagining that their own discourses are superior 'grand narratives' that offer the correct interpretations of events. They are expected to abandon this 'modernist' project and. . . well, they may conclude that there is little else for them to do but to reflect discursively on their postmodern predicament. Their only option, so it might appear from their own theory, is to become a tribe of consenting adults who admit converts to an inner circle upon proving that they accept the articles of faith, can use the language and respect the house rules of discourse.

None of these ideas are new but they have come to the fore in contemporary social thought because a critical mass of postmodern thinkers, represented in most of the social sciences, have taken the radical implications seriously. Some believe that their own frame of mind is shared by increasing numbers of lay groups, in which case postmodernity is held to exist beyond social theory 'out there' in society. However, symbolic interactionists and sociologists influenced by phenomenology have a long record of not only recognizing but insisting that actors' definitions of situations are crucial to how they respond. Mainstream sociology has long been sensitive to there being many possible readings of any situation and to the fact that phenomena such as social classes, deviance, poverty and leisure do not exist as ready-made structures for citizens to access and researchers to study but are constituted and reproduced only because people believe in them and apply these labels to particular times, groups, events, activities and experiences.

Social theorists who believe that 'reality is in the mind of the beholder' have normally sought an escape from the predicament in which they might appear to be locked by their own theory. They have usually tried to claim a privileged position, maybe achieved through reflexivity, taking account of the relative status of truth, building this into their own rules of discourse and thereby gaining knowledge of other groups' realities, which amounts to more than a construction grounded in the theorists' own linguistic conventions. Having 'escaped', they have proceeded just like other 'modern' scientists except, possibly, that they have accepted their need to operate with a heightened sense of permanent and pervasive contradiction (Ang, 1996). If a privileged position is deemed impossible, there would appear to be nothing left for theorists to do except to work discursively within their own theories, attributing truth to or disputing each other's work, but without any pretence of generating objective knowledge about an external world. However, anyone who proceeds to write about leisure 'out there' in society is making an escape attempt, but having decentred the subject the first question that such enquirers are likely to ask is: 'How do people recognize it [leisure] in their own everyday lives?' Investigators cease treating phenomena as things that can be observed independently of laypeople's perceptions and experiences and realize that a thorough understanding must be through these experiences. Many leisure researchers have long believed that the starting point for their enquiries should be lay people's experiences and definitions. The postmodern turn, with its insistence upon decentring, has supported this alternative way of identifying leisure.

Everyday concepts

Many researchers have asked members of the public what leisure means to them. This is a matter of some interest, however leisure is defined by the investigator. In order to explain the leisure behaviour of specific groups, it may be considered useful, if not absolutely essential, to establish what they think leisure is. All the relevant enquiries have produced the same kinds of answers (see Stockdale, 1986; Samdahl, 1988; Mobily, 1989; Kleiber *et al.*, 1993). Some groups, the unemployed and housewives, for example, often query whether the term leisure has any relevance to their own lives, but this implies an understanding of what leisure is like for other people. Leisure has proved a meaningful concept for all groups within modern societies, and their everyday understandings highlight three features. First, it is common for leisure to be distinguished from work but, secondly, when lay people appear to opt for a residual definition they usually state or imply that leisure is different because work is disagreeable or has to be done. Their everyday understandings associate leisure with choice, lack of constraint, being able to express oneself and doing things voluntarily. The word 'freedom' often crops up in these contexts. Thirdly, people also refer to leisure as being pleasurable or enjoyable and sometimes relaxing and to these experiences being immediate or intrinsic. All sections of the populations in all modern societies appear to share very similar understandings of leisure. They may have different views on whether they have enough and the quality of what they have, but there appear to be no fundamental disputes about what leisure is.

Leisure researchers who opt for experiential definitions can claim to be respecting and responding to their subjects' ideas and can recommend their concepts on these grounds. Christine Howe and Ann Rancourt (1990) have proposed a definition of leisure as 'a self-enhancing affective state'. John Neulinger's (1990) definition is 'self-motivated conduct that contains its own reward'. The particular forms of words are less important than how this entire group of definitions tries to respond to ordinary people's conceptions of leisure as self-determining and fulfilling.

Optimal experience

Many writers who operate with experiential concepts have been attracted by the work of Mihaly Csikszentmihalyi (1990, 1993), the American social psychologist who has conducted a series of investigations to explore what people mean when they claim that something is enjoyable (see Box 1.1, p. 7). Some leisure researchers, though not Csikszentmihalyi himself, have sought to associate flow with leisure. When such connections are made, it is not being suggested that when at leisure people experience constant flow. However, it can be claimed that, when this 'optimal experience' is not available in other areas of people's lives, they are likely to seek and achieve it through leisure activities. People may experience flow in sporting contests, where optimal experience depends on meeting an opponent of equal ability, or they can become thoroughly absorbed in dancing, playing music, listening to music, reading or whatever. It is often suggested that optimal experience is most likely to be achieved through leisure. For example, Rojek (1995, p. 187) argues that 'As paid work becomes routinised and mechanised leisure becomes the axis for the development of creativity.' Even if people are not gaining optimal experience through leisure, it can be argued that they could be, and maybe should be at least seeking it.

Whatever view is taken on the merits and relevance of Csikszentmihalyi's flow concept, experiential approaches can be commended for raising questions about what people are seeking and deriving from leisure. Eric Dunning (1996) has criticized the conventional study of leisure (and much else) for failing to pay proper attention to the sensual and emotional aspects of life. In the study of leisure he believes that this neglect is inexcusable since, according to Dunning, one of the principal roles of leisure is to counterbalance the emotional staleness of 'civilized' societies. The figurational sociology Dunning advocates requires behaviour to be analysed in its total context, but only having paid full regard to the minutiae of the immediate setting and the behaviour itself. As soon as we approach leisure in this way, Dunning believes that we cannot fail to recognize that it is all about expressing emotions – in fact, most forms of play are designed to be emotion-raising, and often require sociability and movement also.

Experiential approaches start from the 'inside', with what people at leisure are actually doing and their immediate contexts, motivations, satisfactions and frustrations. Researchers find themselves asking what people mean when they claim to enjoy something, what it means to have fun and what makes people laugh. Detailed studies have shown that laughter can be provoked by exposing the private thoughts that people are likely to harbour but keep to themselves, when an alternative view of everyday situations is suddenly 'switched on' or when normal hierarchies and relationships are abruptly overturned (see Mulkay, 1988; Podilchak, 1991; Mulkay and Howe, 1994). Explanations of fun turn out to be disappointingly sombre!

Leisure and self-development

There is not just one singular experiential approach to studying leisure. In fact, there is a major split between those who use experiential definitions alongside or within and those who propose their concepts as alternatives to residual definitions.

John Kelly, an American sociologist, is associated with the former type of experiential concept. He defines leisure not simply as time that is otherwise uncommitted and which is therefore free for individuals to use in any way they wish, but as a particular kind of way in which this time can be used. Kelly (1983, 1987, 1994) has successively described his approach to leisure as existential, symbolic interactionist and critical constructionist, but his preoccupation has always been with how leisure is experienced. He argues that modern societies create space, leisure space, in which people are not only able to express but create roles and identities for themselves. Leisure is said to provide 'freedom to be'. Kelly argues that our capacity not merely to act parts but actually to create roles and identities for ourselves is uniquely human. Human behaviour is not wholly pro-grammed by biology. Nor are we just social products who do no more than enact the roles into which we are socialized, having been rewarded for compliance and punished for deviance. Along with many other contemporary sociologists, Kelly emphasizes our ability to be 'reflexive', which means that, far from just mirroring our biological natures and social contexts, we are able to stand back, take an 'outside' view of ourselves and the roles that are mapped for us, develop ideas about how both might be changed and act upon these ideas. According to Kelly, this has become possible to a greater extent in leisure than in any other sphere of life. Leisure is said to provide 'freedom to be' or, perhaps more accurately, 'free-dom to become'. Leisure, as stated above, can provide this because, according to Kelly, leisure is 'beyond necessity'; our societies have no reason to restrict us as severely in leisure as in other areas of life, and therefore actors can experiment and let themselves go without dreading the consequences of failure.

Primitive playfulness

Chris Rojek's experiential definition of leisure differs from Kelly's in several ways, including the absence of any social structural accompaniment. In all his work Rojek has criticized the 'social formalism' that treats leisure as a product of a particular kind of society and that seeks explanations of its uses in the actors' other social roles (Rojek, 1985). Rojek regards such treatments of leisure as part of a failed modernist project that has sought to explain everything rationally and which has believed that, once explained, affairs might be brought under rational control. The 'donatory' approach to leisure policy – the idea that good leisure can be delivered to the people by policymakers and programme operators – is another alleged failure of the modernist project. Rojek has tried to persuade leisure researchers to dispense with these illusions. He is sceptical of claims that we are becoming a different kind of postmodern society but is attracted to postmodernist thought insofar as it recovers 'what the illusions of modernity have concealed' (Rojek, 1995, p. 192). Rojek believes that what is nowadays called leisure springs from a pre-social human impulse to seek pleasure. He believes that these impulses are beyond wholly rational control either by individuals themselves or by their societies, and that the impulses are always liable to erupt, often in surprising ways. So leisure experiences are liable to occur chaotically while we are at work, at school, at political or religious gatherings and, of course, in specifically leisure behaviour. The job of leisure research, in Rojek's view, is to identify the outcomes of human pleasure-seeking and to study the ways in which various interest groups endeavour to control other people's pleasure-seeking, to contain it within rules – spatial, temporal and behavioural boundaries – in accordance with the prescribers' particular moral precepts or commercial interests. However, it follows from its elementary nature that pleasure-seeking can never be totally controlled.

Ning Wang (1996) has offered a similar conceptualization of leisure. He suggests that in all societies it has been possible to recognize two broad types of behaviour. First, there is conduct governed by social structures and rules, whose character has varied by time and place. However, all societies have possessed an 'order' with which members have been expected and constrained to comply. Secondly, whatever the social, economic and political order, Ning Wang argues that 'Eros' always finds expression: people always do some things spontaneously simply for diversion, amusement or fun. He argues that part of the modernist project has been the confinement of Eros within particular parts of life that are generally described as leisure. This particular division, he recognizes, has been a characteristic of modern societies. In contrast, he claims, Eros itself, the source of what we call leisure, is not specifically modern.

Universal relevance

An advantage claimed for experiential concepts is that they escape from the notion that only modern societies have leisure. As Ning Wang points out, all peoples seem to have found ways to do things for pleasure, for fun. This was recognized in Chapter 1. Maybe people in pre-modern times had no words corresponding to 'leisure' but it is unnecessary to be able to spell or even say leisure in order to enjoy it. Hultsman (1995) has argued that our preoccupation with definitions is specifically Western. In other civilizations people have been satisfied that something simply 'is'. Leisure may be organized differently in modern societies, channelled through specifically modern time structures and activity patterns, but all cultures have had games and pastimes and have provided some space for people to be self-determining and to enlarge their abilities and self-concepts. In most pre-modern societies the equivalents of modern leisure appear to have been both less commercial and less individualistic. Play was more likely to express communal solidarity than each individual's distinctiveness (de Grazia, 1992; Somnez *et al.*, 1993). Experiential concepts permit comparisons that often suggest that contemporary leisure is relatively impoverished.

Many writers have noted affinities between modern leisure aspirations and a Greek ideal that was expressed clearly by Aristotle (see, for example, Hemingway, 1988). Aristotle approved of the manner in which the free men of Athens had the opportunity to develop all their talents – their aesthetic tastes, physical prowess, intellectual faculties and political skills. The Aristotelian ideal was the fully developed, well-rounded individual who could move gracefully, act, throw, run, read, debate and participate in civic affairs. Marx appeared to share this ideal, with his vision of a society in which people might work in the morning and hunt or write poetry during the rest of the day (see Rojek, 1984). The fact that such ideals echo through history can be offered as proof that it is only the form, not the inner substance, of our leisure today that is distinctively modern.

Policy relevance

Experiential concepts can be inspirational. They highlight some of leisure's positive qualities more successfully than residual, social structural definitions. Experiential concepts draw attention to what leisure does for people and to what it might achieve. The analyses to which residual concepts lead are relatively bland. People are portrayed as using their time to watch television, go on holidays, drink and such-like. These descriptions are unlikely to ignite enthusiasm. Experiential concepts focus not only on what people do with their leisure but also upon how they are driven and affected. Maybe people are not in constant 'flow'. Maybe they feel fully self-determined only on exceptional occasions. Maybe we are not all using our leisure to become everything of which we are capable. Experiential concepts allow for this, but also offer a vision of what leisure could be. There is a messianic tinge to some treatises based on experiential concepts. For example, John Neulinger (1990) claims that the self-expression and fulfilment that were possible only for free men in ancient Athens are now within the reach of everyone. Bringing such a state within everyone's reach can be made into a goal of leisure policy. In comparison, residual concepts look sterile to anyone seeking policy implications. Experiential concepts enable writers to envisage the kinds of leisure opportunities that would be needed for everyone to derive all the benefits that leisure can offer.

Limitations of Experiential Concepts

Experiential definitions have attractive features, but against these must be set a list of problems.

Operability

First, experiential concepts are difficult to incorporate in research covering large representative samples. This is especially the case when leisure is defined solely as a type of experience, with no stipulation that the experience should occur in any particular part of people's lives. Working faithfully with this kind of definition would require researchers to study the whole of their subjects' lives, as in time budget enquiries, but in this case they would need to identify the occasions when individuals felt self-determined, when their behaviour was intrinsically rewarded, when they felt that they were having fun, in flow or whatever the definitive experience was. Obtaining this information is not impossible. Csikszentmihalyi has developed a method called experience sampling. Subjects have to be persuaded to carry bleepers and are equipped with questionnaires. The bleepers are programmed to alert the subjects at random (except that there is usually a guarantee that the process will not operate during night-time). Whenever he or she is bleeped, the subject has to complete a short questionnaire, usually giving details about what he or she is doing, where and with whom, along with answers to a set of questions about his or her feelings.

The method works, but up to now it has been used only with small samples. The costs of large-scale research are prohibitive. This does not invalidate experiential concepts, but being operable is one of the litmus tests of all social science concepts, and some experiential concepts of leisure stumble at this hurdle. A consequence is that, despite their appeal, the definitions have not become the base for systematic and cumulative research. Even researchers who advocate a feminist (experiential) concept of leisure have often resorted to quantitative methods and a 'masculine' residual concept in their own large-scale studies of women (see Green *et al.*, 1990).

Coherence

Another problem is that experiential concepts, when unqualified, do not dovetail tidily with other concepts their authors use. If leisure is a type of experience that can occur anywhere and at any time, it will include pieces of life that are commonly described as work, education, family interaction and so forth. Purely experiential definitions are inconsistent with leisure's everyday popular meanings insofar as these distinguish it from work that has to be done. The scope for confusion is immense. How can we judge which is the more satisfying if an experience can be both work and leisure?

Definition or evidence?

The coherence problem is avoided when leisure is defined as a kind of experience that is obtained or sought in leisure time, but such conceptualizations can be accused of settling by definition matters that should really be left to the evidence. The number one argument for not stipulating the experience when defining leisure is that discovering whether people feel self-determined, enhanced and intrinsically motivated or whether they have created new roles and identities for themselves should be treated as matters for investigation rather than resolved in advance. It appears mischievous to exclude by definition the possibility that leisure might be boring. It is difficult to imagine any good reasons for deciding in advance of any investigation that leisure is where people will be most able or most likely to achieve self-enhancing experiences or states of mind. Ellery Hamilton-Smith (1992) has pointed out that people are likely to seek optimal experience, whatever this might be, in all areas of their lives rather than solely through leisure. Csikszentmihalyi (1993) himself has used experience sampling to investigate where people are most likely to experience 'flow'. His evidence shows that people are more likely to experience flow at work than during their leisure and that the state of mind characteristic of most leisure is apathy (largely because so much leisure time is accounted for by television). Judith Brook (1993), also, has found that in general people find their work more challenging than their leisure, though it is during leisure that they are most likely to feel 'in control'. Rejecting experiential definitions is not the same as rejecting proposals to investigate leisure experience. There is no dispute that leisure experience is important, and residual concepts do not obstruct its investigation. The point at issue is whether it is useful to predefine leisure as any particular kind of experience.

The actual evidence suggests that people seek and obtain not just one but many kinds of experience through their leisure – fun, company, relaxation, exhilaration and so on. They experience and plan for highs and lows, peaks and troughs. Sometimes people want excitement, whereas at other times they wish to 'switch off'. Research can best investigate the variety of leisure experience by avoiding prejudgements or, to put it more bluntly, prejudicial terms of reference.

Experience in Leisure

There is an overwhelming case for studying people's experiences in leisure but, in my view, the balance of advantage lies towards doing this within, rather than at the expense of, the conventional leisure concept. A residual social structural definition merits retention for several crucial reasons.

Modern leisure is distinctive

Modern societies do in fact create a specific kind of leisure time, enable people to spend money for specifically leisure purposes and have goods and services that are targeted specifically at this market segment, in ways that set them apart from pre-modern societies. In this respect present-day societies remain basically modern. This is not to reject the desirability or the possibility of comparisons. Indeed, the very act of defining leisure as specifically modern makes a clear contrast. It remains possible to enquire whether the games, play and overall quality of life in societies with modern leisure are superior or inferior to what was available in earlier times. However, it is unlikely that the relationships between occupations and leisure and unemployment and leisure, for example, which are found in modern Western societies and which have proved broadly similar in all such countries, will have any relevance in pre-modern situations, where there has been no comparable division of life into work and leisure. Modern work–leisure relationships could not have preceded modernity, and a modern definition of leisure ensures that this is recognized.

A dominant pattern of time organization

It is true that residual concepts map perfectly on to hardly anyone's life and are very difficult to apply in many cases. But the residual pattern can still be dominant even if the majority of a population is not in employment. This is because household schedules tend to be organized around the needs of their employed members, which thereby affect all residents. In a similar way, leisure events tend to be scheduled so that the prime wares and widest choices are available during the periods that are leisure for most workers. People without jobs cannot ignore this dominant rhythm. Even if they try to ignore it, the likelihood is that they will still be affected by it. If some of the retired and the unemployed, for example, are completely divorced from this rhythm, they will have difficulty in experiencing normal leisure. This is likely to be their fundamental leisure problem, which can be identified only by using a residual concept.

The persistence of modernity

This is one of this book's central arguments: a post-industrial society certainly, but postmodern? The previous chapters have recognized that there are major changes in process: the destandardization of working time, full-time employees in some Western countries working longer rather than reducing their hours and greater variety in the circumstances and behaviour of men and women in all age groups. If these trends continued indefinitely, all the older divisions and structures would be obliterated, but, as yet at any rate, we are nowhere near such a point. Most of the research-based evidence pointing to the persistence of modernity is scattered throughout all the preceding chapters, but there are additional a priori grounds for scepticism towards claims about the eclipse of modernity. The contrasts between the modern and postmodern that are drawn by those who believe that the former is being superseded by the latter do not suggest that the transformation will be as thorough as the earlier change from traditional to modern society.

Box 8.1 lists some of the key words associated with traditional societies in the left column, modern industrial societies in the centre and postmodern or post-industrial societies on the right. Some of the changes said to be currently in process are broadly equivalent to the earlier shift from tradition to modernity. Work shifting from agriculture into manufacturing and then into service sectors, jobs from agrarian to blue-collar to white-collar and the organization of life from

---

Box 8.1.   Traditional, modern and postmodern societies.

Pre-industrial	Industrial	Post-industrial
	Fordist	Post-Fordist
Traditional	Modern	Postmodern
		Late modern
		High modern
Agriculture	Manufacturing	Services
Peasants	Blue-collar	White-collar
Self-sufficiency	Production	Consumption
Way of life	Work	Leisure
Religion, tradition	Science	Relativism
Community	Structure	Culture
	Groups	Reflexive individualization
Locality	Nation state	Globalization
Villages	Urbanization	Flexible communication networks
Traditional values	Achievement values	Post-materialist values
Extended family	Nuclear family	Negotiated roles
No mass politics	Parties representing large social groups	New social movements
Family and community support dependents	Welfare state	Individualized self-help

---

local to national to global levels are of this order. In contrast, leisure cannot replace work in quite the same way. Nor can consumption replace production in the same way that, earlier on, science displaced religion, and life was divided into work and leisure, thereby superseding the manner in which groups used to produce for their own needs. People can have leisure and consume only if work is done producing things and production continues to be based on the application of science. We are not living in an era of wholesale revolutionary upheaval comparable to the birth of modern society, when the population shifted from rural to urban areas, from agriculture into industry, and built new ways of life, which included modern leisure. The implication is that conventional 'modern' leisure concepts and the findings based upon them are not becoming obsolete. Proceeding as if leisure and consumption were transcending former structures and as if culture were escaping from all its earlier moorings leads to grossly exaggerated claims, fears and hopes for leisure.

Calling for leisure and other phenomena to be decentred reopens a long-running debate in sociology, in which investigators are invited to choose between what, in reality, are perfectly compatible positions, like recognizing the significance of structure and agency in social life. There could be no social structures unless people were sustaining and re-creating them by behaving in appropriate meaningful ways. But the aggregated actions of people who share understandings of social class, religion and leisure give all these phenomena the capacity to confront *every* individual as if they were external realities. There could be no such thing as society without individuals, but this does not mean that there are only individuals and no society.

Whatever the original source of people's leisure motivations – nature or nurture – sociology's principal interest must be in how these motivations are socially shaped and controlled. This shaping and controlling is not solely by the 'rules of pleasure' that various groups seek to prescribe but also by the distribution and organization of time and income, the forms of leisure provision and the particular opportunities and constraints that arise from gender and age roles, types of employment and non-employment and social class positions more generally. People's own ideas about leisure must certainly be taken into account in explaining their leisure behaviour, but these ideas do not exhaust what leisure really is. The extent to which leisure behaviour is amenable to rational, scientific explanation is not a matter that can be settled a priori but only by the success or failure of the efforts, and the results up to now have been encouraging. Up to now, leisure research has been a success story. It is anything but a failed project. It has been successful in charting and explaining how and why leisure has grown and how its distribution and uses are related to social class, age and gender. Paying attention to people's authentic leisure experiences adds a further dimension, leads to more comprehensive answers to older questions and opens up some new ones, but without in any way discrediting more conventional findings or their foundations in residual social structural concepts.

The future of leisure research

Social change always presents new issues. As far as today's new issues involve leisure, they will best be addressed by building on the foundations, the knowledge base already laid by past research into leisure. What are the issues that currently require attention?

First, we need fresh research in order to reduce the speculation in current explanations of why, in Britain and some other countries, some sections of the workforces are working longer and the implications for their outside-work lives. Likewise there is a need for research into the consequences of the destandardization of working time. The effects are unlikely to be exactly the same in all sections of the population. Presuming this would fly in the face of everything we know about age, sex and social class differences. These are issues on which theoretical speculation has raced ahead of our evidence, thereby creating an agenda for a new generation of enquiries and researchers.

Secondly, we need to learn more about the implications for men's and women's lives of more of the latter entering employment, taking shorter career breaks, working longer hours and commanding a higher share of total earnings. Even more pressing, there is a dearth of research into the significance for men, and their partners if they have any, of males taking on more housework and the devaluation of traditional brands of masculinity across much of the labour market. Once again, the implications are most likely to differ for both women and men according to their ages and socio-economic status. Upper middle-class men and women may be leading more similar lives than formerly at work and at home (see Chapter 4, pp. 113–114). If so, their experiences of macro-trends will be very different from those of males and females in the so-called socially and economically excluded groups, where high proportions of the women experience lone-parent situations and many males find themselves redundant, not merely in the labour market but in the domestic sphere also.

Thirdly, we need more systematic exploration and less speculation about the implications of predictable life-cycle sequences, formerly common among broad classes of males and females, being replaced by more individualized life courses and of wider variety within and increasing overlap in the circumstances of people in different age groups. If individuals' leisure behaviour remains stable and predictable over time, as argued earlier (Chapter 5, pp. 156–160), how is this achieved when changes in people's work and family lives require changes in their places of residence and in their daily and weekly time schedules and therefore in where their leisure time can be spent and with whom? If people manage to preserve friendships and group memberships, how do they achieve this? We need typologies of individualized biographies that will identify what are likely to be the diverse implications of life course destandardization for men and women in different social classes.

Fourthly, the growth of consumption and commercial leisure and the continuing spread and deepening of consumer culture need to be taken seriously by leisure research. Deconstructing adverts and making or rejecting extravagant claims about their significance are insufficient. We need enquiries that situate the impact of commercial provisions and processes within lifestyles that also use public- and voluntary-sector provisions and where much leisure is organized privately, and how the nuances vary, as they are most likely to do, by age, sex and socio-economic status.

Fifthly, the issue of leisure and identity needs to be properly investigated now that we know what questions to ask. The real issue is not whether leisure-based lifestyles are replacing older sources of identity but the significance of short-term and longer-term leisure embellishments and, once again, how these vary between different sections of the population.

Previous research has laid secure and substantial foundations from which all the above lines of enquiry can proceed. Perhaps most important of all, we now know that the most powerful explanations arise through investigating types of people rather than types of leisure. This is why the field of enquiry is impoverished and disempowered theoretically when it splinters into studies of sport, tourism, the media and so on. Society is not neatly divided into sport players, tourists, theatre-goers, etc. It is the same people who do all these things. And the most powerful explanations of all their types of leisure behaviour need to take account of the actors' total situations and the broader ways of life or lifestyles to which specific uses of leisure contribute. It will be in the course of investigating the issues listed above that the significance of the continuing growth of tourism, developments in telecommunications, the spread of personal computers, more people using the Internet and developments in sport, film, the printed media and so on will be established.

The reasons given for studying leisure in Chapter 1 are still the best. They have not been superseded by the subsequent evidence and arguments. No new justifications for leisure research are required; just recognition that the old reasons have become even stronger than in the past, simply because leisure grows remorselessly in modern societies: not equally so or in exactly the same ways for all sections of the populations but, even so, the unmistakable, overall, long-term and continuing trend is towards leisure becoming a larger and weightier part of people's lives. Voluntary and commercial organizations need to know about their members, clients and customers, actual and potential. Governments need to grasp why they inevitably become embroiled in leisure, the goals that they can realistically pursue and the likely consequences for different sections of the population. Leisure is socially important on account of its capacity to strengthen some groups, thereby deepening some social divisions and ameliorating others. Overall, the ongoing trends in leisure are tending to blur divisions between age groups, the sexes and occupation-based social classes, thereby contributing to broader processes of individualization. Leisure continues to perform the recuperative, learning and expressive functions that make it vital for individuals' well-being. Then there is leisure's economic significance as a source of business and employment. Its importance in all these respects varies between regions and countries, but there are few places today where leisure can be safely ignored in economic policy and planning. These have always been, and remain, important enough reasons for studying leisure.

Further Reading

For alternatives to the conventional, residual concept of leisure

Kelly, J.R. (1994) The symbolic interaction metaphor and leisure: critical challenges. *Leisure Studies* 13, 81–96.
Rojek, C. (2005) An outline of the action approach to leisure studies. *Leisure Studies* 24, 13–25.

For an external and critical view of modern Western leisure

Somnez, S., Shinew, K., Marchese, L., Veldkamp, C. and Burnett, G.W. (1993) Leisure corrupted: an artist's portrait of leisure in a changing society. *Leisure Studies* 12, 266–276.

Bibliography

Abbott-Chapman, J. and Denholm, C. (2001) Adolescents' risk activities, risk hierarchies and the influence of religiosity. *Journal of Youth Studies* 4, 279–297.

Abrams, M. (1961) *The Teenage Consumer*. London Press Exchange, London.

Abrams, M. (1977) Quality of life studies. In: Smith, M.A. (ed.) *Leisure in the Urban Society*. Leisure Studies Association, Manchester, UK.

Abrams, M. (1980) Class differences in the use of leisure time by the elderly. *Leisure Studies Association Quarterly* 1 (4), 2–3.

Adorno, T. and Horkheimer, M. (1977) The culture industry: enlightenment as mass deception. In: Curran, J., Gurevitch, M. and Woollacott, J. (eds) *Mass Communication and Society*. Edward Arnold, London.

Aitchison, C. (1997) A decade of compulsory competitive tendering in UK sport and leisure services: some feminist reflections. *Leisure Studies* 16, 85–105.

Albermarle Report (1960) *The Youth Service in England and Wales*. HMSO, London.

Albrechtsen, S.J. (2000) Technology and leisure in the new millennium. *Leisure Issues* 3 (1), 3–12.

Alcohol Concern (2002) *The State of the Nation: Britain's True Alcohol Bill*. www.alcoholconcern.org.uk, accessed 12 February 2002.

Allan, G. and Crowe, G. (1991) Privatisation, home centredness and leisure. *Leisure Studies* 10, 19–32.

Andrews, F.M. and Withey, S.B. (1976) *Social Indicators of Well-Being*. Plenum Press, New York.

Ang, I. (1996) *Living Room Wars*. Routledge, London.

Arai, S. and Pedlar, A. (2003) Moving beyond individualism in leisure theory: a critical analysis of the concepts of community and social engagement. *Leisure Studies* 22, 185–202.

Bailey, P. (1978) *Leisure and Class in Victorian England*. Routledge, London.

Bailey, P. (ed.) (1986) *Music Hall: the Business of Pleasure*. Open University Press, Milton Keynes, UK.

Bairner, A. and Shirlow, P. (2003) When leisure turns to fear: fear, mobility and ethno-sectarianism in Belfast. *Leisure Studies* 22, 203–221.

Banks, M., Bates, I., Breakwell, G., Bynner, J., Emler, N., Jamieson, L. and Roberts, K. (1992) *Careers and Identities*. Open University Press, Milton Keynes, UK.

Barrell, G., Chamberlain, A., Evans, J., Holt, T. and Mackean, J. (1989) Ideology and commitment in family life: the case of runners. *Leisure Studies* 8, 249–262.

Batan, C.M. (2002) The social meaning of texting. A sociological account of young cellular phone and text users in the Philippines: the case of Metro-Manila. *International Sociological Associaton Congress*, Brisbane.

Batty, D. (2002) Caught in the net. *Guardian*, 18 July, 21.

Baudrillard, J. (1998) *The Consumer Society: Myths and Structures*. Sage, London.

Bauman, Z. (1998a) *Globalization: The Human Consequences*. Polity Press, Cambridge, UK.

Bauman, Z. (1998b) *Work, Consumerism and the New Poor*. Open University Press, Buckingham, UK.

Baxter, J. (2000) The joys and justice of housework. *Sociology* 34, 609–631.

Beatson, M. (1995) *Labour Market Flexibility*. Research Series 48, Employment Department, Sheffield, UK.

Beck, U. and Beck-Gernsheim, E. (1995) *The Normal Chaos of Love*. Polity Press, Cambridge, UK.

Bell, C. and Healey, P. (1973) The family and leisure. In: Smith, M.A. *et al.* (eds) *Leisure and Society in Britain*. Allen Lane, London.

Bellaby, P. and Lawrenson, D. (2001) Approaches to the risk of riding motor cycles: reflections on the problem of reconciling statistical risk assessment and motorcyclists' own reasons for riding. *Sociological Review* 49, 368–388.

Bennett, A. (2001) *Cultures of Popular Music*. Open University Press, Maidenhead, UK.

Berger, P.A., Steinmuller, P. and Sopp, P. (1993) Differentiation of life courses? Changing patterns of labour market sequences in West Germany. *European Sociological Review* 9, 43–61.

Berrett, T., Burton, T.L. and Slack, T. (1993) Quality products, quality service: factors leading to entrepreneurial success in the sport and leisure industry. *Leisure Studies* 12, 93–106.

Beutel, A.M. and Marini, M.M. (1995) Gender and values. *American Sociological Review* 60, 436–448.

Bianchini, F. and Parkinson, M. (eds) (1993) *Cultural Policy and Urban Regeneration*. Manchester University Press, Manchester, UK.

Bienefeld, M.A. (1972) *Working Hours in British Industry*. Weidenfeld and Nicolson, London.

Bishop, J. and Hoggett, P. (1986) *Organizing Around Enthusiasms*. Comedia, London.

Bittman, M. and Wajcman, J. (1999) *The Rush Hour: the Quality of Leisure Time and Gender Equity*. SPRC Discussion Paper 97, University of New South Wales, Sydney.

Bittman, M., Rice, J.M. and Wajcman, J. (2004) Appliances and their impact: the ownership of domestic technology and time spent on housework. *British Journal of Sociology* 55, 401–423.

Blackshaw, T. (2003) *Leisure Life: Myth, Masculinity and Modernity*. Routledge, London.

Blyton, P. and Trinczek, R. (1996) *The Reincarnation of Worksharing as a Response to Job Cuts: Assessing Recent Developments in Germany*. Hans Bockler Foundation, Dusseldorf, Germany.

Bocock, R. (1993) *Consumption*. Routledge, London.

Bonney, N. (2005) Overworked Britons? Part-time work and work–life balance. *Work, Employment and Society* 19, 391–401.

Boothby, J., Tungatt, M., Townsend, A.R. and Collins, M.F. (1981) *A Sporting Chance?* Study 22, Sports Council, London.

Boseley, S. (2002) Alcohol problem inflicts £3bn bill on NHS. *Guardian*, 1 March, 3.

Bosworth, D. (1994) *Sunday Working: an Analysis of an Employer Survey*. Research Series 33, Employment Department, Sheffield, UK.

Bourdieu, P. (1984) *Distinction: a Social Critique of the Judgement of Taste*. Routledge, London.

Bourdieu, P. and Darbel, A. (1997) *The Love of Art*. Polity, Oxford, UK.

Bowden, S. (1994) The new consumerism. In: Johnson, P. (ed.) *Twentieth Century Britain*. Longman, London.

Bowring, F. (1999) Job scarcity: the perverted form of a political blessing. *Sociology* 33, 69–84.

Bramham, P. and Henry, I.P. (1985) Political ideology and leisure policy in the United Kingdom. *Leisure Studies* 4, 1–19.

Breedveld, K. (1994) Post-Fordist leisure and work. Paper presented at the International Sociological Association Conference, Bielefeld, Germany.

Breedveld, K. (1996a) Working odd hours: revolution in time or storm in a tea-cup? Paper presented at the World Leisure and Recreation Association Conference, Cardiff, UK.

Breedveld, K. (1996b) The double myth of flexibilisation: trends in scattered work hours and differences in time sovereignty. Paper presented at the Conference on New Strategies for Everyday Life, Tilburg, Netherlands.

Brennan, D. (1993) Adolescent girls and disco dancing. In: Brackenridge, C. (ed.) *Body Matters*. Publication 47, Leisure Studies Association, Eastbourne, UK.

Bridges, W. (1995) *Job Shift*. Allen and Unwin, London.

British Medical Association (2003) *Adolescent Health*. British Medical Association, London.

Britton, N.J., Halfpenny, P., Devine, F. and Mellor, R. (2004) The future of regional cities in the information age: the impact of information technology on Manchester's financial and business services sector. *Sociology* 38, 795–814.

Brook, J. (1993) Leisure meanings and comparisons with work. *Leisure Studies* 12, 149–162.

Brown, D. and Charles, N. (1982) *Women and Shiftwork: Some Evidence from Britain*. European Foundation, Dublin.

Brown, H.G. (1959) *Some Effects of Shiftwork on Social and Domestic Life*. Occasional Paper 2, Yorkshire Bulletin of Economic and Social Research.

Brown, P. (1987) *Schooling Ordinary Kids*. Tavistock, London.

Brown, R.K. (1990) A flexible future in Europe? Changing patterns of employment in the United Kingdom. *British Journal of Sociology* 41, 301–327.

Brown, S. (1995) Crime and safety in whose community? *Youth and Policy* 48, 27–48.

Butler, K.N. (1978) Roles of the commercial provider in leisure. In: Talbot, M.A. and Vickerman, R.W. (eds) *Social and Economic Costs and Benefits of Leisure*. Leisure Studies Association, Leeds, UK.

Butler, T. and Savage, M. (eds) (1995) *Social Change and the Middle Classes*. UCL Press, London.

Bynner, J. and Ashford, S. (1992) Teenage careers and leisure lives: an analysis of lifestyles. *Society and Leisure* 15, 499–519.

Cale, L. and Almond, L. (1992) Physical activity levels of secondary aged children: a review. *Health Education Journal* 51, 192–197.

Campbell, C. (1995) The sociology of consumption. In: Miller, D. (ed.) *Acknowledging Consumption*. Routledge, London.

Campbell, C. (1997) Shopping, pleasure and the sex war. In: Falk, P. and Campbell, C. (eds) *The Shopping Experience*. Sage, London, pp. 167–176.

Campbell, D. (2003) With porn outstripping corn, America's black economy is flying high. *Guardian* 2 May, 3.

Carabine, E. and Longhurst, B. (2002) Consuming the car: anticipation, use and meaning in contemporary youth culture. *Sociological Review* 50, 181–196.

Carpenter, G. and Patterson, I. (2004) The leisure perceptions and leisure meanings of a mid-life couple around the time of retirement. *World Leisure Journal* 46 (2), 13–25.

Carr, N. (1998) Gendered differences in young tourists' leisure spaces and times. *Journal of Youth Studies* 1, 279–293.

Carr, N. (2002) Poverty and university students' leisure: a passing relationship. Paper presented at the International Sociological Association Congress, Brisbane, Australia.

Carter, F.A. and Corlett, E.N. (1982) *Review of the European Foundation's Research into Shiftwork, 1977–80*. European Foundation, Dublin.

Cashmore, E. (1994) *And There Was Television*. Routledge, London.

Chambers, D.A. (1983) Symbolic equipment and the objects of leisure images. *Leisure Studies* 2, 301–315.

Champoux, J.E. (1978) Perceptions of work and non-work. *Sociology of Work and Occupations* 5, 402–422.

Chan, T.W. and Goldthorpe, J.H. (2004) Is there a status order in contemporary British society? Evidence from the occupational structure of friendship. *European Sociological Review* 20, 383–401.

Chaney, D. (1996) *Lifestyles*. Routledge, London.

Chaney, D. (2002) *Cultural Change and Everyday Life*. Palgrave, Basingstoke, UK.

Chase, D.R. and Godbey, G.C. (1983) The accuracy of self-reported participation rates. *Leisure Studies* 2, 231–235.

Cherry, G. (1984) Leisure and the home: a review of a changing relationship. *Leisure Studies* 3, 35–52.

Child, E. (1981) Play as a social product. *Leisure Studies Association Quarterly* 2 (4), 2–4.

Clarke, J. and Critcher, C. (1985) *The Devil Makes Work*. Macmillan, London.

Cloke, P., Phillips, M. and Thrift, N. (1995) The new middle classes and the constructs of rural living. In: Butler, T. and Savage, M. (eds) *Social Change and the Middle Classes*. UCL Press, London.

Coalter, F. (1998) Leisure studies, leisure policy and social citizenship: the failure of welfare or the limits of welfare? *Leisure Studies* 17, 21–36.

Cohen, P. (1976) Subcultural concepts and working class community. In: Hammersley, M. and Woods, P. (eds) *The Process of Schooling*. Routledge, London.

Cohen, S. (1972) *Folk Devils and Moral Panics*. MacGibbon and Kee, London.

Coles, B. (1995) *Youth and Social Policy*. UCL Press, London.

Collins, M.F. with Kay, T. (2003) *Sport and Social Exclusion*. Routledge, London.

Coppock, V., Haydon, D. and Richter, I. (1995) *The Illusions of Post-Feminism*. Taylor and Francis, London.

Corcoran-Nantes, Y. and Roberts, K. (1995) We've got one of those: the peripheral status of women in male dominated industries. *Gender, Work and Organisation* 2, 21–33.

Cousins, C.R. and Ning Tang (2004) Working time, work and family conflict in the Netherlands, Sweden and the UK. *Work, Employment and Society* 18, 531–549.

Coveney, L., Jackson, M., Jeffreys, S., Kaye, L. and Mahony, P. (1984) *The Sexuality Papers*. Hutchinson, London.

Crawford, G. (2003) The career of the sport supporter: the case of the Manchester Storm. *Sociology* 37, 219–237.

Crawford, G. (2004) *Consuming Sport: Fans, Sport and Culture*. Routledge, London.

Crewe, I. (1989) *The Decline of labour and the Decline of Labour: Social and Electoral Trends in Post-war Britain*. Essex Papers in Government and Politics 65, University of Essex, Colchester, UK.

Critcher, C. (2000) Still raving: social reactions to ecstasy. *Leisure Studies* 19, 145–162.

Crompton, R., Brockmann, M. and Lyonette, C. (2005) Attitudes, women's employment and the domestic division of labour: a cross-national analysis in two waves. *Work, Employment and Society* 19, 213–233.

Cross, G. (1993) *Time and Money: the Making of Consumer Culture*. Routledge, London.

Csikszentmihalyi, M. (1990) *Flow: the Psychology of Optimal Experience*. Harper and Row, New York.

Csikszentmihalyi, M. (1993) Activity and happiness. *Journal of Occupational Science* 1 (1), 38–42.

Cunningham, H. (1980) *Leisure in the Industrial Revolution*. Croom Helm, London.

Dale, A. (1986) Differences in car usage for married men and married women. *Sociology* 20, 91–92.

Dant, T. (2000) Consumption caught in the cash nexus. *Sociology* 34, 655–670.

Dare, B., Walton, G. and Coe, W. (1987) *Concepts of Leisure in Western Thought*. Kendall/Hunt, Dubuque, Iowa.

Darton, D. (1986) Leisure forecast 1986: the leisured society. *Leisure Management* January, 7–8.

Davidson, P. (1996) The holiday and work experiences of women with young children. *Leisure Studies* 15, 89–103.

Davies, A. (1992) *Leisure, Gender and Poverty*. Open University Press, Buckingham, UK.

Davies, A. (1994) Cinema and broadcasting. In: Johnson, P. (ed.) *Twentieth Century Britain*. Longman, London.

Dawson, D. (1988a) Leisure and the definition of poverty. *Leisure Studies* 7, 221–231.

Dawson, D. (1988b) Social class in leisure: reproduction and resistance. *Leisure Sciences* 10, 193–202.

Deem, R. (1982) Women, leisure and inequality. *Leisure Studies* 1, 29–46.

Deem, R. (1986) *All Work and No Play?* Open University Press, Milton Keynes, UK.

Deem, R. (1996) Women, the city and holidays. *Leisure Studies* 15, 105–119.

de Grazia, S. (1962) *Of Time, Work and Leisure*. Twentieth Century Fund, New York.

de Grazia, V. (1992) Leisure and citizenship. In: *Leisure and New Citizenship*. Actas VIII Congreso, ELRA, Bilbao, Spain.

DeLisle, L.J. (2004) Leisure and tolerance – an historical perspective. *World Leisure Journal* 46 (2), 55–63.

de Lisle, T. (2004) Melody maker. *Guardian*, 1 March, 2–3.

Denzin, N.K. (1991) *Images of Postmodernism*. Sage, London.

Department for Education (1995) *Young People's Participation in the Youth Service*. Statistical Bulletin 1/95, Department for Education, London.

Department for Health (2001) *Health Survey for England*. Department for Health, London.

Devine, F. (1992) *Affluent Workers Revisited? Privatism and the Working Class*. Edinburgh University Press, Edinburgh, UK.

Dickson, T.J. (2004) If the outcome is predictable, is it an adventure? Being in, not barricaded from, the outdoors. *World Leisure Journal* 46 (4), 48–65.

Dixon, R.M. (1991) *Black Arts, Policy and the Issue of Equity*. Race and Social Policy Unit, University of Liverpool, Liverpool, UK.

du Bois-Reymond, M., Dickstra, R., Hurrelmann, K. and Peters, E. (eds) (1995) *Childhood and Youth in Germany and The Netherlands*. De Gruyter, Berlin.

Dumazedier, J. (1967) *Towards a Society of Leisure*. Free Press, New York.

Dumazedier, J. (1974) *Sociology of Leisure*. Elsevier, Amsterdam.

Dumazedier, J. (1989) France: leisure sociology in the 1980s. In: Olszewska, A. and Roberts, K. (eds) *Leisure and Lifestyle*. Sage, London.

Duncombe, J. and Marsden, D. (1993) Love and intimacy: the gender division of emotion and emotion work. *Sociology* 27, 221–241.

Dunning, E. (1996) On problems of the emotions in sport and leisure: critical and counter-critical comments on the conventional and figurational sociologies of sport and leisure. *Leisure Studies* 15, 185–207.

Dunning, E. and Rojek, C. (eds) (1992) *Sport and Leisure in the Civilising Process.* Macmillan, Basingstoke, UK.

Dunning, E., Murphy, P. and Williams, J. (1986) Spectator violence at football matches: towards a sociological explanation. *British Journal of Sociology* 37, 221–244.

Dunning, E., Murphy, P. and Waddington, I. (1992) *Violence in the British Civilising Process.* Discussion Papers in Sociology S92/2, University of Leicester, Leicester, UK.

e-living (2002) *A Cross-Sectional and Comparative Analysis.* www.eurescom.de/e-living/

Elsden, N. (2001) An exploration of the 'ladette' in relation to female football fans. *Leisure Studies Association Newsletter* 58, 32–44.

English Sports Council (1999) *The Development of Sporting Talent 1997.* English Sports Council, London.

Erickson, B.H. (1996) Culture, class and connections. *American Journal of Sociology* 102, 217–251.

Estes, R.J. and Wilenski, H. (1978) *Life-cycle Squeeze and the Morale Curve.* Reprint 422, Institute of Industrial Relations, University of California, Berkeley, California.

European Commission, Directorate-General for Employment and Social Affairs (2003) *Employment in Europe 2003: Recent Trends and Prospects.* European Communities, Luxembourg.

European Foundation for the Improvement of Living and Working Conditions (1980) *The Effects of Shiftwork on Health, Social and Family Life.* European Foundation, Dublin.

Evans, S.T. and Haworth, J.T. (1991) Variations in personal activity, access to categories of experience, and psychological well-being in young adults. *Leisure Studies* 10, 249–264.

Eygendaal, W. (1992) The black heart – a qualitative study of the death metal culture in The Netherlands. Paper presented at the Conference on Internationalisation and Leisure Research, Tilburg, Netherlands.

Facer, K. and Furlong, R. (2001) Beyond the myth of the cyberkid: young people at the margins of the information revolution. *Journal of Youth Studies* 4, 451–469.

Fache, W. (1996) The common weekend is threatened in Belgium. Paper presented at the Conference on New Strategies for Everyday Life, Tilburg, Netherlands.

Fagan, C. (2002) How many hours? Work time regimes and preferences in European Union countries. In: Crow, G. and Heath, S. (eds) *Social Conceptions of Time: Structure and Process in Work and Everyday Life.* Palgrave, Basingstoke, UK, pp. 69–87.

Fagnani, J. and Letablier, M.-T. (2004) Work and family life balance: the impact of the 35-hour laws in France. *Work, Employment and Society* 18, 551–572.

Fajertag, G. (1996) Working time policies in Europe: recent trends. Paper presented at the Conference on New Strategies for Everyday Life, Tilburg, Netherlands.

Fasting, K., Brackenridge, C. and Sundgot-Borgen, J. (2004) Prevalence of sexual harassment among Norwegian female elite athletes in relation to sport type. *International Review for the Sociology of Sport* 39, 373–386.

Featherstone, M. (ed.) (1988) *Postmodernism: Theory, Culture and Society Vol. 5 2–3.* Sage, London.

Featherstone, M. (1991) *Consumer Culture and Post-Modernism.* Sage, London.

Felstead, A., Jewson, N. and Walters, S. (2005a) *Changing Places of Work.* Palgrave Macmillan, Basingstoke, UK.

Felstead, A., Jewson, N. and Walters, S. (2005b) The shifting locations of work: new statistical evidence on the spaces and places of employment. *Work, Employment and Society* 19, 415–431.

Fisher, K. (2002) *Chewing the Fat: the Story Time Diaries Tell About Physical Activity in the United Kingdom*. Working Paper 2002-13, Institute for Social and Economic Research, University of Essex, Colchester, UK.

Fishwick, L. and Hayes, D. (1989) Sport for whom? Differential participation patterns of recreational athletes in leisure time physical activities. *Sociology of Sport Journal* 6, 269–277.

Forrester, V. (1999) *The Economic Horror*. Polity Press, Cambridge, UK.

Fox, K. and Rickards, L. (2004) *Sport and Leisure: Results from the Sport and Leisure Module of the 2002 General Household Survey*. Office for National Statistics, London.

Franzen, A. (2000) Does the internet make us lonely? *European Sociological Review* 16, 427–438.

Freysinger, V.J. and Chen, T. (1993) Family and leisure in China: the impact of culture. *World Leisure and Recreation* 35 (3), 22–24.

Frost, L. (2003) Doing bodies differently? Gender, youth, appearance and damage. *Journal of Youth Studies* 6, 53–70.

Froud, J., Johal, S., Leaver, A. and Williams, K. (2005) Different worlds of motoring: choice, constraint and risk in household consumption. *Sociological Review* 53, 96–128.

Fryer, D. and Payne, R. (1984) Proactive behaviour in unemployment: findings and implications. *Leisure Studies* 3, 273–295.

Furlong, A., Campbell, R. and Roberts, K. (1990) The effects of post-16 experiences and social class on the leisure patterns of young adults. *Leisure Studies* 9, 213–224.

Gabriel, Y. and Lang, T. (1995) *The Unmanageable Consumer: Contemporary Consumption and its Fragmentation*. Sage, London.

Gallie, D., Marsh, C. and Vogler, C. (eds) (1994) *Social Change and the Experience of Unemployment*. Oxford University Press, Oxford, UK.

Garhammer, M. (1998) Time pressure in modern Germany. *Society and Leisure* 21, 327–352.

Garhammer, M. (1999) The institutionalisation of work and shifting boundaries between work and leisure time. Paper presented at the International Institute of Sociology Congress, Tel Aviv, Israel.

Gatenby, R. (2004) *Married Only at the Weekends? A Study of the Amount of Time Spent Together by Spouses*. Office for National Statistics, London.

Gattas, J.T., Roberts, K., Schmitz-Scherzer, R., Tokarski, W. and Vitanyi, I. (1987) Leisure and lifestyles: towards a research agenda. *Society and Leisure* 9, 529–539.

Gershuny, J.I. (1986) Leisure: feast or famine? *Society and Leisure* 9, 431–454.

Gershuny, J. (1992) Are we running out of time? *Futures* January/February, 3–22.

Gershuny, J. (2000) *Changing Times: Work and Leisure in Postindustrial Society*. Oxford University Press, Oxford, UK.

Gershuny, J. (2003) *Time Through the Lifecourse in the Family*. ISER Working Paper 2003-3, University of Essex, Colchester, UK.

Gershuny, J. (2004) Domestic equipment does not increase domestic work: a response to Bittman, Rice and Wajcman. *British Journal of Sociology* 55, 425–431.

Gershuny, J. and Fisher, K. (1999) *Leisure in the UK Across the 20th Century*. Working Paper 99-3, Institute for Social and Economic Research, University of Essex, Colchester, UK.

Gerth, H.H. and Wright Mills, C. (1948) *From Max Weber*. Routledge, London.

Giddens, A. (1991) *Modernity and Self-Identity*. Polity Press, Cambridge, UK.

Gillespie, D.L., Leffler, A. and Lerner, E. (2002) 'If it weren't for my hobby I'd have a life': dog sports, serious leisure, and boundary negotiations. *Leisure Studies* 21, 285–304.

Glyptis, S. (1981) Leisure life-styles. *Regional Studies* 15, 311–326.

Glyptis, S. (1989) *Leisure and Unemployment*. Open University Press, Milton Keynes, UK.

Glyptis, S.A. and Chambers, D.A. (1982) No place like home? *Leisure Studies* 1, 247–262.

Glyptis, S., McInnes, H. and Patmore, J.A. (1987) *Leisure and the Home*. Sports Council/Economic and Social Research Council, London.

Godbey, G. (1975) Anti-leisure and public recreation policy. In: Parker, S. *et al.* (eds) *Sport and Leisure in Contemporary Society*. Leisure Studies Association, London.

Goddard, E. (1991) *Drinking in England and Wales in the late-1980s*. HMSO, London.

Goldthorpe, J.H. (1996) Class analysis and the reorientation of class theory: the case of persisting differentials in educational attainment. *British Journal of Sociology* 47, 481–505.

Goldthorpe, J.H., Lockwood, D., Bechhofer, F. and Platt, J. (1969) *The Affluent Worker in the Class Structure*. Cambridge University Press, Cambridge, UK.

Goodale, T. and Godbey, G. (1988) *The Evolution of Leisure*. Venture, State College, Penn State, Pennsylvania.

Gorz, A. (1999) *Reclaiming Work: Beyond the Wage-Based Society*. Polity Press, Cambridge, UK.

Gratton, C. (1992) A perspective on European leisure markets. Paper presented at the Conference on Internationalisation and Leisure Research, Tilburg, The Netherlands.

Gratton, C. and Taylor, P. (2004) The economics of work and leisure. In: Haworth, J.T. and Veal, A.J. (eds) *Work and Leisure*. Routledge, London, pp. 85–106.

Greater London Council (1986) *A Sporting Chance*. Greater London Council, London.

Green, E. (1998) Women doing friendship: an analysis of women's leisure as a site of identity construction: empowerment and resistance. *Leisure Studies* 17, 171–185.

Green, E., Hebron, S. and Woodward, D. (1990) *Women's Leisure, What Leisure?* Macmillan, London.

Green, E., Mitchell, W. and Bunton, R. (2000) Contextualising risk and danger: an analysis of young people's perceptions of risk. *Journal of Youth Studies* 3, 109–126.

Gregory, S. (1982) Women among others: another view. *Leisure Studies* 1, 47–52.

Griffin, C. (1985) *Typical Girls?* Routledge, London.

Griffiths, V. (1995) *Adolescent Girls and their Friends*. Avebury, Aldershot, UK.

Gvozdeva, G.P. (1994) Changes in free time utilization by rural residents in West Siberia under the ongoing economic reform. Paper presented at the International Sociological Association Conference, Bielefeld, Germany.

Hakim, C. (1993) The myth of rising female employment. *Work, Employment and Society* 7, 97–120.

Halford, S. and Savage, M. (1995) Restructuring organisations, changing people: gender and restructuring in banking and local government. *Work, Employment and Society* 9, 97–122.

Hall, J. and Perry, N. (1974) *Aspects of Leisure in Two Industrial Cities*. Occasional Papers in Survey Research 5, Social Science Research Council, London.

Hall, S. and Jefferson, T. (eds) (1976) *Resistance Through Rituals*. Hutchinson, London.

Hall Aitken Associates (2002) *Evaluation of Pioneer and Pathfinder UK Online Centres: Follow-Up Study*. Research Report 362, Department for Education and Skills, Sheffield, UK.

Hamilton-Smith, E. (1992) Work, leisure and optimal experience. *Leisure Studies* 11, 243–256.

Hantrais, L. (1985) Leisure lifestyles and the synchronisation of family schedules: a Franco-British comparative perspective. *World Leisure and Recreation* 20 (2), 18–24.

Hantrais, L. and Kamphorst, T.J. (1987) *Trends in the Arts: a Multinational Perspective.* Giordano Bruno, Amersfoort, The Netherlands.

Harada, M. (1994) Towards a renaissance of leisure in Japan. *Leisure Studies* 13, 277–287.

Hardey, M. (1990) Family form and leisure opportunities. In: Long, J. (ed.) *Leisure, Health and Well-Being.* Leisure Studies Association, Brighton, UK.

Hargreaves, Jennifer (1982) *Sport, Culture and Ideology.* Routledge, London.

Hargreaves, Jennifer (1994) *Sporting Females.* Routledge, London.

Hargreaves, John (1986) *Sport, Power and Culture.* Polity Press, Cambridge, UK.

Harper, R. (2001) *Social Capital: A Review of the Literature.* Office for National Statistics, London.

Harper, W. (1997) The future of leisure: making leisure work. *Leisure Studies* 16, 189–198.

Harris, J. (2001) Playing the man's game: sites of resistance and incorporation in women's football. *World Leisure Journal* 43 (4), 22–29.

Hassan, R. (2004) *Media, Politics and the Network Society.* Open University Press, Maidenhead, UK.

Havighurst, R.J. and Feigenbaum, K. (1959) Leisure and lifestyle. *American Journal of Sociology* 64, 396–405.

Havitz, M.E., Morden, P.A. and Samdahl, D.M. (2004) *The Diverse Worlds of Unemployed Adults: Consequences for Leisure, Lifestyle and Well-being.* Wilfrid Laurier University Press, Waterloo, Ontario.

Hawkins, B., Foose, A.K. and Binkley, A.L. (2004) Contribution of leisure to the life satisfaction of older adults in Australia and the United States. *World Leisure Journal* 46 (2), 4–12.

Haworth, J.T. (1993) Skill challenge relationships and psychological well-being in everyday life. *Society and Leisure* 16, 115–128.

Haworth, J.T. and Drucker, J. (1991) Psychological wellbeing and access to categories of experience in unemployed young adults. *Leisure Studies* 10, 265–274.

Haworth, J.T. and Veal, A.J. (2004) Work and leisure: themes and issues. In: Haworth, J.T. and Veal, A.J. (eds) *Work and Leisure.* Routledge, London, pp. 213–230.

Hebdige, D. (1979) *Sub-Culture: the Meaning of Style.* Methuen, London.

Hedges, B. (1986) *Personal Leisure Histories.* Economic and Social Research Council/ Sports Council, London.

Helve, H. (1998) Attitudes and values of young people and cultural, economic and political change. Paper presented at the International Sociological Association Congress, Montreal, Quebec.

Hemingway, J.L. (1988) Leisure and civility: reflections on a Greek ideal. *Leisure Sciences* 10, 179–191.

Henderson, K., Bialeschki, M.D., Shaw, S.C. and Freysinger, V.J. (1989) *A Leisure of One's Own.* Venture, Penn State, Pennsylvania.

Hendry, L.B., Raymond, M. and Stewart, C. (1984) Unemployment, school and leisure: an adolescent study. *Leisure Studies* 3, 175–187.

Hendry, L.B., Shucksmith, J., Love, J.G. and Glendinning, A. (1993) *Young People's Leisure and Lifestyles.* Routledge, London.

Hendry, L.B., Kloep, M., Espenes, G.A., Ingebrigtsen, J.E., Glendinning, A. and Wood, S. (2002a) Leisure transitions – a rural perspective. *Leisure Studies* 21, 1–14.

Hendry, L.B., Kloep, M. and Wood, S. (2002b) Young people talking about adolescent rural crowds and social settings. *Journal of Youth Studies* 5, 357–374.

Henley Centre (1993) *Inbound Tourism – a Packaged Future*. Henley Centre, London.

Henry, I.P. (1993) *The Politics of Leisure Policy*. Macmillan, Basingstoke, UK.

Heuser, L. (2005) We're not too old to play sports: the career of women lawn bowlers. *Leisure Studies* 24, 45–60.

Hewitt, P.B. (1993) *About Time: The Revolution in Work and Family Life*. IPPR/Rivers Oram Press, London.

Hey, V. (1986) *Patriarchy and Pub Culture*. Tavistock, London.

Hickman, L. (2003) Missing: 8,000 gym members. *Guardian* 26 August, 6.

Hidy, P. (1982) *Who are being Entertained?* Institute for Culture, Budapest.

Hillman, M. (1991) *One False Move*. Policy Studies Institute, London.

Hilton, M. (2005) Globalising consumers: the history of consumertism as a socio-political movement. Paper presented at the Conference on Politicised Consumption – Consumed Politics, Giessen.

Hinrichs, K., Roche, W. and Sirianni, C. (1991) *Working Time in Transition*. Temple University Press, Philadelphia.

Hirsch, F. (1977) *The Social Limits to Growth*. Routledge, London.

Hobcraft, J. and Kiernan, K. (1995) *Becoming a Parent in Europe*. Welfare State Programme 116, London School of Economics, London.

Hobson, D. (1979) Working class women, the family and leisure. In: Strelitz, Z. (ed.) *Leisure and Family Diversity*. Conference Papers 9, Leisure Studies Association, London.

Hodgson, P. (1988) Why leisure research is different. Paper presented at the 41st ESOMAR Market Research Conference, Lisbon.

Hodkinson, P. (2002) *Goth: Identity, Style and Subculture*. Berg, Oxford, UK.

Hoffman, R. (1996) On the road to lifetime working hours. Paper presented at the Conference on New Strategies for Everyday Life, Tilburg, The Netherlands.

Hogarth, T., Hasluck, C., Pierre, G., Winterbottam, M. and Vivian, D. (2001) *Work–Life Balance 2000: Results from the Baseline Study*. Research Report 249, Department for Education and Employment, Sheffield, UK.

Hollands, R. and Chatterton, P. (2002) Producing youth nightlife in the new urban entertainment economy: corporatisation, branding and market segmentation. Paper presented at the International Sociological Association Congress, Brisbane, Australia.

Hollands, R.G. (1995) *Friday Night, Saturday Night*. Department of Social Policy, University of Newcastle, Newcastle upon Tyne, UK.

Holliday, S. (1996) Trends in British work, leisure and the quality of life. Paper presented at the Conference on New Strategies for Everyday Life, Tilburg, The Netherlands.

Horning, K.H., Gerhard, A. and Michailow, M. (1995) *Time Pioneers: Flexible Working Time and New Lifestyles*. Polity Press, Cambridge, UK.

Howe, C.Z. and Rancourt, A.M. (1990) The importance of definitions of selected concepts for leisure enquiry. *Leisure Sciences* 12, 395–406.

Howkins, A. and Lowerson, J. (1979) *Trends in Leisure, 1919–1939*. Social Science Research Council/Sports Council, London.

Hughes, G. (1993) The self, signification and the superyacht. *Leisure Studies* 12, 253–265.

Hultsman, J. (1995) Spelling leisure. *Leisure Studies* 14, 87–101.

Hunnicutt, B.K. (1988) *Work Without End*. Temple University Press, Philadelphia.

Hutton, W. (1995) High risk. *Guardian*, 30 October.

Huws, U. (1993) *Teleworking in Britain.* Research Series 18, Employment Department, Sheffield, UK.

Inglehart, R. (1977) *The Silent Revolution.* Princeton University Press, Princeton, New Jersey.

Inglehart, R. (1997) *Modernization and Postmodernization: Cultural, Economic and Political Change in 43 Societies.* Princeton University Press, Princeton, New Jersey.

Inkson, K. and Coe, T. (1993) *Are Career Ladders Disappearing?* Institute of Management, London.

Institute of Management (1993) *Managers Under Stress.* Institute of Management, London.

Irwin, S. (1995) *Rights of Passage.* UCL Press, London.

Isao-Ahola, S.E. and Mannell, R.C. (2004) Leisure and health. In: Haworth, J.T. and Veal, A.J. (eds) *Work and Leisure.* Routledge, London, pp. 184–199.

Jackson, J. (2004) Players blow whistle on Sunday soccer. *Observer,* 14 November, 13.

Jackson, P.R. and Taylor, P.E. (1994) Factors associated with employment status in later life. *Work, Employment and Society* 8, 553–567.

Jagger, E. (2001) Marketing Mollie and Melville: dating in a postmodern, consumer society. *Sociology* 35, 39–57.

Jahoda, M. (1982) *Employment and Unemployment: A Social-Psychological Analysis.* Cambridge University Press, Cambridge, UK.

Jansen-Verbeke, M. (1987) Women, shopping and leisure. *Leisure Studies* 6, 71–86.

Jeffreys, S. (1999) Globalising sexual exploitation: sex tourism and the traffic in women. *Leisure Studies* 18, 179–196.

Jeffreys, S. (2003) Sex tourism: do women do it too? *Leisure Studies* 22, 223–238.

Jenkins, C. and Sherman, B. (1981) *The Leisure Shock.* Methuen, London.

Jenkins, S.P. and Osberg, L. (2003) Nobody to play with: the implications of leisure coordination. Paper presented at the IZA Conference of the International Research Consortium on the Economics of Time Use, St Gerlach.

Jones, G. (1995) *Leaving Home.* Open University Press, Buckingham, UK.

Jones, S. (1986) *Workers at Play.* Routledge, London.

Jung, B. (1990) The impact of the crisis on leisure patterns in Poland. *Leisure Studies* 9, 95–105.

Jung, B. (1994) For what leisure? The role of culture and recreation in post-communist Poland. *Leisure Studies* 13, 1–15.

Kaplan, M. (1979) *Leisure: Lifestyle and Lifespan.* W.B. Saunders, Philadelphia.

Karsten, L. (1995) Women's leisure: divergence, reconceptualisation and change. *Leisure Studies* 14, 186–201.

Kay, T.A. (1987) Leisure in the lifestyles of unemployed people: a case study in Leicester. PhD thesis, University of Loughborough, UK.

Kay, T. (1996) Women's work and women's worth: the leisure implications of women's changing employment patterns. *Leisure Studies* 15, 49–64.

Kay, T. (1998) Having it all or doing it all? The construction of women's lifestyles in time-crunched households. *Leisure and Society* 21, 435–454.

Kay, T. (2003) Leisure, gender and self in the analysis of family. *World Leisure Journal* 45 (4), 4–14.

Kelly, J. (1983) *Leisure Identities and Interactions.* Allen and Unwin, London.

Kelly, J.R. (1986) Commodification of leisure: trend or tract? *Society and Leisure* 9, 455–475.

Kelly, J.R. (1987) *Freedom To Be: A New Sociology of Leisure.* Macmillan, New York.

Kelly, J.R. (1991) Commodification and consciousness: an initial study. *Leisure Studies* 10, 7–18.

Kelly, J.R. (1994) The symbolic interaction metaphor and leisure: critical challenges. *Leisure Studies* 13, 81–96.

Kelly, J.R. and Pesavento-Raymond, L.C. (1988) *Leisure Activities of Unemployed Black and Hispanic Urban Youth*. University of Illinois, Urbana-Champaign, Illinois.

Kelly, J.R., Steinkamp, M.W. and Kelly, J.R. (1987) Later-life satisfaction: does leisure contribute? *Leisure Sciences* 9, 189–200.

Kelvin, P., Dewberry, C. and Morley-Bunker, N. (1984) *Unemployment and Leisure*. University College, London.

Kenvyn, I. (2000) The ascribed significance of adolescent free time. PhD thesis, University of Leeds, Leeds, UK.

Kiernan, K.E. (1995) *Transition to Parenthood: Young Mothers, Young Fathers – Associated Factors and Later Life Experiences*. Welfare State Programme 113, London School of Economics, London.

Kilpatrick, R. and Trew, K. (1985) Lifestyles and well-being among unemployed men in Northern Ireland. *Journal of Occupational Psychology* 58, 207–216.

Kleiber, D.A., Caldwell, L.L. and Shaw, S.M. (1993) Leisure meanings in adolescence. *Society and Leisure* 16, 99–114.

Knulst, M. (1992) An elitist rearguard. *Netherlands Journal of Social Science* 28, 72–94.

Koch-Weser, E. (1990) A framework for the quantitative study of leisure styles. Paper presented at the International Sociological Association Conference, Madrid, Spain.

Kohli, M., Rein, M., Guillemard, A.-M. and van Gunsteren, H. (eds) (1992) *Time for Retirement*. Cambridge University Press, Cambridge, UK.

Koseki, S. (1989) Japan: homo ludens Japonicus. In: Olszewska, A. and Roberts, K. (eds) *Leisure and Lifestyle*. Sage, London.

Kraut, R., Lundmark, V., Patterson, M., Kiesler, S., Mukopadhyay, T. and Scherlis, W. (1998) Internet paradox: a social technology that reduces social involvement and psychological well-being. *American Psychologist* 15, 1017–1031.

Kravchenko, S. (2004) The game-ization of society and its influence on consumption: toward substantiating a new sociological paradigm. In: Osadchaya, G. and Meshkova, E. (eds) *Methodology of Sociological Analysis of Social Sphere*. Russian State Social University, Moscow, pp. 100–110.

Laczko, F. and Phillipson, C. (1992) *Changing Work and Retirement*. Open University Press, Milton Keynes, UK.

Laermans, R. (1994) Leisure as making time: some sociological reflections on the paradoxical outcomes of individualization. In: Actas do Congreso Mundial do Lazer, *New Routes for Leisure*. Instituto de Ciencias Socias, University of Lisbon, Lisbon.

Lash, S. (1990) *Sociology of Postmodernism*. Routledge, London.

Lash, S. and Urry, J. (1994) *Economies of Signs and Space*. Sage, London.

Lawrence, L. (2003) These are the voyages – interaction in real and virtual space environments in leisure. *Leisure Studies* 22, 301–315.

Layard, R. (2003) *Happiness: Has Social Science a Clue?* Lionel Robbins Memorial Lectures 2002/03, London School of Economics, London.

Leaman, O. (1984) *Sit on the Sidelines and Watch the Boys Play*. Schools Council Programme Pamphlet, Longman Resources Trust, York, UK.

Lee, J.F.-C. (2002) The exploratory study of youth's behaviour in the Internet chat room in Taiwan. *International Sociological Association Congress*, Brisbane.

Lees, S. (1986) *Losing Out*. Hutchinson, London.

Lenskyj, H. (1988) Measured time, women, sport and leisure. *Leisure Studies* 7, 233–240.

Leonard, D. (1980) *Sex and Generation*. Tavistock, London.

Lewis, S. (2003) The integration of paid work and the rest of life. Is post-industrial work the new leisure? *Leisure Studies* 22, 343–355.

Li, Y., Savage, M. and Tampubolon, G. (2002) Dynamics of social capital: trends and turnover in associational membership in England and Wales, 1972–1999. *Sociological Research Online* 7, 3.

Li, Y., Savage, M. and Pickles, A. (2003) Social capital and social exclusion in England and Wales (1972–1999). *British Journal of Sociology* 54, 497–526.

Linder, S. (1970) *The Harried Leisure Class.* Columbia University Press, New York.

Lindsay, J. (2004) Gender and class in the lives of young hairdressers: from serious to spectacular. *Journal of Youth Studies* 7, 259–277.

Lloyd, N. (ed.) (1986) *Work and Leisure in the 1980s.* Sports Council/Economic and Social Research Council, London.

Lobo, F. (1993) Late career unemployment, leisure and lifestyle. Paper presented at the World Leisure and Recreation Association Conference, Jaipur, India.

Lobo, F. (1999) Young people and unemployment: does job loss diminish involvement in leisure? *Society and Leisure* 22, 145–170.

Long, J. and Wimbush, E. (1985) *Continuity and Change: Leisure Around Retirement.* Economic and Social Research Council/Sports Council, London.

Longhurst, B. (1996) *Popular Music and Society.* Polity Press, Cambridge, UK.

Lunt, P.K. and Livingstone, P.M. (1992) *Mass Consumption and Personal Identity.* Open University Press, Milton Keynes, UK.

Lury, C. (1996) *Consumer Culture.* Rutgers University Press, New Brunswick.

Lynch, R. and Veal, A.J. (1996) *Australian Leisure.* Longman, Melbourne, Australia.

Mac an Ghail, M. (1996) What about the boys? Schooling, class and crisis masculinity. *Sociological Review* 44, 381–397.

McGlone, A.M. and Pudney, S.E. (1986) Personal consumption, gender and marital status. *Sociology* 20, 88–90.

McGoldrick, A.E. (1983) Company early retirement schemes and private pensions schemes: scope for leisure and new lifestyles. *Leisure Studies* 2, 187–202.

McGuire, F.A., Dottavio, F.D. and O'Leary, J.T. (1987) The relationship of early life experiences to later life leisure involvement. *Leisure Sciences* 9, 251–257.

McKeever, E. (1993) Eating out – a family affair. *World Leisure and Recreation* 35(3), 35–38.

McMahon, A. (1999) *Taking Care of Men: Sexual Politics in the Public Mind.* Cambridge University Press, Cambridge, UK.

MacRae, R. (2004) Notions of 'us' and 'them': markers of stratification in clubbing lifestyles. *Journal of Youth Studies* 7, 55–71.

McRobbie, A. (2000) *Feminism and Youth Culture.* Macmillan, London.

Madigan, R. and Munro, M. (1996) House beautiful: style and consumption in the home. *Sociology* 30, 41–57.

Maffesoli, M. (1994) *The Time of the Tribes.* Sage, London.

Maguire, J. (1991) Sport, racism and British society: a sociological study of elite male Afro/Caribbean soccer and rugby union players. In: Jarvie, G. (ed.) *Sport, Racism and Ethnicity.* Falmer, London.

Malcolmson, R.W. (1973) *Popular Recreations in English Society, 1700–1850.* Cambridge University Press, Cambridge, UK.

Mander, J. (1980) *Four Arguments for the Elimination of Television.* Harvester Press, Brighton, UK.

Mannheim, K. (1936) *Ideology and Utopia.* Routledge, London.

Marsden, D. (1982) *Workless.* Croom Helm, London.

Marsh, A. (1979). *Women and Shiftwork.* HMSO, London.

Marshall, G., Rose, D., Newby, H. and Vogler, C. (1988) *Social Class in Modern Britain.* Hutchinson, London.

Martin, B. and Mason, S. (1986) Spending patterns show new leisure priorities. *Leisure Studies* 5, 233–236.

Martin, B. and Mason, S. (1990) Leisure in a less buoyant economy. *Leisure Studies* 9, 1–6.

Martin, B. and Mason, S. (1992) Current trends in leisure: the changing face of leisure provision. *Leisure Studies* 11, 81–86.

Martin, W.H. and Mason, S. (1998) *Transforming the Future: Rethinking Free Time and Work*. Leisure Consultants, Sudbury, UK.

Martino, W. (1999) Cool boys, party animals, squids and poofters: interrogating the dynamics and politics of adolescent masculinities in school. *British Journal of Sociology of Education* 20, 239–263.

Mason, J. (1988) No peace for the wicked: older married women and leisure. In: Wimbush, E. and Talbot, M. (eds) *Relative Freedoms*. Open University Press, Milton Keynes, UK.

Mason, T. (1994) Sport and recreation. In: Johnson, P. (ed.) *Twentieth Century Britain*. Longman, London.

Mattar, Y. (2003) Virtual communities and hip-hop music consumers in Singapore: interplaying global, local and subcultural identities. *Leisure Studies* 22, 283–300.

Melendez, N. (1992) Life satisfaction and leisure activity patterns among the retired elderly in Puerto Rico. Paper presented at the International Sociological Association Conference, New Routes for Leisure, Lisbon.

Meller, H.E. (1976) *Leisure and the Changing City 1870–1914*. Routledge, London.

Miah, A. (2000) Virtually nothing: re-evaluating the significance of cyberspace. *Leisure Studies* 19, 211–225.

Mihalik, B.J., O'Leary, J.T., Maguire, F.A. and Dottavio, T.D. (1989) Sports involvement across the life span: expansion and contraction of sports activities. *Research Quarterly for Exercise and Sport* 60, 396–398.

Miles, S. (1998) *Consumerism – As a Way of Life*. Sage, London.

Miles, S. (2000) *Youth Lifestyles in a Changing World*. Open University Press, Buckingham, UK.

Miles, S., Cliff, D. and Burr, V. (1998) Fitting in and sticking out: consumption, consumer meanings and the construction of young people's identities. *Journal of Youth Studies* 1, 81–96.

Miller, D. (1995) Consumption as the vanguard of history. In: Miller, D. (ed.) *Acknowledging Consumption*. Routledge, London.

Miller, K.A. and Kohn, M.L. (1983) The reciprocal effects of job conditions and the intellectuality of leisure time activities. In: Parker, S. (ed.) *Leisure, Work and Family*. Leisure Studies Association, London.

Mobily, K.E. (1989) Meanings of leisure and recreation among adolescents. *Leisure Studies* 8, 11–23.

Mogenson, G.V. (1990) *Time and Consumption*. Danmarks Statistik, Copenhagen.

Morgan, D.J. (1992) *Discovering Men*. Routledge, London.

Morley, D. (1986) *Family Television: Cultural Power and Domestic Leisure*. Comedia, London.

Morris, K. and Fuller, M. (1999) Heterosexual relationships of young women in a rural environment. *British Journal of Sociology of Education* 20, 531–543.

Mort, F. (1996) *Cultures of Consumption: Masculinities and Social Space in Late-Twentieth Century Britain*. Routledge, London.

Mott, J. (1973) Miners, weavers and pigeon racing. In: Smith, M.A. *et al.* (eds) *Leisure and Society in Britain*. Allen Lane, London.

Mott, P.E. *et al.* (1965) *Shift Work: The Social, Psychological and Physical Conse-quences*. University of Michigan Press, Ann Arbor, Michigan.

Muggleton, D. (2000) *Inside Subculture: the Postmodern Meaning of Style*. Berg, Oxford, UK.

Mulford, M., Orbell, J., Shatto, C. and Stockard, J. (1998) Physical attractiveness, oppor-tunity, and success in everyday exchange. *American Journal of Sociology* 103, 1565–1592.

Mulgan, G. and Wilkinson, H. (1995) Well-being and time. *Demos Quarterly* 5, 2–11.

Mulkay, M. (1988) *On Humour: Its Nature and Place in Modern Society*. Polity Press, Cambridge, UK.

Mulkay, M. and Howe, G. (1994) Laughter for sale. *Sociological Review* 42, 481–500.

Mullett, S. (1988) Leisure and consumption: incompatible concepts? *Leisure Studies* 7, 241–253.

Mungham, G. and Pearson, G. (eds) (1976) *Working Class Youth Culture*. Routledge, London.

Murdock, G. (1994) New times/hard times: leisure participation and the common good. *Leisure Studies* 13, 239–248.

Murphy, H. (2003) Exploring leisure and psychological health and wellbeing: some problematic issues in the case of Northern Ireland. *Leisure Studies* 22, 37–50.

Myerscough, J. (1974) The recent history of the use of leisure time. In: Appleton, I. (ed.) *Leisure Research and Policy*. Scottish Academic Press, Edinburgh, UK.

Nardi, P.M. (ed.) (1992) *Men's Friendships*. Sage, London.

Nare, S. (1996) Girls' and boys' economy of emotions: a comparison with Islamic gender system. In: Helve, H. and Bynner, J. (eds) *Youth and Life Management: Research Perspectives*. Helsinki University Press, Yliopistopaino, Finland.

National Centre for Social Research (2003) *National Survey of Sexual Attitudes and Life-styles II*. National Centre for Social Research, London.

Neulinger, J. (1990) *Eden After All*. Giordano Bruno, Culemborg.

Nickson, D., Warhurst, C., Witz, A. and Cullen, A.M. (1998) Aesthetic labour in the ser-vice economy: an overlooked development. Paper presented at the International Labour Markets Conference, Aberdeen, UK.

Ning Wang (1996) Logos-modernity, Eros-modernity, and leisure. *Leisure Studies* 15, 121–135.

Noon, M. and Blyton, P. (1997) *The Realities of Work*. Macmillan, Basingstoke, UK.

Nyman, C. (1999) Gender equality in the most equal country in the world? Money and marriage in Sweden. *Sociological Review* 47, 766–793.

O'Connor, B. and Boyle, R. (1993) Dallas with balls: televised sport, soap opera and male and female pleasures. *Leisure Studies* 12, 107–119.

Oliver, J. (1998) Losing control. *Management Today* June, 32–38.

O'Malley, P. and Valverde, M. (2004) Pleasure, freedom and drugs: the uses of 'pleasure' in liberal governance of drug and alcohol consumption. *Sociology* 38, 25–42.

Pahl, J. (1990) Household spending, personal spending and the control of money in marriage. *Sociology* 24, 119–138.

Pahl, R. (1995) *After Success*. Polity Press, Cambridge, UK.

Pakulski, J. and Waters, M. (1996) *The Death of Class*. Sage, London.

Parker, H., Williams, L. and Aldridge, J. (2002) The normalization of 'sensible' recre-ational drug use: further evidence from the North-West England longitudinal study. *Sociology* 36, 941–964.

Parker, S. (1971) *The Future of Work and Leisure*. MacGibbon and Kee, London.

Parker, S. (1979) Retirement – leisure or not? *Society and Leisure* 2, 329–340.

Parker, S. (1981) Change, flexibility, spontaneity and self-determination in leisure. *Social Forces.* 60, 323–331.

Parker, S. (1983) *Leisure and Work.* Allen and Unwin, London.

Parker, S., Hamilton-Smith, E. and Davidson, P. (1993) Serious and other leisure: thirty Australians. *World Leisure and Recreation* 35 (1), 14–18.

Parry, N.C.A. and Johnson, D. (1974) *Leisure and Social Structure.* Hatfield Polytechnic, Hatfield, UK.

Pearson, L.F. (1977) *Working Life and Leisure.* Sunderland Polytechnic, Sunderland, UK.

Petolka, P. (1996) Experimenting 6 + 6 shift work in Finland. Paper presented at the Conference on New Strategies for Everyday Life, Tilburg, The Netherlands.

Peterson, R.A. and Kern, R.M. (1996) Changing highbrow taste: from snob to omnivore. *American Sociological Review* 61, 900–907.

Phillips, T. and Western, M. (2005) Social change and social identity: postmodernity, reflexive modernisation and the transformation of social identities in Australia. In: Devine, F., Savage, M., Scott, J. and Crompton, R. (eds) *Rethinking Class: Culture, Identities, Lifestyle.* Palgrave Macmillan, Basingstoke, UK, pp. 163–185.

Pini, M. (2001) *Club Cultures and Female Subjectivity: The Move from Home to House.* Palgrave, Basingstoke, UK.

Platman, K. (2004) 'Portfolio careers' and the search for flexibility in later life. *Work, Employment and Society* 18, 573–599.

Podilchak, W. (1991) Distinctions of fun, enjoyment and leisure. *Leisure Studies* 10, 133–144.

Pollert, A. (ed.) (1991) *Farewell to Flexibility.* Blackwell, Oxford, UK.

Pontinen, P. (1996) Moral panics revisited. In: Helve, H. and Bynner, J. (eds) *Youth and Life Management: Research Perspectives.* Helsinki University Press, Yliopistopaino, Finland.

Poor, R. (1972) *4 Days, 40 Hours.* Pan, London.

Pronovost, G. (1988) The social meanings of leisure. *International Sociology* 3, 89–103.

Putnam, R.D. (2000) *Bowling Alone: the Collapse and Revival of American Community.* Simon and Schuster, New York.

Rapoport, R. and Rapoport, R.N. (1975) *Leisure and the Family Life-Cycle.* Routledge, London.

Rattansi, A. and Phoenix, A. (1997) Rethinking youth identities: modernist and postmodernist frameworks. In: Bynner, J., Chisholm, L. and Furlong, A. (eds) *Youth, Citizenship and Social Change in a European Context.* Ashgate, Aldershot, UK.

Ravenscroft, N. (1998) The changing regulation of public leisure provision. *Leisure Studies* 17, 138–154.

Raymond, L.P. (1984) The effects of unemployment on the leisure activity participation of unemployed steelworkers. In: *Le Temps Libre et le Loisir.* Actes du Congres Mondial de Recherche, Marly-le Roi, France.

Reeves, R. (2002) The Precious Time Poll: about time. *Observer,* 29 June, 4–9.

Riordan, J. (1995) From communist forum to capitalist market – East European sport in transition. *European Physical Education Review* 1, 15–26.

Ritzer, G. (1993) *The McDonaldization of Society.* Pine Forge Press, Thousand Oaks, California.

Ritzer, G. (1998) *The McDonaldization Thesis.* Sage, London.

Ritzer, G. (2004) *The Globalization of Nothing.* Pine Forge Press, Thousand Oaks, California.

Roberts, J. (1987) Buying leisure. *Leisure Studies,* 6, 87–91.

Roberts, K. (1970) *Leisure.* Longman, London.

Roberts, K. (1978) *Contemporary Society and the Growth of Leisure.* Longman, London.

Roberts, K. (1990) Leisure and sociological theory in Britain. *Society and Leisure* 13, 105–127.

Roberts, K. (1996) Young people, schools, sport and government policies. *Sport, Education and Society* 1, 47–57.

Roberts, K. (2001) *Class in Modern Britain*. Palgrave, Basingstoke, UK.

Roberts, K. and Brodie, D. (1992) *Inner-City Sport: Who Plays and What are the Benefits?* Giordano Bruno, Culemborg.

Roberts, K. and Chambers, D.A. (1985) Changing times: hours of work/patterns of leisure. *World Leisure and Recreation* 27 (1), 17–23.

Roberts, K. and Jung, B. (1995) *Poland's First Post-Communist Generation*. Avebury, Aldershot, UK.

Roberts, K. and Parsell, G. (1991) Young people's sources and levels of income, and patterns of consumption in Britain in the late-1980s. *Youth and Policy* 35, 20–25.

Roberts, K. and Parsell, G. (1992) Entering the labour market in Britain: the survival of traditional opportunity structures. *Sociological Review* 30, 727–753.

Roberts, K. and Parsell, G. (1994) Youth cultures in Britain: the middle class take-over. *Leisure Studies* 13, 33–48.

Roberts, K., Noble, M., and Duggan, J. (1982) Youth unemployment: an old problem or a new lifestyle. *Leisure Studies* 1, 171–182.

Roberts, K., Brodie, D. and Dench, S. (1987) Youth unemployment and out-of-home recreation. *Society and Leisure* 10, 281–294.

Roberts, K., York, C. and Brodie, D.A. (1988) Participant sport in the commercial sector. *Leisure Studies* 7, 145–157.

Roberts, K., Dench, S., Minten, J. and York, C. (1989a) *Community Response to Leisure Centre Provision in Belfast*. Study 34, Sports Council, London.

Roberts, K., Lamb, K.L., Dench, S. and Brodie, D.A. (1989b) Leisure patterns, health status and employment status. *Leisure Studies* 8, 229–235.

Roberts, K., Campbell, R. and Furlong, A. (1990) Class and gender divisions among young adults at leisure. In: Wallace, C. and Cross, M. (eds) *Youth in Transition*. Falmer, London.

Roberts, K., Minten, J.H., Chadwick, C., Lamb, K.L. and Brodie, D.A. (1991a) Sporting lives: a case study of leisure careers. *Society and Leisure* 14, 261–284.

Roberts, K., Parsell, G. and Chadwick, C. (1991b) Unemployment and young people's leisure in Liverpool and Swindon. *Society and Leisure* 14, 513–530.

Robinson, J.P. and Godbey, G. (1996) Time inequalities and irrelevancies. Paper presented at the Conference on New Strategies for Everyday Life, Tilburg, The Netherlands.

Robinson, J.P. and Godbey, G. (1999) *Time For Life: The Surprising Ways Americans Use Their Time,* 2nd edn. Pennsylvania State University Press, Penn State, Pennsylvania.

Robson, K. (2003) *Teenage Time Use as Investment in Cultural Capital*. Working Paper 2003-12, Institute for Social and Economic Research, University of Essex, Colchester, UK.

Rojek, C. (1984) Did Marx have a theory of leisure? *Leisure Studies* 3, 163–174.

Rojek, C. (1985) *Capitalism and Leisure Theory*. Tavistock, London.

Rojek, C. (1995) *Decentring Leisure*. Sage, London.

Rojek, C. (1997) Leisure in the writings of Walter Benjamin. *Leisure Studies* 16, 155–171.

Rojek, C. (2000a) *Leisure and Culture*. Macmillan, Basingstoke, UK.

Rojek, C. (2000b) Leisure and the rich today: Veblen's thesis after a century. *Leisure Studies* 19, 1–15.

Rojek, C. (2005) An outline of the action approach to leisure studies. *Leisure Studies* 24, 13–25.

Rojek, C. and Urry, J. (eds) (1997) *Touring Cultures: Transformations of Travel and Theory.* Routledge, London.

Rosducher, J. and Seifert, H. (1996) *The Reduction of Working Hours and Employment: Reduction of Working Hours in Germany and its Significance for Employment Policy.* Hans-Bockler Foundation, Dusseldorf, Germany.

Rose, D. and O'Reilly, K. (1997) *Constructing Classes.* Economic and Social Research Council/Office of National Statistics, Swindon, UK.

Rosenweig, R. (1983) *Eight Hours For What We Will.* Cambridge University Press, New York.

Rowe, D. (1995) *Popular Cultures: Rock Music, Sport and the Politics of Pleasure.* Sage, London.

Russell, H. (1999) Friends in low places: gender, unemployment and sociability. *Work, Employment and Society* 13, 205–224.

Russell, N. and Drew, N. (2001) *ICT Access and Use: Report on the Benchmark Survey.* Research Report 252, Department for Education and Employment, Sheffield, UK.

Russell, N. and Stafford, N. (2002) *Trends in ICT Access and Use.* Research Report 358, Department for Education and Skills, Sheffield, UK.

Salaman, G. (1974) *Community and Occupation.* Cambridge University Press, Cambridge, UK.

Samdahl, D.M. (1988) A symbolic interactionist model of leisure: theory and empirical support. *Leisure Sciences* 10, 27–39.

Samuel, N. (1990) Introduction. In: Samuel, N. (ed.) *Women's Leisure and the Family in Contemporary Society*, CAB International, Wallingford, UK.

Saunders, P. (1990) *A Nation of Home Owners.* Unwin Hyman, London.

Savage, M., Barlow, J., Dickens, P. and Fielding, T. (1992) *Property, Bureaucracy and Culture.* Routledge, London.

Scase, R. (1999) *Britain Towards 2010: The Changing Business Environment.* Foresight, Office of Science and Technology, Department of Trade and Industry, London.

Scheerder, J., Vanreusel, B., Taks, M. and Renson, R. (2002) Social sports stratification in Flanders 1969–1999. *International Review for the Sociology of Sport* 37, 219–245.

Schneider, B., Ainbinder, A.M. and Csikszentmihalyi, M. (2004) Stress and working parents. In: Haworth, J.T. and Veal, A.J. (eds) *Work and Leisure.* Routledge, London, pp. 145–167.

Schor, J.B. (1991) *The Overworked American.* Basic Books, New York.

Schor, J. (1998) Beyond work and spend. *Vrijetijd Studies* 18, 7–20.

Scott, D. and Willits, F.K. (1989) Adolescent and adult leisure patterns: a 37 year follow-up study. *Leisure Sciences* 11, 323–335.

Scraton, S. (1987) Boys muscle in where angels fear to tread – girls' subcultures and physical activities. In: Horne, J., Jary, D. and Tomlinson, A. (eds) *Sport, Leisure and Social Relations.* Routledge, London.

Scraton, S. (1992) *Shaping Up to Womanhood: Gender and Girls' Physical Education.* Open University Press, Buckingham, UK.

Scraton, S. (1994) The changing world of women and leisure: feminism, post-feminism and leisure. *Leisure Studies* 13, 249–261.

Seabrook, J. (1988) *The Leisure Society.* Blackwell, Oxford, UK.

Selwyn, N. (2003) Schooling the mobile generation: the future for schools in the mobile-networked society. *British Journal of Sociology of Education* 24, 131–144.

Shamir, B. (1985) Unemployment and free time – the role of the Protestant work ethic and work involvement. *Leisure Studies* 4, 333–345.

Sharkey, A. (1997) The land of the free. *Weekend Guardian*, 22 November, 14–25.

Sharp, D.J., Greer, J.M. and Lowe, G. (1988) The normalisation of under-age drinking. Paper presented at a meeting of the British Psychological Society, Leeds, UK.

Sharpe, S. (1977) *Just Like a Girl*. Penguin, Harmondsworth, UK.

Shields, R. (ed.) (1992) *Lifestyle Shopping*. Routledge, London.

Shildrick, T. (2002) Young people, illicit drug use and the question of normalization. *Journal of Youth Studies* 5, 35–48.

Siegenthaler, K.L. and O'Dell, I. (2003) Older golfers: serious leisure and successful aging. *World Leisure Journal* 45 (1), 45–52.

Sintas, J.L. and Alvarez, E.G. (2002) Omnivores show up again: the segmentation of cultural consumers in Spanish social space. *European Sociological Review* 18, 353–368.

Smith, D.M. (1981) New movements in the sociology of youth: a critique. *British Journal of Sociology* 32, 239–251.

Smith, J. (1987) Women at play: gender, the life-cycle and leisure. In: Horne, J., Jary, D. and Tomlinson, A. (eds) *Sport, Leisure and Social Relations*. Routledge, London.

Smith, M. and Carroll, M. (2002) Employment patterns for the future: balancing work and family life in two local authorities. In: Crow, G. and Heath, S. (eds) *Social Conceptions of Time: Structure and Process in Work and Everyday Life*. Palgrave, Basingstoke, UK, pp. 109–125.

Somnez, S., Shinew, K., Marchese, L., Veldkamp, C. and Burnett, G.W. (1993) Leisure corrupted: an artist's portrait of leisure in a changing society. *Leisure Studies* 12, 266–276.

Southerton, D. (2002) Boundaries of 'us' and 'them': class, mobility and identification in a new town. *Sociology* 36, 171–193.

Sport England (2003) *Young People and Sport in England: Trends in Participation 1994–2002*. Sport England, London.

Spruijt, E. and de Goede, M. (1995) Changing family structures and adolescent well-being. Paper presented at the Second European Sociological Association Conference, Budapest.

Stanley, L. (1977) Sex, gender and the sociology of leisure. In: Smith, M.A. (ed.) *Leisure and the Urban Society*. Leisure Studies Association, Manchester, UK.

Stebbins, R.A. (1992) *Amateurs, Professionals and Serious Leisure*. McGill-Queens University Press, Montreal, Quebec.

Stebbins, R.A. (1998) *After Work: the Search for an Optimal Leisure Lifestyle*. Temeron Books, Calgary, Alberta.

Stebbins, R.A. (2001) The costs and benefits of hedonism: some consequences of taking casual leisure seriously. *Leisure Studies* 20, 305–309.

Stebbins, R.A. (2005) Project-based leisure: theoretical neglect of a common use of free time. *Leisure Studies* 24, 1–11.

Steger, B. (1996) Hurried work, hurried leisure and time to sleep: the case of Japan. Paper presented at the Conference on New Strategies for Everyday Life, Tilburg, The Netherlands.

Stockdale, J. (1986) *What is Leisure?* Economic and Social Research Council/Sports Council, London.

Stokes, G. (1983) Work, leisure and unemployment. *Leisure Studies* 2, 269–286.

Stolle, D. and Micheletti, M. (2005) What motivates political consumers? Paper presented at the Conference on Politicised Consumption – Consumed Politics, Giessen, Germany.

Streather, J. (1979) One-parent families and leisure. In: Strelitz, Z. (ed.) *Leisure and Family Diversity*. Leisure Studies Association, London.

Street, J. (1993) Global culture, local politics. *Leisure Studies* 12, 191–201.

Sturgis, P. and Jackson, J. (2003a) *Preliminary Analysis of the UK Time Use Survey for the Department of Culture, Media and Sport: Examining Participation in Sporting and Cultural Activities.* London School of Economics, London.

Sturgis, P. and Jackson, J. (2003b) *Examining Participation in Sporting and Cultural Activities: Analysis of the Time Use Survey Phase 2.* London School of Economics, London.

Sulkanen, P. (1997) Introduction: the new consumer society – rethinking the social bond. In: Sulkanen, P., Holmwood, J., Radner, H. and Schulze, G. (eds) *Constructing the New Consumer Society.* Macmillan, London.

Sullivan, O. (1996) Time co-ordination, the domestic division of labour and affective relations: time use and the enjoyment of activities within couples. *Sociology* 30, 79–100.

Sullivan, O. (2000) The division of domestic labour: twenty years of change. *Sociology* 34, 437–456.

Sullivan, O. and Gershuny, J. (2001) Cross-national changes in time use: some sociological (his)stories re-examined. *British Journal of Sociology* 52, 331–347.

Swain, J. (2000) The money's good, the fame's good, the girls are good: the role of playground football in the construction of boys' masculinity in a junior school. *British Journal of Sociology of Education* 21, 95–109.

Sweeting, H. and West, P. (2003) Young people's leisure and risk-taking behaviours: change in gender patterning in the West of Scotland during the 1990s. *Journal of Youth Studies* 6, 391–412.

Talbot, M. (1979) *Women and Leisure.* Social Science Research Council/Sports Council, London.

Talbot, M. (1990) Being herself through sport. In: Long, J. (ed.) *Leisure, Health and Well-Being.* Conference Papers 44, Leisure Studies Association, Brighton Polytechnic, Brighton, UK.

Taylor, J.S. (2001) Dollars are a girl's best friend? Female tourists' sexual behaviour in the Caribbean. *Sociology* 35, 749–764.

Taylor, P. (1992) Commercial leisure: exploiting consumer preferences. In: Sugden, J. and Knox, C. (eds) *Leisure in the 1990s.* Leisure Studies Association, Eastbourne, UK.

Taylor, R. (2002) *Britain's World of Work – Myths and Realities.* Economic and Social Research Council, Swindon, UK.

Taylor-Goodby, P. (1985) Personal consumption and gender. *Sociology* 19, 273–284.

Taylor-Goodby, P. (1986) Women, work, money and marriage. *Sociology* 20, 93–94.

Te Kloetz, J.W. (1998) Between freedom and commitment: the post-modern family discovered. Paper presented at the International Sociological Association Congress, Montreal, Quebec.

Thompson, E.P. (1967) Time, work discipline and industrial capitalism. *Past and Present* 39, 60.

Thompson, S.M. (1990) Thank the ladies for the plates: the incorporation of women into sport. *Leisure Studies* 9, 135–143.

Thornton, S. (1995) *Club Cultures: Music, Media and Subcultural Capital.* Polity Press, Cambridge, UK.

Thrift, N. (1989) Images of social change. In: Hamnett, C., McDowell, L. and Sarre, P. (eds) *The Changing Social Structure.* Sage, London.

Tinsley, H.E.A., Colbs, S.L., Teaff, J.D. and Kaufman, N. (1987) The relationship of age, gender, health and economic status to the psychological benefits older persons report from participation in leisure activities. *Leisure Sciences* 9, 53–65.

Tokarski, W. (1991) Research note: leisure lifestyle careers in old age. *Leisure Studies* 10, 79–81.

Tomlinson, A. (1979) Leisure, the family and the woman's role: observations on personal accounts. In: Strelitz, Z. (ed.) *Leisure and Family Diversity*. Conference Papers 9, Leisure Studies Association, London.

Tomlinson, A. (ed.) (1990) *Consumption, Identity and Style*. Routledge, London.

Tomlinson, M. and Walton, D. (1986) A sporting chance. *Leisure Management* 6 (5), 41–42.

Turner, R.H. (1964) *The Social Context of Ambition*. Chandler, San Francisco, California.

Tyler, M. and Abbott, P. (1998) Chocs away: weight watching in the contemporary airline industry. *Sociology* 32, 433–450.

Urry, J. (1995a) *Consuming Places*. Routledge, London.

Urry, J. (1995b) A middle class countryside? In: Butler, T. and Savage, M. (eds) *Social Change and the Middle Classes*. UCL Press, London.

van den Broek, A., Breedveld, K. and Knulst, W. (2002) Roles, rhythms and routines: towards a new script of daily life in the Netherlands. In: Crow, G. and Heath, S. (eds) *Social Conceptions of Time: Structure and Process in Work and Everyday Life*. Palgrave, Basingstoke, UK, pp. 195–214.

van der Lippe, T. (1996) Trends in time use of men and women. Paper presented at the Conference on New Strategies for Everyday Life, Tilburg, The Netherlands.

van der Poel, H. (1994) The modularisation of daily life. In: Henry, I. (ed.) *Leisure, Modernity, Postmodernity and Lifestyles*. Leisure Studies Association, Eastbourne, UK.

van Eijck, K. (1999) Socialisation, education and lifestyle: how social mobility increases the cultural heterogeneity of status groups. *Poetics* 26, 309–328.

van Eijck, K. and van Rees, K. (1998) The impact of social mobility on patterns of cultural consumption: individual omnivores and heterogeneous status groups. Paper presented at the International Sociological Association Congress, Montreal, Quebec.

van Ophem, J. and de Hoog, K. (1998) Differences in leisure behaviour of the poor and the rich in the Netherlands at the beginning of the 1990s. In: Te Kloeze, J.W. (ed.) *Family and Leisure in Poland and the Netherlands*. Garant, Leuven-Apeldoorn, The Netherlands.

Veal, A.J. (1989) Leisure and life-style: a pluralist framework for analysis. *Leisure Studies* 8, 141–153.

Veal, A.J. (1993) The concept of lifestyle: a review. *Leisure Studies* 12, 233–252.

Veblen, T. (1925) *The Theory of the Leisure Class*. Allen and Unwin, London.

Vester, H.-G. (1987) Adventure as a form of leisure. *Leisure Sciences* 6, 237–249.

Viasanen, M. and Natti, J. (2002) Working time preferences in dual earning households. *European Societies* 4, 307–329.

Vickerstaff, S. and Cox, J. (2005) Retirement and risk: the individualisation of retirement experiences. *Sociological Review* 53, 77–95.

Wait, P. (1996) Social stratification and housing mobility. *Sociology* 30, 533–550.

Wallace, C. and Kovatcheva, S. (1998) *Youth in Society: the Construction and Deconstruction of Youth in East and West Europe*. Macmillan, Basingstoke, UK.

Walter, T. (1985) *Hope on the Dole*. SPCK, London.

Walton, J.K. (1977) Holidays and the discipline of industrial labour. In: Smith, M.A. (ed.) *Leisure and the Urban Society*. Leisure Studies Association, Manchester, UK.

Walton, P. (1996) Enhancing positive attitudes to men working flexible and reduced hours. Paper presented at the Conference on New Strategies for Everyday Life, Tilburg, The Netherlands.

Walvin, J. (1978) *Leisure and Society, 1830–1950*. Longman, London.

Warde, A. (1994) Consumption, identity formation and uncertainty. *Sociology* 28, 877–898.

Warde, A. (1995) Cultural change and class differentiation: distinction and taste in the British middle class, 1968–88. In: Roberts, K. (ed.) *Leisure and Social Stratification*. Publication 53, Leisure Studies Association, Eastbourne, UK.

Warde, A. and Hetherington, K. (1993) A changing domestic division of labour? Issues of measurement and interpretation. *Work, Employment and Society* 7, 23–45.

Warde, A., Martens, L. and Olsen, W. (1999) Consumption and the problem of variety: cultural omnivorousness, social distinction and dining out. *Sociology* 33, 105–127.

Warren, T. (2003) Class- and gender-based working time? Time poverty and the division of domestic labour. *Sociology* 37, 733–752.

Wearing, B. (1993) The family that plays together stays together: or does it? Leisure and mothers. *World Leisure and Recreation* 35 (3), 25–29.

Wearing, B. (1995) Leisure and resistance in an ageing society. *Leisure Studies* 14, 263–279.

Wearing, B. (1998) *Leisure and Feminist Theory*. Sage, London.

Wearing, B. and Wearing, S. (1988) All in a day's leisure: gender and the concept of leisure. *Leisure Studies* 7, 111–123.

Wearing, B. and Wearing, S. (1992) Identity and the commodification of leisure. *Leisure Studies* 11, 3–18.

Wearing, S. and Foley, C. (2002) The mobile phone, a fashion accessory or blanket security: conspicuous consumption, identity and adolescent women's leisure choices. Paper presented at the International Sociological Association Congress, Brisbane, Australia.

Wellman, B. and Haythornwaite, C. (eds) (2002) *The Internet and Everyday Life*. Blackwell, Oxford, UK.

Wernick, A. (1991) *Promotional Culture*. Sage, London.

Whannel, G. (1986) The unholy alliance: notes on television and the remaking of British sport 1965–85. *Leisure Studies* 5, 129–145.

Wheaton, B. (ed.) (2004) *Understanding Lifestyle Sports: Consumption, Identity and Difference*. Routledge, London.

Wilenski, H.L. (1963) The uneven distribution of leisure: the impact of economic growth on free time. In: Smigel, E.O. (ed.) *Work and Leisure*. College and University Press, New Haven, Connecticut.

Willis, P. (1977) *Learning to Labour*. Saxon House, Farnborough, UK.

Willis, P. (1990) *Common Culture*. Open University Press, Milton Keynes, UK.

Willis, P., Bekem, A., Ellis, T. and Whitt, D. (1988) *The Youth Review: Social Conditions of Young People in Wolverhampton*. Avebury, Aldershot, UK.

Wilson, J. (1988) *Politics and Leisure*. Unwin Hyman, London.

Woolgar, S. (ed.) (2002) *Virtual Society? Technology, Cyberbole, Reality*. Oxford University Press, Oxford, UK.

Wright, D. (1994) Boys' thoughts and talk about sex in a working class locality of Glasgow. *Sociological Review* 42, 703–737.

Wright-Mills, C. (1956) *White-Collar*. Galaxy, New York.

Wynne, D. (1990) Leisure, lifestyle and the construction of social position. *Leisure Studies* 9, 21–34.

Wynne, D. (1998) *Leisure, Lifestyle and the New Middle Class*. Routledge, London.

Yorganci, I. (1993) Preliminary findings from a survey of gender relationships and sexual harassment in sport. In: Brackenridge, C. (ed.) *Body Matters*. Leisure Studies Association, Eastbourne, UK.

Young, M. and Schuller, T. (1991) *Life After Work*. Harper Collins, London.

Young, M. and Willmott, P. (1973) *The Symmetrical Family*. Routledge, London.

Yule, J. (1997a) Engendered ideologies and leisure policy in the UK. Part 1: gender ideologies. *Leisure Studies* 16, 61–84.

Yule, J. (1997b) Engendered ideologies and leisure policy in the UK. Part 2: professional ideologies. *Leisure Studies* 16, 139–154.

Zuzanek, J. (2004) Work, leisure, time-pressure and stress. In: Haworth, J.T. and Veal, A.J. (eds) *Work and Leisure.* Routledge, London, pp. 123–144.

Zuzanek, J. and Mannell, R. (1983) Work–leisure relationships from a social psychological perspective. *Leisure Studies* 2, 327–344.

Zuzanek, J. and Mannell, R. (1998) Life cycle squeeze, time pressure, daily stress, and leisure participation: a Canadian perspective. *Leisure and Society* 21, 513–544.

Zuzanek, J., Beckers, T. and Peters, P. (1998) The harried leisure class revisited: a cross-national and longitudinal perspective. Dutch and Canadian trends in the use of time: from the 1970s to the 1990s. *Leisure Studies* 17, 1–19.

Index

Page numbers in **bold** refer to illustrations and tables